Visual Basic®
for DOS Programming

Visual Basic®
for DOS
Programming
With Applications

Douglas A. Hergert

BANTAM BOOKS
NEW YORK • TORONTO • LONDON • SYDNEY • AUCKLAND

Visual Basic ® for DOS Programming: With Applications
A Bantam Book / October 1992

Interior design by Nancy Sugihara
Produced by MicroText Productions
Composed by Context Publishing Services

ISBN 0-553-37099-5

Published simultaneously in the United States and Canada

Bantam Books are published by Bantam Books, a division of Bantam Doubleday Dell
Publishing Group, Inc. Its trademark, consisting of the words "Bantam Books" and the portrayal
of a rooster, is Registered in U.S. Patent and Trademark Office and in other countries. Marca
Registrada, Bantam Books, 666 Fifth Avenue, New York, New York 10103.

PRINTED IN THE UNITED STATES OF AMERICA

0   9   8   7   6   5   4   3   2   1

Acknowledgments

My thanks to Claudette Moore and Jono Hardjowirogo for direction and encouragement; Troy Strain and Bill Nelson for technical advice; and Maureen Drexel and Lauralee Reinke for their editorial and production expertise. Special thanks to Elaine Andersson, Andrew Hergert, Audrey Hergert, and Boubacar Diatta.

D.A.H.

Contents

viii   Contents

PART II
Visual Basic Applications   149

Introduction

Visual Basic is Microsoft's creative new program development environment for DOS—an accessible and dynamic collection of tools for creating high-quality DOS applications. This book introduces you to the steps of application development in Visual Basic, and presents a library of practical Visual Basic programs. If you are already familiar with the Basic language, this book will help you to broaden your programming knowledge and adapt your skills to the unique features of Visual Basic. If you are not a programmer, you can use the applications in this book with Visual Basic to expand your current library of DOS programs.

Part I of this book is a tutorial-style introduction to the tools of the Visual Basic environment. You'll learn how to develop forms-based interfaces for new applications you design—selecting from Visual Basic's ready-made graphical objects such as command buttons, text boxes, lists, labels, and check boxes. Then you'll find out how to complete your application by writing procedures in this powerful new version of the Basic language. You'll also discover the significance of the Visual Basic's *event-driven* programming model, and begin experimenting with a vast library of new programming tools.

Part II presents a collection of complete and working programming projects that you can examine, run, and customize for your own use. All the applications are also included on the exercise disk packaged with this book. The chapters in Part II present applications in the context of major programming topics. Each chapter begins with a description of the application itself, and instructions for running and using the program. You'll load each application into Visual Basic, examine the program's components, and run it. Finally, you can use a Visual Basic menu command named **Make EXE File** to create executable application files—which can then be run directly from DOS. These sample programs are designed to perform a wide variety of useful tasks at home or at work. They will also help you begin formulating your own imaginative ideas for additional Visual Basic applications.

INSTALLING VISUAL BASIC

Visual Basic comes with a **Setup** utility that makes installation on your hard disk a simple process:

1. Insert disk 1 of the Visual Basic product in the floppy disk drive. From the DOS prompt, enter **A:SETUP** or **B:SETUP**, depending on the drive in which you have inserted the disk. On the first screen of the Setup program, select **Install Visual Basic for MS-DOS** and press Enter.

2. Setup presents a dialog box that asks for your name or your company name. After you enter and confirm your name, another series of dialog boxes gives you the opportunity to select the disk drive and directory location for the components of Visual Basic. The default directory for the program is **C:\VBDOS**. Whether you accept this default or enter a different directory name, the Setup program creates the necessary directory and subdirectories on your disk. A final screen in this series summarizes the directories on your disk.

3. Select **No Change** to continue. The Setup utility begins copying files to your hard disk and notifies you when it is time to swap disks. Installation takes several minutes.

4. When installation is complete, a dialog box gives you the option of exiting to DOS or going straight to the Visual Basic tutorial program. Select **Exit** for now. You can work through the tutorial later by choosing the **Tutorial** command from Visual Basic's **Help** menu.

5. To prepare for the exercises in the upcoming chapters, create a new subdirectory for the applications provided on the exercise disk that came with this book. Give the subdirectory a name such as **VBAPPS**. Copy all the files with extension names of MAK, FRM, and BAS from the exercise disk to this directory location.

To start Visual Basic, go to the VBDOS directory and type **VBDOS** from the DOS prompt.

Note: The program listings in this book are the same as the source code stored on the accompanying exercise disk, except that long lines of printed code have occasionally been broken to fit on the page. You can always examine the actual program lines directly on your screen, in Visual Basic's Code window.

PART I

The Visual Basic Development Environment

1

Your First Visual Basic Application

INTRODUCTION

Microsoft Visual Basic for DOS is a dramatic new approach to creating Basic programs. More than a traditional programming language, Visual Basic is an elaborate development environment in which you can design high-quality applications in a shorter time than ever before. Using tools provided in Visual Basic, you will create programs that match the visual and conceptual elegance of the best DOS applications. Your programs can include pull-down menus, dialog boxes, text editing capabilities, mouse control, and many other features that would require great amounts of effort to create in a traditional programming language.

Visual Basic is a multifaceted programming environment, rich in individual tools. The purpose of the environment is to streamline the development process by providing the visual elements of a program's user interface as ready-made *controls* that you can incorporate into your application almost instantly. In the initial steps of creating an application, you use these controls to plan and build your program's interface directly on the screen. In most cases you'll begin writing Basic code at the point when your application's visual interface is already complete. You then can modify the interface—adding or removing controls, or reorganizing your program's visual presentation—at any time during the development process.

You typically use Visual Basic's controls to depict the choices and features you are planning to offer in an application. Conveniently, the appearance and behavior of these controls are predefined. Consider a couple of examples:

- You can use a Visual Basic *command button* to represent an operation that is available in your program. For example, you might provide a command button to depict a calculation or a disk operation that your program can perform. The user performs the operation by clicking the button with a mouse. Clicking a button produces a visual push-button effect on the screen, an effect that is built in to Visual Basic's command button control.

- A *text box* control accepts an input value from the keyboard. To enter an input item, the user selects the text box and types the value. If an application has more than one text box, the user can enter values into them in any order. In addition, a Visual Basic text box possesses built-in editing functions, such as cut and paste and copy and paste.

Along with command buttons and text boxes, Visual Basic provides a complete set of ready-made controls—including *lists, labels, check boxes, option buttons, scroll bars, frames,* and others. These controls vastly simplify your job as a programmer. You can concentrate your efforts on the important computational and data processing procedures of your program. Visual Basic automatically provides the elements of your user interface—including screen presentation, keyboard functions, and mouse operations.

In this first chapter you'll begin exploring the tools and resources available in Visual Basic. This chapter has three main parts:

1. A brief survey of the Visual Basic development environment.

2. A look at a sample Visual Basic application, a database program named *Real Estate.* You'll load the program from the exercise disk included with this book. Then, after running *Real Estate* to see how it works, you'll begin examining the parts of the application.

3. A preview of the steps required for developing an application in Visual Basic. You'll learn much more about these steps in the remaining chapters of Part I.

Begin now by starting up Visual Basic on your computer. (If you haven't yet installed Visual Basic, do so now by following the steps outlined in the introduction.) The Visual Basic programming environment appears on your screen, as shown in Figure 1-1.

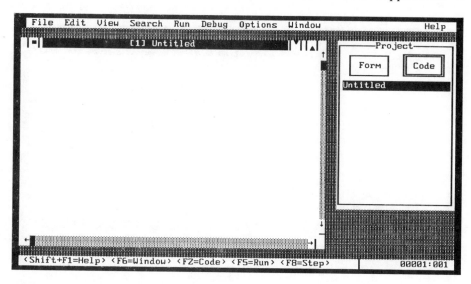

Figure 1-1 Visual Basic's programming environment

THE VISUAL BASIC DEVELOPMENT ENVIRONMENT

Visual Basic for DOS has two main components, called the programming environment and the Form Designer. You typically begin your work in the Form Designer component, where you plan the visual interface of your application. Then in the programming environment you write the code that will take control when the user makes selections and performs other actions in the interface you design. As you develop an application, you may find yourself switching back and forth frequently between the programming environment and the Form Designer. At first glance, these two components together may seem crowded with a bewildering assortment of windows and menus, but you will quickly become as comfortable with this environment as you are with your favorite word processor or spreadsheet program.

As shown in Figure 1-1, Visual Basic starts out in the programming environment. A code window appears on the left side of the screen; this is where you'll eventually develop Basic procedures for your application. Next to the code window is the Project window, where Visual Basic lists the parts of your application. You'll examine the programming environment

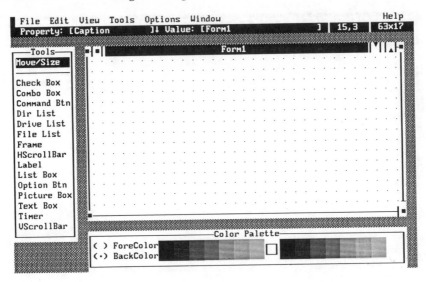

Figure 1-2 The Form Designer

in greater detail later. For now, take a first look at the Form Designer by following these steps:

1. Pull down the **File** menu by clicking this name in the menu bar. Then click the **New Form** command. (Or, from the keyboard, press the Alt key to activate the menu bar, then press F to pull down the **File** menu and F again to choose the **New Form** command.) The New Form dialog box appears.

2. Click the **OK** button.

The Form Designer environment takes over the screen, as shown in Figure 1-2. Visual Basic is ready for you to begin designing the user interface for an application.

Forms and Projects

A window named **Form1** takes up most of the screen space in the Form Designer. This empty window is the starting point for your work on a new application. The windows in which you build a Visual Basic application are called *forms*. You can use a form for any number of different purposes, depending on the needs of your application. For example, a form can become a dialog box. You design a dialog box by selecting controls and placing them inside a form. Alternatively, your program can use a form as an area to display text output or tables of numerical data. You can add as many forms to a program as are required in the plan of your application.

You design one application at a time in Visual Basic. Each form that you add to your application is stored on disk as a separate file. During development time a given application can therefore consist of many different files on disk. The file components of an application are together called a *project*. Visual Basic keeps track of the files of a given project and can open them all in a single operation.

In this chapter, you'll focus on the general characteristics of several major tools that appear in the two components of the Visual Basic environment:

- The *Toolbox*, located at the left side of the Form Designer (Figure 1-2), lists the assortment of visual controls that you can select for use in your application.

- The *Properties bar*, beneath the menu bar at the top of the Form Designer screen, gives you tools for identifying and changing the initial characteristics of the controls that you select for your application.

- The *Project window*, at the right side of the programming environment (Figure 1-1), lists the components of the application that you are currently creating.

- The menu bars of both the programming environment and the Form Designer provide a variety of tools for you to use during program development.

As you examine these tools, you'll also perform a few introductory hands-on exercises in the Visual Basic environment.

The Toolbox and the Properties Bar

As you can see at the left side of the Form Designer screen (Figure 1-2), the Toolbox items are presented as abbreviated descriptions in alphabetical order. These tools represent the visual controls you put in an application. You can insert any number of controls into a form, and you arrange those controls in whatever way suits your application design.

Each of the controls represented in the Toolbox has its own special characteristics. Learning how to use controls successfully is one of the major tasks ahead of you as you begin developing applications. For now, take a brief look the items in the Toolbox, and consider the purpose of each control:

- A *check box* depicts an option that can be turned on or off. A dialog box might contain a list of check boxes; each option in the list can be switched on or off independently.

- A *combo box* is a text box with an attached list that can drop down beneath the input area. To make an entry into such a box, the user can either type text directly from the keyboard or select an entry from the drop-down list.

- A *command button* is a control that the user can click to perform a specific operation.

- A *directory list* displays the hierarchy of directories on a disk.

- A *drive list* allows the user to view the valid disk drives in the system and to activate a new drive.

- A *file list* displays file names from a directory.

- A *frame* can be used to group together a collection of other controls in a form.

- A *horizontal scroll bar* is a control that depicts a value or a position in relation to a minimum and a maximum. Arrows appear on the left and right ends of the bar, and a scroll box moves back and forth across the bar. One typical use of this control is to allow the user to scroll inside a text box.

- A *label* is typically a short text item that identifies an element in a dialog box. You can also use a label to display longer blocks of text.

- A *list box* control is a list of entries, any one of which can be selected as an input item.

- An *option button* is another control that represents an *on-off* option. However, a list of option buttons always represents a group of mutually exclusive options. Only one of the options in the list can be switched on at a time; the other options in the list are off.

- A *picture box* control can display text or combinations of ASCII graphics characters in an application.

- A *text box* is an input box designed to accept text that the user enters from the keyboard.

- A *timer* control represents timed events in an application.

- The *vertical scroll bar* contains arrows at the top and bottom of the bar and a scroll box that moves up and down.

You'll see examples of some of these controls in the sample application presented later in this chapter. Meanwhile, the following brief exercise will show you how simple it is to put a control on a form.

Hands-on Exercise: Placing a Control on a Form

The form currently displayed in the Form Designer environment is initially named **Form1**. You can practice placing controls on this form, as if you were planning to create a dialog box for an application. Start out now by performing the following steps:

1. Move the mouse pointer to the **Command Btn** item in the Toolbox list.

2. Double-click the left mouse button. A button named **Command1** immediately appears in the center of **Form1**, as shown in Figure 1-3. Notice the small squares displayed at the four corners of the command button. These squares are called *sizing handles*. Their presence indicates that this control is currently selected for a subsequent action.

3. Type the uppercase letters **OK** from the keyboard, and press Enter. As a result, **OK** becomes the button's new caption. In the Properties bar above **Form1**, notice that the Property box displays the word **Caption** and the Value box displays **OK**.

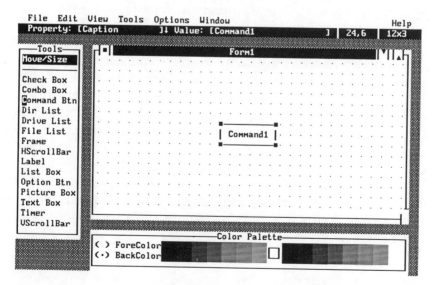

Figure 1-3 Placing a command button on the form

4. Now drag the command button to a new position near the upper-left corner of **Form1**: Position the mouse pointer over the control, and hold down the left mouse button while you drag the control up and to the left. As you drag the button, you'll see an outline of the control move to the new position. You'll also notice that the movement occurs in vertical and horizontal jumps within the dotted grid background of the form. When you release the mouse button the repositioning is complete.

5. Decrease the size of the command button: Position the mouse pointer over the sizing handle located at the lower-right corner of the command button. Hold down the left mouse button and move the sizing handle to the left until the button is just wide enough to display its current caption, **OK**. Release the mouse button, and the sizing operation is complete.

6. Click the mouse anywhere inside the **Form1** to deactivate the command button control.

You have just placed your first control on a form. If you were actually planning an application, this command button might ultimately represent a particular operation that your program would perform on demand—for example, saving a record, calculating a mathematical value, clearing values from the screen, displaying a new dialog box of options, or exiting from the current program. You'll see buttons that represent operations like these in this chapter's sample application. To perform one of these operations during a run of the program, the user simply clicks the appropriate command button.

As you begin adding controls to an application, you'll want to be able to specify the characteristics of each control—its appearance and location, its name, and its behavior. These and other characteristics are called *properties* in Visual Basic. Each property has a name and a *default setting*. Interestingly enough, you have just changed several of the properties of the command button control in **Form1**: the **Width** property, representing the size of the control; the **Left** and **Top** properties, representing the position of the control; and the **Caption** property, representing the text caption displayed on the button itself. You have used the mouse and the keyboard to change these particular properties directly on the screen. However, other properties are controlled via the important Form Designer tool called the Properties bar.

Controls and Their Properties

Each of the fifteen different controls listed in the Toolbox has its own set of properties. In addition, the forms of an application also have properties.

To modify the appearance, position, or behavior of a given control or form, you have to change the setting of the appropriate property. Some properties—such as the ones named **Top** and **Left**—are common to most or all controls. Others are special-purpose properties that are relevant only to specific controls. The Properties bar gives you simple techniques for working with properties. You use the Properties bar to perform any of these actions:

- View the list of properties that apply to a given control or form.

- Determine the current setting of a particular property for a selected control or form.

- View the list of available settings for a property.

- Change the setting of a property for a selected control or form.

The Properties bar is located on the second line of the Form Designer screen, just beneath the menu bar, as you can see in Figure 1-4.

The line on which the Properties bar is located contains four boxes. Here are descriptions of these four boxes, from left to right:

- The *Property box* is a drop-down list that displays all the properties of a selected control or form. As you have seen, this box initially displays the **Caption** property when you add a new command button to the form.

- The *Value box* displays the setting of the current property. For a property that has a fixed group of settings, the drop-down list attached

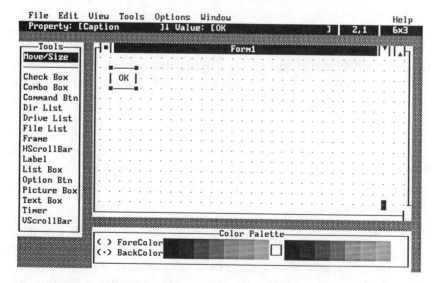

Figure 1-4 The Properties bar

to this box displays those settings. Otherwise, the Value box accepts a setting as input from the keyboard.

- The *Location box* displays the position coordinates of the selected control or form. The first coordinate is the horizontal position and the second is the vertical position. For a control, the coordinates represent the position in relation to the upper-left corner of the form that contains it. For example, the coordinates **2, 1** mean that the control is located at column 2 and row 1 of the form. (Coordinates begin at 0, 0.) For a form, the coordinates are in relation to the upper-left corner of the screen.

- The *Size box* shows the dimensions of the selected control or form. The first dimension is the width and the second is the height. For example, **6x3** means that a control is six columns wide by three lines long.

When you pull down the list attached to the Properties list box, you see the complete set of properties definable for the selected control. After you select a property, you use the Value box to change the setting of that property. Every property for a given control has a default setting—that is, a setting that remains in effect unless you explicitly change it.

Hands-on Exercise: Using the Properties Bar

For a quick introduction to the Properties bar, you'll now change two more properties of the command button control that you have already placed on **Form1**. First you'll assign the control a new name by changing a property called **CtlName**. The **CtlName** setting is the name by which you identify a given control inside the code of your program. As you'll see shortly, the default **CtlName** setting of the command button is **Command1**. Then you'll change the appearance of the mouse pointer when it is positioned over the control. The property that controls this characteristic is called **MousePointer**.

Changing the **CtlName** property requires that you enter a new name directly from the keyboard into the Value box. In contrast, the **Mouse-Pointer** property has a fixed list of available settings; to choose a setting, you pull down the list attached to the Value box. Follow these steps to make these two changes:

1. Click the command button to select the control. The sizing handles reappear at the corners of the button. In the Properties bar, the Location box shows the position to which you have moved this button, and the Size box shows the dimensions of the button.

2.   Click the down-arrow icon next to the Property list box to pull down the list of available properties for the command button. In the pull-down list, click the **CtlName** property. The list closes and the Value box displays the default setting of the **CtlName** property: **Command1**.

3.   From the keyboard, type the new name **OKButton** and press Enter. You can supply any **CtlName** setting that conveniently identifies the purpose of the control itself.

4.   Now click the down-arrow icon next to the Property list box again. This time click in the vertical scroll bar to scroll up or down the list, and take a look at the entire list of properties defined for a command button. Then scroll to the **MousePointer** property. At this point in your work, the screen looks like Figure 1-5.

5.   Click the **MousePointer** property in the list. It becomes the current property.

6.   Click the down-arrow icon located at the right of the Value box, pulling down the list of available settings. If you scroll down the list, you'll find that there are twelve different settings for the mouse pointer. Each setting gives the pointer a different appearance when you move the mouse to the current control.

7.   Select setting 4, named **Icon**, as shown in Figure 1-6. Press Enter to close the Value list. The **Icon** setting now appears in the Value box, along with its corresponding pointer icon—a happy face character.

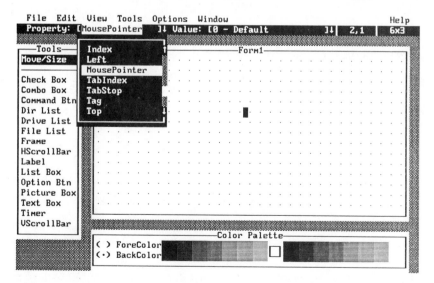

Figure 1-5 Using the Properties bar

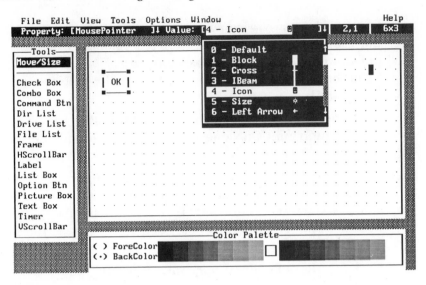

Figure 1-6 The Value list

To see the effect of this second property selection, move the mouse pointer over the command button. As you'll see, the pointer appears as a happy face character.

For most new controls that you add to an application, typically you will need to change only a few of the default property settings during your work in the Form Designer. Later on you'll see that properties also can be changed by the code in your program, in response to events that take place during *run time*.

So far you have worked with several elements of the Form Designer environment: the Toolbox, the Properties bar, a form, and a control. Next you'll return to the programming environment and examine its elements. As you switch from one component to the other, Visual Basic will give you the opportunity to save the form you've been creating in the Form Designer:

1. Pull down the File menu in the Form Designer and choose the Exit command. A box appears on the screen with the following message and prompt: "Project or source files have changed. Save them now?"

2. Click the Yes button to save the form to disk. Visual Basic saves the form under the default file name FORM1.FRM.

The programming environment reappears on the screen, and once again you see the code window and the Project window.

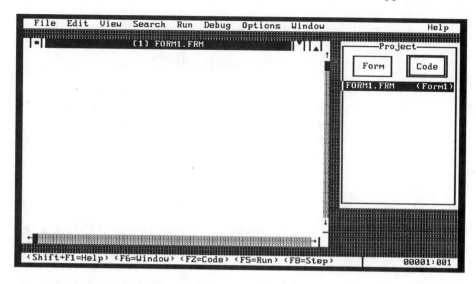

```
   File   Edit   View   Search   Run   Debug   Options   Window                  Help
  ┌─■─┬───────────────────[1]  FORM1.FRM──────────────────▼│▲┐        ┌─Project─────────┐
  │                                                              ↑     │  ┌──────┐ ┌──────┐│
  │                                                              █     │  │ Form │ │ Code ││
  │                                                                    │  └──────┘ └──────┘│
  │                                                                    ├────────────────────┤
  │                                                                    │FORM1.FRM   (Form1)│
  │                                                                    │                    │
  │                                                                    │                    │
  │                                                                    │                    │
  │                                                                    │                    │
  │                                                                    │                    │
  │                                                                    │                    │
  │                                                              ↓     │                    │
  │◄█▒▒▒▒▒▒▒▒▒▒▒▒▒▒▒▒▒▒▒▒▒▒▒▒▒▒▒▒▒▒▒▒▒▒▒▒▒▒▒▒▒▒►│        └────────────────────┘
  └<Shift+F1=Help> <F6=Window> <FZ=Code> <F5=Run> <F8=Step>────────────│ 00001:001 │
```

Figure 1-7 The Project window

The Project Window

As shown in Figure 1-7, the Project window lists the files of the application you are currently creating. Your current project contains one file, named FORM1.FRM. The Project window shows two items for each file in its list: the file name on disk (or the default file name, if the file has not yet been saved to disk) and, in parentheses, the setting of a property called **FormName**. You can move and resize the Project window at any time during your work in the programming environment.

Projects contain forms and *modules*. As you've already seen, a form is a visual part of an application. A module is a file for storing code.

Forms and Modules

You can write and store Visual Basic procedures and declarations for an application in two locations:

- A form generally contains the procedures that are related to its own controls. As you've seen, the form window in the Form Designer environment shows the visual controls that you have placed in a form. Likewise, a Code window in the programming environment displays the declarations and procedures you write for the form. The Code window also operates as a full-function text editor for developing procedures.

- A module contains procedures that you write for use by more than one form. Like the Code window for a form, a module window serves as an editor for entering and modifying code.

You'll find out more about these code areas later. For now, concentrate on the tools that the Project window gives you for working with forms and modules. Notice first that there are two command buttons at the top of the Project window: **Form** and **Code**. These two buttons give you access to the parts of a form.

Hands-on Exercise: Using the Project Window

The **Form** and **Code** buttons apply to the currently selected file in the Project window. You select a file in the list by clicking the file with the mouse or by pressing the up- or down-arrow key when the Project window is active. For now, **Form1** is the only file in your project. With this file selected, perform the following steps:

1. Click the **Form** button. This action switches you back to the Form Designer. **Form1** reappears on the screen along with the command button that you have already placed on the form.

2. Pull down the Form Designer's Edit menu and choose the Event Procedures command—or simply press the F12 function key, the shortcut for this command. A message box appears on the screen asking if you want to exit to the programming environment.

3. Click OK. When you return to the programming environment, Visual Basic displays a dialog box named Event Procedures, as shown in Figure 1-8. An event procedure is code that you write to respond to a specific action that the user performs with a control. Notice the boxes labeled **Files, Objects,** and **Events** in this dialog box. These lists are designed to help you organize your code as you begin developing a program. You'll learn more about these lists later in this chapter.

4. For now, click Cancel to close the dialog box.

Visual Basic uses three different extensions for the names of the files in your project:

- The **FRM** extension identifies a form file.
- The **BAS** extension identifies a module file.
- The **MAK** extension identifies *project file*. This file keeps track of the various parts of your application.

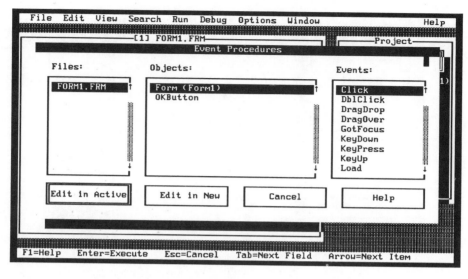

Figure 1-8 The Event Procedures dialog box

A project can consist of a single form or many forms and modules. The list of file names in the Project window increases in length as you add new forms and modules to your application. You use commands listed in the **File** menu to add files to your program.

Menus in the Programming Environment

The menu system in the programming environment provides many tools that you'll use during the process of developing an application. There are nine pull-down menus in the system: the **File** menu, the **Edit** menu, the **View** menu, the **Search** menu, the **Run** menu, the **Debug** menu, the **Options** menu, the **Window** menu, and the **Help** menu, shown in Figures 1-9 to 1-17. (The Form Designer has its own set of menus, which you'll explore in Chapter 2.)

As you have already seen, you can pull down a menu by clicking an item in the menu bar or by pressing the Alt key on the keyboard and then striking the first letter of the menu name. For example, pressing Alt and then F displays the **File** menu. Once a menu is displayed, you select a command by clicking the command name with the mouse or by pressing the appropriate key on the keyboard. In addition, some menu commands have keyboard shortcuts that you can use to invoke them without pulling down a menu.

Brief summaries of the commands and tools provided in each menu follow.

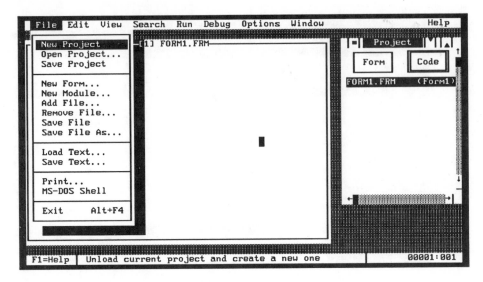

Figure 1-9 The **File** menu

The File Menu

The **File** menu contains commands for working individually or collectively with the files of a project. For example, the **Open Project...** command opens all the files of an existing project in one efficient operation. Likewise, the **Save Project** command saves all the files of the current project to disk. The **New Project** command starts you out fresh with a new project. The **File** menu also contains commands that add new forms and modules to your current application and that save forms and modules individually to disk. You can use the **Load Text...** command to add code to your current application from a text file on disk. Conversely, the **Save Text...** command stores code from the current form to a text file on disk. The **Print...** command allows you to print the code of an open file. Finally, the **Exit** command closes the Visual Basic window, ending your current session with the program.

The Edit Menu

The **Edit** menu contains an assortment of tools that are useful during the process of writing the text of a Basic program. The **Undo** command allows you to restore the original text after a mistaken editing operation. The **Cut**, **Copy**, and **Paste** commands together provide the cut-and-paste and copy-and-paste operations. The **New Sub...**, **New Function...**, and **Event Procedures...** commands simplify the process of adding new procedures and viewing existing procedures in your program.

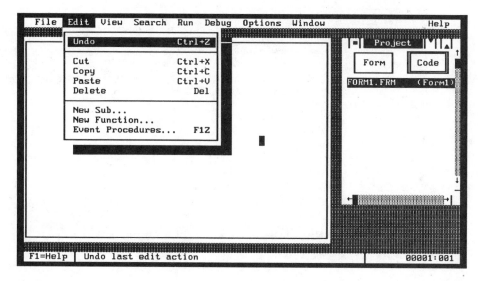

Figure 1-10 The **Edit** menu

The View Menu

The **View** menu supplies miscellaneous tools for working with code and forms. You can use the **Code...** command to select a procedure from an open form or module. The **Form...** command switches you to the Form Designer. (These two commands are equivalent to the **Code** and **Form**

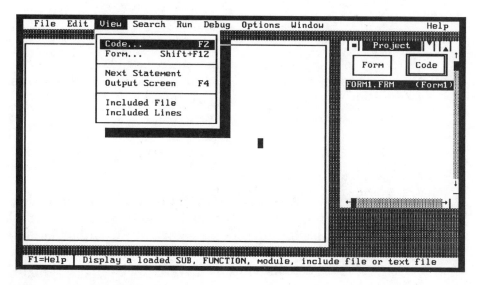

Figure 1-11 The **View** menu

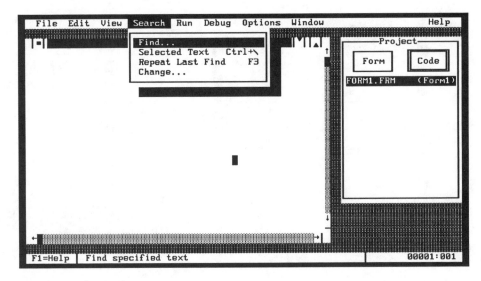

Figure 1-12 The **Search** menu

buttons on the Project window.) The **Next Statement** command selects the next executable statement after an interruption in a program. The **Output Screen** command displays the current output screen—that is, the last screen created by a program run. Finally, the **View** menu provides two commands for working with *include files*—code files that are designed to be loaded into memory when you run your program.

The Search Menu

The **Search** menu provides find and replace operations for use in a Code window. The **Find...** command is useful for locating a particular passage of code in your program. The **Change...** command allows you to make global replacements in the text of your code.

The Run Menu

The **Run** menu contains the commands that you use when you are ready to try running an application that you have developed. For example, the **Start** command begins a performance of the current application. The **Make EXE File...** command creates a single compiled EXE file from the parts of the current application.

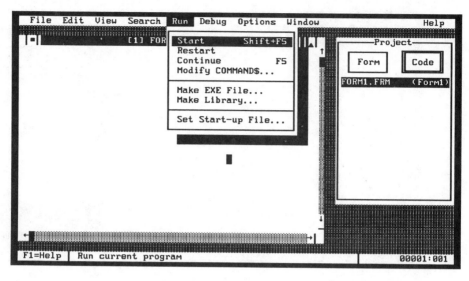

Figure 1-13 The **Run** menu

The Debug Menu

The **Debug** menu has a variety of tools that are useful in finding and correcting logical errors in a program. Once a performance is underway, you can use commands in the **Debug** menu to perform *debugging* opera-

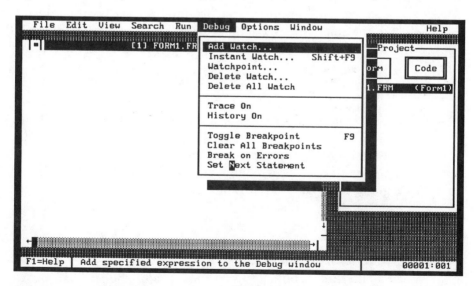

Figure 1-14 The **Debug** menu

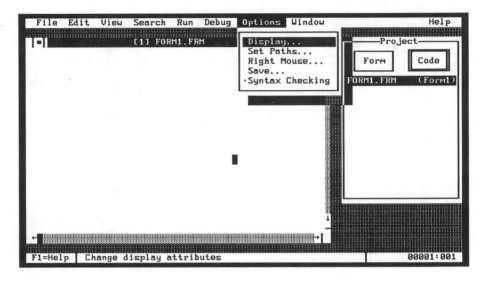

Figure 1-15 The **Options** menu

tions if you find that your program is not working the way you expected it to. (You'll have a chance to work with some of these tools in Chapter 5.)

The Options Menu

The **Options** menu allows you to modify the appearance and operation of the Visual Basic programming environment itself. For example, you can select new display colors, establish default file paths, change the effect of a mouse click, and turn Basic syntax checking on or off in the Code window.

The Window Menu

The **Window** menu gives you quick access to the windows available in the programming environment, including debugging, output, and project windows. In addition, you can use the **New Window** command to open multiple windows for viewing the code of a given form or module and the **Arrange All** command to rearrange multiple windows on the screen.

The Help Menu

The **Help** menu provides a variety of entry points into the Visual Basic help system: The **Index** command provides an alphabetically arranged list of help topics. The **Contents** command directs you to major categories of information about the programming environment and the Visual Basic

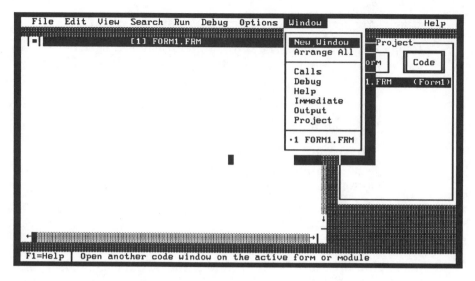

Figure 1-16 The **Window** menu

language. The **Keyboard** command displays a **Keyboard Guide**, providing access to keyboard techniques in the Visual Basic environment. In addition, the **Tutorial** command starts the on-line Visual Basic tutorial. You should take the time to go through this tutorial at some time when you begin your work with Visual Basic.

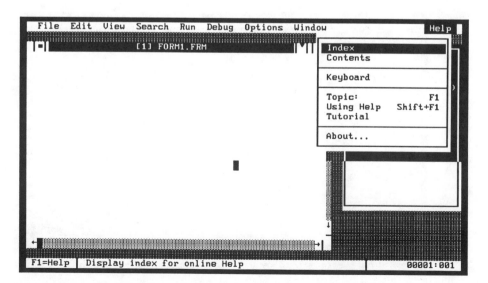

Figure 1-17 The **Help** menu

Hands-on Exercise: Using Commands from the File Menu

Imagine that you have been building a dialog box in **Form1**, which is currently the only form in your application. You now decide to add a module in which to write general-purpose procedures that will be used in the project. Here are the steps for adding this new file to your application:

1. Pull down the **File** menu and choose the **New Module** command.

2. In the resulting **New Module** dialog box, enter the file name **Test** for the module. Then press Enter. Visual Basic assigns the file name TEST.BAS to the module. As shown in Figure 1-18, the Project window now lists the two files that are currently in your application, and the Code window is available for entering code into the TEST.BAS module.

3. Now close this project without saving it. (Normally you would choose the **Save Project** command from the **File** menu to save this project as a MAK file. But you don't need to save this exercise.) Pull down the **File** menu and choose the **New Project** command. Visual Basic displays a message box on the screen asking you if you wish to save the files of your project. Respond by clicking the **No** button.

4. Finally, to prepare for the next section of this chapter, you'll now open a sample application from disk: Pull down the **File** command and select **Open Project**. In the **Directories** box, double-click the

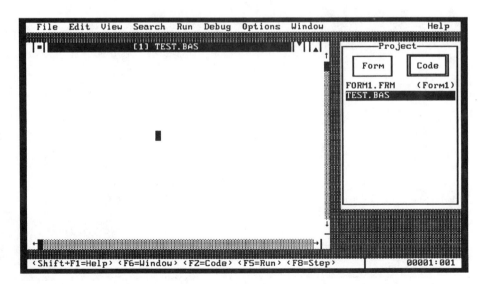

Figure 1-18 Adding a module to the project

directory in which you have stored the sample programs from the exercise disk that came with this book. To move up the directory path, double-click the two periods at the top of the **Directories** list. (Alternatively, select the appropriate disk drive if you have elected to keep these sample programs on a floppy disk.) In the **Files** box, scroll down to **REALEST.MAK** and double-click the project's file name.

A FIRST APPLICATION EXAMPLE

In response to your final step in the previous exercise, Visual Basic opens the application you have selected. The application contains one form, named REALEST.FRM, as shown in the Project window in Figure 1-19. The Code window shows the beginning of the program. This sample application, called the *Real Estate* program, will be the focus of your attention throughout most of the remainder of this chapter.

In fact, the program consists of two files on disk. REALEST.MAK is the project file and REALEST.FRM is the form file. You'll try running this program shortly; when you do so, you'll see the program's form appear on the screen. This form contains examples of the Visual Basic controls that you've been learning about in this chapter.

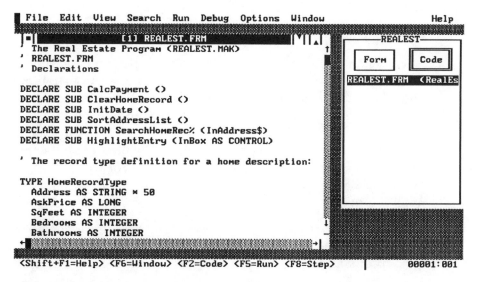

Figure 1-19 Opening the *Real Estate* Application

The *Real Estate* Application

Real Estate is a database application, designed for a user who is in the process of searching for a house to buy. Imagine that you are selling your current home and looking for a new one to buy. It might take you weeks or even months to find the right house, and along the way you might inspect dozens of houses that are on the market. At some point in this process, the houses you've already seen may become a mental blur of remodeled kitchens, garden decks with built-in hot tubs, and panoramic views of the city.

The *Real Estate* application gives you a quick way to keep track of essential information about the homes you've seen, along with your own evaluative notes. You can also use the program to review the information about a given house at any time. The program maintains a database on disk, storing the house records as you enter them into the program's main dialog box. Each time you run the *Real Estate* application, the program provides you with a list of all the addresses you have stored in the database so far. To look at the description of a given home, you simply select an address from the list. Alternatively, you can enter new addresses into the database, or you can revise existing records.

In addition, the program calculates the monthly mortgage payment you would have to make after the purchase of a particular house. The program has a payment calculator that displays the loan payment calculated from a given principal amount, a down payment, an interest rate, and the term of the loan in years.

Running the Application

The best way to start examining this sample application is to run it. As you do so, keep in mind that the program's dialog box—with all its input boxes and labels, command buttons and options, and all the other elements of this application's user interface—was designed and built inside Visual Basic's Form Designer environment. (In Chapter 2 you'll work through the steps of creating dialog boxes; and in Chapter 3 you'll explore the techniques for establishing the appropriate control properties.)

The following steps will guide you through a sample run of the *Real Estate* application:

1. Press F5 to begin the performance. This key is the keyboard shortcut for the **Continue** command in the **Run** menu. When you press it, the program's input dialog appears, as shown in Figure 1-20. As you can

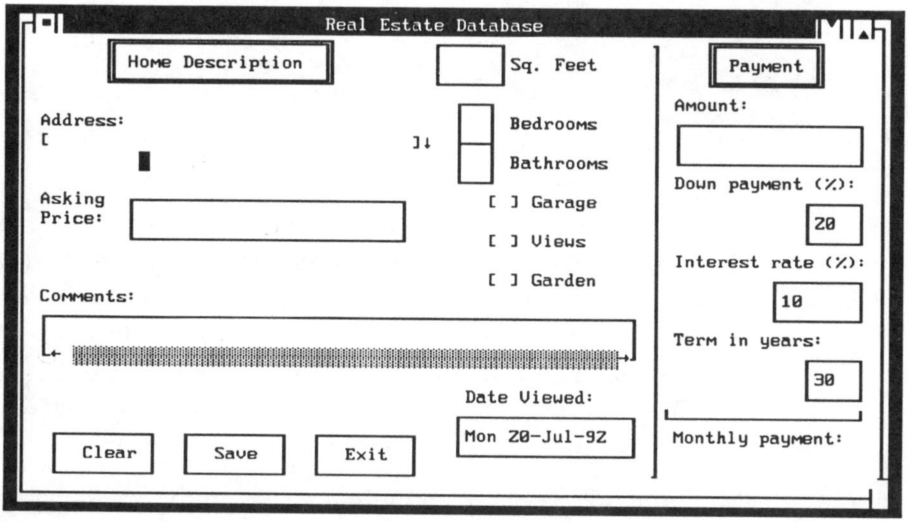

Figure 1-20 The dialog box of the *Real Estate* application

see, there are about a dozen controls that you will use to enter the information about a recently viewed house.

- A combo box labeled **Address** is for the address of the house. As you begin entering records into the database, the drop-down list attached to this box provides the complete list of addresses that you have visited so far. You can select an address from this list to view the corresponding house record.

- Text boxes labeled **Asking Price**, **Sq. Feet**, **Bedrooms**, and **Bathrooms** are for entering basic information about the house. In addition, there is a scrollable text box labeled **Comments** for you to enter a line of descriptive information and impressions; and a text box labeled **Date Viewed**, which initially displays the current date. (You can change the date entry if you wish.)

- There are three check boxes, labeled **Garage**, **Views**, and **Garden**. Initially these boxes are unchecked; you check them if the current house has these features.

2. Enter the following imaginary home record into the dialog box:

    Address: 980 Orange Drive, Berkeley
    Asking Price: 195500
    Sq. Feet: 2250
    Bedrooms: 3

```
Bathrooms: 2
Garage: (checked)
Views: (unchecked)
Garden: (checked)
Comments: Built in the 1920's; nicely renovated;
big kitchen.
```

You can use the Tab key or the mouse to select the text box for each data entry. Click a check box with the mouse to toggle between the checked and unchecked status. Examine your work after you complete the entries, and correct any errors that you find.

3. Click the **Save** button to save this record in the database. Then click the **Clear** button to clear the current record from the dialog box, so you can begin entering a new record.

4. Enter the following two additional records into the database, one at a time. (Click **Save** and then **Clear** after entering each record.)

```
Address: 50 Main Street, Albany
Asking Price: 237000
Sq. Feet: 2650
Bedrooms: 4
Bathrooms: 2
Garage: (checked)
Views: (checked)
Garden: (checked)
Comments: Comfortable ranch house; large yard; bay
views.
```

```
Address: 1350 32nd Avenue, El Cerrito
Asking Price: 259000
Sq. Feet: 2425
Bedrooms: 3
Bathrooms: 1
Garage: (checked)
Views: (unchecked)
Garden: (unchecked)
Comments: Overpriced; small bedrooms; needs major
repairs.
```

5. Click the arrow at the right side of the **Address** box to view the drop-down list of existing address records. The list is shown in Figure 1-21. Click the third address in the list (980 Orange Drive). The program reads the corresponding home record from the database and displays its data in the dialog box.

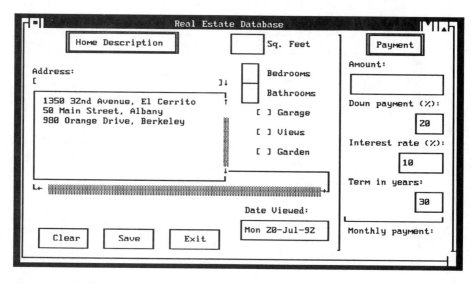

Figure 1-21 The drop-down list of addresses

6. Examine the right side of the *Real Estate* application's dialog box. The program has automatically entered the current home's asking price into the Amount text box and has calculated a monthly mortgage payment of $1,372.52, displayed at the lower-right corner of the dialog box. This calculation is based on the program's default mortgage terms: a 20% down payment, a 10% interest rate for the loan, and a 30-year term. In the next steps you'll make changes in these defaults and see how the program recalculates the mortgage payment.

7. Enter a value of **30** in the **Down Payment** box, a rate of **8.75** into the text box labeled **Interest Rate**, and a value of **15** into the box labeled **Term in Years**. Then press Tab to reactivate the **Address** box. Given these new terms, the program recalculates the monthly payment as $1,367.75, as shown in Figure 1-22.

8. Click the **Exit** button to end the program performance, and then press any key to return to the programming environment.

Examining the Elements of the Application

The dialog box of the *Real Estate* application illustrates several of the controls from the Visual Basic Toolbox, including labels, text boxes, command buttons, check boxes, combo boxes, and a horizontal scroll bar. (Review Figure 1-22 and find the examples of each of these controls.) An

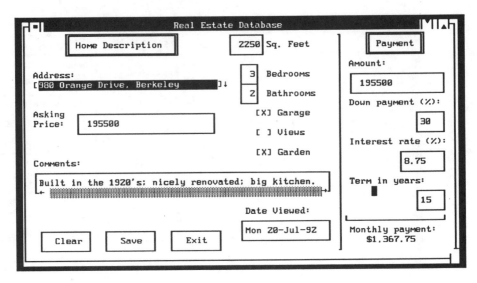

Figure 1-22 Recalculating the monthly mortgage

interesting exercise at this point is to examine the property settings for controls used in this application. You could choose almost any control in the **RealEst** form for this exercise, but first you have to switch to the Form Designer environment. Follow these steps:

1. Click the Form button in the Project window. Because this project contains only one form, Visual Basic immediately makes the switch to the Form Designer and displays the form. The form looks almost the same as it did during the program performance, except for the presence of a grid of background dots that the Form Designer supplies.

2. Click the text box labeled Comments to select this control. Then press the Alt key. The Form Designer's menu bar and Properties bar appear at the top of the screen, superimposed over the top lines of the **RealEst** form.

3. Pull down the Property list and use the up- and down-arrow keys on your keyboard to examine the property settings for the selected control. As you highlight each property in turn, the current setting for the property appears in the Value box to the right of the Property list, as shown in Figure 1-23. Several properties have been explicitly reset from their default values for this text box control:

    • The **CtlName** property provides a name for the control; this name serves to identify the control in the application's code.

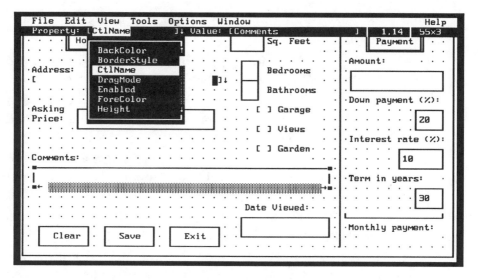

Figure 1-23 Examining the controls in the **RealEst** form

The **CtlName** setting for this text box is **Comments**. As you have already seen, **CtlName** is an important property that you will set for most of the controls that you add to a form.

- The **ScrollBars** property determines whether the text box will have a scroll bar. The setting here is **1-Horizontal**. (An associated property named **Multiline** has a setting of **True**.)

- The **Text** property gives the initial text value displayed inside the box. The setting for this property is empty, meaning that no text appears inside the box when the program begins.

- The **Height**, **Width**, **Top**, and **Bottom** settings determine the dimensions and the position of the text box.

You'll learn more about the settings for these and other properties in Chapter 3. For now, keep in mind that these particular property settings apply to only one control, the **Comments** text box. As you develop the interface for an application, you'll establish property settings individually for each control in your program. (Press Escape to close the Property list.)

Viewing the Code behind the Application

Before leaving the *Real Estate* application, you should first take a look at some of the code that lies behind the application's form. Think of the major tasks that the program must perform in response to your input and selections during run time:

- As you enter the information about a given house, the program organizes all of the data together as a complete record.

- When you click the **Save** button, the program stores the current house record in the database on disk and adds the home's address to the list attached to the **Address** combo box.

- If you select an existing address from the **Address** list, the program searches for that address in the database, reads the corresponding record from the file, and displays the record's data in the dialog box.

- If you make changes in the loan terms, the program recalculates the monthly payment.

- When you click the **Clear** button, the program erases the information for the current home record from the main dialog box, thus preparing for a new record input.

- Finally, the program performance ends when you click the **Exit** button on the main dialog box.

Notice that all these operations and calculations occur *in response to* your actions during run time. You enter a value into a text box, you select an entry from a list, or you click a command button—and the application produces an appropriate programmed response to your activity. Visual Basic is an *event-driven* language. Each programmed action that takes place during a performance is in response to an anticipated event—usually an event that is initiated by the user.

This event-driven language model determines to a large extent how you organize your programs in Visual Basic. A program consists primarily of *event procedures* that define the action of the application in response to specific events that are anticipated during run time. When you place a control in a form, you have to think about the associated events that might take place around the control. If you want your program to respond to a potential event, you write an event procedure that defines the response.

The *Real Estate* application has many interesting event procedures. For now, take a look at one fairly simple example—the procedure that takes control when you click the **Clear** button during run time. From your current position in the Form Designer, here are the steps for viewing the code:

1. Press Alt, if necessary, to view the menu bar for the Form Designer. Then pull down the **Edit** menu and choose the **Event Procedures** command. (Alternatively, you can simply press F12, the shortcut key

for this command.) A message box appears on the screen, asking you if you want to exit to the programming environment.

2. Click OK. The programming environment takes over the screen, and the Event Procedures dialog box appears.

3. In the Objects list, scroll down to the **ClearButton** control and select this name in the list. In response, the Events list displays the complete list of event procedures available for a command button control. Procedures that exist for the current control are displayed in all-uppercase letters.

4. Select the **Click** procedure in the Events list if it is not already selected. Then click the **Edit in Active** button. Visual Basic displays the **ClearButton_Click** procedure in the code window, as shown in Figure 1-24.

Your goal in looking at this procedure now is not to master the details of the code but rather to begin understanding the significance of Visual Basic's event-driven programming model. This procedure's name, **ClearButton_Click**, describes its purpose in the program: Quite simply, it is performed when the **ClearButton** control is clicked by the user.

The procedure performs several actions, all of which you can see by scrolling down the code window: First, it assigns empty string values to the **Text** properties of the text boxes that describe a home. Then, it resets the date, restores the **Value** properties of the program's three check boxes to

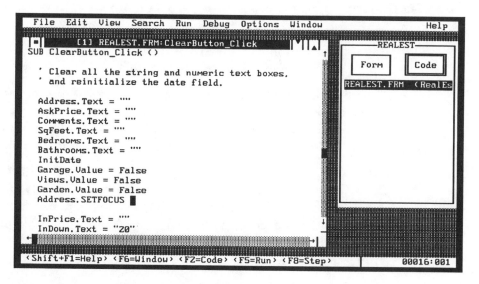

Figure 1-24 The **ClearButton_Click** procedure

False, and activates the **Address** box. Finally, it reestablishes the program's default values for the terms of the loan calculation. (Near the top of the procedure you can see a *comment* that briefly describes the action of the routine. As in other versions of Basic, a comment in a Visual Basic program begins with a single-quote character.) When these actions are complete, the program performance pauses, waiting for the next event that requires a response.

You can now look at the code behind other controls if you want to. Just press F12 to reopen the **Event Procedures** dialog box. Select an object and a corresponding event procedure, and then click the **Edit in Active** button. In particular, you may be interested in looking at the event procedures behind the other command buttons in the dialog box form.

When you are finished looking at the *Real Estate* application, pull down the **File** menu and select the **Exit** command to leave Visual Basic. You'll return to this application in Chapter 8, where you'll have the opportunity to examine the program's code in detail.

SUMMARY: THE STEPS OF APPLICATION DEVELOPMENT IN VISUAL BASIC

Application development in Visual Basic is essentially a three-step process. In the first two steps you design an interface, using the tools provided in the Form Designer environment—the Toolbox and the Properties bar. The third step is writing code. Here is a brief summary of these steps:

1. Create a form and switch to the Form Designer. Select visual controls (command buttons, text boxes, lists, and so on) to represent the options and operations of your application.

2. Establish the initial properties of these controls—in other words, specify how the elements of your application will appear on the screen and how they will behave while your program is running.

3. Finally, write the event procedures for some or all of the controls that you have built into your application. These procedures will ultimately determine how your program will respond to events that take place while the program is running. Events include a wide range of user-initiated actions, such as clicking a button with the mouse, selecting a menu option, or entering a data value into a text box from the keyboard.

Only the last of these three steps involves the process traditionally called *programming*. The first two steps take place within the interactive environment of the Form Designer.

In the upcoming chapters of this book you'll learn about these three essential steps in greater detail. Take a moment now to reflect on the learning process that you are about to begin. There are many tools to master, some of them simple and mechanical, others conceptual and subtle. But because these tools are all interrelated, the process of learning to use them may sometimes seem remarkably circular. At the outset you'll want to become familiar with the controls that Visual Basic offers for your applications, and you'll want to understand the significance of their properties. Then you'll begin writing code to respond to events in your applications. You'll expand what you know about programming while you master the elements of the Visual Basic environment.

As you develop your own understanding of the relationships among the various elements of a Visual Basic application—controls, properties, and code—you will eventually go back to learn more about each one of these features individually. In short, the process of learning about Visual Basic is much like the process of developing and fine-tuning an application: You alternately focus your attention on individual controls, the properties and events that relate to those controls, and the procedures that govern your program's response to events.

2

Building an Application:
Step 1—Selecting Forms
and Controls

INTRODUCTION

In the first phase of Visual Basic application development, you select the tools and design the windows for your program's on-screen presentation. During this process you are also laying the structural foundation for the event-driven program that will define your program's behavior. This step takes place in Visual Basic's Form Designer component, in an interactive, dynamic, and efficient process. As you create the forms that will eventually become your program's dialog boxes and windows—and you place appropriate controls on these forms—you can see your application taking shape in front of you.

While the results of this step are impressive, they are neither complete nor final. When you move on to the subsequent steps of application development, you can go back to the Form Designer and make changes in the visual interface at any point, fine-tuning the initial concept of your program as you proceed. But by the end of this stage, you already have a very satisfying sense that your programming project is underway. You also have a clear plan for organizing the work remaining ahead of you.

As a hands-on introduction to the process of building a visual interface, this chapter guides you through the initial development of a financial application called the *Loan Calculator*. This program is designed to compute the monthly payment for a bank loan of any size and to produce a payment comparison table for a range of nearby principal amounts and interest rates. You'll work with a variety of controls in the application, including labels, text boxes, command buttons, frames, option buttons, and a combo box. You'll begin planning the use of these controls to depict the input requirements, the options, and the operations of the application.

The variety of tools available in Visual Basic gives you great flexibility in planning the style of your application's interface. To explore this idea, you'll also begin developing a second version of the *Loan Calculator* application, presenting the program's options in a rather different way from the first version. You'll combine several of the program's original controls in a pull-down menu located at the top of the main dialog box. To build this menu system, you'll work with Visual Basic's menu-planning tool, called the *Menu Design Window*. In the end, you'll be able to compare the two different approaches and decide which interface you prefer.

Although the focus of this chapter is on forms and controls, occasionally you'll find yourself looking ahead at properties and code as well. The three steps of program development in Visual Basic are not always independent, neatly sequential processes. More typically, you will find yourself alternately focusing your attention on different levels of your application, or even concentrating on multiple elements of the program at once.

In Chapters 3, 4, and 5 you'll continue working on versions of this application. You'll define properties for most of the program's forms and controls, and you'll continue writing code to define the program's reactions to events. Finally, you'll work on some of Visual Basic's debugging techniques. At various stages in your work you'll load parts of the *Loan Calculator* application from the exercise disk that came with this book. This will allow you to focus on each specific task in its turn. As you complete this program, you'll develop the essential skills you need to build applications in Visual Basic.

The *Loan Calculator* Application

Before you begin developing the application, here is a brief preview of the finished project. (If you want to see the finished program on your screen while you go through this preview, choose the **Open Project** command from the **File** menu and load the LOANCALC.MAK project from the directory where you have copied the files from this book's exercise disk. Then press F5 when you are ready to run the program.) The *Loan Calculator* includes three forms—two designed as dialog boxes and one as a window for displaying a table of monthly payments. The main dialog box has controls for the expected input parameters of a loan: the principal amount, the interest rate, and the term of the loan. The **Term** control is a combo box with a list of likely loan periods, expressed in years.

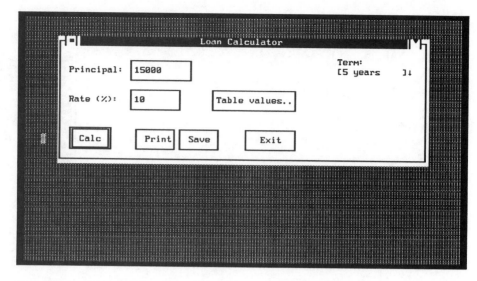

Figure 2-1 The main dialog box of the *Loan Calculator*

In this application you begin by entering the three major input values that describe your anticipated loan. For example, imagine that you are buying a new car and you are planning to finance about $15,000 of the purchase price as a five-year loan from your bank. You expect the interest rate to be about ten percent. To enter these values you can click each of the three text boxes in turn with the mouse—Principal, Rate, and Term— and type a value into each box from the keyboard. Or you can press the Tab key to move from one box to the next. (To enter the term of the loan, you can also click the down-arrow next to the Term box and select an option from the resulting drop-down list.) Figure 2-1 shows the *Loan Calculator* dialog box, with the car loan parameters already entered into the appropriate input controls.

Before viewing an output table, you now have the option of selecting appropriate increments for the payment comparison table that the program will produce. To open the program's second dialog box, you click the **Table values...** button or press Alt+T. The resulting dialog box has two sets of option buttons, representing table increments for the principal and the interest rate. You select **$100** for the principal increment and **0.25%** as the interest increment (Figure 2-2).

When you click the **OK** button (or press Enter), the second dialog box disappears from the screen, and the program produces the output table. As you can see in Figure 2-3, the monthly payment for a five-year $15,000 loan at a 10% interest rate is $318.71. The table also shows a nearby range

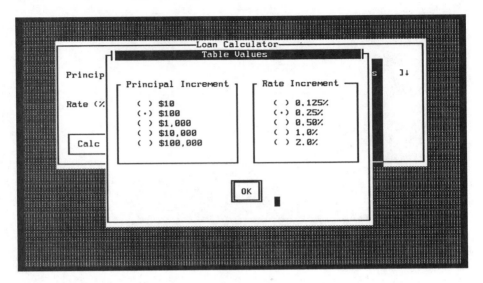

Figure 2-2 The **Table Values** dialog box

of other calculated monthly payments, varying by the amount of the principal and the interest rate.

Once you have produced the table that you want, you can select one or both of the other output destinations, represented by the **Print** and **Save** buttons in the dialog box: Clicking the **Save** button (or pressing Alt+S)

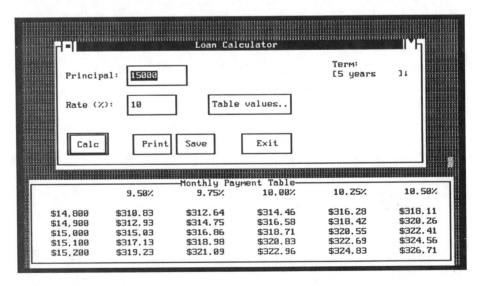

Figure 2-3 The payment table

produces a text file on disk for your payment table. Alternatively, clicking the **Print** button (or pressing Alt+P) sends the output to your printer. During a run of the program you can produce as many different output tables as you want. After changing one or more of the three loan parameters, you click the **Calc** button or press Enter to view the resulting payment table. When you are finished, click the **Exit** button (or press Alt+X) to terminate the program performance.

The job ahead of you in this chapter is to create the three forms of this application and to place the appropriate controls on the two dialog boxes. You'll find that several of the controls—labels, text boxes, and control buttons—are very simple to create and put in place. The others—the combo box and the groups of option buttons—require some extra steps.

You'll create temporary files for the forms you design in this chapter's first exercise. (The forms for the final version of the *Loan Calculator* appear on the exercise disk as LOANINPT.FRM, LOANOPTS.FRM, and LOANTABL.FRM. In this chapter you'll save your work instead as TEMP-INPT.FRM, TEMPOPTS.FRM, and TEMPTABL.FRM.) Then, in Chapters 3, 4, and 5, you'll load the same project—progressively closer to completion—from files provided on the exercise disk. In this way you avoid having to perform repetitive steps that may not be central to the learning process.

Start up Visual Basic now if you have not already done so. If you've already been working in the Visual Basic environment, pull down the **File** menu and select the **New Project** command to begin a new project.

PLANNING AN APPLICATION

You'll begin this exercise by preparing the three forms for your project. For each form you will:

- Add the form to the project and supply an appropriate file name for saving the form on disk.

- Use the mouse to move the form to its correct position and to adjust its size.

In addition to saving the three forms individually on disk as FRM files, you'll also create the project's MAK file.

In Chapter 1 you had your first look at the Form Designer. Now as you prepare the first form for the *Loan Calculator,* you'll also take the opportunity to examine the Form Designer's menu system in greater detail. Here are the steps for creating the first form:

1. In the programming environment, pull down the **File** menu and choose the **New Form** command. The **New Form** dialog box appears on the screen. As you've seen before, it contains a text box labeled **File Name** and a **Directories** list box where you can choose the directory in which you want to save the new FRM file you are about to create.

2. Optionally, select the directory where you want to save the files you are about to create. To open a directory, double-click its name with the mouse. (To move up the directory hierarchy, double-click the two dots displayed at the top of the **Directories** list. These dots disappear when you reach the root directory for the current drive.) The name of the current directory is displayed just beneath the **File Name** label.

3. Activate the **File Name** text box by clicking it with the mouse or by pressing Alt+N. Enter the name **TEMPINPT** into the text box. Then click the **OK** button or press Enter to create the form file and switch to the Form Designer environment. Visual Basic expands the form's file name to TEMPINPT.FRM.

4. Use the mouse to size the form: Notice that a sizing handle is displayed at each of the form's four corners. Position the mouse pointer over the handle at the lower-left corner of the form, and drag the handle five columns to the left and four rows up. The size and shape of the form change accordingly. When you release the mouse button, the current dimensions of the form are displayed in the size box, at the right side of the Properties bar: **68x13**. (If you don't get the dimensions right at first, try dragging the size handle again.)

5. Use the mouse to reposition the frame: Point to the frame's title bar and drag the frame up to the position just beneath the Properties bar. Then drag again to center the frame horizontally on the screen. The coordinates **6,2**—representing the frame's row and column position relative to the upper-left corner of the screen—appear in the location box, just to the left of the size box in the Properties bar.

6. Pull down the **File** menu and choose the **Save Form** command. In response, Visual Basic saves the form as TEMPINPT.FRM.

By the way, Visual Basic also supplies simple keyboard techniques that you can use instead of the mouse to move or resize a form in the Form Designer environment:

- To move a form, press any combination of arrow keys (up, down, left, or right).

- To resize a form, hold down the shift key and then press any combination of arrow keys to increase or decrease the dimensions of the form.

Your next job is to add the other two forms to the project. But before you do, take a moment now for a brief survey of the menu commands available in the Form Designer.

The Form Designer Menus

Some of the menus in the Form Designer component contain lists of commands that are similar to menus in the programming environment. For example, the **File** menu contains commands for opening and saving projects and forms, and for exiting from the Form Designer environment; and the **Edit** menu has commands for cut-and-paste and copy-and-paste operations that you can perform on the controls you add to a form. The **Edit** menu also has the **Event Procedures** command, which switches you back to the programming environment and opens the **Event Procedures** dialog box.

The **View** menu's **Code** command (Figure 2-4) also moves you back to the programming environment. The **Form** command loads an existing form into the Form Designer from the current project. As you've seen, a project can consist of multiple forms; however, you can load only one form at a time into the Form Designer. If you need to edit several forms belonging to a particular project, you must work on them one at a time: Load a form into the Form Designer, make the necessary changes, save the revisions to disk, and then load the next form.

The **Menu Bar** command in the **View** menu is a toggle that allows you to hide or display the Form Designer's menu bar. You may want to hide the menu bar if you are working on a form that takes up the full screen. You can always bring back the menu bar by pressing F10 or activate it by pressing the Alt key. Finally, the **Grid Lines** command is another toggle that hides or displays the grid of dots in the background of a form. By

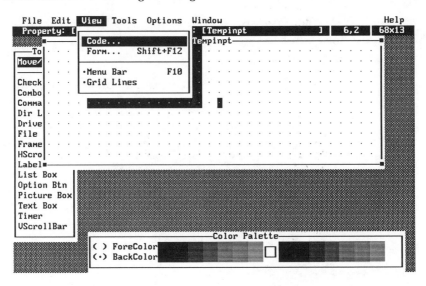

Figure 2-4 The **View** menu in the Form Designer environment

default, the Form Designer displays this grid in each form for the convenience of positioning controls.

The **Tools** menu (Figure 2-5) contains a complete list of the controls
available in the Form Designer. This list is identical to the Toolbox list.
Again, if you are working with a full-screen form, you may find it more

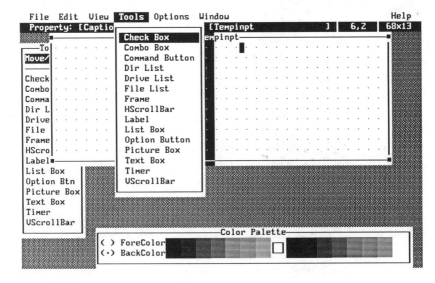

Figure 2-5 The **Tools** menu in the Form Designer environment

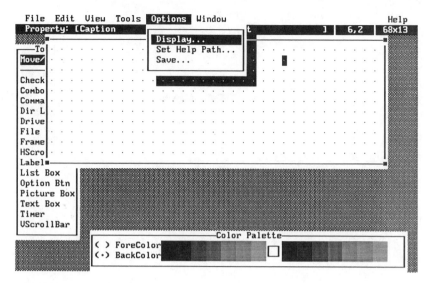

Figure 2-6 The **Options** menu in the Form Designer environment

convenient to select controls from the **Tools** menu rather than from the Toolbox.

The **Options** menu (Figure 2-6) contains three commands that change the behavior or appearance of the Form Designer. The **Display...** command allows you to select colors for the elements of the Form Designer environment. The **Set Help Path...** command specifies the directory location of help files. And the **Save...** command allows you select automatic save or backup options for saving files from the Form Designer environment.

The **Window** menu (Figure 2-7) lists all the windows available in the Form Designer and allows you to activate any of them. In particular, this menu gives you a convenient way to activate a window from the keyboard: Press Alt+W to pull down the Window menu, and then press the first letter of a window name. The Window menu also gives you access to the Menu Design Window, as you'll see later in this chapter.

Finally, the Form Designer's Help menu gives you a variety of entry points into the Visual Basic help system. You can press the F1 function key at any time during your work in the Form Designer to view information about the currently selected window, menu command, or control.

Adding Forms

You have created the first of three forms needed in the *Loan Calculator* application. Now you're ready to add the other two. You can add new forms

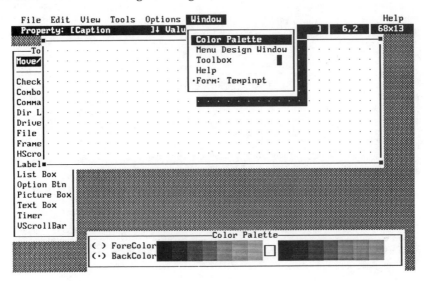

Figure 2-7 The **Window** menu in the Form Designer environment

to the current project from either the Form Designer or the programming environment. In the following steps you'll begin by returning to the programming environment to examine the project window and to create a MAK file:

1. Pull down the **File** menu and choose the **Exit** command. Because you have already saved the TEMPINPT form, Visual Basic switches you directly to the programming environment. The Project window now contains only one file in its list: TEMPINPT.FRM, as shown in Figure 2-8.

2. In the programming environment, pull down the **File** menu and choose **Save Project**. In the **Save Project** dialog box, select a directory if necessary and then enter **TEMPCALC** into the File Name text box. Then click OK. Visual Basic saves your project as TEMPCALC.MAK.

3. Pull down the **File** menu and choose **New Form**. In the **New Form** dialog box, select a directory if necessary and then enter TEMPOPTS as the file name for the new form you are about to create. Click OK. Once again Visual Basic switches you to the Form Designer.

4. Size the new form, giving it the dimensions **49x18**.

5. Move the form to the position **15, 3**.

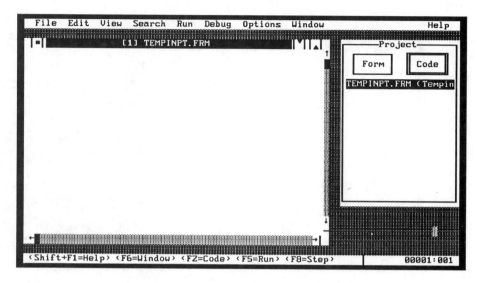

Figure 2-8 One form in the project window

6. Choose **Save Project** from the Form Designer's **File** menu. In response, Visual Basic saves the TEMPOPTS form and adds it to the TEMPCALC.MAK project file.

7. Select the **New Form** command again—but this time from the Form Designer's **File** menu—to add a third form to the project. Select a directory if necessary and enter TEMPTABL as the file name for the new form. Then click OK. This form is to be the output window for the payment table that the program generates.

8. Size the form, giving it the dimensions **78x9**, and move it to **1, 16**.

9. Choose **Save Project** again from the **File** menu, and then choose the **Exit** command to switch back to the programming environment.

When you complete all these steps, the project list will contain three FRM files, as shown in Figure 2-9. (You can use the mouse to change the size and the position of the Project window, just as you have done for the forms in this application.) The entire application consists of four files on disk: the three FRM files and one MAK file.

Because you have saved each form individually on disk, subsequent save operations will be much simpler when you make new changes in this application. Once each part of a project has a file name, you can save the entire project quickly by selecting the **Save Project** command. To avoid

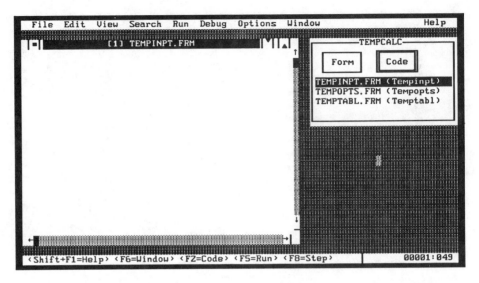

Figure 2-9 Three forms in the Project window

losing any work, you should periodically pull down the **File** menu and select **Save Project** as you proceed through the steps of application development.

WORKING WITH CONTROLS

You are ready to begin placing controls on the two forms that will become the application's dialog boxes. The Form Designer gives you two techniques for adding a control to a selected form from the list of controls in the Toolbox:

- The simpler technique is the one you have already practiced in Chapter 1: Double-click the appropriate control in the Toolbox. The corresponding control appears immediately in the center of the active form.

- Another technique is to select a control in the Toolbox list and then drag the mouse over the area where you want to place the control in the current form. This technique is required in some special situations, as you'll see later in this chapter.

Using the first of these two techniques, you can quickly place several controls on a form in succession by double-clicking the controls in the Toolbox. Then when you have added all the controls you want, you can start moving and sizing the controls inside the form. However, this approach calls for a little advance planning. When you eventually run your program, the order in which controls are activated by the Tab key matches the order in which you originally placed the controls on the form. You can change the Tab order during design time by changing the setting of a property named **TabIndex** for each of the controls on your form. But it is easier to anticipate this order while you are first adding controls to your application. Keep this property in mind as you begin adding controls to the *Loan Calculator* application.

Placing Controls on a Form

Select the TEMPINPT form in the Project window and click the **Form** button. The Form Designer reappears on the screen and displays the TEMPINPT form. This empty form will be the main dialog box of your application. When your work is complete, the form will contain eleven controls in all: three labels, two text boxes, one combo box, and five command buttons. You'll begin this exercise by double-clicking an item in the Toolbox list for each of these controls. Each time you do so, the newest control will appear in the center of the form, superimposed over the previous control. In effect, Visual Basic piles all eleven controls, one in front of another, in the middle of the form.

At the moment the Toolbox window is partially covered by the TEMP-INPT form. To activate the Toolbox, click its title bar with the mouse, or pull down the **Window** menu and choose **Toolbox**. Here are the steps for placing controls on the form:

1. Double-click **Label** in the Toolbox list three times. As you do so, the controls named **Label1**, **Label2**, and **Label3** appear in succession in the middle of the form.

2. Double-click **Text Box** twice in the Toolbox. Controls named **Text1** and **Text2** appear in the form.

3. Double-click **Combo Box** in the Toolbox. **Combo1** appears.

4. Double-click **Command Btn** five times. The controls named **Command1**, **Command2**, **Command3**, **Command4**, and **Command5** appear in the form.

5. Use the mouse to drag the eleven controls from the center of the form to their *approximate* positions inside the form. Use Figure 2-10 as your guide, but don't spend too much time on this task; you'll adjust the controls to their exact sizes and locations in the next step.

Table 2-1   Locations and Sizes of Controls in the Main Dialog Box

Control	Location	Size
Label1	1, 2	11x1
Label2	1, 5	11x1
Label3	50, 1	10x1
Text1	12, 1	12x3
Text2	12, 4	10x3
Combo1	50, 2	14x1
Command1	1, 8	8x3
Command2	26, 4	17x3
Command3	33, 8	10x3
Command4	12, 8	8x3
Command5	21, 8	8x3

6. Select each control in turn and drag the control to its correct location, as shown in Table 2-1. Then drag the sizing handles to give the control its correct size, also specified in Table 2-1.

7. Choose the **Save Project** command from the **File** menu to save your work to disk.

When you complete these steps, the TEMPINPT form appears as in Figure 2-10. An interesting exercise at this point is to try running the application, just to examine some of the features that Visual Basic builds into your dialog box before you write any of your own code. Of course, the application itself doesn't do anything useful yet, but you can still run it to see how the interface looks.

Here are the steps for running the program:

1. Pull down the **File** menu and choose **Exit** to return to the programming environment.

2. Now pull down the **Run** menu and select the **Start** command, or simply press the F5 shortcut key. The application's main dialog box appears on the screen, and the program is now running. Try the following experiments on the controls in the TEMPINPT form:

   • Press the Tab key several times to see the order in which controls are activated. An active control is said to have the *focus*

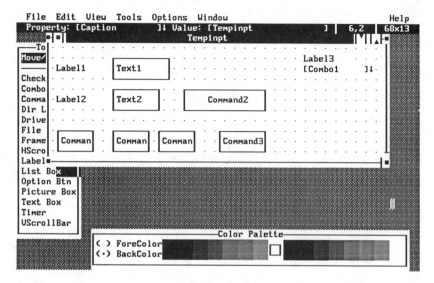

Figure 2-10 TEMPINPT with its controls in place

of the program. Notice how each type of control changes in appearance when it receives the focus. Also note that the label controls do not receive the focus at all.

- Try entering, editing, inserting, and deleting text inside either of the two text boxes. (You can even try a cut-and-paste operation: Select some text and press Ctrl+X to cut, then reposition the insertion point and press Ctrl+V to paste the text to a new location.) As you can see, these text boxes have a complete set of built-in editing functions.

- Click a command button, and notice the graphic push-button effect on the screen.

- Click the small down-arrow icon at the right side of the combo box. This is the arrow you normally press to view the drop-down list attached to a combo box control. While the list is empty at this point in the development of the application, you will nonetheless see a frame drop down from the box.

The application does not yet have an exit routine, so you have to use the form's built-in *control menu* to terminate the program performance. There are several ways to do this:

- Double-click the control menu box, located at the upper-left corner of the form.

- Press Alt+ – (minus sign) to pull down the control menu, and then choose **Close** from the menu.
- Press Ctrl+F4 from the keyboard.

After any one of these actions, press any key to return to the programming environment. If you now switch again to the Form Designer, you'll see that the TEMPINPT form is unchanged, regardless of any entries you may have made in text boxes during the experimental run of the application. Run-time activities never affect the original design-time definition of an application. Switch back to the programming environment now for the next step in this exercise.

Defining the Combo Box List

The combo box in the TEMPINPT form still seems vaguely defined, even for this stage of the development process. As you've seen, the drop-down list attached to the combo box is still empty. Further development of this control requires you to work with code, a topic introduced in later chapters. But taking the time to define this control now, at this early point in your work, will give you a preview of some of the skills you'll master later. In the following exercise you'll define the combo box list.

The drop-down list for a combo box is created at run time rather than development time. The list in the *Loan Calculator* application is a simple case, because the entries in the drop-down list remain fixed during the entire program performance. (Contrast this with the drop-down list that you saw in the *Real Estate* application: The **Address** combo box in that program has a list that gets longer each time you add a new home record to the database.)

The simplest way to define a fixed list for a combo box is at the time the startup form is first "loaded" onto the screen, at the beginning of the program performance. In many applications this action—displaying the first form on the screen—is the first event the program recognizes. It is called the **Load** event for the form. As with other events that occur during a program's performance, Visual Basic always looks for a corresponding event procedure when the **Load** event takes place. The event procedure in this case is named **Form_Load**.

In other words, the **Load** event triggers a performance of the **Form_Load** procedure at the time a form is first displayed on the screen. Any instructions that you include in the **Form_Load** procedure of the startup form are therefore performed at the beginning of the program run. This procedure is a perfect place to put instructions that initialize conditions in your program—including the instructions that build a fixed list for a combo box.

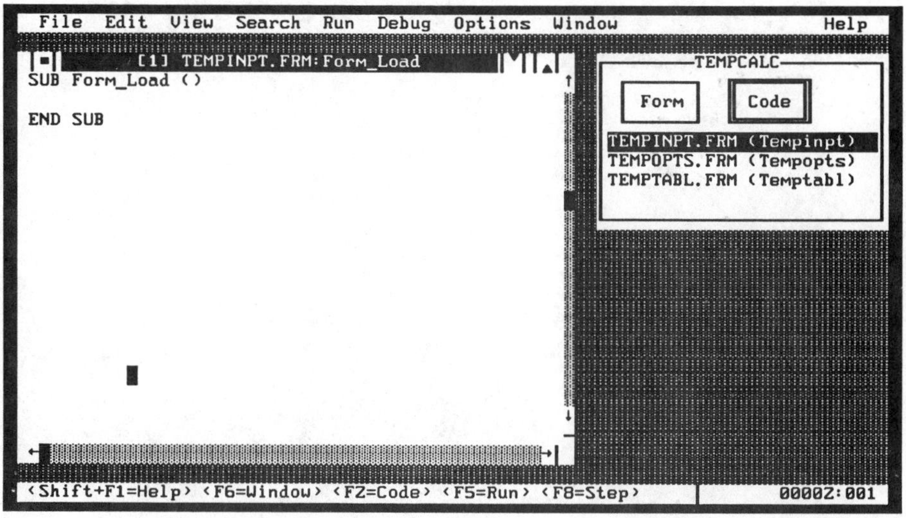

```
 File   Edit   View   Search   Run   Debug   Options   Window                    Help
┌─■──────────[1] TEMPINPT.FRM:Form_Load─────────────────┐▼│▲│┌──────────TEMPCALC──────────┐
SUB Form_Load ()                                              │ ┌──────┐  ┌──────┐
                                                              │ │ Form │  │ Code │
END SUB                                                       │ └──────┘  └──────┘
                                                              │ TEMPINPT.FRM (Tempinpt)
                                                              │ TEMPOPTS.FRM (Tempopts)
                                                              │ TEMPTABL.FRM (Temptabl)




              ■



 <Shift+F1=Help> <F6=Window> <FZ=Code> <F5=Run> <F8=Step>              00002:001
```

Figure 2-11 The **Form_Load** procedure in the Code window

Follow these steps to create the **Form_Load** procedure in TEMPINPT:

1. Select TEMPINPT in the Project window.

2. Pull down the **Edit** menu and choose **Event Procedures** (or press F12, the shortcut for this command). In the resulting **Event Procedures** dialog box, TEMPINPT.FRM is selected in the **Files** list, and **Form** is selected in the **Objects** list.

3. Click **Load** in the **Events** list and then click the **Edit in Active** button. As you can see in Figure 2-11, the resulting code window is named TEMPINPT.FRM:Form_Load. In this window Visual Basic has already prepared a template for the **Form_Load** procedure by entering the first and last lines of code.

4. Between the **Sub** and **End Sub** lines, type the following six lines of Visual Basic code:

    ```
    Combo1.ADDITEM "4 years"
    Combo1.ADDITEM "5 years"
    Combo1.ADDITEM "10 years"
    Combo1.ADDITEM "15 years"
    Combo1.ADDITEM "20 years"
    Combo1.ADDITEM "30 years"
    ```

5. Check your typing carefully for errors. Then press F5 to try running the program again. When the dialog box appears on the screen, click the down-arrow icon at the right of the **Combo1** control. You'll see

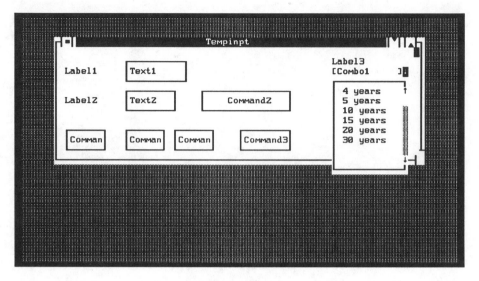

Figure 2-12 The drop-down list defined for the **Combo1** control

the drop-down list that you have just defined (Figure 2-12). Click any one of the entries in the list. Your selection becomes the new text displayed inside the combo box.

6. Press Ctrl+F4 to terminate the program run, and press any key to return to the programming environment.

You've now written your first event procedure. As you've guessed, each of the **Combo1.ADDITEM** statements in the **Form_Load** procedure appends a text item to the drop-down list of the **Combo1** control. **ADDITEM** is known as a *method,* a built-in Visual Basic procedure whose action is applied to a specific object. In this case the relevant object is the **Combo1** control. The usual syntax for calling a Visual Basic method is:

```
ObjectName.METHODNAME
```

where *ObjectName* identifies the object to which the method applies. The name of the object and the name of the method are separated by a period.

You'll learn much more about methods and event procedures in later chapters. After this brief detour into Visual Basic code, you can now return to developing the interface of your application. At this point in your work, the TEMPINPT dialog box contains all the controls you have planned for it. But for the most part, the controls all still have their default properties. Most glaringly, none of the labels, captions, or initial text values have been set in ways that are relevant to this application. You'll work on these and other properties in Chapter 3. For now, pull down the **File** menu and select the **Save Project** command to save your work. (Recall that **Save Project** saves changes you have made in any of the project's forms.)

Frames and Option Buttons

Your next task is to prepare the application's second dialog box, saved as TEMPOPTS.FRM. Looking back at Figure 2-2, you'll recall that this form is to contain two groups of option buttons, each group enclosed in a frame. In addition, there is a command button at the bottom of the form.

Option buttons are always defined in groups. Only one option can be selected at a given time; all the other buttons are switched off. The active option button contains a solid black bullet; inactive option buttons are represented by empty parentheses. These controls are sometimes called radio buttons.

Any option buttons inside a form are automatically defined as a group. But when you want to include more than one group of options in a given dialog box, you need a way to separate the groups from each other. One way is to enclose each group of options inside a frame. This is the approach you'll use in the *Loan Calculator* application.

You'll begin the following exercise by placing two frames and a command button on the TEMPOPTS form:

1. Select TEMPOPTS in the Project window, and click the **Form** button. This action switches you to the Form Designer environment and displays the TEMPOPTS form.

2. In the Toolbox list, double-click **Frame** twice. Then double-click **Command Btn** once. Move the three controls from their original positions at the center of the form to their approximate new positions: Place the command button, **Command1**, at the bottom of the form. The two frames, **Frame1** and **Frame2**, belong at the upper-left and upper-right sides of the form.

3. Move and resize the three controls according to the measurements provided in Table 2-2.

Now you are ready to place the option buttons inside each of the frames. Note that the double-clicking technique is not available for inserting Toolbox controls into a frame. If you double-click the option button icon, the resulting control will be located inside the *form* but not inside a *frame*. Even if you later move the control to a position that appears to be inside one of the two frames, the control will still belong to the form, not the

Table 2-2 Locations and Sizes of the Controls in the Second Dialog Box

Control	Location	Size
Frame1	1, 2	23x9
Frame2	26, 2	20x9
Command1	22, 12	6x3

frame. For this reason, you have to drag each option button manually to its position inside a frame in order to create the two groups of options correctly.

Here are the steps for placing the first option button, initially named **Option1**, inside **Frame1**:

1. Inside the Toolbox list, select **Option Btn** by clicking it once with the mouse.

2. Without pressing the mouse button, move the pointer to a position near the upper-left corner of **Frame1**.

3. To create the option button control, hold down the left mouse button and drag the mouse to the right. A shadow of the control appears inside **Frame1**. When the control is approximately the correct size (see Figure 2-13), release the mouse button. **Option1** appears inside the frame.

You now need to repeat these three steps for each of the remaining four option buttons in **Frame1** and then for the five option buttons in **Frame2**. Start out by creating the option buttons in their approximate locations and sizes. Then when all ten buttons are in place, adjust the positions and sizes according to the measurements in Table 2-3. All ten option buttons have the same size. The positions are measured in relation to the upper-left corner of the *containing frame,* not the form. For this reason, corresponding option buttons in each of the two frames have the same location measurements.

As you work on positioning these option buttons inside their frames, you might want to use a special Visual Basic technique for selecting multiple controls. If you hold down the Ctrl key when you select a series of controls, the controls become a multiple selection. You can then move all of the controls in the selection at once by dragging them with the mouse. (To deactivate the multiple selection, click the mouse anywhere inside the

**Table 2-3   Locations and Sizes of the Option Buttons in the
Second Dialog Box**

Frame1	Frame2	Location	Size
Option1	Option6	3, 1	14x1
Option2	Option7	3, 2	14x1
Option3	Option8	3, 3	14x1
Option4	Option9	3, 4	14x1
Option5	Option10	3, 5	14x1

form.) When you finish your work, the TEMPOPTS form appears as shown
in Figure 2-13. You'll return to this form in Chapter 3 to define the
properties of its controls. For now, choose the **Save Project** command to
save your work. Then choose **Exit** from the **File** menu to return to the
programming environment.

   In this chapter's final exercise, you'll begin developing the interface for
a new version of the *Loan Calculator* application. In the new interface,
several of the options from the original version will be reorganized as
commands in a pull-down menu. To create this menu, you'll use the Menu
Design Window in the Form Designer.

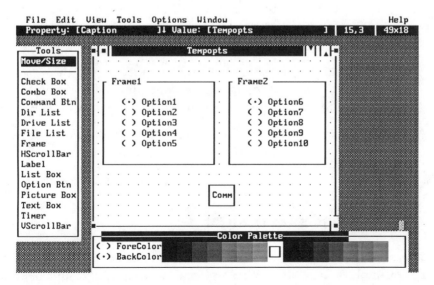

Figure 2-13 The second dialog box with all its controls in place

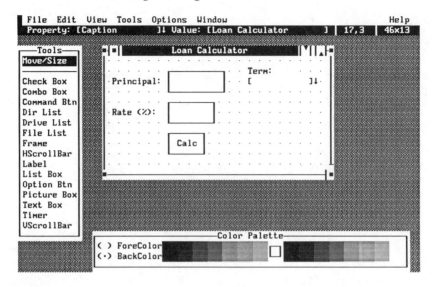

Figure 2-14 Starting point for the second version of the *Loan Calculator* application

So you can focus on creating the menu for this new version, the beginning stage of the application is available as a project on the exercise disk. Follow these steps to open this project and prepare for the work ahead:

1. Pull down the **File** menu and select the **Open Project...** command.

2. In the **Directories** box, select the directory in which you have stored the files from the exercise disk.

3. In the **Files** box, double-click the file named CH2EX2.MAK.

4. When the project is loaded into memory, select the form CH2-EX2A.FRM in the Project window and click the **Form** button. This form is the starting point for your work in the upcoming exercise.

As you can see in Figure 2-14, the form is a simplified version of the *Loan Calculator* application. Four of the five command buttons have been removed.

ALTERNATIVE PROGRAM DESIGN

There are always many different ways to design dialog boxes in Visual Basic. For example, you've already seen several controls and groups of controls that represent options in a dialog box, including:

- Command buttons.
- Groups of option buttons or check boxes.
- Combo boxes with their attached drop-down lists.

Your own style of designing dialog boxes will depend on what you judge to be the most efficient and visually pleasing presentation for a given application—and on your familiarity with the needs and abilities of the people who ultimately will be using your program. In some instances you might find yourself designing a dialog box in one way, only to change the organization altogether after you've worked with the application for a while. For example, you might decide to reorganize a crowded dialog box into a menu-driven application. This sort of change is illustrated in the upcoming exercise.

Working with the Menu Design Window

Comparing Figures 2-1 and 2-14, you can see that four features are missing from the second version of the *Loan Calculator*: the **Exit** button, the **Print** and **Save** buttons, and the **Table values** button. The options represented by these controls all can be placed conveniently in pull-down menus. For example, a menu that offers a variety of output options—along with a command that exits from the application itself—is typically called the **File** menu. Here are the commands that the **File** menu will include in the *Loan Calculator:*

```
File
Print Table
Save Table
Exit
```

You create menus for Visual Basic applications in the Form Designer's Menu Design Window. To open this window, pull down the **Window** menu now and select the **Menu Design Window** command. The window that appears on the screen is shown in Figure 2-15.

This window contains options for defining the commands, properties, and characteristics of an entire menu bar, with one or more pull-down menus. The resulting menu bar becomes part of the active form in your application. The top half of the Menu Design Window contains text boxes and check boxes for command names and a variety of properties. For example, the **Caption** box is for the name of a menu as it appears in the menu bar or for the name of one of the commands that appears in a menu list. The **CtlName** box is for the corresponding *control name.* As you learned

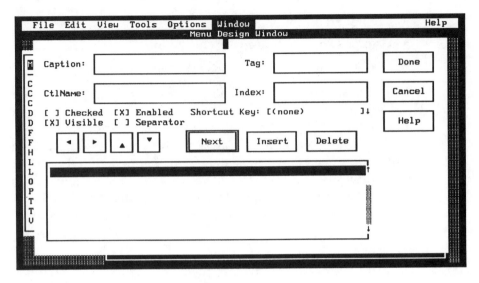

Figure 2-15 The Menu Design Window

in Chapter 1, the **CtlName** property is an identifier that you assign to each control or menu entry for programming purposes. The bottom half of the Menu Design Window contains a large list box, which displays the hierarchy of your menu system as you begin designing it.

In this introductory exercise, you'll supply only two items of information for each menu entry: the **Caption** and the **CtlName** values. Here are the steps for defining the **File** menu for the *Loan Calculator:*

1. Enter **&File** into the **Caption** box. The ampersand character indicates that the *next* character will be the *access key* for the menu and will be highlighted in the menu name. This means that the user can press Alt+F to pull down the **File** menu that you are creating. The menu name appears at the top of the menu list box in the Menu Design Window (Figure 2-16).

2. Enter **FileMenu** into the **CtlName** box.

3. Click the **Next** button to begin defining the next entry in the menu.

4. Click the right-arrow icon above the list box, or press Alt+right arrow. An ellipses symbol appears at the beginning of the new caption in the menu list box, indicating that this entry is a command within the **File** menu.

5. Enter **&Print Table** as the caption of the new entry. Then enter **PrintTableCommand** as the control name.

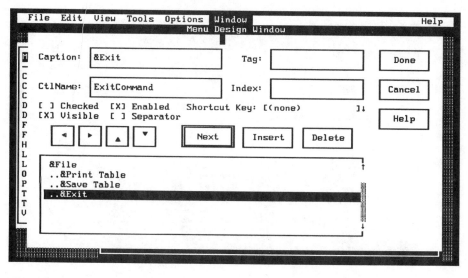

Figure 2-16 A menu definition in the Menu Design Window

6. Click the **Next** button. You don't need to click the right-arrow icon again; the new entry is assumed to be at the same menu level as the previous entry.

7. Enter **&Save Table** as the new caption and **SaveTableCommand** as the new control name.

8. Click the **Next** button.

9. Enter **E&xit** as the final caption and **ExitCommand** as the control name. Figure 2-16 shows the Menu Design Window at this point in your work.

10. Click the **Done** button to complete your work in the Menu Design Window.

11. Choose the **Save Project** command from the Form Designer's **File** menu to save your work to disk.

After these steps, you can pull down the new **File** menu that now appears in your dialog box. You'll see the three commands that you included in the menu, as shown in Figure 2-17.

There is much more to learn about menus and the Menu Design Window. You'll work more with this particular menu later. But for now, you can already see that the application's pull-down **File** menu is a reasonable alternative to the original design of the *Loan Calculator* application.

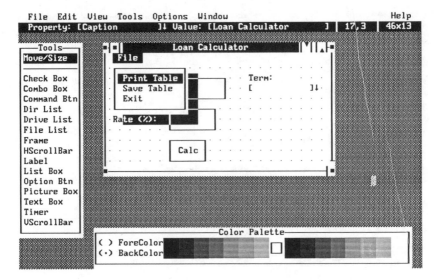

Figure 2-17 The new **File** menu, as created in the Menu Design Window

SUMMARY: FORMS AND CONTROLS

The first stage of application development moves quickly and produces satisfying results. In the Form Designer environment, you create the forms for your application and you begin adding controls to represent the features of your program. You use the mouse to move each form and control to its initial location and to adjust the size of each object that will appear on the screen. As you do so, Visual Basic assigns numeric settings to the corresponding properties: **Top** and **Left** for the location measurements and **Width** and **Height** for the size dimensions. An additional property, **TabIndex**, is determined by the order in which you place controls on a form.

But many other important properties still need to be defined. The command buttons and labels on your forms need text captions. Text boxes require appropriate initial values. The forms themselves need titles and possibly background colors. Along with these visual characteristics, you need to set other properties to prepare the way for the programming tasks that lie ahead. All these changes take place in the Form Designer's Properties bar, which is the focus of Chapter 3.

3

Building an Application:
Step 2—Assigning Properties

INTRODUCTION

The objects of a Visual Basic application—forms and controls—have properties that you can change during either design time or run time. These properties determine an object's characteristics—its visual appearance on the screen, its functional elements, its *value*, and its treatment during run time. In this chapter you'll continue exploring the properties available for forms and controls. You'll learn to recognize the range of appropriate settings for a given property, and you'll practice the mechanical steps for selecting settings in the Form Designer's Properties bar.

Begin by reviewing the features of the Properties bar. You've seen that it consists of four boxes, arranged from left to right across the width of the Form Designer environment. At the far left is the Property box, with its attached drop-down list of properties. You view this list by clicking the down-arrow icon at the right of the box. For example, Figure 3-1 shows the scrollable list of properties for a form.

To the immediate right of the Property list box is the Value box. For a property that has a fixed group of settings, this box has an attached list of those settings. A down-arrow icon at the right of the Value box indicates that a settings list exists for the current property. To view the list, you click the down arrow. For example, in Figure 3-2 you can see the settings list for a form property named **BorderStyle**. This property determines the appearance and function of the form's border during run time. The default

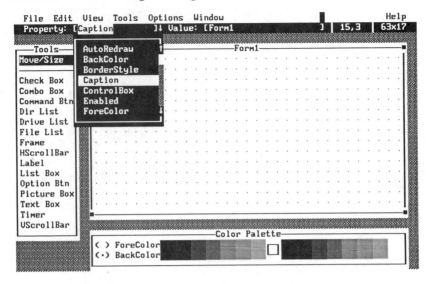

Figure 3-1 The drop-down properties list for a form

setting is **Sizable Single**, which means that the user can drag the border to change the size and shape of the form.

Sometimes there are no fixed settings for a given property. In this case, no settings list is available; the down-arrow icon does not appear at the right of the Value box. For example, Figure 3-3 shows the Value box for the **FormName** property. To set this property, you enter a text value directly into the Value box.

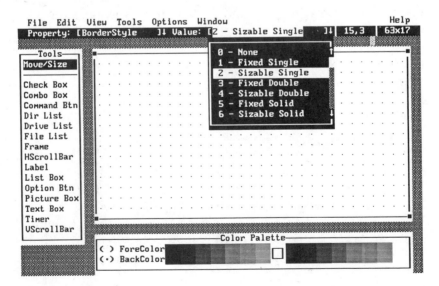

Figure 3-2 The drop-down list attached to the Value box

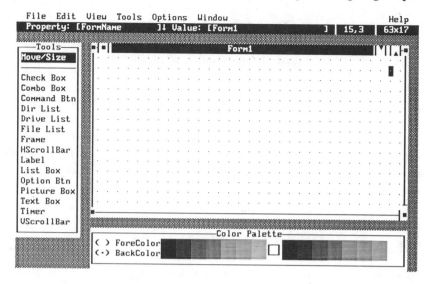

Figure 3-3 A property that has no fixed settings

These are the two main ways to establish the setting of a property in the Form Designer: Select a value from the drop-down list attached to the Value box, or enter a value directly into the box. Sometimes, however, Visual Basic presents other techniques for selecting a property setting. For example, you have seen that you can set the **Left**, **Top**, **Width**, and **Height** properties of a form or control simply by dragging the object with the mouse. In this chapter you'll see another example of a special technique—this time for setting the display colors of a form or control.

As you've learned, the remaining two boxes on the Properties bar give the location and size measurements (expressed in screen columns and rows) of the selected form or control. These are the current settings of **Left**, **Top**, **Width**, and **Height**.

In the hands-on exercises for this chapter, you will continue developing the *Loan Calculator* application that you began in Chapter 2. As your starting point in this chapter, you'll load the application from files supplied on the exercise disk. The project named CH3EX1.MAK contains the first version of the *Loan Calculator* application as you left it in Chapter 2.

1. Start up Visual Basic and choose the **Open Project** command from the **File** menu.

2. Open the CH3EX1 project from the directory where you have copied the files of the exercise disk. The three forms in the project are stored in files named CH3EX1A.FRM, CH3EX1B.FRM, and CH3EX1C.FRM. They are the same as the forms you created in

Chapter 2, except with different file names. You are ready to begin setting properties in the forms of this project; as you do so, you'll be opening and reopening each of these forms several times in the Form Designer environment.

This chapter is merely a first introduction to the subject of properties. You'll continue to discover new properties as you proceed in your work with Visual Basic. Keep in mind that all properties have default settings—that is, settings that remain in effect unless they are changed during either design time or run time. In a typical application, you'll leave many properties—for both forms and controls—unchanged from their default settings.

ASSIGNING PROPERTIES TO FORMS

To work with the properties of a form, you begin by opening the form in the Form Designer environment and selecting the form itself. If a control inside the form is selected, click the mouse over an empty area inside the form; this action deselects the control and selects the form for subsequent property definitions.

One of the first form properties you might think of setting is **FormName**. This property defines the name by which a form can be identified in an application's code. The name also appears in the Project window, next to the file name for a form. By default, Visual Basic for DOS uses the first part of a form's file name as the setting for the **FormName** property. You can keep this default name, or you can change the **FormName** setting to something clearer. As your first exercise with this chapter's version of the *Loan Calculator* files, take the following steps to supply new **FormName** settings for the three forms of the project:

1. Select the form CH3EX1A in the project window and click the **Form** button. Visual Basic opens the form into the Form Designer environment.

2. Pull down the Property list and select the **FormName** property.

3. Type **LoanInpt** as the **FormName** setting for this form and press Enter.

4. Choose the **Save Form** command from the **File** menu to save this change to disk.

5. Pull down the **View** menu and choose the **Form** command. In the **Form** dialog box, select the CH3EX1B form and click OK. Change this form's name to **LoanOpts** and then save the change to disk.

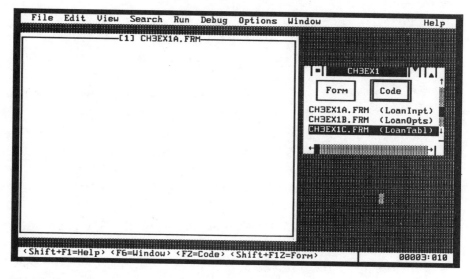

Figure 3-4 New form names displayed in the Project window

6. Finally, use the **Form** command in the **View** menu to open the third form, CH3EX1C. Assign the name **LoanTabl** to the form and save the change.

7. Pull down the **File** menu and choose **Exit** to return to the programming environment. As shown in Figure 3-4, the Project window now displays the three new form names, next to the original file names. (Keep in mind that you can move and resize the Project window to view its contents.)

Now you can refer to the three forms in this exercise by their new **FormName** settings, **LoanInpt**, **LoanOpts**, and **LoanTabl**.

In Chapter 4 you'll begin to see some of the programming situations in which the **FormName** property is important. In general, any operation that involves an entire form is performed via a reference to the **FormName** setting. For example, operations that hide or display a form, or send text or graphics to a form, identify the form by its **FormName**.

Visual Properties of Forms

One important property that changes the visual appearance of a form is **Caption**. The text you enter for this property appears in the title bar at the top of the selected form. In other words, the **Caption** setting provides the title that will describe or identify the purpose of the form itself to the user. Here are the steps for changing the caption settings of the three forms:

1. Select the **LoanInpt** form in the Project window and click the **Form** button to switch back to the Form Designer. The **Caption** property should be the current selection in the Property box. (If not, pull down the property list and select the **Caption** property.)

2. Type **Loan Calculator** as the new caption setting for this form and then press Enter. (This title indicates to the user that **LoanInpt** is the main dialog box for the application.) Notice that the characters of this text appear in the title bar of the form even as you type them into the Value box.

3. Choose the **Save Form** command from the **File** menu to save this change to disk. The newly titled form is shown in Figure 3-5.

4. Choose the **Form** command from the Form Designer's **View** menu and select the **LoanOpts** form from the list. Click OK to open the form. Enter **Table Values** as the form's caption, because this is the dialog box in which the user specifies the increments for the principal and interest rates in the resulting payment table. Choose **Save Form** from the **File** menu.

5. Choose the **Form** command from the **View** menu once again and open the **LoanTabl** form. Type **Loan Table** as the form's caption and then save the form. This is the form in which the output table will appear.

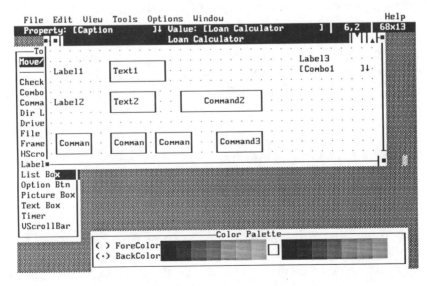

Figure 3-5 The **LoanInpt** form with a new **Caption** setting

A property that can result in rather dramatic changes in the appearance of a form is **BackColor**. As its name suggests, this property controls the background color displayed inside a form—that is, the surface surrounding any controls that are contained in the form. Visual Basic supplies several convenient ways to represent colors in the code of a program. But during design time, the best tool for changing the color of a form or control is the Color Palette in the Form Designer.

Using the Color Palette

The **LoanOpts** form is a convenient object in which to experiment with the Color Palette:

1. Choose the **Form** command from the **View** menu and select the **LoanOpts** form. Click OK to open the form.

2. In the Color Palette window at the bottom of the Form Designer screen, click the **BackColor** option. On a color screen, the Color Palette shows the range of colors from which you can choose for the background and foreground of a selected form or control. (See Figure 3-6.)

3. Click the last color in the row of colors. This selection gives the **LoanOpts** form a bright white background. Notice that the Value

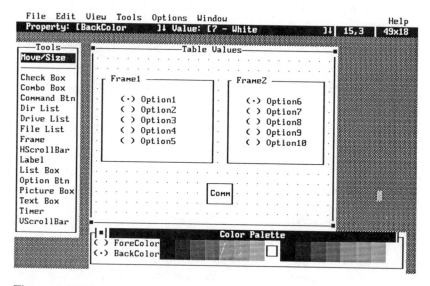

Figure 3-6 The Color Palette box

box in the Properties bar identifies this color selection as 15 - Bright White. (Experiment with other colors if you wish.)

4.   Pull down the **File** menu and choose the **Save Form** command.

While the Color Palette is open, you can select any sequence of forms and controls in your current project and make changes in their display colors. If you want to close the Color Palette box, activate the window and press Ctrl+F4, or double-click the control menu box located at the upper-left corner of the window. (You can reopen the palette at any time by pulling down the **Window** menu and choosing the **Color Palette** command.)

Functional Properties of Forms

Several properties specify how a Visual Basic form will operate as a window:

- The **BorderStyle** property controls the appearance and function of the form's border; specifically, this setting determines whether the user can drag borders to change the size and shape of the window.

- The **MinButton** property specifies whether a minimize button will appear at the upper-right corner of the form. (Clicking this button reduces the form to an icon.)

- The **MaxButton** property specifies whether a maximize button will appear at the upper-right corner of the frame. (Clicking this button enlarges the form window to the full amount of space available on the screen.)

- The **ControlBox** property determines whether there will be a control menu box at the upper-left corner of the frame.

- The **Enabled** property specifies whether the form will react to user events such as mouse clicks.

- The **AutoRedraw** property determines whether Visual Basic will redisplay the form's contents if necessary.

Except for **BorderStyle**, these properties all have fixed Value lists consisting of two possible settings—**True** or **False**. The default setting is **True** for all but **AutoRedraw**.

In the *Loan Calculator* application, you have carefully defined appropriate sizes for each dialog box and for the form that displays the output table. You can therefore disable the properties that would allow the user to drag borders or to maximize the window size. Furthermore, it is reasonable to eliminate the control menu box in all but the main dialog box.

In the following steps you change the functional elements of the three forms:

1. Choose the **Form** command from the **View** menu and open the **LoanInpt** form. Pull down the Property list and select the **BorderStyle** property. Pull down the Value list and select **1-Fixed Single**.

2. Select **MaxButton** from the Property list and then select **False** from the value list. Choose the **Save Form** command from the **File** menu to save these changes to disk.

3. Open the **LoanOpts** form and select settings of **False** for the **ControlBox**, **MaxButton**, and **MinButton** properties. Also, select the **1-Fixed Single** setting for the **BorderStyle** property. Save the changes to disk.

4. Open the **LoanTabl** form. This form does not need to respond to any user events; therefore you can select settings of **False** for four properties: **ControlBox**, **Enabled**, **MaxButton**, and **MinButton**. However, the contents of the form may sometimes need to be refreshed, so you should select **True** for the **AutoRedraw** property. Finally, select the **1-Fixed Single** setting for this form's **BorderStyle** property. Save the changes to disk.

The **BorderStyle** property affects only the run-time characteristics of a form, not the characteristics of the form in the Form Designer. During the design stage, you can always continue to make changes in the size and shape of any form.

ASSIGNING PROPERTIES TO CONTROLS

While you are working on the controls in a given form, you can use a shortcut for changing property settings: Make a selection in the Property list and then activate any number of controls in sequence to change their individual settings for the current property. This is a good way to organize your work when there are many properties to set. You'll use this technique in the upcoming exercise, as you change the **Caption** and **Text** settings for the controls in this application.

Visual Properties of Controls

The **Caption** property applies to several different types of controls in the *Loan Calculator*. This property defines the text of a label, the name of a

Table 3-1   The New *Caption* Settings for Controls on the
***LoanInpt* Form**

Default Caption setting	New Caption setting
Label1	Principal:
Label2	Rate (%):
Label3	Term:
Command1	Calc
Command2	&Table values...
Command3	E&xit
Command4	&Print
Command5	&Save

command button, the title of a frame, and the description attached to an option button. **Caption** is therefore a good property to start with as you turn your attention to the controls in the application's two dialog boxes.

Table 3-1 shows the new **Caption** settings for controls on the **LoanInpt** form, and Table 3-2 shows the **Caption** settings for the **LoanOpts** form. You can quickly establish all of these settings in sequence, beginning with the following steps:

1. Open the **LoanInpt** form and select the **Label1** control.

2. Pull down the properties list and select the **Caption** property if it is not already the current property.

3. Type **Principal:**, the new text for the label, and press Enter.

4. Click **Label2** and enter **Rate (%):** as its new text.

5. Repeat step 4 for each of the remaining controls listed in Table 3-1. (Notice the use of the ampersand character—&—to define shortcut keys for the command buttons in this form.) Save the changes to disk.

6. Open the **LoanOpts** form and set the **Caption** properties as listed in Table 3-2. Save the changes to disk.

Next you should set the initial text values to be displayed in the three text boxes in the **LoanInpt** form. The setting of the **Text** property specifies the value displayed inside these boxes. In some applications there may be a predictable input value for a particular text box. When you design such an application, you might decide to assign this value as the initial

Table 3-2   The New *Caption* Settings for Controls on the *LoanOpts* Form

Default Caption setting	New Caption setting
Option1	$10
Option2	$100
Option3	$1,000
Option4	$10,000
Option5	$100,000
Option6	0.125%
Option7	0.25%
Option8	0.50%
Option9	1.0%
Option10	2.0%
Frame1	Principal Increment
Frame2	Rate Increment
Command1	OK

Text setting for the box. This is not the case in the *Loan Calculator.* The application does not try to suggest values for the principal, interest rate, and term of the loan—the actual input values for these parameters could fall within wide ranges of numbers. For this reason, you'll supply blank values for the two text boxes and the combo box. Here are the steps for changing the **Text** setting for the three text boxes:

1. Open the **LoanInpt** form and select the first text box, for the principal of the loan. The default text value inside this box is **Text1**.

2. Pull down the Property list and select the **Text** property.

3. Highlight the current text in the Value box and then press the Delete key on your keyboard to delete the text. Press Enter to confirm the revision.

4. Select the second text box, **Text2**. Repeat step 3 to clear the text from this box.

5. Select the combo box, which displays the text **Combo1**. Repeat step 3 to clear the text. Save the changes to disk.

After these steps, you've specified values for almost all the properties that determine the *appearance* of the two dialog boxes. The main dialog box

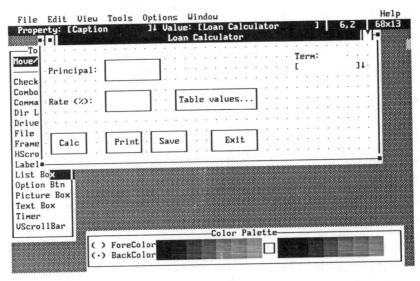

Figure 3-7 The main dialog box with appropriate property settings

now appears as shown in Figure 3-7. However, several properties remain to be set.

Functional Properties of Controls

Think back to the steps you originally took to place controls on the main dialog box (in Chapter 2). You took care to add controls in a specific order. You learned that the order of placement during design time determines the run-time *tab order* —that is, the order in which controls are activated when the user repeatedly presses the Tab key. Here is the current Tab order for the controls of the **LoanInpt** form: first the two text boxes, then the combo box, then the command buttons—**Calc, Table values, Exit, Print,** and **Save**.

Suppose you decide to change this order. You now want the **Print** and **Save** buttons to be activated after the combo box and before the other command buttons. You make this change by resetting the values of the **TabIndex** property. **TabIndex** has an integer value for each control in a form. The sequence of integers represents the tab order.

Before you try to change the **TabIndex** sequence, you have to make sure you know what the current sequence is. You'll begin the following exercise by examining the current **TabIndex** value for the combo box:

1. Activate the combo box in the **LoanInpt** form.

2. Pull down the Property list and select the **TabIndex** property. The setting for the combo box is 5. To make the **Print** and **Save** buttons

next in the sequence, you have to set the **TabIndex** property to 6 and **7** for these two controls.

3. Activate the **Print** button and enter **6** as the new **TabIndex** setting for this control.

4. Activate the **Save** button and enter **7** as the new **TabIndex** setting.

5. Activate the other three command buttons—**Calc**, **Table values**, and **Exit**—one at a time. Notice that Visual Basic has adjusted their **TabIndex** settings to **8**, **9**, and **10**, respectively.

The next time you run the program, you'll see that these changes in the **TabIndex** property have produced the tab order that you wanted.

Another important control for command buttons is **Default**. By setting this property to **True** for a button, you give the user the option of pressing the Enter key to select the button. Only one command button on a given form can have a **Default** setting of **True**.

In the LoanInpt form, it would be useful to establish **Calc** as the default button. That way the user can type a new entry into the **Principal, Rate,** or **Term** box and then press Enter to see the resulting changes in the payment table. Here are the steps for changing the **Default** status of the **Calc** button:

1. Select the **Calc** button.

2. Choose **Default** from the Property list.

3. Choose **True** from the Value list and then save this change to disk. Visual Basic places a double border around the **Calc** button to indicate that this control is now the default.

Now open the **LoanOpts** form again. Recall the main functional characteristic of a group of option buttons: Exactly one option in the group is selected at a given time. If the user makes a new selection, the previously selected option is deactivated. To conform to this rule, you must select one of the options in each group as the default selection.

Option buttons have a **Value** property that determines whether an option is selected or not selected. As you might guess, the available settings of the **Value** property are **True** and **False**. During design time, Visual Basic allows you to set the **Value** property to **True** for one option in a group. (If you then set **Value** to **True** for another option in the same group, Visual Basic automatically resets the **Value** to **False** for the other option buttons in the group.)

For the *Loan Calculator* application, you will set the middle option in each group to **True**. This means that the selected principal increment will

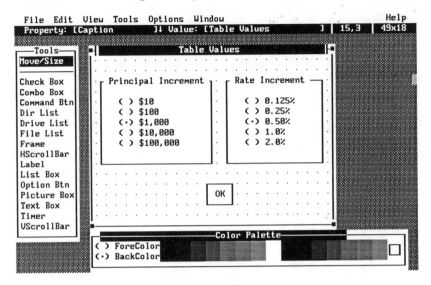

Figure 3-8 The **LoanOpts** form with option buttons activated

be **$1,000** and the selected rate increment will be **0.50%**. To establish this setting, follow these steps:

1. Select the middle option in the first group, **$1,000**. Select **Value** in the Property list and then press Enter to change the setting to **True**.

2. Perform the same step to change the **Value** setting for the middle option in the second group.

3. Save this change to disk.

The **LoanOpts** form now appears as in Figure 3-8.

Code-Related Properties for Controls

Some Visual Basic properties are designed to help you prepare for the code that you will eventually write for your program. One of the most important properties in this regard is **CtlName**. Like **FormName** for forms, the **CtlName** property supplies the name that you will use to identify a particular control inside your code. You'll work with this property in the next exercise.

Assigning Control Names

You should assign a meaningful **CtlName** setting to every control that will appear in the code of your program. In the *Loan Calculator* application, this includes all the controls that supply input values to your program—the text boxes, the combo box, and the option buttons—along with the command buttons that represent procedures that your program can perform. Of course, it would be legal to use Visual Basic's default **CtlName** settings (such as **Text1, Combo1, Option1**, and **Command1**), but default names are not at all descriptive of the roles these controls play in your application. Supplying your own **CtlName** settings gives you the opportunity to devise meaningful names for the elements of your program, making your code more readable and easier to understand.

Table 3-3 provides a list of the new **CtlName** settings you'll assign to the controls of the **LoanInpt** form. Missing from this list are the label controls, which have no role in the program code. The label controls can therefore keep their default names, such as **Label1**.

Here are the steps for assigning these control names:

1. Open the **LoanInpt** form and select the **Text1** control.

2. Pull down the properties list and select **CtlName** if this property is not already selected.

3. Type **InPrinc** as the setting for this control, then press the Enter key.

4. Select the next control, **Text2**. Enter the new **CtlName** setting for this control, **InRate**.

5. Repeat step 4 for the remaining controls in Table 3-3 and then save these changes to disk.

As an example of the use of a control name in code, turn back to the **Form_Load** procedure that you wrote in Chapter 2. You'll recall that you

Table 3-3 The New CtlName Settings for the
Loan Calculator **Controls**

Default CtlName setting	New CtlName setting
Text1	InPrinc
Text2	InRate
Combo1	InTerm
Command1	Calc
Command2	Options
Command3	ExitButton
Command4	PrntTabl
Command5	SaveTabl

entered code into this procedure to create the drop-down list for the combo box in the **LoanInpt** form. To view this procedure, pull down the **View** menu in the Form Designer environment and choose the **Code** command. Click OK in the resulting message box. Visual Basic switches you to the programming environment and displays the **Code** dialog box on the screen, as shown in Figure 3-9. In the **Choose item to edit** box, select **Form_Load**, then click the **Edit in Active** button. This is how the procedure looks at the moment:

```
Sub Form_Load ()
   Combo1.AddItem "4 years"
   Combo1.AddItem "5 years"
   Combo1.AddItem "10 years"
   Combo1.AddItem "15 years"
   Combo1.AddItem "20 years"
   Combo1.AddItem "30 years"
End Sub
```

The default control name **Combo1** no longer has meaning in your application, because you have changed the name of the combo box to **InTerm**. Normally you do not write code for your application until you have already assigned **CtlName** settings to your controls. But in this special case the code already exists, and therefore it has to be modified to adjust to the new control name.

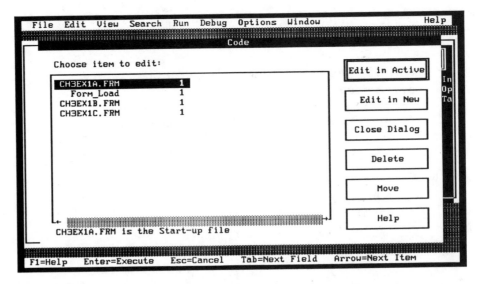

Figure 3-9 The **Code** dialog box in the programming environment

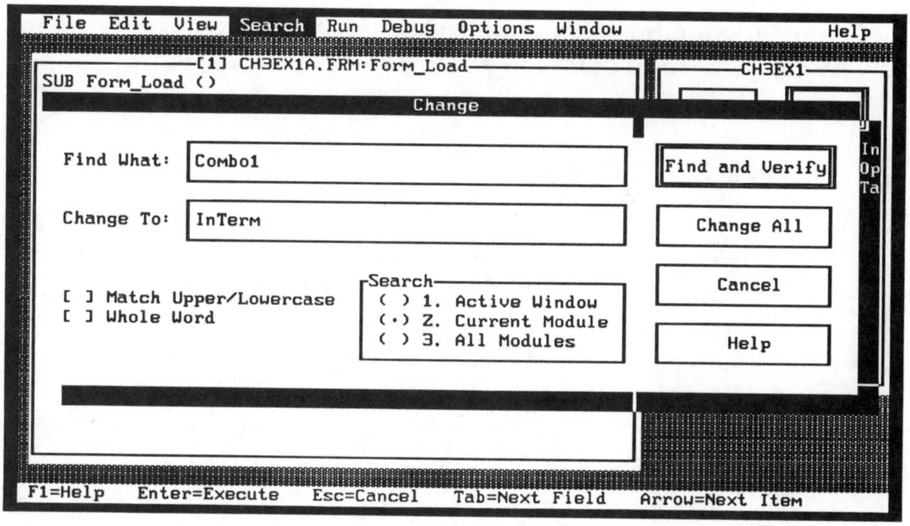

```
 File   Edit   View   Search   Run   Debug   Options   Window                    Help
┌─────────────────────[1] CH3EX1A.FRM:Form_Load────────────────────┐ ┌───CH3EX1───┐
│SUB Form_Load ()                                                   │ │            │
│                               Change                              │ │            │
│                                                                   │ │          In│
│   Find What:  Combo1                               ┌────────────┐ │ │          Op│
│                                                    │Find and Verify│ │          Ta│
│   Change To:  InTerm                               └────────────┘ │ │            │
│                                                    ┌────────────┐ │ │            │
│                                                    │ Change All │ │ │            │
│                               ┌─Search─────────┐   └────────────┘ │ │            │
│   [ ] Match Upper/Lowercase   │ ( ) 1. Active Window  ┌────────┐  │ │            │
│   [ ] Whole Word              │ (·) 2. Current Module │ Cancel │  │ │            │
│                               │ ( ) 3. All Modules    └────────┘  │ │            │
│                               └─────────────────┘   ┌────────┐   │ │            │
│                                                     │  Help  │   │ │            │
│                                                     └────────┘   │ │            │
└──────────────────────────────────────────────────────────────────┘ └────────────┘
 F1=Help    Enter=Execute    Esc=Cancel    Tab=Next Field    Arrow=Next Item
```

Figure 3-10   The dialog box for the **Replace** command

You can use Visual Basic's search-and-replace feature to replace all the instances of the name **Combo1** to **InTerm** in this procedure. Here are the steps:

1. Pull down the **Search** menu and choose the **Change** command. In the resulting **Change** dialog box (Figure 3-10), enter **Combo1** in the **Find What** box and **InTerm** in the **Change To** box.

2. Leaving all the other settings unchanged, click the **Change All** button. Click OK in response to the **Change Complete** message.

When you complete this operation, the **Form_Load** procedure appears as follows:

```
Sub Form_Load ()
  InTerm.AddItem "4 years"
  InTerm.AddItem "5 years"
  InTerm.AddItem "10 years"
  InTerm.AddItem "15 years"
  InTerm.AddItem "20 years"
  InTerm.AddItem "30 years"
End Sub
```

The statements in the procedure now refer correctly to **InTerm,** which is the new name for the combo box control. Save these changes to disk and then try running the program again. You will find that the combo box list appears just as it did when you first created this code.

Creating Control Arrays

For some event procedures, it is convenient to assign a single name to an entire group of controls. Individual controls in the group are then identified by the common name plus an *index* number. For example, in the upcoming exercise, you'll assign the control name **PInc** to five option buttons. In your code, the names of the five individual buttons will be:

```
PInc(0)
PInc(1)
PInc(2)
PInc(3)
PInc(4)
```

A group of controls identified in this way—with an indexed name—is called a *control array*. There are many reasons for creating control arrays. In general, they simplify operations with controls that have a common purpose. For example, structuring a group of option buttons as a control array makes it very easy to identify and react to the option that the user selects at run time.

The following exercise will help you master the mechanical details of setting up a control array during design time. You'll establish both groups of option buttons in the **LoanOpts** form as control arrays. The common name for the first array is **PInc** (for "principal increment"), and the name of the second array is **RInc** (for "rate increment").

Here are the steps for creating these two control arrays:

1. Select the **LoanOpts** form in the Project window and click the **Form** button. Visual Basic displays the selected form in the Form Designer environment.

2. Select the first option button (**Option1**) in the frame on the left side of the form.

3. Pull down the properties list and select the **CtlName** property.

4. Enter the name **PInc** as the control name.

5. Select the next option button down the same frame and again enter **PInc** as the control name. Visual Basic displays a message box on the screen (Figure 3-11) asking you to confirm that you intend to create a control array. Click the **Yes** button to confirm.

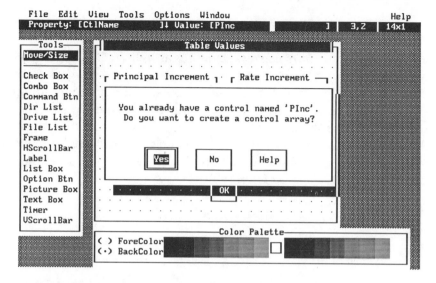

Figure 3-11 Confirmation for creating a control array

6. Continue assigning the same **CtlName** setting—**PInc**—to the remaining option buttons in the current frame.

7. Repeat steps 2 through 6 for the option buttons in the other frame, but this time assign the name **RInc** to all five of the option buttons in the frame.

8. Select the **OK** button at the bottom of the form and enter **OKOpts** as its **CtlName** setting.

When you create a control array, Visual Basic automatically assigns appropriate settings to a property named **Index**. To examine this property, select the first of the controls in the **RInc** array; then select **Index** in the properties list. The setting is **0**. If you now look at each of the next **RInc** controls in turn, you'll see that they have **Index** values of **1**, **2**, **3**, and **4**. In other words, the controls in this group have the following names:

```
RInc(0)
RInc(1)
RInc(2)
RInc(3)
RInc(4)
```

Likewise, the controls in the **PInc** array have the same sequence of **Index** settings. This confirms that your control arrays have been created successfully. You'll see code examples illustrating the use of control arrays in Chapter 4. Before leaving the **LoanOpts** form, save the changes in the form to disk. Choose **Exit** from the **File** menu to switch to the programming environment.

You can define control arrays in menus as well. In Chapter 2 you began building an alternative menu-driven version of the *Loan Calculator* application. Now you'll continue developing this example by adding menus that represent the options currently appearing on the **LoanOpts** form.

To prepare for the next exercise, load the project from files supplied on the exercise disk: CH3EX2.MAK is the name of the project. It includes two forms: CH3EX2A.FRM has a **FormName** setting of **LoanInpt**, and CH3EX2B.FRM is named **LoanTabl**.

PROPERTIES IN MENUS

During a performance of the first version of the *Loan Calculator,* the user can call up a separate dialog box to select increment values for the payment table. To view the dialog box, the user clicks the **Table Values...** command button. The window has two groups of option buttons, for setting the principal increment and the rate increment.

An alternative design is to place these two groups of options in two pull-down menus on the main dialog box. In the second version of the application, the dialog box already has one pull-down menu, named **File**. The two additional menus could be named **Principal** and **Rate**. This expanded menu system eliminates the need for a second dialog box and places the options closer at hand.

In Chapter 2 you used Visual Basic's Menu Design Window to create the **File** menu. Now you'll return to this window to expand the menu hierarchy, adding the two new menus. In designing the **File** menu, you dealt with only two of the property options in the Menu Design Window—**Caption** and **CtlName**. For these new menus you'll work with two additional properties, named **Index** and **Checked**. In the Menu Design Window, **Index** is represented as a text box and **Checked** is a check box:

- The **Index** text box is for specifying the index of each element in a control array that you create for the menu. In the context of a menu, a control array is a group of commands that have the same control name.

- The **Checked** property specifies whether a given command will have a bullet displayed next to it in the menu list. In the *Loan Calculator* you'll use this property to indicate the default selection in each of the new menus.

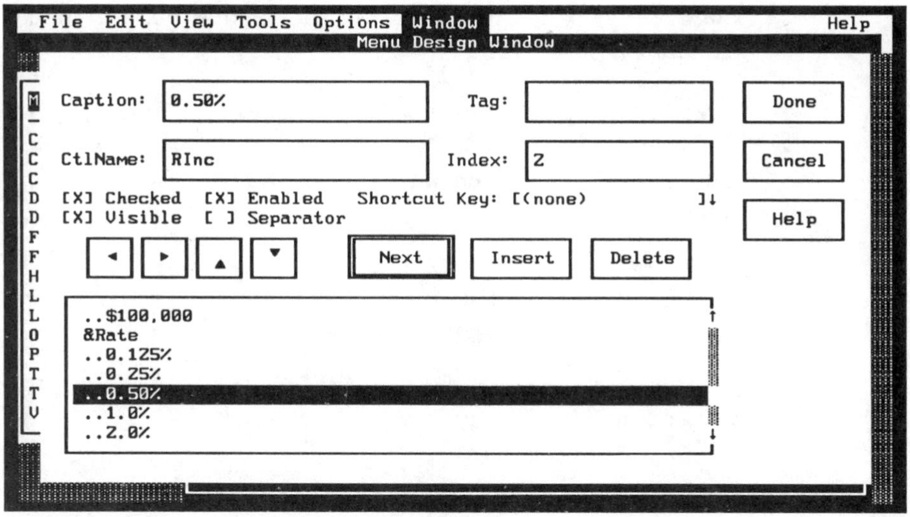

```
 File   Edit   View   Tools   Options  Window                          Help
                           Menu Design Window
┌─┐
│M│  Caption:  ┌─────────────┐         Tag:  ┌─────────────┐      ┌────────┐
│─│            │ 0.50%       │              │             │      │  Done  │
│C│            └─────────────┘              └─────────────┘      └────────┘
│C│  CtlName:  ┌─────────────┐       Index: ┌─────────────┐      ┌────────┐
│C│            │ RInc        │              │ 2           │      │ Cancel │
│D│            └─────────────┘              └─────────────┘      └────────┘
│D│  [X] Checked  [X] Enabled   Shortcut Key: [(none)        ]↓
│F│  [X] Visible  [ ] Separator                                  ┌────────┐
│F│                                                              │  Help  │
│H│   ┌───┐ ┌───┐ ┌───┐ ┌───┐   ┌───────┐ ┌────────┐ ┌────────┐  └────────┘
│L│   │ ◄ │ │ ► │ │ ▲ │ │ ▼ │   │ Next  │ │ Insert │ │ Delete │
│L│   └───┘ └───┘ └───┘ └───┘   └───────┘ └────────┘ └────────┘
│O│  ┌──────────────────────────────────────────────────────────┐↑
│P│  │ ..$100,000                                                │
│T│  │ &Rate                                                     │
│T│  │ ..0.125%                                                  │
│V│  │ ..0.25%                                                   │
│ │  │ ..0.50%                                                   │
│ │  │ ..1.0%                                                    │
│ │  │ ..2.0%                                                    │↓
└─┘  └──────────────────────────────────────────────────────────┘
```

Figure 3-12 The Menu Design Window with new menu entries

Select the **LoanInpt** form in the Project window and click the **Form** button. Then pull down Visual Basic's **Window** menu and select the **Menu Design Window** command. When the window appears on the screen, you'll see the definition for the **File** menu that you created in Chapter 2. Notice the locations of the **Index** text box and the **Checked** check box (Figure 3-12).

The new menu entries for this application are described in Table 3-3. Here is an outline of the steps for defining these new menus:

1.   Click the **Next** button four times, placing the menu list highlight just after the last of the existing entries.

2.   Click the left-arrow icon or press Alt+left arrow to start again at the highest menu level.

3.   Activate the **Caption** box and enter the name of the first of the two new menus: **&Principal**.

4.   Activate the **CtlName** box and enter the menu's control name, **PrincMenu**. Leave the **Index** box blank for this entry, and leave the **Checked** box unchecked.

5.   Click the **Next** button to start a new entry, and then click the right-arrow icon to indicate that this entry is to appear as a command inside the **Principal** menu.

6.   Enter the text **$10** into the **Caption** box and the name **PInc** into the **CtlName** box. Because this entry is to be the first element of a control

Table 3-4 New Menu Entries for the Second Version of the *Loan Calculator* Application

Level	Caption	CtlName	Index	Checked
menu name	&Principal	PrincMenu	–	no
..command	$10	PInc	0	no
..command	$100	PInc	1	no
..command	$1,000	PInc	2	yes
..command	$10,000	PInc	3	no
..command	$100,000	PInc	4	no
menu name	&Rate	RateMenu	–	no
..command	0.125%	RInc	0	no
..command	0.25%	RInc	1	no
..command	0.50%	RInc	2	yes
..command	1.0%	RInc	3	no
..command	2.0%	RInc	4	no

array, enter the number **0** into the **Index** box. The **Checked** box remains unchecked. Click **Next** to begin the next entry.

7. Continue creating the remaining entries described in Table 3-4. Remember to check the **Checked** box for the third entries (with **Index** values of **2**) in the **PInc** and **RInc** arrays. Also, take care to place each entry at its correct level in the menu hierarchy.

When you finish your work in this exercise, the Menu Design Window will appear as shown in Figure 3-12. The two new menus are outlined in the menu list in the lower half of the window. In effect, you have created two control arrays for this menu. The array named **PInc** represents the five entries in the **Principal** menu, and the array named **RInc** represents the five entries in the **Rate** menu. Check your work to make sure that each entry is correct. (The Menu Design Window allows you to edit menu entries at any time.) Then click the **Done** button to complete the menu definitions.

Returning to the **LoanInpt** form, you can examine the two new menus that you have defined. Click each menu in turn to view the drop-down menu lists. Figure 3-13 shows the **Principal** list and Figure 3-14 shows the **Rate** list. Notice that a bullet is displayed next to the middle entry in each

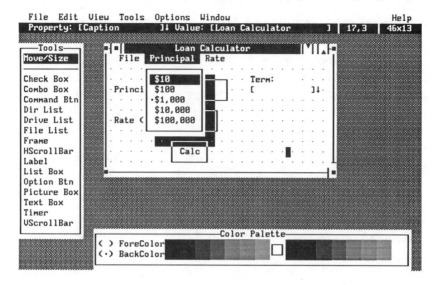

Figure 3-13 The **Principal Increment** menu list

list. In both cases this bullet identifies the default increment value at the time the program begins its performance. To make a new selection, the user will simply pull down a menu and click the desired increment amount.

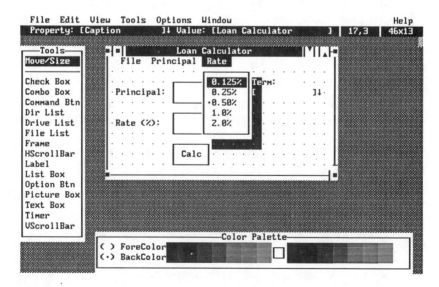

Figure 3-14 The **Rate Increment** menu list

SUMMARY: PROPERTIES IN A VISUAL BASIC APPLICATION

So far you've examined a handful of properties that apply to forms, controls, and menu entries, and you've seen how various settings can change the appearance and the functional elements of your application. Here is a summary of the form properties that you have learned about in this chapter:

- **FormName** is a name that you use to identify a form in code. (The setting is a one-word text value.)

- **Caption** is a descriptive name displayed in the form's title bar. (The setting is a text value.)

- **BackColor** is the color displayed in the background area of a form. (The setting is an integer, but you can use the **Color Palette** to select a color.)

- **BorderStyle** determines whether the form can be sized by dragging the border during run time; it also specifies the graphic style of the border. (A fixed list of several settings is available.)

- **MaxButton** specifies whether there will be a maximize button at the upper-right corner of the form. (Settings are **True** or **False**.)

- **MinButton** specifies whether there will be a minimize button at the upper-right corner of the form. (Settings are **True** or **False**.)

- **ControlBox** determines whether there will be a control-menu box at the upper-left corner of the form. (Settings are **True** or **False**.)

- **Enabled** determines whether the form will respond to events that the user initiates. (Settings are **True** or **False**.)

- **AutoRedraw** instructs Visual Basic to refresh or not to refresh the form's contents when necessary. (Settings are **True** or **False**.)

These are the control properties that you have worked with in applications up to this point:

- **Caption** is a text value displayed on a control; it applies to labels, command buttons, frames, check boxes, and option buttons.

- **Text** is the initial text value in a text box or a combo box.

- **TabIndex** specifies the order in which controls will be selected when the user presses the Tab key during run time. (The setting is an integer.)

- **Default** allows you to establish a default command button in a form. (The user can select this button by pressing the Enter key.)

- **Value** is the status of an option button or a check box. (Settings for an option button are **True** or **False**. Settings for a check box are **0-Unchecked, 1-Checked,** or **2-Grayed.**)
- **CtlName** is the name that you use to identify a control in code.
- **Index** is the index number of a control that is an element of a control array.

Here are the menu properties that you have seen illustrated in this chapter and the previous one:

- **Caption** is the name of a menu or the name of a command in a pull-down menu list.
- **CtlName** is the name that you use to identify a menu element in code.
- **Index** is the index number of a command that is an element of a control array.
- **Checked** specifies whether a given command in a menu list is checked. (The setting is **True** or **False.**)

You'll learn about other properties and settings as you continue working with Visual Basic applications.

4

Building an Application: Step 3—Writing Code

INTRODUCTION

In the third stage of application development, you write code to handle the specific events that you want your program to recognize. The controls you have placed in your project—and the properties you have defined for them—give your application its visual and functional qualities. The code you now write will determine what the program can actually do.

If you are an experienced Basic programmer, you might be surprised at how little code you have to write in a Visual Basic application to achieve impressive results. In a traditional version of the Basic language, you spend much of your programming effort on the detailed task of developing an interface for your programs—creating menus, developing input and output techniques, and generally finding ways to make your program work as simply as possible. In Visual Basic these design tasks are already complete by the time you reach the coding stage.

This chapter guides you through the process of planning and writing code for a Visual Basic application. You'll continue working on the *Loan Calculator* application you've been developing in the previous two chapters. For this chapter's hands-on exercise, you'll once again open the project from files supplied on the exercise disk that came with this book. The first version of the exercise—which includes all the work you completed in Chapter 3—is stored on the exercise disk as CH4EX1.MAK.

Your goals in this chapter are, first, to learn how to create procedures and to practice entering code; and second, to gain a broad understanding of Visual Basic program organization. After a brief hands-on exercise, you'll have the chance to examine the complete code for the *Loan Calculator* in both its versions. (The final versions of the program are stored on the exercise disk as LOANCALC.MAK and LOANCA2.MAK.) Before you begin, take a moment to review the concepts behind Visual Basic and to compare this new language with what you know about Basic programming in other environments.

THE EVENT-DRIVEN PROGRAMMING MODEL

During run time, a Visual Basic application waits for events to take place before performing code. A given procedure is performed when triggered by a specific event. This *event-driven* operating mode governs the action in a Visual Basic application.

Visual Basic defines groups of relevant events for each type of control. Most events are actions performed by the person using the program—actions as simple as clicking a mouse button or pressing a key on the keyboard. Each event has a name, such as **Click**, **Load**, and **GotFocus**. The same name identifies the corresponding event procedure that Visual Basic looks for when the event takes place. The full name of an event procedure is:

```
ObjectName_EventName
```

where *ObjectName* identifies the form or control that is the object of the action and *EventName* identifies the event that has occurred. For example, consider the command button named **Options** in the *Loan Calculator*. The action of clicking this control with the mouse initiates a **Click** event. When this event takes place, Visual Basic performs the event procedure named **Options_Click** in your code.

The event procedures for a form always use the object name **Form**, no matter what the actual name of the form is. For example, **Form_Load** is the name of the procedure that is called at the time a form is first loaded into memory at run time.

Not every event is followed by execution of code. When an event occurs, Visual Basic looks for a procedure you have written to define the program's reaction to the event. If the event procedure is found—that is, if you have supplied the target code—it is performed. If not, nothing happens. In short, an application loops repeatedly through the following process during run time:

1. Wait for the next event.

2. When an event occurs, look for the corresponding event procedure in the program's code.

3. If the event procedure exists, perform it; otherwise do nothing.

4. Start again at step 1.

Your job in this final stage of program development is to anticipate events and to plan your program's reactions to them. You organize your code around forms and controls you have already defined. Before writing code, you select the objects that will be central to the action of your program, and you choose the events that you want the application to recognize for those objects. You then write event procedures to define the response to each anticipated event.

You will probably not write event procedures for every control in your application. Some screen objects have inherently simple roles, defined entirely by the built-in characteristics of the controls themselves. For example, consider some of the controls you have placed in the *Loan Calculator*. The labels in the main dialog box—with captions of **Principal**, **Rate**, and **Term**—describe the program's input requirements. No recognized events will take place around these label controls; you therefore do not need to write code for them. Likewise, the frame controls on the second dialog box—labeled **Principal Increment** and **Text Increment**—serve only as containers for the groups of option buttons. Again, no event procedures are required for these controls.

By design, the initial action of the *Loan Calculator* takes place when the user enters a value or clicks a command button in the **LoanTabl** form. For example, clicking the command button labeled **Table values...** opens a second dialog box of options. Clicking the **Calc** button produces a payment table on the screen. Clicking the **Print** or **Save** button sends the output to a selected destination—the printer or a text file on disk. Therefore, these controls are the objects around which you'll organize the code for the application.

LoanTabl is this application's *startup file*—that is, the form around which Visual Basic recognizes events from the start of the program run. In a multifile application, the startup file can be a form or a module, and is always listed first in the Project window. If you want to change the startup file in an application, follow these steps:

1. Pull down the **Run** menu and choose the **Set Start-up File** command.

2. In the resulting dialog box, choose the form or module that you want to designate as the startup file and then click **OK**.

VISUAL BASIC AND OTHER VERSIONS OF BASIC

If you are already an experienced Basic programmer, your first task is to adjust yourself to Visual Basic's object-oriented, event-driven programming model. After that, your previous programming experience—however brief or extensive—becomes an asset.

Traditional versions of the Basic programming language are *procedure oriented* rather than event oriented. In a procedure-oriented language, a program consists of a structured hierarchy of procedures. At the top of the structure is a main program section that controls the action by making *calls* to the program's procedures. In general, the action is sequential: The main program calls procedures one after another in a prescribed order, and the program performance ends after the last call. The sequence of procedure calls is determined by the logic and structure of the program itself.

By contrast, the order and sequence of a Visual Basic program depends on the events that occur at run time. Some event procedures may be called many times—each time the user performs an action and triggers the corresponding event. Some procedures may never be performed at all if the anticipated event never takes place.

Other versions of Basic do allow you to set up *event traps* to anticipate specific events during a program performance. In this sense you can create event-driven programs even in previous versions of the language, but you have to write the code to control all the mechanical details of the event. What is new in Visual Basic is the match between visual objects on the screen—objects that you select for your application without programming—and the predefined events associated with those objects.

Despite the differences between Visual Basic and other Basics, many of the keywords, tools, and built-in procedures in Visual Basic are the same as in other versions. For example, here is a selective list of Visual Basic programming structures and tools that you will recognize as identical, or almost identical, to equivalent features in other Basics:

- *Procedures* and *functions*, the two structures designed for organizing individual sections of code.

- Numeric and string *data types*, and the operations and functions that are available for these data types.

- *Variables*, names that represent individual data values in a program.

- Data structures—*arrays* and *records*—representing multiple data values by a single name.

- *Assignment statements* for storing values in variables.

- Control structures, such as *loops* and *decisions*.

- Data file procedures, including *sequential* and *random-access* file input and output.

- *Error-trapping* techniques.

In many of the chapters of this book you'll find special **Review Boxes** that will help you reexamine Basic programming topics such as these. The first, **Review Box 4-1**, covers the general syntax of procedures and functions. In the upcoming sections of this chapter you'll begin exploring the different ways of using procedures and functions to organize your code in a Visual Basic application.

PROGRAM ORGANIZATION

Visual Basic distinguishes between two categories of code: *event procedures* and *general procedures*. The main distinction lies in the way procedures are called for execution:

- A call to an event procedure occurs automatically whenever the corresponding event occurs. Event procedures are always **Sub** procedures and appear only in forms.

- A call to a general procedure is performed explicitly via a procedure call, never triggered by an event. General procedures include both **Sub** procedures and **Function** procedures, and may appear in either forms or code modules. (**Review Box 4-1** describes the difference between **Sub** and **Function** procedures.)

You can write general procedures to help organize your program into small, manageable parts. Small procedures—with carefully limited tasks to perform—are always easier to work with than large ones. As a general rule of thumb, a complex procedure that grows much longer than about a page of code should be divided into a sequence of smaller routines. Another reason for writing general procedures is to avoid repetition of code. A

Review Box 4-1:

Procedures and Functions

Code in Visual Basic is organized in sections known as **SUB** procedures and **FUNCTION** procedures. A procedure performs a disinct task and has its own unique name in an application. A *call* is a statement or expression that results in a performance of a procedure.

A **SUB** procedure—also known simply as a *procedure*—is a block of code enclosed within **SUB** and **END SUB** statements:

```
SUB ProcedureName (ArgumentList)
  ' Block of statements.
END SUB
```

The optional *ArgumentList* is a list of variables that will receive argument values sent to the procedure at the time of a call. Variables in the list are separated by commas. The type of each variable can be identified by a type-declaration character (**%** for an integer, **&** for a long integer, **!** for a single-precision floating-point value, **#** for a double-precision floating-point value, **@** for a currency value, or **$** for a string), or by an **As** *Type* clause:

```
Argument1 AS Type, Argument2 AS Type
```

A call to a **SUB** procedure is a statement consisting of the name of the procedure followed by a list of the argument values sent to the procedure:

```
ProcedureName ArgumentValueList
```

As a result of the call statement, each argument value is assigned to its corresponding argument variable in the procedure definition, and then the block of statements in the procedure is performed. Argument values in a call can be expressed as literal values, expressions, or variables. By

---

general procedure can be called from any number of different locations in your program.

When you are ready to write code for any kind of procedure, Visual Basic takes care of creating the appropriate procedure *template,* consisting of the **Sub** and **End Sub** statements or the **Function** and **End Function** statements.

Review Box 4-1: *(continued)*

default, argument values that appear as variables are sent *by reference.* This means that any change the procedure makes in the value of the argument is passed back to the variable in the original call. You can protect a variable from such a change by passing the argument *by value* instead. To do so, include the keyword **BYVAL** in the argument list of the **SUB** procedure definition:

```
SUB ProcedureName (BYVAL Argument1 AS Type)
```

Alternatively, you can enclose an individual argument in parentheses in the call statement; this also prevents the procedure from changing the value of the variable:

```
ProcedureName (ArgumentVariable1)
```

A **FUNCTION** procedure—also known simply as a *function*—is a block of code enclosed within **FUNCTION** and **END FUNCTION** statements. Like a **SUB** procedure, a function has an optional list of argument variables. Unlike a **SUB** procedure, a function returns a value of a specified data type:

```
FUNCTION FunctionName (ArgumentList) AS ReturnType
  ' Block of statements.
  FunctionName = ReturnValue
END FUNCTION
```

An assignment statement inside the function block specifies the function's return value by assigning an expression to the function name. A call to a function never stands alone as a statement by itself, but always appears as an expression that represents the function's return value.

You have already seen how to open the template for an event procedure. Here is a quick review of the steps:

1. In the Project Window, select the form for which you want to open an event procedure.

2. Pull down the **Edit** menu and choose the **Event Procedures** command (or simply press the F12 function key). The **Event Procedures** dialog box appears on the screen.

3. Use the **Object** and **Events** list boxes to select the event procedure: First choose the name of an object from the **Object** list and then the name of the event from the **Events** list.

4. Click the **Edit in Active** button.

When you complete these steps, the template for the event procedure you have selected appears inside the Code window, ready for you to begin writing the code.

For example, suppose you want to write the **Calc_Click** procedure for the *Loan Calculator*. When you choose the **Calc** object and the **Click** event in the **Event Procedures** dialog box, the event procedure template appears in the window as follows:

```
Sub Calc_Click ()
|
End Sub
```

The flashing edit cursor appears between these two lines, ready for you to type your first line of code. Figure 4-1 shows the Code window at this point in the process.

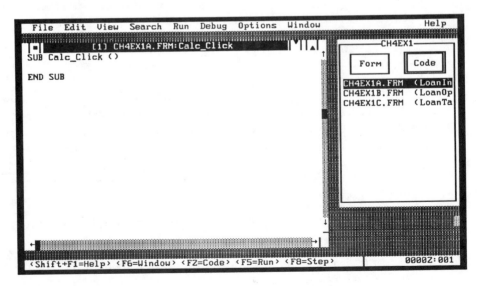

Figure 4-1 Opening the **Calc_Click** procedure template

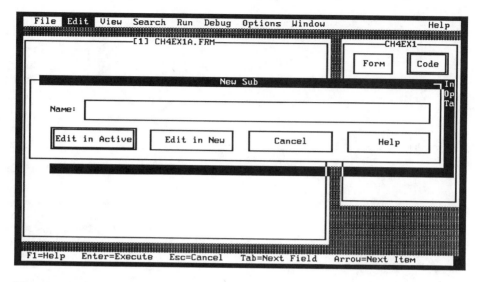

Figure 4-2 The **New Sub** dialog box

To create the template for a general procedure, you use the **New Sub** or **New Function** command from the **Edit** menu in the programming environment. Here are the steps for creating a template for a new general procedure or function:

1. Pull down the **Edit** menu and select **New Sub** or **New Function**. A dialog box appears on the screen, as shown in Figure 4-2 or 4-3.

2. Enter the name you want to give to the new procedure or function in the **Name** text box.

3. Click the **Edit in Active** button. The new procedure template appears in the Code window.

Whether the template in the Code window is for an event procedure or a general procedure, the next step is to begin writing code. The first lines you write should be a brief comment explaining the procedure's purpose. As you know, comments in Visual Basic begin with the single-quote character; for example:

```
Sub Calc_Click ()

    ' Produce the output table when
    ' the user clicks the Calc button.
```

The more carefully and consistently you document your code in this way, the more easily you will be able to revise and debug your program later.

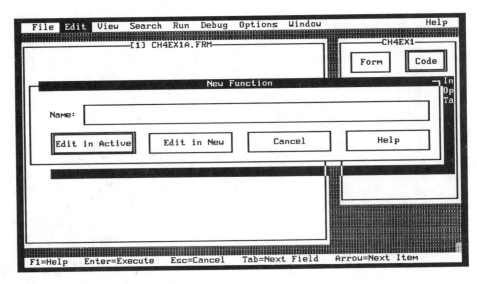

Figure 4-3 The **New Function** dialog box

Hands-on Exercise: Entering Code

The **LoanInpt** form, which displays the main dialog box of the *Loan Calculator,* will eventually require several event procedures. You'll have the opportunity to examine all of these procedures later in this chapter. But for this first programming exercise, you'll create three procedures yourself:

- An abbreviated version of **Calc_Click**, designed temporarily to display single payment calculations in the **LoanTabl** form rather than entire payment tables.

- A short function named **Payment**, which the program uses to calculate all monthly payment figures.

- The **ExitButton_Click** procedure, which consists of one line of code allowing the user to stop the program performance.

Load the CH4EX1.MAK project into memory now from the directory where you have copied the files of the exercise disk. Follow these steps to create the three procedures:

1. Select the **LoanInpt** form in the Project window and press F12 to view the **Event Procedures** dialog box.

2. Select **Calc** from the **Object** list and **Click** from the **Events** list, and then click **Edit in Active** to display the template for the **Calc_Click** procedure.

3. Type the lines of this procedure in its initial form:

```
SUB Calc_Click ()

    ' Produce the output table when
    ' the user clicks the Calc button.

    DIM Princ AS CURRENCY, Rate AS SINGLE, Term AS INTEGER

    ' Read the input values and convert them to
    ' numbers.

    Princ = VAL(InPrinc.Text)
    Rate = VAL(InRate.Text) / 100
    Term = VAL(InTerm.Text)

    TempPmt = Payment(Princ, Rate / 12, Term * 12)
    LoanTabl.SHOW
    LoanTabl.PRINT FORMAT$(TempPmt, "$#,#####.00")

END SUB
```

4. Press F12 again, and use the **Event Procedures** dialog box to open the template for the **ExitButton_Click** procedure.

5. The procedure consists of a comment and one line of code, the keyword **End**. Type this keyword into the procedure template, preceded by a comment:

```
SUB ExitButton_Click ()

    ' Terminate the program performance.

    END

END SUB
```

6. Choose the **New Function** command from the **Edit** menu to create a template for the **Payment** function. Enter **Payment** into the **Name** text box and click **Edit in Active**.

7. Type the lines of the function, including the argument list and the type identifier on the **Function** line itself:

```
FUNCTION Payment (P@, MoRate!, Months%) AS CURRENCY

  ' Calculate the monthly payment.

  Payment = (P@ * MoRate!) / (1 - (1 + MoRate!) ^ (-Months%))

END FUNCTION
```

As you type these first lines of the program, you may encounter a useful feature that is part of the Visual Basic code editor. If you attempt to enter a line that contains a syntax error, the "smart" editor immediately spots the problem and displays an error message on the screen. For example, imagine that you inadvertently enter the following line from the **Payment** function without its final closing parenthesis character:

```
Payment = (P@ * MoRate!) / (1 - (1 + MoRate!) ^ (-Months%)
```

When you do so, the warning box shown in Figure 4-4 appears on the screen. This is the first of several Visual Basic features designed to help you correct errors in your programs.

You are ready to try running this abbreviated version of the *Loan Calculator* application. Press the F5 function key to begin a performance. At this point, Visual Basic finds any structural errors that might exist in

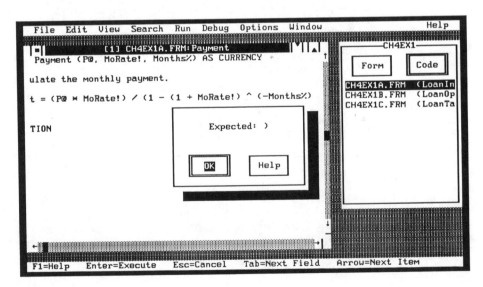

Figure 4-4 A message from the smart editor

your code—errors that prevent the program from running. If such errors exist, you will see appropriate error messages on the screen. For example, imagine that you have omitted one of the arguments in the call to the **Payment** function (a call made from within the **Calc_Click** procedure):

```
TempPmt = Payment(Rate / 12, Term * 12)
```

The first argument, **Princ**, is missing from this function call. The function itself requires three arguments, not two:

```
Function Payment (P@, MoRate!, Months%) As Currency
```

When you press F5 to run the program, Visual Basic immediately finds this inconsistency. It scrolls to the **Calc_Click** procedure in your code, highlights the mistaken function call, and displays the error message shown in Figure 4-5.

Before you can run the program, you must examine the highlighted line of code, determine exactly what is wrong with it, and correct the error. Additional errors might be highlighted in your subsequent attempts to run the program. But when you have corrected the final error, the program performance begins. The main dialog box for the *Loan Calculator* appears on the screen, ready for your input.

To test the program, enter the following three values as the parameters of an imaginary loan: a principal of **15000**; an interest rate of **10**; and a term of **5** years. Click the **Calc** button, and the value **$318.71** appears in the **Loan Table** form at the bottom of the screen. This is the monthly

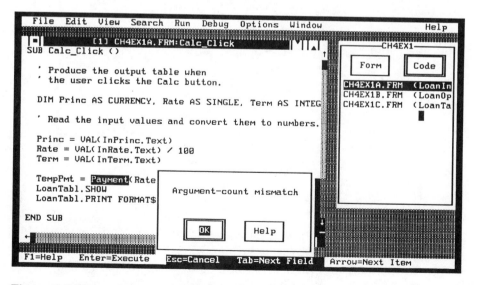

Figure 4-5 Error message after an attempt to run the program

payment for the loan. Try additional calculations if you wish. When you are finished, click the **Exit** button. The performance stops, and you can press any key to return to the Visual Basic programming environment.

Examining the Code

Now take a brief look at the three procedures you have created. The **Calc_Click** procedure, called when the user clicks the **Calc** button, has the initial tasks of reading input from the text boxes and combo box and converting the input into numeric form. Then the procedure sends these three input values as arguments in a call to the **Payment** function, to calculate the monthly payment amount. Finally, **Calc_Click** displays the calculated payment in the **LoanTabl** form.

A value entered into a text box or a combo box is always stored as a string—that is, a sequence of alphabetic and digital characters. When the input value is actually meant as a number—as in the *Loan Calculator* application—your program has to convert the string input into a numeric form before attempting to perform arithmetic operations on the number. (See **Review Box 4-2** for a description of data types and variables in the Visual Basic programming language.) Like most versions of the language, Visual Basic has a built-in function named **VAL** that performs this conversion. This function takes one string argument, *NumStr*:

```
VAL(NumStr)
```

Assuming *NumStr* is a string of digits, the **VAL** function returns the numeric equivalent of its argument.

Here are the three lines in the **Calc_Click** procedure that read the input and perform the data-type conversions:

```
Princ = VAL(InPrinc.Text)
Rate = VAL(InRate.Text) / 100
Term = VAL(InTerm.Text)
```

Each of these three lines is designed to accomplish three separate tasks:

1. Read a value from a text box or combo box.

2. Convert the text value into a number.

3. Assign the number to a numeric variable.

The first of these tasks, reading an input value, is done by a reference to the current **Text** property setting for each of the three controls, **InPrinc**, **InRate**, and **InTerm**. During design time you assigned a blank string as the **Text** setting for these three controls. When the user enters a value into one of these controls, the new **Text** property setting represents the input value.

A program uses the following general format to read the current setting of a property defined for any object in the application:

```
ObjectName.PropertyName
```

Given this format, you can see that **InPrinc.Text**, **InRate.Text**, and **InTerm.Text** represent the three input values that the user has entered into the text boxes and the combo box. Sending each of these values as arguments to the **VAL** function results in the actual numeric loan parameters. For example, here is the principal of the loan:

```
VAL(InPrinc.Text)
```

An assignment statement stores this value in the variable named **Princ**:

```
Princ = VAL(InPrinc.Text)
```

The two additional assignment statements store the interest rate and the term of the loan in the variables **Rate** and **Term**. Notice that the program divides the user's input for the interest rate by 100, to convert the percentage into a decimal value:

```
Rate = VAL(InRate.Text) / 100
```

After reading and converting the three input values and storing them in the variables **Princ**, **Rate**, and **Term**, the **Calc_Click** procedure sends these values to the **Payment** function to calculate the monthly payment:

```
TempPmt = Payment(Princ, Rate / 12, Term * 12)
```

Actually, the **Rate** value must first be divided by 12 to produce a monthly interest rate amount, and the **Term** value must be multiplied by 12 to give the loan term in months. Given these three arguments, the **Payment** function calculates the montly loan payment, which is stored in the variable **TempPmt**.

Finally, the **Calc_Click** procedure displays the **LoanTabl** form on the screen and prints the result of the payment calculation in the form. These two tasks are performed by calls to two of Visual Basic's built-in *methods*. You'll recall that a method is a procedure that performs an operation on a particular object. (In Chapter 2 you used the **ADDITEM** method to build the drop-down list for the combo box in the *Loan Calculator*.) The format for calling a method is:

```
ObjectName.METHODNAME
```

Calc_Click uses two methods that apply to forms: The **SHOW** method brings a hidden form to the screen, and the **PRINT** method displays one

Review Box 4-2:

Data Types, Operations, Variables, and Constants

Visual Basic supports five numeric data types—named **INTEGER,**
LONG, SINGLE, DOUBLE, and **CURRENCY**—along with a related
group of numeric operations. In addition, Visual Basic has two **STRING**
types—variable length and fixed length.

A *variable* is a name that represents a data value belonging to a specific
type. You can define the type of a variable by appending a type-
declaration character as a suffix at the end of the variable name (%, &,
!, #, and @ for the five numeric types, or $ for a string) or by declaring
the variable in a **DIM** statement. The default type of an undeclared
variable that has no type-declaration character is **SINGLE**.

The *integer* types represent whole numbers within specific ranges of
values. Integer representation is always perfectly precise and also provides the fastest operations. Operations available for integers include ^
(exponentiation), * (multiplication), / (division), \ (integer division),
MOD (modulo arithmetic), + (addition), and – (subtraction). The
following table summarizes the characteristics of the two integer types:

Name	Variable Suffix	Storage	Low Value	High Value
INTEGER	%	2 bytes	–32768	32768
LONG	&	4 bytes	–2147483648	2147483647

The *floating-point* types represent numbers with decimal points, within
very large ranges but with limited precision. Operations are exponentiation, multiplication, division, addition, and subtraction. This table
summarizes the two floating-point types:

Name	Variable Suffix	Storage	Precision
SINGLE	!	4 bytes	6 digits
DOUBLE	#	8 bytes	10 digits

Review Box 4-2: (continued)

The **Currency** type represents *fixed-decimal* values without loss of precision. Values belonging to this type may have up to fourteen digits to the left of the decimal point and four digits after the decimal point:

Name	Variable Suffix	Storage	Low Value	High Value
CURRENCY	@	8 bytes	−9.22E+14	9.22E+14

A *string* value is a sequence of characters, which may include letters of the alphabet, digits from "0" to "9", punctuation characters, and other special characters as defined in the ASCII code. Visual Basic defines one string operation, *concatenation*, represented by the + operator. Concatenation combines two strings to form a third string. In addition, Visual Basic has a large library of string procedures and functions. The **LEN** function returns the length, in characters, of a string. A variable-length string can contain any number of characters up to 32K bytes. A fixed-length string has a predeclared length. You use a **DIM** statement to declare a fixed-length string:

```
DIM StringVarName AS STRING * StringLength
```

where *StringLength* is an integer representing the length of the string.

An *assignment statement* stores a value in a variable. This statement has the general form:

```
VariableName = value
```

The value stored in a variable can—and often does—change frequently during a program performance. In contrast, a *constant* is a name that represents an unchanging value throughout the performance. Visual Basic supplies the **CONST** statement for declaring constants. This statement can appear in form or module declaration sections, or in procedures.

or more text values inside a form. The following two instructions show the **LoanTabl** form and display the calculated payment value inside the form:

```
LoanTabl.SHOW
LoanTabl.PRINT FORMAT$(TempPmt, "$#,#####.00")
```

A built-in Visual Basic function named **FORMAT$** produces an output string in dollar-and-cent format. The **PRINT** method and the **FORMAT$** function together operate much like the PRINT USING statement in traditional Basic. The primary difference is that **PRINT** is a method that applies to a particular object in Visual Basic.

In this shortened version of the *Loan Calculator,* each click of the **Calc** button displays a single payment value in the **LoanInpt** form. Finally, clicking the **Exit** button ends the program performance. As you saw, the exit is performed by a single Visual Basic command, **END**:

```
SUB ExitButton_Click ()
  END
END SUB
```

These three short procedures illustrate many features of Visual Basic programming. Here is a summary of what you have learned so far:

- The code you write in a Visual Basic program is divided into event procedures and general procedures. The format for naming an event procedure is *ObjectName_EventName*—for example, **Calc_Click**. An event procedure is called when the corresponding event occurs during run time. A general procedure (such as the **Payment** function) is performed as a result of an explicit call.

- The Visual Basic language has many *built-in* general procedures and functions. Examples you have seen illustrated so far are **VAL** and **FORMAT$**. Tools such as these are likely to be familiar to you from your work in other versions of Basic.

- Visual Basic also has a group of built-in procedures called methods. Each method performs an operation on a particular object. The format for calling a method is *ObjectName.METHODNAME*. For example, **LoanTabl.SHOW** calls the **SHOW** method for the **LoanTabl** form.

- A program uses the format *ObjectName.PropertyName* to access the current setting of any property. Much like a variable name, this format represents a value belonging to a specified data type; for example, **InPrinc.Text** represents a string value.

As you now turn to the complete code listings of the *Loan Calculator* application, you'll see more examples of each of these features. For now, don't worry about specific details, but concentrate instead on broad categories of programming tools. Event procedures, general procedures, methods, and properties—these are the elements of Visual Basic programming that you'll be studying and using in the chapters ahead.

Procedures in the *Loan Calculator*

You can now open the complete *Loan Calculator* application from the files supplied on the exercise disk. The name of the project file is LOAN-CALC.MAK. Run the application now if you wish, and review the program's various operations. Enter an initial set of values into the **Principal**, **Rate**, and **Term** boxes, and click the **Calc** button (or press the Enter key) to see the resulting payment table. Then click the **Table values** button and change the increment values for the table. Finally, try saving the table as a text file on disk and sending the table to the printer. Click the **Exit** button when you are finished experimenting with the program and then press any key to return to the programming environment.

This version of the application has procedures stored in both the **LoanInpt** and **LoanOpts** forms. Begin by focusing on the first of these forms, **LoanInpt**. Select the form and click the **Code** button on the Project Window (or press the F2 function key) to view the **Code** dialog box. As shown in Figure 4-6, this dialog box displays a list of all the procedures in

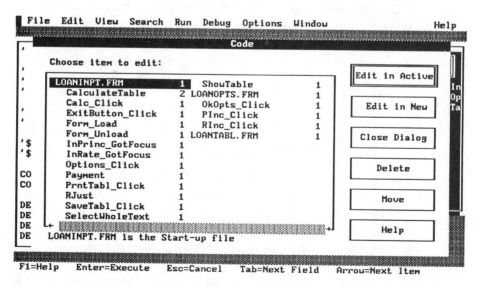

Figure 4-6 The **Code** dialog box for the *Loan Calculator* application

the project. To view any procedure, you simply select its name in the list and click the **Edit in Active** button.

Examining the **Code** dialog box, you'll find that the form contains the following nine event procedures:

- **Form_Load** performs several initialization tasks at the beginning of the program's performance. (You've already seen part of this procedure; it contains the sequence of **ADDITEM** method calls that build the drop-down list in the **InTerm** combo box.)

- **Form_Unload** terminates the program if the user chooses the **Close** command from the control menu of the LOANINPUT form.

- **Options_Click** is called when the user clicks the command button labeled **Table values**. It displays the application's second dialog box on the screen.

- **Calc_Click** is called when the user clicks the **Calc** command button. It creates and displays the payment table in the **LoanTabl** form.

- **SaveTabl_Click** is called when the user clicks the **Save** button. It saves the payment table to disk in a text file named LOANTEMP.TXT.

- **PrntTabl_Click** is called when the user clicks the **Print** button. It sends the payment table to the printer.

- **InPrinc_GotFocus** is called when the user selects the **InPrinc** text box. This procedure selects (and highlights) the entire text currently in the text box so the user can enter a new value easily.

- **InRate_GotFocus** is called when the user selects the **InRate** text box. Again, it highlights the entire text inside the text box.

- **ExitButton_Click** is called when the user clicks the button labeled **Exit**. As you have seen, it terminates the program performance.

In addition, the form contains a collection of five general procedures. Again, you can view any of these procedures by pressing F2, selecting a name in the **Code** list, and clicking the **Edit in Active** button. There are two function procedures: **Payment**, which performs the monthly payment calculation; and **RJust**, which the program uses for aligning columns of figures in the payment table. The three **Sub** procedures are designed to simplify the program's overall organization: **CalculateTable** builds the entire table and stores it in convenient ways for the actual output procedures. **ShowTable** displays the table in the **LoanTabl** form. **SelectWholeText** is a general procedure for highlighting the current text in a text box.

You can examine all the program's procedures in Listings 4-1 to 4-8. In the sections ahead you'll survey a few of the most important programming techniques represented in this code.

Declaring and Initializing Variables

As in other advanced versions of Basic, the *scope* of variables is always an important issue. Scope refers to the level at which a given variable is recognized and available for use. Broadly speaking, there are three ranges of scope in Visual Basic:

- Variables that are shared among multiple forms and modules in a project. Visual Basic provides the **COMMON SHARED** statement for declaring this kind of variable.

- Variables that are available only within the form or module that declares them—including all the procedures that the form or module contains. The **DIM SHARED** statement declares a variable of this scope. Each form or module has its own *declarations section* in which such variables can be declared.

- Variables that are declared by a **DIM** statement inside a procedure and are available only within the procedure that declares them.

The *Loan Calculator* illustrates all three of these levels. Listing 4-1 shows the declarations section (sometimes called the "form-level declarations") of the **LoanInpt** form. To view the declarations section of a form, press F2 and select the form's name in the **Code** dialog box; then click the **Edit in Active** button.

The program has two variables that are shared by both the **LoanInpt** and the **LoanOpts** forms. The variables are named **CurPrincInc** and **CurRateInc**. They represent the current settings for the two increment values that determine the range of the payment table—the principal increment from one row to the next in the table and the interest rate increment from one column to the next. Here are the **COMMON SHARED** statements that declare **CurPrincInc** and **CurRateInc**:

```
COMMON SHARED CurPrincInc AS CURRENCY
COMMON SHARED CurRateInc  AS SINGLE
```

These lines appear as form-level declarations in both the **LoanInpt** and the **LoanOpts** forms (Listings 4-1 and 4-8). The **As** clause declares the data type of each variable. The two variables are *initialized* in the **Form_Load** procedure (Listing 4-2):

```
CurPrincInc = 1000
CurRateInc = .005
```

Form_Load is always a good place to assign first values to a program's shared variables. In the *Loan Calculator* these values remain fixed until the user clicks the **Table values** button and selects new settings on the **LoanOpts** form. Later you'll see how the values of the two variables are reset in the **LoanOpts** procedures. But you can already understand why these two variables are defined in **COMMON SHARED** statements: Procedures in both the **LoanInpt** and the **LoanOpts** forms need access to them.

Notice the other kinds of statements located in the form-level declarations of the **LoanInpt** form. First, the following $FORM statements appear at the beginning of the code:

```
'$FORM LoanTabl
'$FORM LoanOpts
```

Although these lines look like comments, they actually represent a special kind of code called *metacommands*. The $FORM metacommand is an essential part of a multiform project; it allows one form to gain access to the controls and properties of the other forms in the project. Interestingly enough, Visual Basic inserts $FORM metacommands into your program automatically if they are needed.

Another kind of code that Visual Basic takes care of placing in your program is the DECLARE statement. DECLARE provides an advance declaration of procedures and functions that your program uses, and activates argument checking for calls to the procedures. Here are two examples of DECLARE statements that appear in the form-level declarations of the **LoanInpt** form:

```
DECLARE SUB CalculateTable (P AS CURRENCY, R AS SINGLE,
T AS INTEGER)
DECLARE FUNCTION Payment (P@, MoRate!, Months%) AS
CURRENCY
```

Displaying the Table

In this complete version of the *Loan Calculator,* the **Calc_Click** procedure (Listing 4-3) performs some input validation checks before attempting to create the output table. If any of the three input values is equal to zero, the procedure assumes that the user has made a mistake. Note that the **VAL** function returns a value of zero if its string argument cannot be successfully converted to a number. In this case, **Calc_Click** displays an error message on the screen, as shown in Figure 4-7.

On the other hand, if **Calc_Click** finds that all three input values are usable, the event procedure makes calls to two general procedures that do all the work of calculating and displaying the output table:

```
CalculateTable Princ, Rate, Term
ShowTable
```

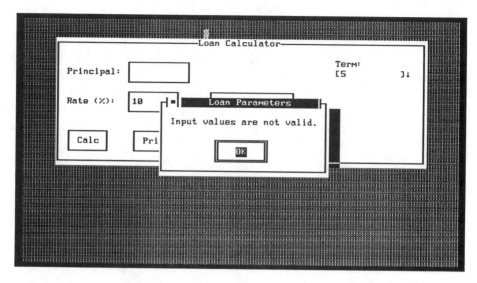

Figure 4-7 Error message for invalid input

The **CalculateTable** procedure (Listing 4-4) builds the entire table of monthly payment figures and stores it in two different formats—one for the convenience of the procedure that displays the table on the screen and another for the procedures that save and print the table. For this work, the procedure makes extensive use of Visual Basic's built-in **FORMAT$** function and also the **Payment** function, which is one of the general procedures in the **LoanInpt** form.

Once the figures of the output table have been calculated and stored in memory, the **ShowTable** procedure (Listing 4-5) has the job of displaying the table in the **LoanTabl** form. The procedure contains illustrations of three methods that apply to forms—the **SHOW** method, which displays the form on the screen; the **CLS** method, which clears all information from the form; and the **PRINT** method, which displays values in the form.

Saving and Printing the Table

The **PrntTabl_Click** and **SaveTabl_Click** procedures (Listing 4-6) both begin by calling the **Calc_Click** procedure, to make sure that the current payment table is based on the latest input data:

```
Calc_Click
```

This call illustrates an important point: Although an event procedure is normally called when the corresponding event takes place, you can also force a performance of an event procedure by writing a regular call statement.

The **PrntTabl_Calc** procedure then goes on to send the payment table to the printer. For this task, Visual Basic provides an object called **Printer**. Unlike other objects you've worked with up to now, the **Printer** object is not visible on the screen; however, it has properties and methods, which you access in familiar ways. For example, you can use the following format to call a **Printer** method:

```
Printer.METHODNAME
```

The **PrntTabl_Click** procedure has two examples of **Printer** method calls. The **PRINT** method, as you might expect, sends items and lines of information to the printer; and the **NEWPAGE** method moves the printing position to the top of the next page.

The **SaveTabl_Click** procedure uses standard Basic tools for creating a sequential file on disk. The output is saved in a text file named LOAN-TEMP.TXT. The first step in the process is to open the file for output:

```
Open FileName$ for Output as #1
```

Then a sequence of **Print#** statements send the table to the open file, one line at a time; for example:

```
Print #1, OutTable$(i%)
```

And finally, the procedure closes the file when the entire table has been saved:

```
Close #1
```

Listing 4-6 also shows two additional event procedures from the **LoanInpt** form—**Options_Click** and **ExitButton_Click**. The first of these uses the **SHOW** method to display the **LoanOpts** form on the screen:

```
LoanOpts.SHOW 1
```

The **SHOW** method takes an optional numeric argument; in this example, the value of 1 specifies that the **LoanOpts** form will have exclusive control of the program until the user closes the dialog box by clicking the **OK** button.

Changing the Increment Values

The **LoanOpts** form contains three event procedures, all of which are shown in Listing 4-8. When the user clicks one of the option buttons in the **Principal Increment** frame, the event procedure named **PInc_Click** is called. Likewise, clicking a button in the **Rate Increment** frame results in a call to **RInc_Click**. To understand these two procedures, recall that you defined these two groups of buttons as *control arrays*. For this reason, a single event procedure is sufficient for handling each group of buttons. When one of these two procedures is called, Visual Basic automatically passes the procedure an argument representing the **Index** number of the option button that the user has clicked. **PInc_Click** and **RInc_Click** use this number to determine the new values for the variables **CurPrincInc** and **CurRateInc**.

The third event procedure, **OkOpts_Click**, simply closes the **LoanOpts** form when the user clicks the **OK** button.

Controlling the Text Boxes

The remaining three procedures in the **LoanInpt** form (Listing 4-7) address a small detail in the behavior of the two text boxes. In short, these procedures highlight the entire contents of a text box as soon as the box is activated. This highlighting allows the user to enter a new value into a box without first erasing the old value. (Any new typing from the keyboard automatically replaces the highlighted text.)

The procedures are interesting for a number of reasons. First, they illustrate an event named **GotFocus**. This event occurs when a control receives the focus. (During run time, one control has the focus at a given time.) The **InPrinc_GotFocus** and **InRate_GotFocus** procedures are called when one of these text boxes is activated. Each procedure makes a call to a general procedure named **SelectWholeText**.

The **SelectWholeText** procedure illustrates an important feature: You can write a procedure that accepts a control as an argument:

```
SelectWholeText (InTextBox As Control)
```

This arrangement allows you to write general-purpose procedures for controls, to perform a given set of operations on any object received as an argument. For example, **SelectWholeText** highlights the text contained in any text box. To do so, it uses two Visual Basic properties named **SelStart** and **SelLength**, which set the starting point and the length of the text highlight.

Code in the Second Version of the *Loan Calculator*

Now that you have a sense of how the first version of the *Loan Calculator* works, you might want to take a look at the code in the second version. You can load the second version from files supplied on the exercise disk; the project name is LOANCA2.MAK. Run the program, and notice the differences in the way the two versions operate. The second version has only one command button, **Calc**. All the other options—including output destinations and table increments—are presented in the pull-down menu system.

The code for the second version is similar to the first, but organized differently. For one thing, all the code in the second version is contained in one form, named **LoanIn2**. In addition, the event procedures that save and print the form—and other procedures that change the table increments—are associated with menu objects rather than command buttons and icons.

As you look at the code for the second version, you might also want to review the structure of the menu system. Select the **Menu Design Window** command from the **Window** menu in the Form Designer. As you'll recall, this window shows you all the properties of each element in the menu.

You'll return to the second version of the *Loan Calculator* for debugging exercises in Chapter 5.

SUMMARY: THE ELEMENTS OF VISUAL BASIC PROGRAMMING

A Visual Basic program is centered around events—and the forms and controls that are the objects of events.

The code you write is organized into two general kinds of procedures. An *event procedure* is called whenever the corresponding event takes place during run time. A *general procedure*—which may be structured as a **Sub** or **Function** procedure—is performed by a call statement or a call expression. Interestingly, Visual Basic also allows you to force a performance of an event procedure even when the corresponding event has not taken place.

As in other versions of Basic, data in a Visual Basic program are represented by variable names. But a program also can access another variety of data—the properties of each form and control in the application, identified as *ObjectName.PropertyName*. A program can *read* the current setting of a property or *change* the setting by placing the property name at the left side of an assignment statement:

```
ObjectName.PropertyName = Value
```

Visual Basic provides many built-in routines. A large library of general functions and procedures is available. In addition, Visual Basic provides *methods*—procedures that operate on specific categories of objects. Each object—including forms, controls, and special objects such as **Printer**—has its own library of associated methods.

Listing 4-1 Form-level declarations from the LoanInpt form

```
' The LoanCalc program.

' Produces a table of monthly payment calculations
' from loan terms that the user enters into the
' LoanInpt form.

' LoanInpt.FRM
' Declarations

'$FORM LoanTabl
'$FORM LoanOpts

COMMON SHARED CurPrincInc AS CURRENCY
COMMON SHARED CurRateInc  AS SINGLE

DECLARE SUB Calc_Click ()
DECLARE SUB CalculateTable (P AS CURRENCY, R AS SINGLE, T AS
INTEGER)
DECLARE FUNCTION RJust$ (InString$, JustWidth%)
DECLARE FUNCTION Payment (P@, MoRate!, Months%) AS CURRENCY
DECLARE SUB ShowTable ()
DECLARE SUB SelectWholeText (InTextBox AS CONTROL)

' Define True and False constants.

CONST False = 0
CONST True = NOT False

' Declare output table arrays.

DIM SHARED FormTable$(5, 5)
DIM SHARED OutTable$(5)

' Declare flag for input errors.

DIM SHARED BadInput AS INTEGER

' End of LoanInpt declarations.
```

Listing 4-2 The Form_Load and Form_Unload procedures for the LoanInpt form

```
SUB Form_Load ()

  ' Build the drop-down list for
  ' the Term combo box.

  InTerm.ADDITEM "4 years"
  InTerm.ADDITEM "5 years"
  InTerm.ADDITEM "10 years"
  InTerm.ADDITEM "15 years"
  InTerm.ADDITEM "20 years"
  InTerm.ADDITEM "30 years"

  ' Initialize the increment values.

  CurPrincInc = 1000
  CurRateInc = .005

END SUB   ' Form_Load



SUB Form_Unload (Cancel AS INTEGER)
  END
END SUB
```

Listing 4-3 The Calc_Click procedure

```
SUB Calc_Click ()

  ' Produce the output table when
  ' the user clicks the Calc button.

  DIM Princ AS CURRENCY, Rate AS SINGLE, Term AS INTEGER

  ' Read the input values and convert them to numbers.

  Princ = VAL(InPrinc.Text)
  Rate = VAL(InRate.Text) / 100
  Term = VAL(InTerm.Text)
```

```
' Check for input errors or missing values,
' and display an error message if necessary.

BadInput = (Princ = 0) OR (Rate = 0) OR (Term = 0)
IF BadInput THEN
  Msg$ = "Input values are not valid."
  Title$ = "Loan Parameters"
  MSGBOX Msg$, 48, Title$
ELSE

' If input is OK, calculate and display the loan table.

  CalculateTable Princ, Rate, Term
  ShowTable
END IF

END SUB  ' Calc_Click
```

Listing 4-4 The CalculateTable procedure and the Payment function

```
SUB CalculateTable (P AS CURRENCY, R AS SINGLE, T AS INTEGER)

  ' Build the payment table in the output arrays:
  '    -- FormTable$ is for displaying the table.
  '    -- OutTable$ is for printing and saving the table.

  CONST W = 12
  DIM StartPrinc AS CURRENCY
  DIM StartRate AS SINGLE
  DIM PRange(5) AS CURRENCY
  DIM RRange(5)  AS SINGLE
  DIM Pmt AS CURRENCY

  ' Calculate the starting principal and rate for the
  ' table, given the current increment values.

  StartPrinc = P - 2 * CurPrincInc
  StartRate = R - 2 * CurRateInc

  ' Compute the first column and row of the table.

  OutTable$(0) = SPACE$(W)
```

(continued)

```
   FOR i% = 1 TO 5
     PRange(i%) = StartPrinc + CurPrincInc * (i% - 1)
     RRange(i%) = StartRate + CurRateInc * (i% - 1)

     FormTable$(i%, 0) = FORMAT$(PRange(i%), "$#,######")
     FormTable$(0, i%) = FORMAT$(RRange(i%), "0.00%")

     OutTable$(0) = OutTable$(0) + RJust$(FormTable$(0, i%), W)
     OutTable$(i%) = RJust$(FormTable$(i%, 0), W)
   NEXT i%

   ' Fill in the rest of the table.

   FOR i% = 1 TO 5
     FOR j% = 1 TO 5
       Pmt = Payment(PRange(i%), RRange(j%) / 12, T * 12)
       FormTable$(i%, j%) = FORMAT$(Pmt, "$#,####.00")
       OutTable$(i%) = OutTable$(i%) + RJust$(FormTable$(i%,
j%), W)
     NEXT j%
   NEXT i%

END SUB   ' CalculateTable



FUNCTION Payment (P@, MoRate!, Months%) AS CURRENCY

   ' Calculate the monthly payment.

   Payment = (P@ * MoRate!) / (1 - (1 + MoRate!) ^ (-Months%))

END FUNCTION   ' Payment
```

Listing 4-5 The ShowTable procedure and the RJust$ function

```
SUB ShowTable ()

   ' Display the payment table in the LoanTabl form.

   CONST W = 10   ' Output width
```

```
    LoanTabl.SHOW
    LoanTabl.CLS

    FOR i% = 0 TO 5
      FOR j% = 0 TO 5
        LoanTabl.PRINT TAB((W + 3) * j%);
        LoanTabl.PRINT RJust$(FormTable$(i%, j%), W);
      NEXT j%
      LoanTabl.PRINT
      IF i% = 0 THEN LoanTabl.PRINT
    NEXT i%

    LoanInpt.SETFOCUS

END SUB   ' ShowTable



FUNCTION RJust$ (InString$, JustWidth%)

  ' Right-justify a string within a width.

  TempStr$ = SPACE$(JustWidth%)
  RSET TempStr$ = InString$
  RJust$ = TempStr$

END FUNCTION   ' RJust$
```

Listing 4-6 PrntTabl_Click, SaveTabl_Click, Options_Click, and ExitButton_Click

```
SUB PrntTabl_Click ()

  ' Print the payment table.

  Calc_Click

  IF NOT BadInput THEN
    Printer.PRINT OutTable$(0)
    Printer.PRINT
    FOR i% = 1 TO 5
      Printer.PRINT OutTable$(i%)
    NEXT i%
```

(continued)

```
      Printer.NEWPAGE
   END IF

   InPrinc.SETFOCUS

 END SUB  ' PrntTabl_Click


SUB SaveTabl_Click ()

   ' Save the table as a text file.

   CONST FileName$ = "LoanTemp.Txt"

   Calc_Click
   IF NOT BadInput THEN
     OPEN FileName$ FOR OUTPUT AS #1
     PRINT #1, OutTable$(0)
     PRINT #1,
     FOR i% = 1 TO 5
       PRINT #1, OutTable$(i%)
     NEXT i%
     CLOSE #1
   END IF

   InPrinc.SETFOCUS

 END SUB  ' SaveTabl_Click


SUB Options_Click ()

   ' Give the user the opportunity to select
   ' new increment values for the payment table.

   LoanOpts.SHOW 1

   ' When control returns to the LoanInpt form,
   ' set the focus on the InPrinc text box and
   ' force a call to the Calc_Click event procedure.

   InPrinc.SETFOCUS
   Calc_Click

 END SUB  ' Options_Click
```

```
SUB ExitButton_Click ()

  ' Terminate the program performance.
  END

END SUB   ' ExitButton_Click
```

Listing 4-7 The GotFocus event procedures and SelectWholeText procedure

```
SUB InPrinc_GotFocus ()

  ' Highlight current entry when
  ' text box is selected.

  SelectWholeText InPrinc

END SUB   ' InPrinc_GotFocus



SUB InRate_GotFocus ()

  ' Highlight current entry
  ' when text box is selected.

  SelectWholeText InRate

END SUB   ' InRate_GotFocus



SUB SelectWholeText (InTextBox AS CONTROL)

  ' Highlight current entry when the
  ' user selects a text box.

  InTextBox.SelStart = 0
  InTextBox.SelLength = LEN(InTextBox.Text)

END SUB   ' SelectWholeText
```

Listing 4-8 Declarations and event procedures from the LoanOpts form

```
' LoanOpts.FRM
' Declarations.

COMMON SHARED CurPrincInc AS CURRENCY
COMMON SHARED CurRateInc  AS SINGLE



SUB OkOpts_Click ()

    ' When the user clicks the OK button,
    ' close the Table Values dialog box
    ' and recalculate the payment table.

    LoanOpts.HIDE

END SUB  ' OkOpts_Click



SUB PInc_Click (Index AS INTEGER)

    ' Calculate the principal increment
    ' value using the Index number of the
    ' currently selected option button.

    CurPrincInc = 10 ^ (Index + 1)

END SUB  ' PInc_Click



SUB RInc_Click (Index AS INTEGER)

    ' Determine the rate increment value
    ' using the Index number of the currently
    ' selected option button.

    SELECT CASE Index
        CASE 0
            CurRateInc = .00125
```

```
        CASE 1
            CurRateInc = .0025
        CASE 2
            CurRateInc = .005
        CASE 3
            CurRateInc = .01
        CASE 4
            CurRateInc = .02
    END SELECT

END SUB   ' RInc_Click
```

5

Debugging and Compiling an Application

INTRODUCTION

Mistakes are a fact of life in programming. Like all programming languages, Visual Basic demands a level of perfection that seldom emerges from the first version of code—or even the second or third versions—however skillful the programmer. For just this reason, the Visual Basic programming environment includes a collection of tools and commands that will help you find the bugs in an application.

You've already seen two kinds of error correction that take place in the Visual Basic environment. At the first and most immediate level, the smart editor catches syntax errors as you enter declarations and commands into the Code window. Given a line that contains an error, the editor displays an error message on the screen explaining what is wrong with the line. (See Figure 4-4 in Chapter 4 for an example.) In the Code window, the edit cursor appears at the location of the error. This kind of error takes place while you are writing code and is usually easy to correct.

At the next stage of application development—when you first try running your new program—Visual Basic finds and describes any structural inconsistencies that prevent the performance from beginning. For example, in Chapter 4 you saw what happens when the number of arguments in a procedure call does not match the number of arguments actually required by the procedure itself (Figure 4-5). Again, you will seldom need much time to fix this kind of error.

Bugs that you discover during your program's performance are often much more troublesome, and can launch you into long and detailed investigations of your own code. Broadly speaking, two kinds of problems show up during a program's performance:

- A *run-time* error interrupts the program because of some condition that Visual Basic cannot handle in any other way. A common example is an attempt to perform division by zero. In response to such an error, Visual Basic stops the program and displays an error message on the screen.

- A *logical error* does not interrupt the program but creates unexpected and unwanted results. This kind of error can be the most difficult to correct. Your program completes its performance from beginning to end but produces bad output, incorrect calculations, or an inappropriate sequence of operations.

In this chapter you'll learn to use Visual Basic's debugging tools to correct errors in your code. In particular, you'll focus on the commands offered in the **Debug** menu, shown in Figure 5-1. You'll also learn ways to use features called the *Immediate* window and the *Debug* window.

This chapter guides you through a sequence of hands-on exercises designed to help you experiment with debugging features. The context for these exercises is a version of the *Loan Calculator* stored on the exercise disk as CH5EX1.MAK. Begin now by opening this project into the Visual

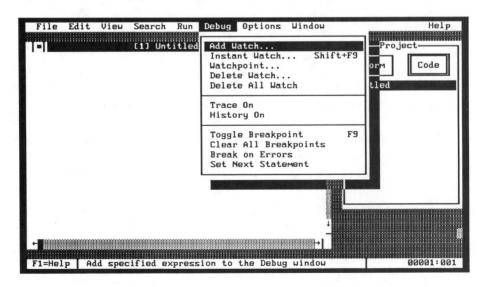

Figure 5-1 The **Debug** menu

Basic environment. In the declarations section of the **LoanInpt** form you will find the following message, presented as a sequence of comment lines:

```
' ******************************************
' ***        Debugging Exercise        ***
' ***           (Chapter 5)            ***
' ***      ----------------------      ***
' ***      This program has errors.    ***
' ******************************************
```

The deliberate errors introduced into this version of the program will give you opportunities to try out Visual Basic's debugging tools.

CORRECTING PERFORMANCE ERRORS

When you notice something going wrong with a program, your first task is to stop the program so you can take advantage of debugging tools. There are a number of ways to do this. Perhaps the simplest—but often least helpful—way is to press the Ctrl-Break combination on your keyboard. The Code window then shows you what part of your program was being performed when you stopped. The problem with this technique is that you can't easily control the point at which the break occurs. In fact, you are most likely to break during a time when Visual Basic is waiting for an event to take place. In general, you need a more precise way to find the code that is causing the problem.

Visual Basic automatically provides an appropriate break when a run-time error interrupts the program performance. You can see how this happens by starting up this chapter's version of the *Loan Calculator* now:

1. Press F5 to start the program. (Keep in mind that this version—CH5EX1.MAK—has some built-in errors.)

2. Enter values for the three loan parameters: **15000** for the principal, **10** for the rate, and **5 years** for the term.

3. Click the **Calc** button.

You may be surprised by what happens next. Rather than producing the payment table at the bottom of the screen, Visual Basic stops your program and displays an error box with the one-word message **Overflow** (Figure 5-2). When you click the **OK** button on the error box, you see a Code window that displays part of your code—specifically, the **Payment** function. Clearly something has gone wrong.

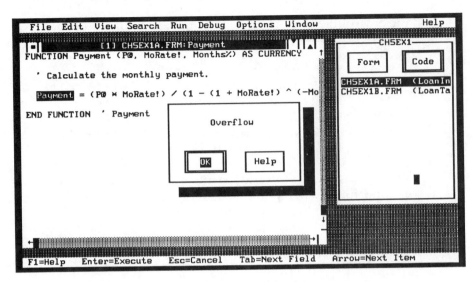

Figure 5-2 Interruption of the program due to an **Overflow** error

An *overflow* error occurs when a variable is assigned a value outside the range of the variable's defined data type. One of the common causes of an overflow error is division by zero. As you examine the **Payment** function for errors, division by zero is the first possibility that comes to mind. But no matter how carefully you look, you can't see anything wrong with the function itself. It *looks* just like the code that worked perfectly well before. (It *is*.) You conclude that the problem must be elsewhere in your program—probably somewhere in the routine that *calls* the **Payment** function, which you know is the **CalculateTable** procedure. Apparently this procedure has passed one or more inappropriate arguments to the function.

So here is your problem: You need to see exactly what is happening to the data passed to the **Payment** function. Then you'll want to investigate the program's activities at some point *before* this overflow error occurs.

Visual Basic Debugging Features

The Immediate window is one place to find out the current values of variables when your program performance is interrupted automatically or when you stop the program by pressing Ctrl-Break. To control debugging activities once you are in a break mode—and to designate subsequent break points in the program—you use the commands in the **Debug** menu.

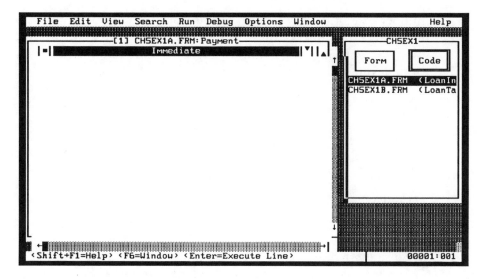

```
   File   Edit   View   Search   Run   Debug   Options   Window                Help
╔══════════════════════════════════════════════════════════════╗ ╔═══CH5EX1═══╗
║                ─[1] CH5EX1A.FRM:Payment────────────║ ║            ║
║ │■│███████████████Immediate██████████████████│▼│▐│▲│ ║ ║ ┌──────┐ ┌──────┐ ║
║                                                      ↑ ║ ║ │ Form │ │ Code │ ║
║                                                        ║ ║ └──────┘ └──────┘ ║
║                                                        ║ ║ CH5EX1A.FRM (LoanIn║
║                                                        ║ ║ CH5EX1B.FRM (LoanTa║
║                                                        ║ ║                    ║
   <Shift+F1=Help> <F6=Window> <Enter=Execute Line>           00001:001
```

Figure 5-3 The Immediate window

The Immediate Window

To view the Immediate window, pull down the **Window** menu and choose
the **Immediate** command. It starts out empty (Figure 5-3), but you can use
it along with the output screen to investigate the current values of variables
that were defined at the moment the break occurred in the program.

To view values in the Immediate window, you type **Print** statements
directly into the window, in this format:

```
Print expression
```

When you do so, Visual Basic evaluates the *expression* and displays its value
directly on the output screen, sometimes superimposed over whatever is
already on the screen. You can see why this tool is called the *Immediate*
window: Commands you type in it are performed as soon as you press the
Enter key.

For now you would like to know the values of the variables that were
passed to the **Payment** function—on the theory that one of these values
has probably caused the overflow error. The function's argument variables
are **P@** (a currency-type variable representing the principal of the loan),
MoRate! (a single-precision floating-point variable representing the
monthly interest rate), and **Months%** (an integer variable representing the

number of months in the term of the loan). The **Payment** function does not change the values of these variables, so you can view the original three values by entering the following three statements into the Immediate window, one at a time:

```
Print P@
Print MoRate!
Print Months%
```

After each statement, the value of the variable appears on the output screen, as follows:

```
13000
0
60
```

Because these output lines are superimposed over the still-displayed *Loan Calculator* dialog box, you may have to look carefully at the output screen— or even issue the **Print** statements more than once from the Immediate window—to find the information you want. Press any key to return to the programming environment from the output screen.

Two of these argument variables have the values you would have predicted: The value of **P@**, 13000, has been reduced by two thousand-dollar increments from the original **Principal** entry of 15000. (Keep in mind that the payment table displays two rows of monthly payment calculations for principal amounts that are *smaller* than the target amount and two for *larger* ones.) The value of **Months%**, 60, is also correct—it represents the number of months in a five-year loan term.

But the value displayed for **MoRate!**, 0, cannot be right. **MoRate!** should contain a reasonable interest rate amount, never zero. Obviously the **CalculateTable** procedure has sent an unusable value to the **Payment** function for this argument. Furthermore, a quick review of the function's formula for monthly payment calculations shows why the overflow error occurred:

```
Payment = (P@ * MoRate!) / (1 - (1 + MoRate!) ^ (-Months%))
```

A **MoRate!** value of zero produces a zero in the denominator of this division operation—in short, division by zero.

Thanks to the Immediate window, you've identified the problem quickly. The next step is to trace the error back to its source and correct it. Close the Immediate window now (double-click the window's control-menu box). In the Code window, place a single-quote character just before the assignment statement in the **Payment** function:

```
' Payment = (P@ * MoRate!) / (1 - (1 + MoRate!) ^ (-Months%))
```

This is sometimes known as *commenting out* a line of code. It is a convenient way to deactivate a statement temporarily while you are trying to find out what is going wrong in your program.

Now press F2, select the general procedure named **CalculateTable** in the **Code** dialog box, and click the **Edit in Active** button. The calls to the **Payment** function occur within a pair of nested **FOR** loops, located near the end of the procedure. Here is how these loops appear in the current version of the program:

```
FOR i% = 1 TO 5
  FOR j% = 1 TO 5
    Pmt = Payment(PRange(i%), RRange(h%) / 12, T * 12)
    FormTable$(i%, j%) = FORMAT$(Pmt, "$#,####.00")
    OutTable$(i%) = OutTable$(i%) + RJust$(FormTable$(i%, j%), W)
  NEXT j%
NEXT i%
```

This passage will be the focus of your attention in the next exercise as you continue searching for the bug. (**Review Box 5-1** describes the variety of loop structures available in Visual Basic.)

Take a close look at the loops. For convenience, the **CalculateTable** procedure arranges the calculated data for the payment table in a group of one-dimensional and two-dimensional arrays. (**Review Box 5-2** discusses arrays in Visual Basic.) Two of these arrays—named **PRange** and **RRange**— are defined locally for the **CalculateTable** procedure. The remaining two—**FormTable$** and **OutTable$**—are created for the benefit of other procedures in the program. They are therefore defined in the declaration section of the **LoanInpt** form, making them available to all procedures in the program.

You need to understand how these arrays are organized in order to proceed with this debugging session:

- The one-dimensional array **PRange** contains the range of principal amounts that appear in the first column of the output table. (These numbers, calculated earlier in the **CalculateTable** procedure, are stored in **PRange(1)** to **PRange(5)**.)

- Likewise, the one-dimensional array **RRange** contains the range of interest rates that appear in the top row of the output table (in **RRange(1)** to **RRange(5)**).

- The two-dimensional array **FormTable$** is designed to store formatted string versions of each individual value in the table. The first dimension represents the rows of the table and the second dimension the columns. The **ShowTable** procedure uses this array to display the table in the **LoanTabl** form.

- The one-dimensional string array **OutTable$** is for storing each row of the table as a single string. The program builds this array for use in the procedure that prints the table (**PrintTableCommand_Click**) and also for use in the procedure that saves the table on disk as a text file (**SaveTableCommand_Click**).

The role of the **FOR** loops shown at the end of the **CalculateTable** procedure is to calculate the monthly payment amounts one at a time and to store them as formatted strings in the **FormTable$** and **OutTable$** arrays. The control variables of the loops—**i%** and **j%**—are meant to be used as indexes into the four arrays. By the time the performance reaches these loops, the one-dimensional arrays **PRange** and **RRange** already contain the range of principal amounts and interest rates for the first column and first row of the payment table. Individual elements of these arrays—**PRange(i%)** and **RRange(j%)**—can therefore be sent as arguments to the **Payment** function.

Consider the numbers represented by **RRange(j%)**—the range of interest rates. Because you already know that these interest rates are not reaching the **Payment** procedure, you can conclude that one of the following two situations is the source of the problem:

- The range of interest rates has not been stored successfully in the **RRange** array, or

- The correct elements of **RRange** are not actually being sent to the **Payment** function.

To discover which of these hypotheses is true, you need to monitor three values in the **CalculateTable** procedure: the control variable **j%**, the array element **RRange(j%)**, and the expression **RRange(j%) / 12**—the calculation for the *monthly* interest rate. In the next steps of this exercise, you'll establish these three items as *watch expressions* whose values you can monitor during the course of a program performance. (If you have already spotted the error in the **CalculateTable** procedure, continue along through the following exercise anyway.)

The Debug Window

The Debug window is available in the Visual Basic programming environment to display items that you define as watch expressions. You can open this window either by defining one or more watch expressions or by choosing **Debug** from the **Window** menu. Once the window is open, you'll

Review Box 5-1:

Loop Structures

Structures that control repetition in a program are known as *loops*. Visual Basic's two categories of repetition structures are **FOR** loops and **DO** loops. Both kinds of loops repeat the performance of a block of code for a controlled number of *iterations*. In some programming situations you can conveniently choose either kind of loop, but the general difference between them lies in the way they control the number of iterations:

- A **FOR** loop has a *counter*—or *control variable*—that keeps track of the number of iterations. The looping stops when the counter reaches an expressed stopping point.
- A **DO** loop is controlled by a conditional expression. The iterations continue until the value of the expression changes—from true to false, or false to true.

In a **FOR** loop, the block of statements is marked off by a **FOR** statement and a **NEXT** statement:

```
FOR Counter = FirstValue TO LastValue
    ' Block of statements.
NEXT Counter
```

This is the simplest form of the **FOR** loop: At the beginning of the loop performance, *FirstValue* is assigned to the *Counter* variable. If *Counter* is less than or equal to *LastValue*, Visual Basic performs the block of statements one time. At the end of the block, the value of *Counter* is increased by one and again compared with *LastValue*. Iterations continue until *Counter* is greater than *LastValue*.

The optional **STEP** clause allows you to specify an increment or decrement amount for the counter variable:

```
FOR Counter = FirstValue TO LastValue STEP ChangeValue
```

At the end of each iteration, *ChangeValue* is added to the current value of *Counter*. If *ChangeValue* is a positive number (and *FirstValue* is less than *LastValue*), the looping stops when *Counter* is greater than *LastValue*. If *ChangeValue* is a negative number (and *FirstValue* is greater than *LastValue*), the looping stops when *Counter* is less than *LastValue*. Without a **STEP** clause, the default increment amount is 1.

Review Box 5-1: *(continued)*

The block of code in a **DO** loop is enclosed between the **DO** statement and a **LOOP** statement. The loop usually contains either a **WHILE** condition or an **UNTIL** condition to control the repetition. Traditionally, a **WHILE** clause appears at the top of the loop in the **DO** statement; or the **UNTIL** clause appears at the bottom of the loop in the **LOOP** statement. But Visual Basic is flexible on this point: Either clause can be placed at the top or the bottom of the loop.

In a **DO WHILE** loop, the repetition continues as long as the condition is true:

```
DO WHILE Condition
   ' Block of statements.
LOOP
```

In a **DO...UNTIL** structure, looping continues as long as the condition is false:

```
DO
   ' Block of statements.
LOOP UNTIL Condition
```

The looping stops when the value of the *Condition* changes from false to true in an **UNTIL** clause, or from true to false in a **WHILE** clause.

A *nested* loop appears completely inside another loop structure. Nested loop structures can perform complex and powerful operations in very economical blocks of code.

---

want to rearrange the programming environment so that you can view both the Debug and Code windows at once. Then you can start defining watch expressions.

In the following steps, you'll create watch expressions for monitoring the three items that you want to examine in the **CalculateTable** procedure:

1. Pull down the **Window** menu and choose **Debug**. The Debug window opens onto the screen.

2. Use the mouse to change the shapes and positions of the Debug and Code windows, as shown in Figure 5-4.

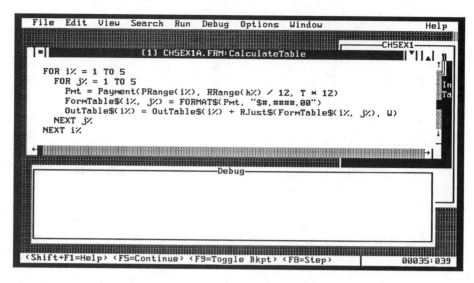

Figure 5-4 Arranging the Code and Debug windows in the programming environment

3. If the **CalculateTable** procedure is not already displayed, press F2 and select it from the **Code** dialog box. Then click the **Edit in Active** button.

4. Pull down the **Debug** menu and choose the **Add Watch** command. The **Add Watch** dialog box appears on the screen, as shown in Figure 5-5.

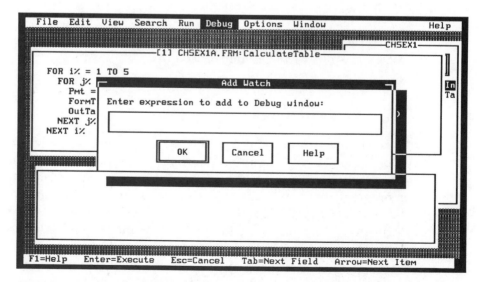

Figure 5-5 The **Add Watch** dialog box

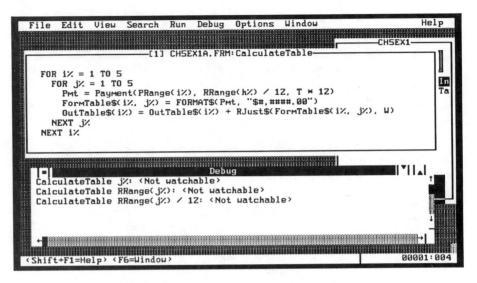

```
 File   Edit   View   Search   Run   Debug   Options   Window              Help
                                                                   CH5EX1
                    [1] CH5EX1A.FRM:CalculateTable
   FOR i% = 1 TO 5
     FOR j% = 1 TO 5
       Pmt = Payment(PRange(i%), RRange(h%) / 12, T × 12)
       FormTable$(i%, j%) = FORMAT$(Pmt, "$#,####.00")
       OutTable$(i%) = OutTable$(i%) + RJust$(FormTable$(i%, j%), W)
     NEXT j%
   NEXT i%


                                   Debug
   CalculateTable j%: <Not watchable>
   CalculateTable RRange(j%): <Not watchable>
   CalculateTable RRange(j%) / 12: <Not watchable>



 <Shift+F1=Help> <F6=Window>                                    00001:004
```

Figure 5-6 Adding watch expressions to the Debug window

5. Enter **j%** in the text box, and click **OK**. The Debug window shows the watch expression, along with the temporary notation **<Not watchable>**. This notation will disappear when you run the program.

6. Repeat steps 4 and 5 to create two additional watch expressions in the Debug window: **RRange(j%)** and **RRange(j%) / 12**. When you are finished, the programming environment appears as shown in Figure 5-6.

Now you are ready for the next step in the debugging process—defining a *breakpoint* in the **CalculateTable** procedure.

Breakpoints

Once you have narrowed your search down to a particular passage of code, you need a way to stop the program when the performance reaches the target passage. *Breakpoints* are the answer. A breakpoint is a statement in your program that you designate as a temporary stopping point in the performance. Upon reaching a breakpoint, Visual Basic stops the program performance. More precisely, the program is interrupted *just before* the breakpoint statement is performed. At the point of the interruption, Visual Basic returns you to the programming environment, where you can examine both the current Code window and the contents of the Debug window.

Review Box 5-2:

Arrays

An *array* is a data structure that represents a list, table, or multidimensional arrangement of data values. The name of an array is followed by one or more *indexes,* enclosed in parentheses and separated by commas. For example, a one-dimensional array reference has one index—in the format *ArrayName(i)*—referring to the *i*th *element* in a list of values. A two-dimensional array has two indexes—in the format *ArrayName(i, j)*—referring to the element in the *i*th row and the *j*th column of a table; and so on. All values in an array belong to the same data type.

In addition to arrays of data, Visual Basic also recognizes *control arrays,* which represent groups of visual controls in a frame—for example, an array of option buttons, text boxes, or menu items. The discussion that follows applies to data arrays (sometimes also called *variable arrays*), not to control arrays.

Visual Basic supports *fixed* arrays and *dynamic* arrays. The length of a fixed array is set for the entire duration of the program. In contrast, the length of a dynamic array can be adjusted at run time, to meet changing requirements for data storage. **DIM** is the most commonly used declaration for an array:

```
DIM CodeNum(5)
```

By default, the first *element* in an array has an index of zero. The example just given has six elements, from **CodeNum(0)** to **CodeNum(5)**. However, you can define a nondefault indexing system by specifying the upper and lower bounds in the array's declaration statement. The syntax for defining the bounds uses the keyword **TO**; for example:

```
DIM PM%(13 TO 24)' A one-dimensional array with 12
                  elements.
```

You can declare the data type of an array either by appending a type-declaration character to the end of the array name or by declaring the type in an **AS** clause.

A dynamic array is declared in two steps. First, a **DIM SHARED** statement establishes the scope of the array, using the following syntax:

```
DIM SHARED ArrayName()
```

Review Box 5-2: *(continued)*

Notice that the parentheses are empty in this statement; the length of the array is not yet defined. Next, a **REDIM** statement gives the length of the array and the number of dimensions:

```
REDIM ArrayName(Length)
```

REDIM is an executable statement and therefore must appear inside a procedure. The length of a dynamic array can be changed at any time by another **REDIM** statement, but the number of dimensions remains fixed after the original declaration. By default, **REDIM** has the side effect of reinitializing all the elements of the array—numeric elements to zero, or string elements to empty strings. However, you can include the **PRESERVE** keyword in a **REDIM** statement to prevent this effect:

```
REDIM PRESERVE ArrayName(Length)
```

There is an important functional relationship between arrays and **FOR** loops in Basic programming. For example, you can use the counter variable of a **FOR** loop as the index into a one-dimensional array; this gives you an efficient way to process all the elements of the array in very economical code. Likewise, you can use the counter variables in a pair of nested **FOR** loops as the indexes into a two-dimensional array.

Establishing a breakpoint takes two simple steps:

1. Position the cursor on the target line of code.

2. Pull down the **Debug** menu and select the **Toggle Breakpoint** command, or simply press the F9 function key.

Visual Basic highlights the line. (When you finish working with a particular breakpoint, you use these same two steps to toggle the line of code back to its normal status.)

In this stage of the debugging process, you want the program performance to stop just before the call to the **Payment** function in the **CalculateTable** procedure. Move the cursor to the assignment statement that contains this call, and press F9. When you do so, your Code window appears as shown in Figure 5-7.

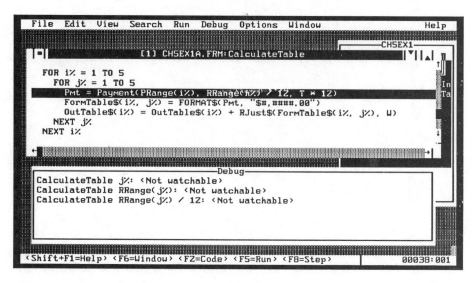

Figure 5-7 A breakpoint

Review the changes you have made in the code to meet the needs of your investigation:

- The statement that originally caused the error in the **Payment** function is commented out.

- A set of watch expressions from **CalculateTable** will allow you to see what should be happening in the **FOR** loops at the end of the procedure.

- A breakpoint in the **CalculateTable** procedure will stop the performance just before the function call.

You are now ready to try running the program again. Choose the **Start** command from the **Run** menu to begin. When the dialog box appears on the screen, enter the same three input values as before (**15000** for the principal, **10** for the interest rate, and **5** for the term). Then click the **Calc** button. As expected, the performance stops at the breakpoint you have established. The Code window displays the target passage from the **CalculateTable** procedure, and the Immediate window displays the current values of **j%**, **RRate(j%)**, and **RRate(j%) / 12**.

Single-Step Performance

After a break in the performance, you can press F5 to continue from the point of the break. At this point in the debugging session, you can use F5 to step through the loops that build the payment table. As you do so, the

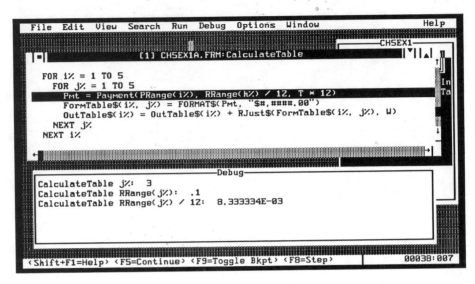

Figure 5-8 Examining the values of watch expressions

Debug window will show you the changing values of the three watch expressions.

Press F5 several times now and examine the information displayed in the Debug window. The window—shown in Figure 5-8—displays the sequence of values that you would expect to find in the **RRange** array and the values that should have been sent to the **Payment** function as the interest-rate argument.

Press F5 repeatedly to step through several more iterations of the loop. For each iteration you see the same results: The **RRange** array contains the correct values, and the **CalculateTable** procedure always calculates appropriate interest rates. But you already know that these values are not reaching the **Payment** function. From this you conclude definitively that the error is somewhere in the function call itself. Finally, a close examination of the function call reveals the problem:

```
Pmt = Payment(PRange(i%), RRange(h%) / 12, T * 12)
```

The **RRange** array is indexed here by an undefined variable, **h%**. The correct index variable is **j%**. Mistakes like this one commonly occur as the result of simple keystroke errors during coding. You can correct the mistake now. Delete the **h%** index and type the correct one, **j%**:

```
Pmt = Payment(PRange(i%), RRange(j%) / 12, T * 12)
```

In retrospect, the detailed debugging process you have just completed—just to correct a one-letter typographical error—may seem excessive. But errors as simple as this one do occur often, and programmers spend many hours trying to find and correct them. The process is much more efficient with the tools you have used in this exercise: watch expressions, breakpoints, and the Debug window.

Now you have several small tasks to perform to return the program to its normal condition:

1. Position the cursor over the call to the **Payment** function, and press F9 to toggle the statement out of the breakpoint mode.

2. Choose **Delete all Watch** from the **Debug** menu, then close the Debug window by pulling down its control menu and choosing **Close**. Resize the Code window back to its original dimensions on the screen.

3. Display the **Payment** function in the Code window and remove the single-quote character from the beginning of the assignment statement. The function is now operational again.

4. Choose **Start** from the **Run** menu to restart the program.

5. Once again enter the three loan parameters and click the **Calc** button on the dialog box. Watch as the program displays a correctly calculated payment table.

Now you should continue testing all the program's operations. Pull down the **Rate** menu and select a new value for the table's interest rate increments. Check the resulting table to make sure it is correct.

Then try an equivalent change with the **Payment** menu: Select **$100** as the new increment for the rows of principal amounts. Check the output table (Figure 5-9). There seems to be something wrong here. The principal amounts in the table increase by $10 for each new row, not $100. Another bug.

Correcting a Logical Error

This time the error does not prevent the program from completing its performance, but the output is wrong. You know that the principal increment is calculated in a short event procedure named **PInc_Click**, so the error shouldn't be too difficult to correct. Follow these steps to get started:

1. Exit from the *Loan Calculator* by choosing the **Exit** command from the program's **File** menu. Press any key to return to the programming environment.

2. Press F2 and select the **PInc_Click** procedure from the **Code** dialog box. Click the **Edit in Active** button.

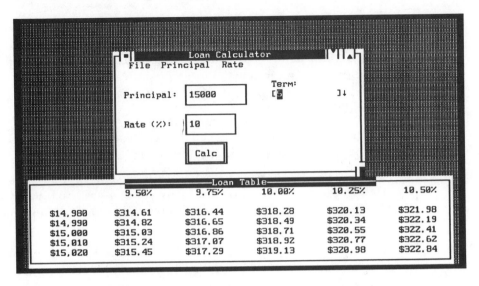

Figure 5-9 A mistake in the **Principal** menu

3. In the procedure, find the statement that calculates the global
   CurPrincInc value:

   ```
   CurPrincInc = 10 ^ Index
   ```

4. Place the cursor on the next executable statement after this assignment statement—a **FOR** statement—and press F9 to make this line
   a breakpoint. Visual Basic highlights the line.

5. Press F5 to restart the program performance. In the dialog box,
   enter the three loan parameters and then pull down the **Principal**
   menu. Click the **$1,000** option. The performance stops at the line
   in **PInc_Click** that you established as a breakpoint.

6. Open the Immediate window and enter the following two lines, one
   after another, in the window:

   ```
   ? Index
   ? CurPrincInc
   ```

   (Note that the **?** command is a shorthand equivalent for **Print** in the
   Immediate window.)

After these statements the output screen shows you the values of the
Index argument—that is, the integer representing the most recent menu
selection—and the calculated value of **CurPrincInc**:

2
100

You can see the likely source of the problem right away. The **Index** values for the menu selections range from 0 to 4, but the formula for calculating **CurPrincInc** should be based on powers of 10 from 1 to 5. A value of 1 needs to be added to **Index** to compute the correct exponent of 10 in the formula:

```
CurPrincInc = 10 ^ (Index + 1)
```

The next step illustrates another important feature of the Immediate window. During a break in the performance, you can perform individual commands that relate to your program—including assignment statements and procedure calls—by entering those statements directly into the Immediate window. Using this technique, you can test the effect of a command on your program before you actually change your code.

To see how this works, enter the following two commands into the Immediate window:

```
CurPrincInc = 10 ^ (Index + 1)
Calc_Click
```

The first of these statements performs the **CurPrincInc** calculation over again, this time using the correct formula. The second actually makes a call to the **Calc_Click** procedure so that you can view the resulting payment table. Examining the output table, you can see that the new formula for **CurPrincInc** is correct—the principal increment amount is now $1,000.

Complete this exercise by correcting the formula in the code of the **PInc_Click** command. (You can actually use the **Copy** and **Paste** commands from the **Edit** menu in the programming environment to copy the formula from the Immediate window to the Code window.) Then clear the breakpoint from the procedure. Press F5 to continue the program performance. Test the **Principal** menu again to make sure it works properly now.

Now the program seems to be working correctly. But part of your job as a developer of Visual Basic applications is to test each program as thoroughly as possible. This means trying out as many different combinations of input data as you can—even combinations that may seem unlikely to you.

For example, in the *Loan Calculator* application you can still generate a run-time error with the following input:

1.   Enter a value of **2** as the interest rate.

2.   Pull down the **Rate** menu and select **1.0%** as the increment.

In response, the program attempts to start the payment table with an interest rate of 0, and an overflow error occurs when the **Payment** function is called.

When you find a bug like this one, you have to rethink the design of your application and decide how you want the program to react to this particular combination of input parameters. Should the program reject the input and refuse to create a table? Should a special error message be displayed on the screen? Or should the program make an automatic adjustment in the increment amount—not quite following the user's instructions, but avoiding a run-time error? Once you decide how you want your application to react, your next step is to write the appropriate code to implement your decision. Then the testing process begins again. Try correcting this design problem now as an additional exercise with the *Loan Calculator*.

COMPILING AN APPLICATION

After you design, write, test, and debug your application, the final step is to compile the program as an EXE file that can be run directly from DOS. To accomplish this you use the **Make EXE File...** command in the **File** menu.

As an exercise with this command, open the project named LOAN.MAK from the exercise disk. Then pull down the **Run** menu and select **Make EXE File**. The dialog box shown in Figure 5-10 appears on the screen. The box suggests a default value for the program's file name, LOAN.EXE. Among the other options in the dialog box, the **EXE Type** frame allows

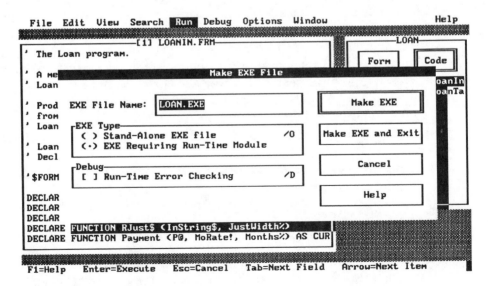

Figure 5-10 The **Make Exe File** dialog box

you to choose between a stand-alone EXE file or an EXE program that depends on the presence of the Visual Basic run-time module stored on disk as VBDRT10.EXE. Choose between these options and then click the **Make EXE and Exit** button.

When the compilation is complete, Visual Basic stores the LOAN.EXE file in the current directory. To run the program, simply type **LOAN** at the DOS prompt.

Reading Parameters from the Command Line

An additional design feature that you can program into an application is the ability to read input parameters directly from the DOS prompt. For example, imagine being able to enter the principal, interest rate, and term of a loan at the time you start up the *Loan Calculator* from DOS. Your command line might appear as follows:

```
C>LOAN 129600 9.75 30
```

If the program is properly designed to read these values from the command line, the three numbers will appear as the initial input parameters in the dialog box when the program begins.

This feature does not happen automatically. You have to include code in your program to read the command line string and to parse the string into individual data values. Visual Basic has a number of tools that help you in this process. First, the built-in **COMMAND$** function returns the *command-line string*—that is, everything the user types at the DOS prompt after the name of the program itself. In the example just given, **COM-MAND$** returns the string "129600 9.75 30". In the procedure you create to read the command line, you can use tools from Visual Basic's library of string functions—for example, the **LEFT$**, **RIGHT$**, and **MID$** functions, which return substring portions from a larger string.

The following procedure, named **ReadCommandLine**, is included in the **LoanIn** form of LOAN.MAK:

```
SUB ReadCommandLine ()

    ' Read the user-supplied command line.
    ' The line should be in the format:

    '       principal rate term
    ' where one or more spaces separate each
    ' numeric data item. This routine ignores
    ' any command line that does not conform
    ' to this format.
```

```
DIM InLine AS STRING, S1%, S2%

    InLine = LTRIM$(RTRIM$(COMMAND$))

    ' Continue only if InLine is not blank.

    IF LEN(InLine) <> 0 THEN

        ' Find locations of two space-character
        ' separators. Eliminate any extra spaces.

        S1% = INSTR(InLine, " ")
        DO WHILE MID$(InLine, S1% + 1, 1) = " "
            S1% = S1% + 1
        LOOP

        S2% = INSTR(S1% + 1, InLine, " ")
        DO WHILE MID$(InLine, S2% + 1, 1) = " "
            S2% = S2% + 1
        LOOP

        ' Continue only if separators are present.

        IF (S1% <> 0) AND (S2% <> 0) THEN

            ' Enter the loan parameters from the command
            ' line. Use Val and Str$ to convert any
            ' nonnumeric input value into "0".

            InPrinc.Text = STR$(VAL(LEFT$(InLine, S1% - 1)))
            InRate.Text = STR$(VAL(MID$(InLine, S1% + 1, S2% - S1%)))
            InTerm.Text = STR$(VAL(RIGHT$(InLine, LEN(InLine) - S2%)))

        END IF
    END IF
END SUB   ' ReadCommandLine
```

This procedure reads the principal, rate, and term from the command line and copies these input values to the application's input controls, **InPrinc**, **InRate**, and **InTerm**. In addition, a call to **ReadCommandLine** appears in the program's **Form_Load** procedure.

While you are developing a procedure like this one, you can use another Visual Basic feature to test the code designed to read the command line.

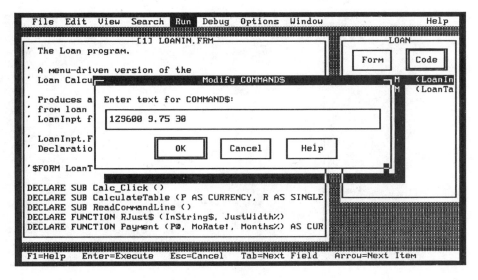

Figure 5-11 The **Modify COMMAND$** dialog box

The **Modify COMMAND$** command in the **Run** menu presents a dialog box in which you can enter a command-line string. The **COMMAND$** function then returns this string to your program as if the string had been entered from the DOS command line.

This final exercise with the *Loan Calculator* (LOAN.MAK) gives you the opportunity to see how **Modify COMMAND$** works:

1. Start up Visual Basic again and load the LOAN.MAK project into memory.

2. Pull down the **Run** menu and select the **Modify COMMAND$** command. In the resulting dialog box (Figure 5-11), enter the following line of data:

    ```
    129600 9.75 30
    ```

    Make sure each number is separated from the next by one or more spaces. Click **OK** or press the Enter key to complete your entry.

3. Press the F5 function key to run the *Loan Calculator* application. Figure 5-12 shows the opening dialog box. The program has copied your command-line input into the appropriate text boxes.

This is a simulation of what will occur when you enter command-line values directly from the DOS prompt.

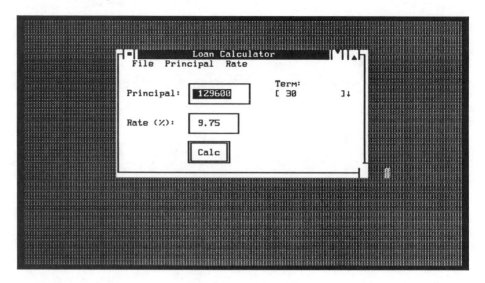

Figure 5-12 Input values from the command line

SUMMARY: THE FINAL STEPS OF APPLICATION DEVELOPMENT

Even in a relatively simple application like the *Loan Calculator,* you may find yourself spending a long time testing and debugging—and sometimes redesigning—your program after you have finished writing the code. As you now turn to more ambitious programming projects, the tools and features you have used in this chapter will prove their value and flexibility over and over again:

- The Immediate window lets you move aside temporarily from your program's code—to perform commands and to view the data that your program is working with.

- Watch expressions and the Debug window allow you to examine the values that your program is working with.

- Breakpoints give you flexible control over breaks in your program's performance.

When all the testing and debugging is complete, the **Make EXE File** command efficiently transforms your program into an independent DOS application, stored in an EXE file. This step meets the final goal of program development in Visual Basic—creating a working application that you can place alongside the other DOS tools you use every day.

PART II

Visual Basic Applications

6

Input and Output Techniques: The Sales Week Application

INTRODUCTION

Input and *output* operations in Visual Basic take place interactively inside the windows you create for an application. In a typical dialog box, you designate some controls for receiving the user's input from the keyboard and others for presenting the information your program generates. Sometimes the two operations may even seem to blend together, when the same controls from which your program *reads* input data later become the tools for *displaying* output data. In this way Visual Basic's controls take the place of specific input and output commands you may be familiar with in other versions of Basic.

For example, traditional Basic programs use the INPUT statement for displaying an input prompt and reading a data item from the keyboard:

```
INPUT "Sales"; InSales
```

When this statement is executed, Basic displays a prompt on the screen— *Sales?*—and waits for the user's keyboard entry. The resulting input value is stored in the variable *InSales*. As you have seen, the approach to this input operation is very different in Visual Basic. You might plan for an equivalent event by placing a label and a text box on a form (Figure 6-1) and assigning settings to the relevant properties: **InSales** as the **CtlName** property of the text box and **Sales** as the label's **Caption** property. During run time, your program reads the user's input as **InSales.Text**, a reference to the **Text** property of the text box.

151

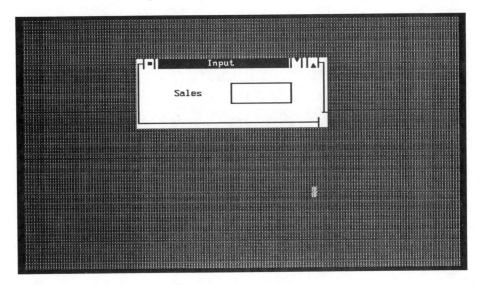

Figure 6-1 An input operation in Visual Basic for DOS

The advantages of the Visual Basic approach are immediately clear to the user. During run time, a text box is a versatile input object: Entries can be edited, deleted, inserted, selected with the mouse, or even copied from one place to another. In an application containing several text boxes, the user can skip around between boxes, entering values in any order. In short, the event-driven programming model gives the user greater control over interactive input operations.

There are also advantages from your point of view as designer of the application. For one, a text box that serves as an input control in one operation can be used later for displaying output. The following assignment statement resets the **Text** property of the **InSales** text box:

```
InSales.Text = NewSalesVal$
```

As a result of this statement, a new value appears inside the text box.

As a context for studying input and output techniques, this chapter presents a business database application named *Sales Week*. You can use this program for recording, reviewing, and analyzing sales figures. When you examine the elements of this application—its controls, properties, and code—you'll see several interesting examples of input and output activities:

- Reading data from text boxes and performing specific validation tests.

- Providing the user with different ways to issue instructions to the program—using the mouse, the keyboard, and menu selections.

- Reading data from and writing data to a sequential data file on disk.

- Displaying text, data, and graphics in a variety of Visual Basic controls—labels, text boxes, and picture boxes.

- Providing textual information in special Visual Basic windows called *message boxes.*

These events and operations will be the focus of your work in this chapter.

THE SALES WEEK APPLICATION

The *Sales Week* program is a simple tool for recording the daily and weekly sales activity of a retail business. The data you enter is saved as a database on disk, giving you a permanent chronological record of weekly sales. The program also builds bar graphs—representing sales for a given week or for a series of consecutive weeks.

The program is set up to work with a directory named \SALESWK on the C drive. All weekly sales files that the program creates are saved in this directory. One of the program's first actions is to search for the directory and to create it if it does not yet exist.

Load the program from the exercise disk now. Its project name is SALESWK.MAK. When you open it, you'll see that the entire program is contained within a single form named SALEGRPH.FRM. Press the F5 function key to run the program, and the program's dialog box immediately appears on the screen, as shown in Figure 6-2.

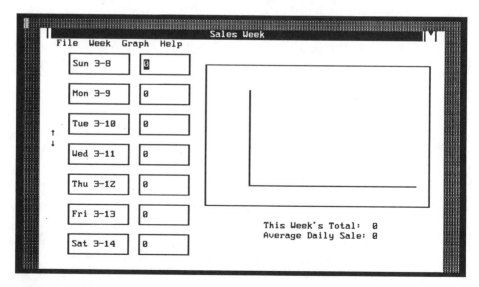

Figure 6-2 The initial dialog box from the *Sales Week* application

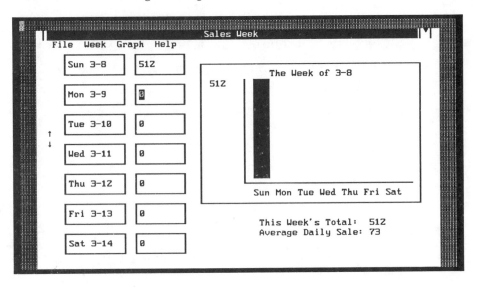

Figure 6-3 The first sales entry

At the left side of the dialog box you see two columns of cells for the current week's sales data. The days of the week, from Sunday to Saturday, appear in the first column, and seven zeros appear initially in the second column. Imagine that you are ready to begin using the program to record this week's daily sales figures. In the cell for Sunday, type a value of 512 (representing $512 or 512 units, the total sales for the day). Press the Tab key or the down-arrow key to move the focus to the next cell down. In the picture box at the right side of the window, the program displays a single vertical bar representing the sales figure you have entered (Figure 6-3).

The graph becomes more significant as you enter more sales figures for the week. For example, try entering the following data into the cells for Monday through Saturday:

420
388
480
535
677
759

Each time you complete a new entry, the program adds a bar to the graph. The label at the top of the graph's vertical axis always shows the value of the largest sales figure for the week. The total sales for the week and the average daily sale are displayed beneath the picture box. Figure 6-4 shows

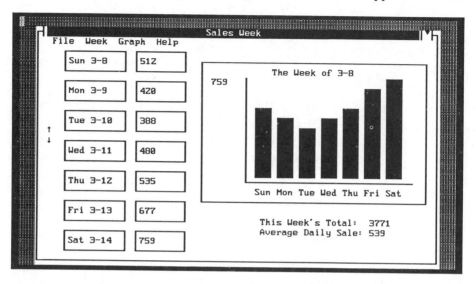

Figure 6-4 An entire week's sales data

what the dialog box looks like when you have completed the sales entries for the week. (Of course, the dates you see will be different.)

You can make changes in the data at any time, and the program automatically redraws the bar graph in response. For example, suppose you discover an error in the data for Thursday: The correct sales figure is 700. Enter this number into the appropriate cell and the new graph reflects your correction.

Now imagine that you have been using this program to record weekly sales data for some time, and you want to review the figures for previous weeks. To move backward in time by one week, you can use the keyboard or the mouse:

- On the keyboard, press the PgUp key to view the data for the previous week. Press PgDn for the next week.

- With the mouse, click the up arrow at the left side of the dialog box to view the previous week. Click the down arrow for the next week.

Whenever you move to the display of another week's data, the program saves the current week's sales figures in the database on disk. The saved figures reappear when you scroll back again to the current week.

To experiment fully with the features of the *Sales Week* application you'll need at least ten weeks of sales data. The program is designed for quick and easy data entry. Go back nine weeks from the current week, and enter

Table 6-1 Nine Weeks of Sales Data

Day	Week								
	1	**2**	**3**	**4**	**5**	**6**	**7**	**8**	**9**
Sun.	237	219	195	119	139	151	225	288	388
Mon.	312	288	347	245	225	235	301	369	463
Tue.	288	315	265	259	201	215	255	342	425
Wed.	366	395	310	305	292	310	319	425	519
Thu.	432	399	405	391	355	376	400	490	588
Fri.	488	450	382	400	410	419	452	550	637
Sat.	450	488	401	391	388	410	429	515	619

a set of imaginary sales data for each week up to the current week. Use the data shown in Table 6-1.

When you have entered all the data, return to this week's sales figures. The program has a convenient shortcut key for displaying this week's sales: Simply press the F5 function key. Now you can view another kind of bar graph, comparing this week's sales with the nine weeks in the immediate past. The program calls this a *trend* graph. To display this graph, press the F8 function key. The result is shown in Figure 6-5. Examining the new

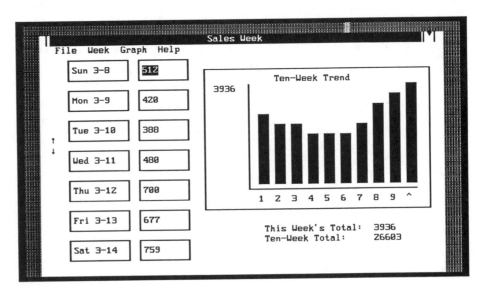

Figure 6-5 A ten-week graph of sales

graph, you see an increase in sales over the last few weeks; you may conclude that your recent advertising campaign in local newspapers has been a success. The *Sales Week* program displays totals for the current week and for the entire ten-week period just beneath the graph itself. To toggle back to the one-week graph for the current week, press the F7 function key.

Menus in the Sales Week Application

You'll notice that the main dialog box includes a menu line with four pull-down menus, named **File, Week, Graph,** and **Help**. These menus offer a variety of commands designed to make the application more convenient and versatile.

The **File** menu (Figure 6-6) has a **Print** command, which prints the data currently displayed in the dialog box; and an **Exit** command, which ends the program performance. Both of these commands—like several of the other commands in the application's menu system—have shortcut keyboard combinations, or *accelerator* keys. To print a screen of data, you can press Ctrl+P; to exit from the program, press Ctrl+X.

The four commands in the **Week** menu (Figure 6-7) help you select a particular week's data. The commands named **This Week** and **Last Week** have accelerator keys of F5 and F6. The **Move Backward** and **Move Forward** commands are equivalent to pressing the PgUp or PgDn keys on the keyboard or clicking the up or down arrows displayed in the dialog box.

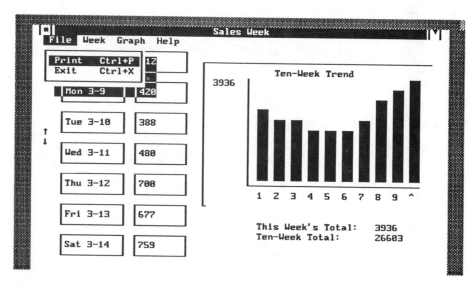

Figure 6-6 The **File** menu of the *Sales Week* application

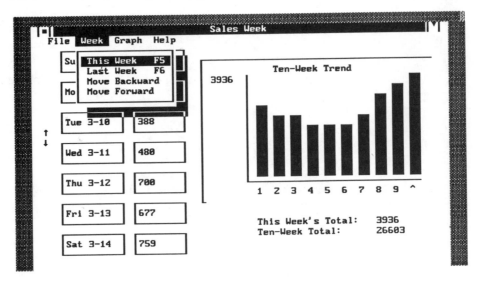

Figure 6-7 The **Week** menu of the *Sales Week* application

The **Graph** menu (Figure 6-8) lets you select the kind of graph that you want to view in the application's picture box. As you have already seen, the **One Week** and the **Ten-Week Trend** commands have keyboard shortcuts of F7 and F8. A third command in the **Graph** menu—named **Current Week's Position**—results in a submenu with three selections, **Beginning**, **Middle**, and **End**. These selections control the position in the trend graph of the week that is currently displayed on the screen. The default is **End**,

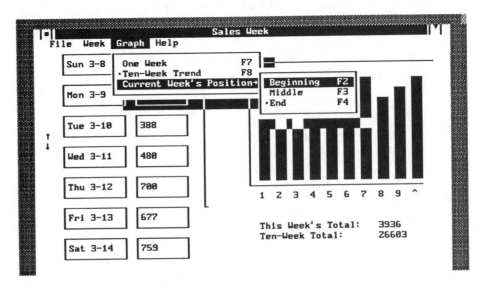

Figure 6-8 The **Graph** menu of the *Sales Week* application

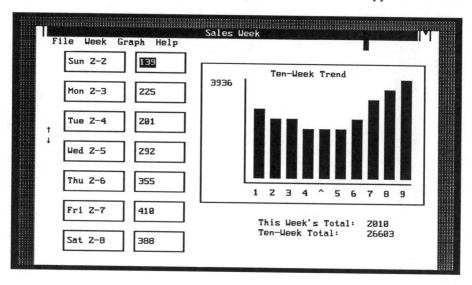

Figure 6-9 Using the **Middle** option

which means that the currently displayed week of data appears as the last column of the graph. Figure 6-9 shows what happens when you move back five weeks in time and then select the **Middle** option: The displayed data appears in the middle of the graph. The currently displayed week is always represented by a caret character (^) along the graph's horizontal axis.

Finally, the **Help** menu (Figure 6-10) offers two help screens. The **About Sales Week** command displays a succinct description of the program

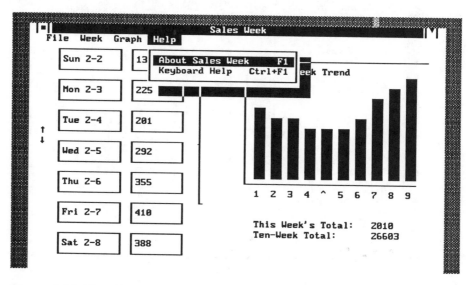

Figure 6-10 The **Help** menu of the *Sales Week* application

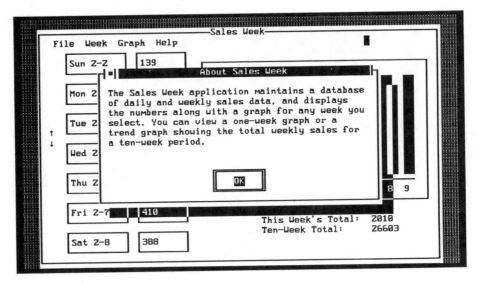

Figure 6-11 The **About Sales Week** help window

(Figure 6-11), and the **Keyboard Help** command displays a list of the program's accelerator keys (Figure 6-12). You can view these help windows by pressing F1 or Ctrl+F1.

As you continue experimenting with the *Sales Week* application, try out all of the various menu commands and make sure you understand the function each one serves.

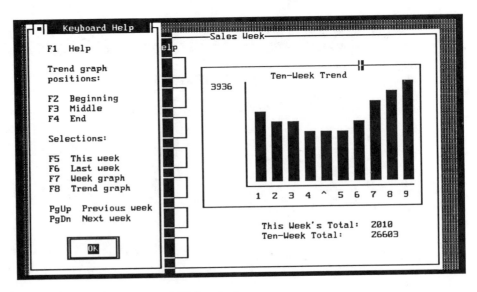

Figure 6-12 The **Keyboard Help** window

The Filing System for the Sales Database

The *Sales Week* application saves the sales database as a series of small text files rather than one large random-access file. Each individual file contains the sales data for one week. The program creates the file for a given week as soon as you enter the data and move on to another week.

File names are derived from the date of the first day of the week, Sunday. Each file has an extension name of SLS. For example, the file for the week of May 31, 1992, is named 05-31-92.SLS. The file contains the seven sales figures entered for this week:

```
512
420
388
480
700
677
759
```

As you have learned, the program is set up to store these files in the directory named C:\SALESWK. If you want to change this default directory location, you can revise the following **CONST** declaration, located in the declaration section of the **SaleGrph** form:

```
CONST PathName$ = "C:\SalesWk"
```

Because the database is stored in text files, you can use the TYPE command to view the contents of any file from the DOS prompt.

THE STRUCTURE OF THE SALES WEEK PROGRAM

The central input controls in the *Sales Week* application are organized as an array of text boxes named **SalesDay**. Actually, the program uses the **SalesDay** boxes for both input and output. They form the column of text boxes in which you originally enter the sales data for a given week. Then, when you later scroll to weeks for which you have previously saved data, the program uses these same text boxes to display the existing sales figures.

Other controls in the program's dialog box include an array of labels, a picture box, a vertical scroll bar, pairs of labels for displaying totals and averages, and, of course, the system of menu commands. Figure 6-13 shows what these controls look like in the form design environment. Before you begin studying the program's code, take a brief look at these controls and their property settings.

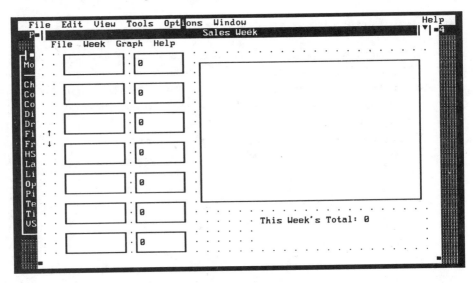

Figure 6-13 The controls of the *Sales Week* application

Controls and Properties

The **SalesDay** text boxes have **Index** settings from **0** to **6**. As you can see in Figure 6-13, each box has an initial **Text** value of **0**. The column of controls just to the left of these text boxes is an array of labels named **WkDay**. During run time, the program displays a day of the week and a date in each one of these label controls. Like the **SalesDay** array, the **WkDay** labels have **Index** settings from **0** to **6**. Their initial **Caption** settings are blank.

Just below the picture box are two pairs of labels. The first label on the left displays the words **This Week's Total:** as its fixed **Caption** setting. The first label on the right is designed to display the total sales for a given week. Its **CtlName** setting is **Total**, and its initial **Caption** setting is **0**. The second pair of labels have **CtlName** settings of **StatLabel** and **StatVal** and blank **Caption** settings. The program uses these labels to display the average daily sale for a one-week graph or the ten-week total for a trend graph.

The picture box in which the program displays bar graphs has a **CtlName** setting of **GraphBox**. As you'll see later, Visual Basic provides ways to display text and ASCII graphics characters inside a picture box.

The application also contains a vertical scroll bar, located at the left side of the dialog box. The bar's **CtlName** setting is **ScrollWeek**. This control has been sized down to a very small height setting; as a result, it looks like nothing more than a pair of arrows. Normally a vertical scroll bar has a *scroll box* that slides up and down the bar; but the **ScrollWeek** bar is too small to display the scroll box. You'll recall that the purpose of this scroll bar is to allow the user to scroll forward or backward by one week at a time.

Several properties determine the behavior and value of a vertical scroll bar in Visual Basic:

- The **Value** property is the numeric equivalent of a selected position on the scroll bar.

- The **Min** property represents the scroll bar's smallest possible value— that is, the **Value** setting when the scroll box is positioned at the top of the bar.

- The **Max** property is the scroll bar's largest possible value—that is, the **Value** setting when the scroll box is positioned at the bottom of the bar.

- The **SmallChange** property is the increment by which the scroll bar's value changes when the user clicks one of the two arrows located at opposite ends of the bar. (Scroll bars also have a **LargeChange** property, representing the increment of change when the user clicks inside the bar.)

The **ScrollWeek** control in the *Sales Week* application has only three possible **Value** settings:

- **1** is the default setting.

- **0** is the **Min** setting. This value means that the user has just clicked the up-arrow icon.

- **2** is the **Max** setting. This value means that the user has just clicked the down-arrow icon.

The control's **SmallChange** setting is **1**. As you'll see shortly, changes in the value of this control are monitored by an event procedure named **ScrollWeek_Change**.

Finally, the application's menu system is designed to give the user a variety of mouse and keyboard techniques for selecting options and operations. As usual, the menu is created at design time in the Menu Design Window. In Figure 6-14 you can see definitions for the **File** and **Week** menus.

Notice that the shortcut keys for individual menu commands are displayed in a column at the right side of the menu list box. As you are creating a menu, you use the **Shortcut Key** option in the Menu Design Window to select an appropriate key for any menu command. This option has a drop-down list (Figure 6-15) displaying the available shortcut keys, including function keys and various keyboard combinations that use the Ctrl and

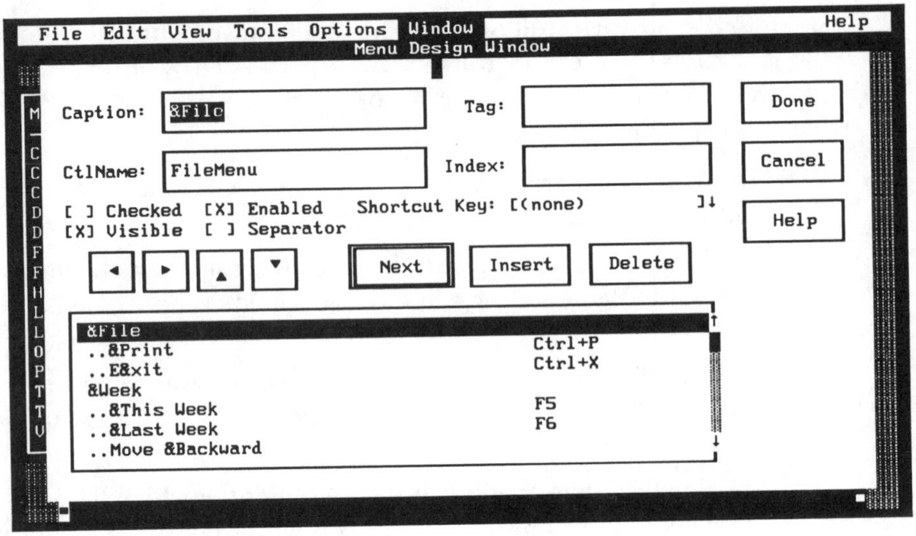

Figure 6-14 Menu definitions for the *Sales Week* application

Shift keys. To assign a shortcut key to a command, you simply select the key from this drop-down list.

Table 6-2 shows the **CtlName** settings and the shortcut keys assigned to the menu commands. A number of important events in the *Sales Week* application are associated with menu commands and menu selections. To understand these events, you should be familiar with the property settings defined for the menu.

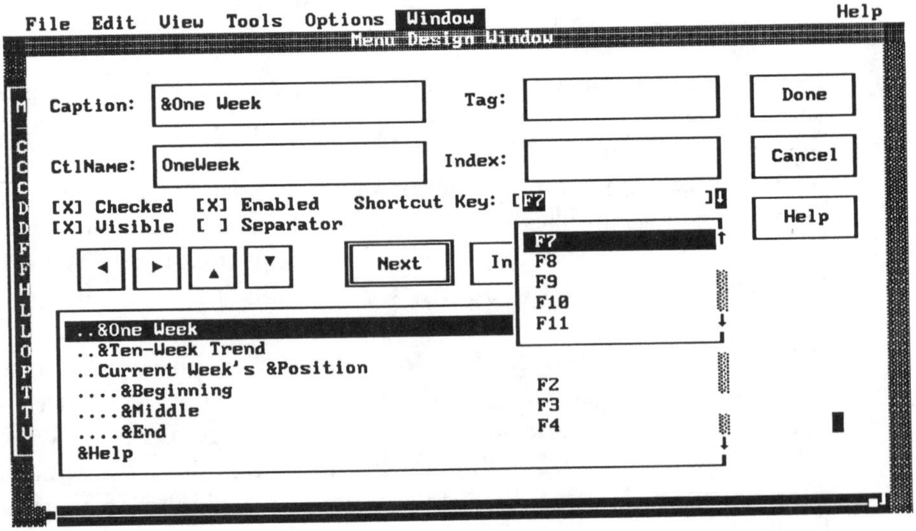

Figure 6-15 The drop-down list of the **Shortcut Key** option

Table 6-2   Properties and Shortcut Keys in the *Sales Week* Menu

Level	Caption	CtlName	Shortcut
menu	**&File**	FileMenu	—
..command	**&Print**	PrintSales	Ctrl+P
..command	**&Exit**	Quit	Ctrl+X
menu	**&Week**	WeekMenu	—
..command	**&This Week**	ThisWeek	F5
..command	**&Last Week**	LastWeek	F6
..command	**Move &Backward**	Backward	—
..command	**Move &Forward**	Forward	—
menu	**&Graph**	GraphMenu	—
..command	**&One Week**	OneWeek	F7
..command	**&Ten-Week Trend**	TenWeeks	F8
..command	**&Current Week's Position...**	Position	—
....command	**&Beginning**	BeginPos	F2
....command	**&Middle**	MidPos	F3
....command	**&End**	EndPos	F4
menu	**&Help**	HelpMenu	—
..command	**&About Sales Week**	GeneralHelp	F1
..command	**&Keyboard Help**	KeyboardHelp	Ctrl+F1

Events

The user's keyboard and mouse activities are monitored and captured by a variety of event procedures in the *Sales Week* application. Broadly, the application recognizes two categories of user input—data entries into the daily sales boxes and commands to perform the program's operations and procedures.

As you have seen, many of the program's operations are presented as menu entries. Each menu command has an associated **Click** procedure in the program's code. This procedure is called when the user selects a menu command. From the user's point of view, there are several different ways to perform menu commands:

- Click a menu with the mouse and then click a command in the drop-down menu list.

- Use the Alt key to pull down a menu and select a command or option by its *access key*. For example, to pull down the **Graph** menu and select the **Ten-Week Trend** option, you can press Alt+G and then T.

- Press one of the defined shortcut keys to invoke a menu command. For example, pressing the F8 function key selects the **Ten-Week Trend** option.

All these user actions trigger the same **Click** event for a given menu command. No matter how the user selects a menu command—using the mouse or one of the keyboard techniques—the corresponding **Click** procedure is called and performed. From your point of view as an application developer, a menu is a powerful programming tool that allows you to monitor several varieties of user activity at once, with a minimum of code. This is particularly true when you include access keys and shortcut keys in a menu.

Aside from menu commands and their associated **Click** procedures, the *Sales Week* application recognizes several other events. First of all, the **Form_Load** event procedure is performed at the beginning of a program run and accomplishes several important initialization tasks. Once the dialog box appears on the screen, a **Change** event procedure is available for the vertical scroll bar, **ScrollWeek**. The **Change** event takes place in the application whenever the user clicks the up- or down-arrow icon on the scroll bar. In response, the program scrolls backward or forward to a new week in the sales database.

Finally, the program recognizes three events associated with the array of text boxes, **SalesDay**:

- The **LostFocus** event takes place when the user activates a new cell in the array of text boxes. The text box that *loses* the focus in this action is the object of the event. The program reads the value in the text box and checks to see if the value has changed—that is, if the user has entered a new sales figure. If so, the program updates the graph display to reflect the new figure.

- The **GotFocus** event is triggered by the same action, but now the object of the event is the text box that *receives* the focus. When this event takes place, the program highlights the entire text currently stored in the newly selected text box.

- The **KeyDown** event takes place when the user presses a key at the keyboard. The object of the event is the text box that currently has the focus. The purpose of the corresponding event procedure, **Sales-Day_KeyDown**, is to trap an up- or down-arrow keypress or a PgUp or PgDn keypress. In response to one of these keys, the program selects a new text box or scrolls to a new week in the database.

You'll have the opportunity to examine all these event procedures now as you turn your attention to the application's code, shown in Listings 6-1 to 6-15.

Procedures and Methods

The declarations in the **SaleGrph** form define several variables and arrays that are central to the program's operations. You can examine the declarations along with the **Form_Load** procedure in Listing 6-1.

Form-Level Variable Declarations

Two of the most important form-level variables are **WeekRef&** and **FileName$**. **WeekRef&** is a long integer that always represents a date within the week that is currently displayed on the screen. **FileName$** is the name of the data file for the displayed week:

```
DIM SHARED WeekRef&, FileName$
```

WeekRef& is a *serial* date. A serial date is a positive or negative long integer that specifies a number of days forward or backward from an arbitrarily defined starting point. The starting date in Visual Basic's serial date system is December 30, 1899, which has a serial value of zero. Prior dates have negative serial values and subsequent dates have positive values.

Extending this idea by a step, a complete serial value is a double-precision number in which the decimal portion represents the time of day. Visual Basic has an extremely valuable library of date and time functions, all based on the representation of chronological values as serial numbers. For example, the **NOW** function returns a complete serial value representing the current date from the system calendar and the time from the system clock. The **Form_Load** procedure uses this function to initialize the value of **WeekRef&**:

```
WeekRef& = INT(NOW)
```

Because the time portion of the value returned by **NOW** is not relevant to the *Sales Week* application, the program uses **INT** to drop the decimal part of the serial value. (Chapter 9 discusses serial numbers and their use in representing date and time values in greater detail.)

Another variable declared in the form-level declarations section is **Back-Weeks**:

```
DIM SHARED BackWeeks AS Integer
```

In a ten-week graph, this integer determines the position of the bar representing the current week. The variable's initial value is established in the **Form_Load** procedure:

```
BackWeeks = 63
```

This value represents nine weeks—9 weeks times 7 days equals 63. It means that nine weeks will appear before the current week in the ten-week graph.

Finally, two important arrays are declared in the form-level declarations section:

```
DIM SHARED WeekOnDisk(6), WeekOnScreen(6)
```

As you can infer from their names, these numeric arrays represent a week's sales data as currently stored on disk and as displayed on the screen. Comparisons between these two arrays give the program a simple way to determine when and if a week's data need to be updated on disk.

Displaying a Week's Sales Data

The **Form_Load** procedure makes a call to a general procedure named **ShowWeek** (Listing 6-2) to display the current week's data in the dialog box. This procedure is called whenever the user selects a new week. The procedure displays the dates of the selected week as the **Caption** settings of the array of labels named **WkDay**. Because **WeekRef&** can represent any date within the week, the first task is to determine the date of the first day of the week, Sunday:

```
WeekStart& = WeekRef& - (WEEKDAY(WeekRef&) - 1)
```

Visual Basic's **WEEKDAY** function receives a serial date as its argument and returns an integer from 1 to 7 representing the corresponding day of the week. **WeekStart&** is thus the serial date for Sunday of the currently selected week. Given this starting date, the following **FOR** loop sets the **Caption** properties for the array of labels in the dialog box:

```
FOR i% = 0 TO 6
  WkDay(i%).Caption = FORMAT$(WeekStart& + i%, "ddd m/d")
NEXT i%
```

Notice the use of Visual Basic's **FORMAT$** function to produce displayable dates from the serial date values. **FORMAT$** offers a variety of date and time formats; in this case the format "ddd m/d" is the one you see displayed in the dialog box.

The **ShowWeek** procedure uses **FORMAT$** again to create the file name for the current week's data on disk:

```
FileName$ = PathName$ + "\" + FORMAT$(WeekStart&,
"mm-dd-yy") + ".SLS"
```

Given this file name, a call to the **ReadNewWeek** procedure reads the week's sales data from disk, if it exists.

Reading Sales Data from Disk and Writing Data to Disk

The **ReadNewWeek** procedure (Listing 6-3) uses an error trap to determine whether a data file exists yet for the currently selected week. The **OPEN** statement normally causes a run-time error if an attempt is made to open a nonexistent file for input. The error trap is triggered if this error occurs:

```
CannotRead = False
ON LOCAL ERROR GOTO FileProblem
  OPEN FileName$ FOR INPUT AS #1
ON ERROR GOTO 0
```

The file exists if the **CannotRead** variable still has a value of **False** after this passage.

The **ReadNewWeek** procedure next assigns **Text** property settings for the array of text boxes named **SalesDay**. The procedure displays a column of zeros in the **SalesDay** text boxes if the file does not exist, or a column of sales data—read from the file on disk—if the file does exist:

```
IF CannotRead THEN
  SalesDay(i%).Text = "0"
ELSE
  INPUT #1, SalesText$
  SalesDay(i%).Text = SalesText$
END IF
```

After displaying the sales data, **ReadNewWeek** sets the values of the arrays **WeekOnDisk** and **WeekOnScreen**. At this point—before the user has had an opportunity to make changes in the data—the two arrays contain the same values:

```
WeekOnDisk(i%) = VAL(SalesDay(i%).Text)
WeekOnScreen(i%) = WeekOnDisk(i%)
```

When the user later selects a new week, the **SaveCurWeek** procedure (Listing 6-4) uses these two arrays to determine whether the current week

needs to be updated on disk—that is, whether there are any new data values
to save:

```
FOR i% = 0 To 6
  IF WeekOnScreen(i%) <> WeekOnDisk(i%) THEN
SomethingtoSave% = True
NEXT i%
```

The **ReadNewWeek** and **SaveCurWeek** procedures use Visual Basic's
OPEN, INPUT#, PRINT#, and **CLOSE#** statements to manage the sequen-
tial-access data files on disk. You can read about these statements in **Review
Box 6-1.**

Drawing the Graphs

After reading a new week's sales data from disk, the **ReadNewWeek**
procedure makes a call to the **UpdateTotal** procedure (Listing 6-5) to
compute the week's total sales and to draw the appropriate bar graph.
UpdateTotal begins by assigning the total sales value to **Total.Caption.**
Then a call to the **DrawAxes** procedure (also in Listing 6-5) draws the
vertical and horizontal axes for the graph.

You'll recall that the picture box in the *Sales Week* application has a
CtlName setting of **GraphBox.** The **DrawAxes** procedure illustrates two
properties and two methods that apply to picture boxes: The **CLS** method
clears all text currently displayed in the box; the **CurrentX** and **CurrentY**
properties together represent the position where the next character will
appear in the picture box; and the **PRINT** method displays a character or
a string at the current position. Because pixel graphics are not available
for Visual Basic picture boxes, the *Sales Week* program uses ASCII graphics
characters to build the axes and the bar graphs. For example, the following
passage clears the picture box and draws the vertical axis for the graph:

```
GraphBox.CLS
FOR y% = 1 TO 10
  GraphBox.CurrentX = 7
  GraphBox.CurrentY = y%
  GraphBox.PRINT CHR$(179);
NEXT y%
```

Note that 179 is the ASCII code for a vertical line character. The **DrawAxes**
procedure also uses ASCII 196 to build the horizontal axis and ASCII 192
to display the square corner where the two axes meet.

Finally, **UpdateTotal** chooses between a call to the **DrawWeekGraph** or the **DrawTrendGraph** procedure, depending on the current **Checked** setting of the **OneWeek** menu command:

```
If OneWeek.Checked Then DrawWeekGraph Else DrawTrendGraph
```

The kind of graph actually drawn therefore depends on the user's current selection in the **Graph** menu.

The **DrawWeekGraph** procedure (Listing 6-6) and the **DrawTrend-Graph** procedure (Listing 6-7) both use **FOR** loops to draw the bar graphs. Within these loops, the **PRINT** method displays a column of ASCII 219 characters for each bar. The graphic character represented by the ASCII code 219 is a solid black rectangle.

Comparing Figures 6-4 and 6-5, you can see that the bars in the one-week graph are thicker than the bars in the ten-week graph. The **DrawWeek-Graph** procedure uses Visual Basic's **STRING$** function to display a bar width of three characters:

```
GraphBox.PRINT STRING$(3, 219)
```

Similarly, the **DrawTrendGraph** procedure produces a bar width of two characters:

```
GraphBox.PRINT STRING$(2, 219)
```

To prepare for displaying a label at the proper position along the x-axis, each procedure resets the **CurrentX** and **CurrentY** properties of the picture box. A call to the **PRINT** method then displays the label. For example, here is how the **DrawWeekGraph** procedure displays abbreviations for the days of the week along the x-axis:

```
GraphBox.CurrentX = 9 + i% * 4
GraphBox.CurrentY = 12
GraphBox.PRINT LEFT$(WkDay(i%).Caption, 3);
```

Notice that the abbreviation is copied from the first three characters of the corresponding **WkDay** caption.

Reading Data from the Keyboard

The **SalesDay_LostFocus** event procedure (Listing 6-8) is called whenever the user selects a new text box in the dialog box. Several keyboard and mouse actions trigger this event in the application, including:

- Pressing the Tab key or Shift+Tab.
- Pressing the up- or down-arrow key.
- Clicking a new text box with the mouse.

Review Box 6-1:

Sequential Data Files

Read and write operations in a text file are performed *sequentially*—that is, one value at a time from the beginning to the end of the file. To open a text file for a reading operation, use the **OPEN** statement as follows:

```
OPEN FileName FOR INPUT AS #FileNum
```

FileName is the name of an existing file on disk, and *FileNum* is an integer that you use to identify the open file in subsequent I/O statements. If *FileName* cannot be found on disk, an attempt to open the file for input results in a run-time error. However, you can prevent an interruption in the program performance by setting up an error trap:

```
ON LOCAL ERROR GOTO ErrorTrapLabel
   OPEN FileName FOR INPUT AS #FileNum
ON ERROR GOTO 0
```

ErrorTrapLabel is a line label that identifies the beginning of the error-trap routine. Typically the routine sets a flag variable indicating the **OPEN** failure.

The **INPUT#** statement reads individual data values from a text file open for reading:

```
INPUT #FileNum, VariableList
```

FileNum is the number assigned to the open file in the corresponding **OPEN** statement. *VariableList* consists of one or more variable names, with data types corresponding to the data expected from the file. **INPUT#** recognizes a comma or an end-of-line marker—CHR$(13) + CHR$(10)—as a delimiter between any two data values; in addition, a space character serves as a valid delimiter between two numeric values.

The object of the **LostFocus** event in this case is the text box that *previously* had the focus. The program uses this event as an opportunity to read and validate the number in the previously selected text box and to update the total and the graph if the value represents a new or revised sales entry.

The **SalesDay_LostFocus** procedure uses the **VAL** and **STR$** functions to perform a simple validation check on the input value. First, the **VAL**

Review Box 6-1: *(continued)*

The **LINE INPUT#** statement reads an entire line of text from the file, regardless of commas or spaces contained in the line:

```
LINE INPUT #FileNum, VariableName
```

The **EOF** function returns a value of true after an **INPUT#** or **LINE INPUT#** statement reads the last data value from the file. Before this point, **EOF** gives a value of false:

```
EOF(FileNum)
```

You can use this function in a **DO** loop to read a file whose length is not known in advance.

To open a file for writing, use the **OPEN** statement in one of these forms:

```
OPEN FileName FOR OUTPUT AS #FileNum
OPEN FileName FOR APPEND AS #FileNum
```

The **OUTPUT** mode creates a new file and opens it for writing. The **APPEND** mode opens an existing file and prepares to append data values to the end of the file.

The **PRINT#** and **WRITE#** statements both send individual data items to a file that is open in one of these two modes:

```
PRINT #FileNum, DataList
WRITE #FileNum, DataList
```

PRINT# sends the items as is, without delimiters. **WRITE#** encloses each string value in quotation marks, and separates each data item from the next by a comma.

The **CLOSE#** statement closes an open file:

```
CLOSE #FileNum
```

function supplies the numeric equivalent of the **Text** value stored in the box:

```
CurVal = VAL(SalesDay(Index).Text)
```

(Keep in mind that the **Index** argument refers to the text box that has lost the focus in the **SalesDay** array.) The **VAL** function reads digital characters to the end of the string, or up to the first nondigital character if the string contains characters that cannot be converted to numbers. For example, if the user happens to enter the value **123abc** into a text box, **VAL** reads only the first three characters and returns the numeric value **123**. If the user enters a string that *begins* with a nondigital character—for example, **q1234**—the **VAL** function returns a value of zero.

The next statement in the **SalesDay_LostFocus** procedure uses the **Str$** function to redisplay the value in the text box:

```
SalesDay(Index).Text = LTRIM$(STR$(CurVal))
```

The purpose of this statement is to eliminate any nondigital characters from the display. In the case where the user enters **123abc**, the display will now be simply **123**. If the entry was **q1234**, this statement replaces the display with **0**.

Next the **LostFocus** procedure compares the text box entry with the value that was originally stored there. The previous value is recorded in the program's **WeekOnScreen** array. If the current value is not the same as the original value, the program copies the new value to **WeekOnScreen** and calls the **UpdateTotal** procedure to recompute the total and redraw the graph:

```
IF CurVal <> WeekOnScreen(Index) THEN
   WeekOnScreen(Index) = CurVal
   UpdateTotal
END IF
```

When a new text box receives the focus, the **SalesDay_GotFocus** event procedure (also in Listing 6-8) highlights the entire text currently stored in the box. This operation, performed by changing the settings of the **SelStart** and **SelLength** properties, is designed to simplify subsequent data entry into the text box. Anything the user types replaces the current selection in the text box.

Reading Commands from the Keyboard

The third event procedure that applies to the **SalesDay** array is **SalesDay_KeyDown**, shown in Listing 6-9. The **KeyDown** event—and its counterpart, the **KeyUp** event—monitor the keyboard for all keys the user presses; but these two events are especially useful for recognizing special keys, such as editing and navigation keys. The *Sales Week* program uses **KeyDown** to give the user extra ways to make selections in the dialog box. In particular, the **SalesDay_KeyDown** procedure responds to four keys:

- The up-arrow and down-arrow keys, for moving the focus to the previous or the next text box in the **SalesDay** array.
- The PgUp and PgDn keys, for scrolling backward or forward to a new week of sales data.

Each of these keys has its own keyboard code number, as recorded in **CONST** statements in the application's form-level declarations section:

```
CONST PgDn = &H22
CONST PgUp = &H21
CONST Up = &H26
CONST Down = &H28
```

The **KeyDown** event procedure passes an argument named **KeyCode**, which gives the keyboard code of the key that has been pressed. The **SalesDay_KeyDown** procedure uses a **Select Case** decision structure respond to this key code:

```
SELECT CASE KeyCode
```

For the up-arrow and down-arrow keys, the procedure uses the **SETFOCUS** method to move the focus to the previous or the next text box. If the current focus is on the first or the last text box, the procedure circles around to the opposite end of the column of boxes. For example, here is the response to the up-arrow key:

```
CASE Up
  IF Index = 0 THEN
    SalesDay(6).SETFOCUS
  ELSE
    SalesDay(Index - 1).SETFOCUS
  END IF
```

For the PgUp and PgDn keys, the procedure changes the setting of the **ScrollWeek.Value** property, thus triggering a **Change** event for the vertical scroll bar:

```
CASE PgUp
  ScrollWeek.Value = ScrollWeek.Min
```

The **ScrollWeek_Change** procedure (also shown in Listing 6-9) responds to a change in the setting of **ScrollWeek.Value**. This change usually takes place when the user clicks the up- or down-arrow icon on the scroll bar—but as you've now seen, it can also be caused by a special call from the **SalesDay_KeyDown** procedure. **ScrollWeek_Change**, in turn, calls either **Backward_Click** or **Forward_Click**—two of the event procedures designed for responding to menu selections.

Responding to Menu Commands

Most of the remaining routines in the *Sales Week* application are event procedures for the menu commands. The procedures for the **File** menu appear in Listing 6-10. Listing 6-11 shows the **Week** menu procedures; Listings 6-12 and 6-13, the **Graph** menu; and Listing 6-14, the **Help** menu. Each of these procedures responds to the **Click** event that occurs when the user selects a menu command. (The procedure shown in Listing 6-15 is designed to search for the directory in which weekly sales files are to be stored. If no such directory exists, one will be created.)

The **PrintSales_Click** procedure prints the sales data from the week that is currently displayed in the *Sales Week* window. To accomplish this task, a **FOR** loop makes a call to the PRINT method for the PRINTER object to print each line of output:

```
PRINTER.PRINT "Sales Week"
PRINTER.PRINT
FOR i% = 0 TO 6
  PRINTER.PRINT WkDay(i%).Caption, SalesDay(i%).Text
NEXT i%
```

Then a call to the NEWPAGE method sends a form-feed signal to the printer:

```
PRINTER.NEWPAGE
```

The **Quit_Click** procedure terminates the program performance when the user selects the **Exit** command from the **File** menu. Before doing so, however, the program calls the **SaveCurWeek** procedure to save to disk any new data in the currently displayed sales week.

The four event procedures for the **Week** menu are designed to display a newly selected week's data and graph on the screen. Each procedure makes an appropriate adjustment in the serial date stored in the **WeekRef&** variable and then makes a call to **ShowWeek**.

The **OneWeek_Click** and **TenWeeks_Click** procedures adjust the **Checked** properties of the two menu commands, **OneWeek** and **TenWeeks**. Then each procedure makes a call to **UpdateTotal** to display the newly selected graph on the screen. You'll recall that **UpdateTotal** reads the settings of the two commands' **Checked** properties to decide which graph to create.

The **BeginPos_Click, EndPos_Click**, and **MidPos_Click** procedures also switch the **Checked** properties of the appropriate menu selections. Then each procedure assigns a new value to **BackWeeks**, the variable used to determine the current week's position in the ten-week graph. A call to **UpdateTotal** redraws the graph.

Finally, the two procedures that display help messages are named **KeyboardHelp_Click** and **GeneralHelp_Click**. Each one of these builds a help string and then calls Visual Basic's **MSGBOX** procedure to display the message box on the screen. A call to **MSGBOX** takes three arguments:

```
MSGBOX MessageString, TypeCode, TitleString
```

The first argument is the string that will be displayed inside the message box. End-of-line markers (**CHR$**(13) + **CHR$**(10)) can be included explicitly in this string; otherwise, Visual Basic controls line wrapping in the message box. The second argument is a code number, selecting from among the various message box styles available. (For example, an argument of 0 displays an OK button at the bottom of the message box, as you can see in Figures 6-11 and 6-12.) The third argument is the string that will appear in the title bar for the message box.

SUMMARY: INPUT AND OUTPUT IN VISUAL BASIC

The *Sales Week* application illustrates a number of techniques for reading data and commands from the user who is operating the keyboard and the mouse:

- Reading the **Text** property of a text box.
- Monitoring **Click** events for commands in a menu system.
- Recognizing shortcut keys and access keys in a menu definition.
- Using the **KeyDown** (or **KeyUp**) event to read special keys from the keyboard.
- Monitoring the **Change** event for a scroll bar.

In addition, this application has many interesting examples of output techniques, including:

- Using text boxes for both output and input.
- Drawing graphs and displaying text in a picture box.

- Performing sequential-access file operations to save data to disk in a text file.
- Sending data to the printer.

Input and output operations are central to every program, and programmers never stop experimenting with new techniques for simplifying and improving these procedures. You'll see many more examples of I/O operations in other applications presented in this book.

Listing 6-1 Declarations and the Form_Load procedure

```
' The Sales Week Program (SALESWK.MAK)
' SALEGRPH.FRM
' Declarations

DECLARE SUB ShowWeek ()
DECLARE SUB Backward_Click ()
DECLARE SUB Forward_Click ()
DECLARE SUB ReadNewWeek ()
DECLARE SUB SaveCurWeek ()
DECLARE SUB UpdateTotal ()
DECLARE SUB DrawAxes ()
DECLARE SUB DrawWeekGraph ()
DECLARE SUB DrawTrendGraph ()
DECLARE SUB SearchForPath ()

' The directory for weekly sales files.

CONST PathName$ = "C:\SalesWk"

' Logical values.

CONST False = 0
CONST True = NOT False

' Keyboard navigation keys.

CONST PgDn = &H22
CONST PgUp = &H21
CONST Up = &H26
CONST Down = &H28
```

```
' Serial number and file name for the current week.

DIM SHARED WeekRef&, FileName$

' Position of current week in trend graph.

DIM SHARED BackWeeks AS INTEGER

' Arrays for current week's sales amounts.

DIM SHARED WeekOnDisk(6), WeekOnScreen(6)


SUB Form_Load ()

  ' Initialize this week's serial number
  ' and show the week's graph.

  SearchForPath
  WeekRef& = INT(NOW)
  ShowWeek

  ' Initialize the position value
  ' for the trend graph.

  BackWeeks = 63

END SUB   ' Form_Load
```

Listing 6-2 The ShowWeek procedure

```
SUB ShowWeek ()

  ' Display the data for a new week.

  ' First save the data for the current week.

  SaveCurWeek

  ' Calculate the serial value for the first day
```

(continued)

```
' of the week and display the day captions.

WeekStart& = WeekRef& - (WEEKDAY(WeekRef&) - 1)
FOR i% = 0 TO 6
  WkDay(i%).Caption = FORMAT$(WeekStart& + i%, "ddd m/d")
NEXT i%


' Build the file name for the new week's data
' and read the data from disk.

FileName$ = PathName$ + "\" + FORMAT$(WeekStart&,
"mm-dd-yy") + ".SLS"
  ReadNewWeek

END SUB   ' ShowWeek
```

Listing 6-3 The ReadNewWeek procedure

```
SUB ReadNewWeek ()

  ' Read data from disk for the newly selected week.

  ' First check to see if the week's file exists yet.

  CannotRead = False
  ON LOCAL ERROR GOTO FileProblem
    OPEN FileName$ FOR INPUT AS #1
  ON ERROR GOTO 0

  ' If the file exists, read it and display individual
  ' data values in the SalesDay text boxes. Otherwise,
  ' display a value of zero in each box.

  FOR i% = 0 TO 6
    IF CannotRead THEN
      SalesDay(i%).Text = "0"
    ELSE
      INPUT #1, SalesText$
      SalesDay(i%).Text = SalesText$
    END IF
```

```
      WeekOnDisk(i%) = VAL(SalesDay(i%).Text)
      WeekOnScreen(i%) = WeekOnDisk(i%)
   NEXT i%
   CLOSE #1


   ' Update the total for the week.


   UpdateTotal
   EXIT SUB


 ' Error trap to handle nonexistent file.


 FileProblem:
   CannotRead = True
 RESUME NEXT


 END SUB   ' ReadNewWeek
```

Listing 6-4 The SaveCurWeek procedure

```
SUB SaveCurWeek ()

   ' Save the revised data for the current week.

   ' First check to see if there are any new data to save.

   SomethingToSave% = False
   FOR i% = 0 TO 6
      IF WeekOnScreen(i%) <> WeekOnDisk(i%) THEN
SomethingToSave% = True
   NEXT i%

   ' If there are any new data, save the entire
   ' week's data as a sequential text file.

   IF SomethingToSave% THEN
      OPEN FileName$ FOR OUTPUT AS #1
      FOR i% = 0 TO 6
         PRINT #1, SalesDay(i%).Text
         WeekOnDisk(i%) = VAL(SalesDay(i%).Text)
```

(continued)

```
      NEXT i%
      CLOSE #1
   END IF

END SUB   ' SaveCurWeek
```

Listing 6-5 The UpdateTotal and DrawAxes procedures

```
SUB DrawAxes ()

  ' Draw the horizontal and vertical
  ' axes in the graph box.

  GraphBox.CLS

  FOR y% = 1 TO 10
     GraphBox.CurrentX = 7
     GraphBox.CurrentY = y%
     GraphBox.PRINT CHR$(179);
  NEXT y%

  FOR x% = 8 TO 37
     GraphBox.CurrentY = 11
     GraphBox.CurrentX = x%
     GraphBox.PRINT CHR$(196);
  NEXT x%

  GraphBox.CurrentX = 7
  GraphBox.CurrentY = 11
  GraphBox.PRINT CHR$(192);

END SUB   ' DrawAxes


SUB UpdateTotal ()

  ' Update the data total after new input.

  Total.Caption = "0"
  FOR i% = 0 TO 6
```

```
      Total.Caption = STR$(VAL(Total.Caption) + WeekOnScreen(i%))
   NEXT i%


   ' Redraw the graph.


   DrawAxes
   IF OneWeek.Checked THEN DrawWeekGraph ELSE DrawTrendGraph


END SUB   ' UpdateTotal
```

Listing 6-6 The DrawWeekGraph procedure

```
SUB DrawWeekGraph ()

   ' Draw the graph for a single week's data.

   CONST MaxHeight = 10
   DIM MaxDay, x%, y%, i%

   ' Find the largest single day's sales amount.

   MaxDay = WeekOnScreen(0)
   FOR i% = 1 TO 6
      IF WeekOnScreen(i%) > MaxDay THEN MaxDay = WeekOnScreen(i%)
   NEXT i%

   ' Draw the seven bars of the graph.

   IF MaxDay <> 0 THEN
      FOR i% = 0 TO 6
         BarTop% = CINT(MaxHeight * (1 - (WeekOnScreen(i%) /
MaxDay))) + 1

         FOR j% = 10 TO BarTop% STEP -1
            GraphBox.CurrentY = j%
            GraphBox.CurrentX = 9 + i% * 4
            GraphBox.PRINT STRING$(3, 219)
         NEXT j%

         ' Display x-axis label.
```

(continued)

```
      GraphBox.CurrentX = 9 + i% * 4
      GraphBox.CurrentY = 12
      GraphBox.PRINT LEFT$(WkDay(i%).Caption, 3);
   NEXT i%

   ' Display y-axis label and title.

   GraphBox.CurrentX = 0
   GraphBox.CurrentY = 1
   GraphBox.PRINT MaxDay;
   GraphBox.CurrentX = 12
   GraphBox.CurrentY = 0
   GraphBox.PRINT "The Week of"; MID$(WkDay(0).Caption, 4);

 END IF

 ' Display the average daily sale.

 StatLabel.Caption = "Average Daily Sale:"
 StatVal.Caption = STR$(CINT(VAL(Total.Caption) / 7))

END SUB   ' DrawWeekGraph
```

Listing 6-7 The DrawTrendGraph procedure

```
SUB DrawTrendGraph ()

  ' Draw the ten-week trend graph.

  CONST MaxHeight = 10
  DIM CurWeekStart AS LONG, MaxTrendWeek, TotTrendWeeks
  DIM TrendWeeks(10), WeekChar$(10)

  SaveCurWeek
  WeekStart& = WeekRef& - (WEEKDAY(WeekRef&) - 1)
  MaxTrendWeek = 0
  FOR i% = 0 TO 9

    ' Build the file name for each week's data.
```

```
    CurWeekStart = WeekStart& - (BackWeeks - (i% * 7))
    TrendFileName$ = PathName$ + "\" + FORMAT$(CurWeekStart,
"mm-dd-yy")
    TrendFileName$ = TrendFileName$ + ".SLS"

    ' Determine the x-axis label for the week.

    IF CurWeekStart = WeekStart& THEN
      WeekChar$(i%) = "^"
    ELSEIF CurWeekStart < WeekStart& THEN
      WeekChar$(i%) = FORMAT$(i% + 1, "#")
    ELSE
      WeekChar$(i%) = FORMAT$(i%, "#")
    END IF

    ' Check to see if file exists.

    FileFound% = True
    ON LOCAL ERROR GOTO NoTrendFileName
      OPEN TrendFileName$ FOR INPUT AS #1
    ON ERROR GOTO 0

    ' Read the file and compute the total sales for the week.

    TrendWeeks(i%) = 0
    IF FileFound% THEN
      FOR j% = 1 TO 7
        INPUT #1, dayVal
        TrendWeeks(i%) = TrendWeeks(i%) + dayVal
      NEXT j%
      CLOSE #1
      IF TrendWeeks(i%) > MaxTrendWeek THEN MaxTrendWeek =
TrendWeeks(i%)
      TotTrendWeeks = TotTrendWeeks + TrendWeeks(i%)
    END IF
  NEXT i%

  ' Draw the bar for each week.

  IF MaxTrendWeek <> 0 THEN
    FOR i% = 0 TO 9
      BarTop% = CINT(MaxHeight * (1 - (TrendWeeks(i%) /
MaxTrendWeek))) + 1
```

(continued)

```
        FOR j% = 10 TO BarTop% STEP -1
          GraphBox.CurrentX = 9 + i% * 3
          GraphBox.CurrentY = j%
          GraphBox.PRINT STRING$(2, 219)
        NEXT j%
        GraphBox.CurrentX = 9 + i% * 3
        GraphBox.CurrentY = 12
        GraphBox.PRINT WeekChar$(i%);
      NEXT i%

      ' Display the y-axis label and the title.

      GraphBox.CurrentX = 0
      GraphBox.CurrentY = 1
      GraphBox.PRINT MaxTrendWeek;
      GraphBox.CurrentX = 12
      GraphBox.CurrentY = 0
      GraphBox.PRINT "Ten-Week Trend";
    END IF

    ' Display the ten-week total.
    StatLabel.Caption = "Ten-Week Total:"
    StatVal.Caption = STR$(TotTrendWeeks)

    EXIT SUB

  ' The error trap for a nonexistent file.

NoTrendFileName:
  FileFound% = False
RESUME NEXT


END SUB    ' DrawTrendGraph
```

Listing 6-8 The SalesDay_LostFocus and SalesDay_GotFocus procedures

```
SUB SalesDay_GotFocus (Index AS INTEGER)

   ' Extend the highlight over the entire text
   ' entry when the user selects an input box.
```

```
      SalesDay(Index).SelStart = 0
      SalesDay(Index).SelLength = LEN(SalesDay(Index).Text)

  END SUB   ' SalesDay_GotFocus


  SUB SalesDay_LostFocus (Index AS INTEGER)

    ' Read a new daily sales figure from a text box.

    DIM CurVal

    ' Read the text value and convert it to a number.

    CurVal = VAL(SalesDay(Index).Text)

    ' Eliminate any invalid characters from the display.

    SalesDay(Index).Text = LTRIM$(STR$(CurVal))

    ' Update the graph only if this is a new input value.

    IF CurVal <> WeekOnScreen(Index) THEN
      WeekOnScreen(Index) = CurVal
      UpdateTotal
    END IF

  END SUB
```

Listing 6-9 The SalesDay_KeyDown procedure and the ScrollWeek_Change procedure

```
  SUB SalesDay_KeyDown (Index AS INTEGER, KeyCode AS INTEGER,
  Shift AS INTEGER)

    ' Respond to navigation keys for selecting the daily
    ' values in a week's data and for scrolling through weeks.

    SELECT CASE KeyCode
```

(continued)

```
      ' Scroll back to the previous week.

      CASE PgUp
        ScrollWeek.Value = ScrollWeek.Min

      ' Scroll forward to the next week.

      CASE PgDn
        ScrollWeek.Value = ScrollWeek.Max

      ' Select the previous day's text box.

      CASE Up
        IF Index = 0 THEN
          SalesDay(6).SETFOCUS
        ELSE
          SalesDay(Index - 1).SETFOCUS
        END IF

      ' Select the next day's text box.

      CASE Down
        IF Index = 6 THEN
          SalesDay(0).SETFOCUS
        ELSE
          SalesDay(Index + 1).SETFOCUS
        END IF
    END SELECT

END SUB   ' SalesDay_KeyDown


SUB ScrollWeek_Change ()

  ' Scroll backward or forward to a new week.

  ' ScrollWeek.Min (0) is the setting for an
  ' up-arrow click, and ScrollWeek.Max (2) is
  ' the setting for a down-arrow click. The
  ' neutral ScrollWeek.Value setting is 1.

  IF ScrollWeek.Value = ScrollWeek.Min THEN
    Backward_Click
```

```
    ELSEIF ScrollWeek.Value = ScrollWeek.Max THEN
      Forward_Click
    END IF

    ' Reset the ScrollWeek value.

    IF ScrollWeek.Value <> 1 THEN
      ScrollWeek.Value = 1
      SalesDay(0).SETFOCUS
    END IF

END SUB   ' ScrollWeek_Change
```

Listing 6-10 The PrintSales_Click procedure and the Quit_Click procedure

```
SUB PrintSales_Click ()

  ' Print the current week's data.

  PRINTER.PRINT "Sales Week"
  PRINTER.PRINT
  FOR i% = 0 TO 6
    PRINTER.PRINT WkDay(i%).Caption, SalesDay(i%).Text
  NEXT i%
  PRINTER.NEWPAGE

END SUB   ' PrintSales_Click



SUB Quit_Click ()

  ' Exit from the program but save the
  ' current week's data first.

  SaveCurWeek
  END

END SUB   ' Quit_Click
```

Listing 6-11 Event procedures for the Week menu commands

```
SUB Backward_Click ()

  ' Scroll back to the previous week.

  WeekRef& = WeekRef& - 7
  ShowWeek

END SUB   ' Backward_Click


SUB Forward_Click ()

  ' Move forward by one week.

  WeekRef& = WeekRef& + 7
  ShowWeek

END SUB   ' Forward_Click


SUB LastWeek_Click ()

  ' Display last week's data and graph.

  WeekRef& = INT(NOW) - 7
  ShowWeek

END SUB    ' LastWeek_Click


SUB ThisWeek_Click ()

  ' Display the current week's data and graph.

  WeekRef& = INT(NOW)
  ShowWeek

END SUB    ' ThisWeek_Click
```

Listing 6-12 The event procedures for the Graph menu

```
SUB OneWeek_Click ()

  ' Display the graph for one week's data.

  OneWeek.Checked = True
  TenWeeks.Checked = False
  UpdateTotal

END SUB  ' OneWeek_Click


SUB TenWeeks_Click ()

  ' Switch to the ten-week trend graph.

  TenWeeks.Checked = True
  OneWeek.Checked = False
  UpdateTotal

END SUB  ' TenWeeks_Click
```

Listing 6-13 The event procedures for the Position options

```
SUB BeginPos_Click ()

  ' Establish new setting for Position submenu.

  BeginPos.Checked = True
  MidPos.Checked = False
  EndPos.Checked = False

  ' Assign correct number of days to the
  ' global variable BackWeeks.

  BackWeeks = 0

  ' Redisplay graph to show new position.
```

(continued)

```
    IF TenWeeks.Checked THEN UpdateTotal

END SUB  ' BeginPos_Click


SUB EndPos_Click ()

   ' Establish new setting for Position submenu.

   EndPos.Checked = True
   MidPos.Checked = False
   BeginPos.Checked = False

   ' Assign correct number of days to the
   ' global variable BackWeeks.

   BackWeeks = 63

   ' Redisplay graph to show new position.

   IF TenWeeks.Checked THEN UpdateTotal

END SUB  ' EndPos_Click


SUB MidPos_Click ()

   ' Establish new setting for Position submenu.

   MidPos.Checked = True
   BeginPos.Checked = False
   EndPos.Checked = False

   ' Assign correct number of days to the
   ' global variable BackWeeks.

   BackWeeks = 28

   ' Redisplay graph to show new position.

   IF TenWeeks.Checked THEN UpdateTotal

END SUB  ' MidPos_Click
```

Listing 6-14 The event procedures for the Help menu

```
SUB GeneralHelp_Click ()

   ' Display a message box with general help.

   CrLf$ = CHR$(13) + CHR$(10)

   Help$ = "The Sales Week application maintains a database " + CrLf$
   Help$ = Help$ + "of daily and weekly sales data, and displays " +
   CrLf$
   Help$ = Help$ + "the numbers along with a graph for any week you " +
   CrLf$
   Help$ = Help$ + "select. You can view a one-week graph or a " +
   CrLf$
   Help$ = Help$ + "trend graph showing the total weekly sales for " +
   CrLf$
   Help$ = Help$ + "a ten-week period. " + CrLf$

   MSGBOX Help$, 0, "About Sales Week"

END SUB   ' GeneralHelp_Click


SUB KeyboardHelp_Click ()

   ' Display a message box with keyboard help.

   DIM HelpMsg$

   CrLf$ = CHR$(13) + CHR$(10)
   HelpMsg$ = "  F1   Help                " + CrLf$ + CrLf$

   HelpMsg$ = HelpMsg$ + "  Trend graph        " + CrLf$
   HelpMsg$ = HelpMsg$ + "  positions:         " + CrLf$ +
   CrLf$
   HelpMsg$ = HelpMsg$ + "  F2  Beginning      " + CrLf$
   HelpMsg$ = HelpMsg$ + "  F3  Middle         " + CrLf$
   HelpMsg$ = HelpMsg$ + "  F4  End            " + CrLf$ +
   CrLf$

   HelpMsg$ = HelpMsg$ + "  Selections:        " + CrLf$ +
   CrLf$
```

(continued)

```
   HelpMsg$ = HelpMsg$ + "  F5   This week        " + CrLf$
   HelpMsg$ = HelpMsg$ + "  F6   Last week        " + CrLf$
   HelpMsg$ = HelpMsg$ + "  F7   Week graph       " + CrLf$
   HelpMsg$ = HelpMsg$ + "  F8   Trend graph      " + CrLf$ +
CrLf$

   HelpMsg$ = HelpMsg$ + "  PgUp  Previous week" + CrLf$
   HelpMsg$ = HelpMsg$ + "  PgDn  Next week      " + CrLf$ +
CrLf$

   HelpMsg$ = HelpMsg$ + "  Ctrl-P  Print        " + CrLf$
   HelpMsg$ = HelpMsg$ + "  Ctrl-X  Exit         "

   MSGBOX HelpMsg$, 0, "Keyboard Help"

END SUB  '  KeyboardHelp_Click
```

Listing 6-15 The SearchForPath procedure

```
SUB SearchForPath ()

   ' Search for the directory in which weekly sales files
   ' are to be stored. Create the directory (on drive C)
   ' if it does not exist yet.

   ' Note: PathName$ is declared at the declarations-level
   ' of the SaleGrph form.

   DIM CDir$

   ' Record the current directory.
   CDir$ = CURDIR$("C")

   ' Set up an error-handling mode.
   ON LOCAL ERROR RESUME NEXT

   ' Attempt to change to the target directory.
```

```
CHDIR PathName$

' If the directory doesn't exist, create it.
MKDIR PathName$

' Restore the original directory.
CHDIR CDir$

END SUB   ' SearchForPath
```

7

Data Structures and Control Arrays: The Address File Application

INTRODUCTION

A *data array* is an efficient way to organize multiple data items under one variable name. Likewise, a *control array* simplifies your work with certain groups of Visual Basic controls on a form. Although data arrays and control arrays are not identical in usage, the two structures are parallel in concept. In both cases, you refer to an individual array element by its indexed position in the array. The index appears as an integer in parentheses after the array name:

```
DataArray(Index)
ControlArray(Index)
```

A **FOR** loop is useful for focusing successively on the individual elements of a data array or a control array. The loop's control variable serves as the index into the array.

You have seen examples of data arrays and control arrays—and the **FOR** loops that process them—in earlier chapters. For example, the *Sales Week* application uses an array of text boxes to display sales figures on the screen and a pair of data arrays to store the same values in memory. Significantly, each of the arrays in the *Sales Week* program has a fixed length—seven elements, representing the seven days of the week. Fixed-length, or *static,* arrays are ideal in any context where the dimensions of the data are known in advance.

In contrast, data arrays and control arrays both can be used *dynamically* in Visual Basic—as structures that increase or decrease in length during run time. For data arrays, this means that you can design a structure to store any group of data items, even if you do not know how many items there will ultimately be. You create a dynamic array by declaring its name, but not its length, in an initial **DIM** statement. A pair of empty parentheses after the array name indicates that the size of the array will be defined later:

```
DIM DataArray()
```

Then, inside a procedure that uses the array, you use the **ReDim** statement to define the necessary length for the array:

```
REDIM DataArray(NewLength)
```

REDIM is an executable statement that allocates space during run time for an array of the indicated length. A dynamic array can be resized any number of times during a program performance. By default, the **REDIM** statement initializes numeric array elements to zero or string elements to empty strings, resulting in a loss of data. Alternatively, you can use the PRESERVE keyword in a REDIM statement when you want to avoid losing the data stored in the array.

A comparable dynamic quality in control arrays allows you to create and display entirely new controls *at run time* in response to specific events that occur during program execution. As you know, you normally create a control array at design time by giving the same **CtlName** setting to a group of controls. When you do so, Visual Basic automatically assigns a sequential **Index** setting to each control you add to the array.

To create a control array whose length will change during run time, you can begin by placing a single control on a form at design time. You then assign a numeric setting to the control's **Index** property, thus defining the control explicitly as an element of an array. Given this initial control, your program uses a special Visual Basic statement named **LOAD** to create new elements of the control array at run time. The **LOAD** statement takes as its argument the name and index number of a control element that will be created:

```
LOAD ControlArray(NewIndex)
```

As a result of the **LOAD** statement, a new control element, numbered **NewIndex**, is added to the array. But keep in mind that **ControlArray** must already exist as a defined array—containing one or more controls—for this statement to work properly.

Try the following brief experiment to see how controls can be created at run time:

1. Create a new form in the Form Designer and place a single option button on the form. Assign the form a **Caption** setting of **Test** and **Width** and **Height** settings of **17** and **23**.

2. Assign the button a **CtlName** setting of **OptionButton,** an **Index** setting of **0, Width** and **Height** settings of **12** and **3, Left** and **Top** settings of **2** and **0,** and a **Caption** setting of **0.**

3. Switch to the programming environment and enter the following lines of code into the form's **Form_Load** procedure:

```
SUB Form_Load ()
  FOR i% = 1 TO 9
    LOAD OptionButton(i%)
    OptionButton(i%).Visible = -1
    OptionButton(i%).Enabled = -1
    OptionButton(i%).Height = 3
    OptionButton(i%).Width = 12
    OptionButton(i%).Left = 2
    OptionButton(i%).Top = i% * 2
    OptionButton(i%).Caption = LTRIM$(STR$(i%))
  NEXT i%
END SUB
```

4. Now press F5 to run the program. The resulting form displays an array of ten option buttons, as shown in Figure 7-1.

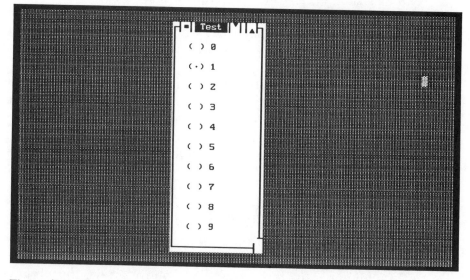

Figure 7-1 Controls created at run time

Only the first of these ten option buttons was created at design time. The remaining nine were placed on the screen by the **LOAD** statement, performed repeatedly by a **FOR** loop in the **Form_Load** procedure. After creating each control, the **Form_Load** procedure also establishes the new control's properties.

Another common place for dynamic controls is in a menu system you create for an application. You can use this powerful feature to make changes during run time in the list of commands offered by particular menu.

THE ADDRESS FILE APPLICATION

This chapter's *Address File* application illustrates control arrays and data arrays that change size during program execution. The application is a menu-driven database program, designed to manage a personal or business address file stored on disk. You can use this program to:

- Add new addresses to your file.
- Retrieve and view the address and phone number for any person you have already entered into the file.
- Revise or update existing addresses.
- Print envelopes on a laser printer.

To search for specific records, the program uses an alphabetized index list—similar in many ways to the index at the end of a book—to keep track of the location of each address in the database. Because the database and its index can increase in size whenever you run the application, this list is stored in memory as a dynamic data array. Each time you add a new record to the database, the program resizes the index array to accommodate the new database length.

The *Address File* application also contains an important example of a control array. The program displays an array of option buttons—named **Title**—from which you can choose an appropriate title for the person in an address record. Initially the array offers a list of five titles: *Mr., Ms., Mrs., Miss,* and *Dr.;* but the program allows you to add more titles to this list to meet the requirements of your own address database. For example, you might add option buttons for new titles such as *The Honorable* for writing to representatives in Congress; *Professor* or *Dean* for academic correspondence; and *The Reverend* or *Rabbi* for religious leaders. Each time you add an entry to this list, the *Address File* program increases the length of the **Title** array.

In addition to its data arrays and control arrays, the program also illustrates another type of data structure: the user-defined type, also known as the *record* type. A record is a variable that represents multiple data *fields*—values that may belong to different data types. **Review Box 7-1** describes Visual Basic's user-defined record type. A record structure is a particularly effective way to organize information in a database management program such as the *Address File* application. (See Chapter 8 for a more detailed look at file techniques associated with database management.)

Data arrays, control arrays, and data records—these structures are the focus of your work in this chapter. Begin now by loading the *Address File* application from the exercise disk. The name of the project file is AD-DRESS.MAK. Use the **Open Project...** command in Visual Basic's **File** menu to open the application, then press F5 to begin a performance.

Running the Program

The *Address File* application offers simple keyboard techniques for saving, retrieving, and printing addresses. When you first run the program, an input form appears on the screen, with eight empty text boxes—labeled *First Name, Last Name, Company Name, Address, City, State, Zip Code,* and *Phone Number.* To the left of these text boxes is a vertical group of option buttons labeled *Mr., Ms., Mrs., Miss,* and *Dr.* You create an address record by entering information into the text boxes and clicking one of the option buttons with the mouse.

A complete sample entry appears in Figure 7-2. When you complete an address entry like this one and you are ready to store the record, a single

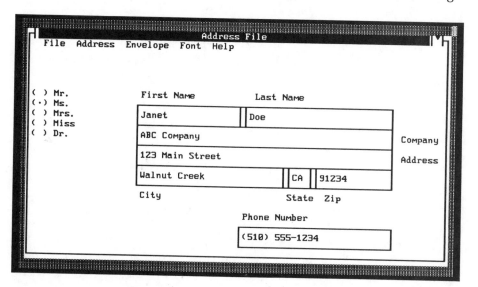

Figure 7-2 An address entry

Review Box 7-1:

Record Structures

A *user-defined type* is a compound structure representing multiple data *fields*. Programmers sometimes refer to this data type as a *record structure*. Two steps are necessary for defining a record variable. The first is to write a **TYPE** definition that outlines the field structure of the record type. The second component is a **DIM** statement that declares a variable belonging to the defined record type.

The **TYPE** statement supplies a name for the user-defined type, followed by a list of field definitions:

```
TYPE RecordTypeName
    FieldName1 AS type
    FieldName2 AS type
    FieldName3 AS type

    ' ...
END TYPE
```

Each field definition consists of a field name followed by an **AS** clause giving the field's data type. The *type* specification can be any of Visual Basic's numeric or string data types, or even a previously defined record type. String fields must be of fixed length. Visual Basic also allows static arrays as fields.

The **DIM** statement for a record variable may appear in the declaration section of a form or in a procedure—depending on the scope you want to establish for the variable. To declare a variable representing a single record, the **DIM** syntax is:

```
DIM VariableName AS RecordTypeName
```

---

keystroke instructs the program to write the address to the database file: *Press the F2 function key to save the current address entry.* The program saves the address, creates a new entry in the index, and leaves the address displayed in the input form.

You can leave some of the text boxes blank and still save a record to the database. All the fields of the address record are optional except for *First Name* and *Last Name,* the two fields that the program uses for identifying a

Review Box 7-1: *(continued)*

You can also define an array of records, in which each array element represents a separate record. In this case, the **DIM** syntax is:

```
DIM ArrayName(length) AS RecordTypeName
```

for a static one-dimensional array, or:

```
DIM ArrayName() As RecordTypeName
```

for a dynamic array of records.

Visual Basic recognizes a special format for references to individual fields in a record variable. In this format, the record variable name is followed by a period and then the field name:

```
VariableName.FieldName
```

The format for a record element in an array of records is only slightly more complicated:

```
ArrayName(Index).FieldName
```

In both cases, this field reference can be used in any statement that normally takes a simple variable name. For example, the following assignment statement stores a value in a field:

```
AddrRec.CityField = "Dakar"
```

Programmers can easily confuse field references with Visual Basic property references. For this reason, you should try to name records and fields in a way that clearly identifies their structural roles:

```
City.Text = AddrRec.CityField
```

record in the index to the database. Normally you'll probably fill most of the text boxes with information, but in some cases you might omit a field such as *Company Name* or *Phone Number*.

After saving an address, you may want to clear the input form so you can enter a new address or view an address already stored in the database. Again, the action takes a single keystroke: *Press F3 to clear the current address*

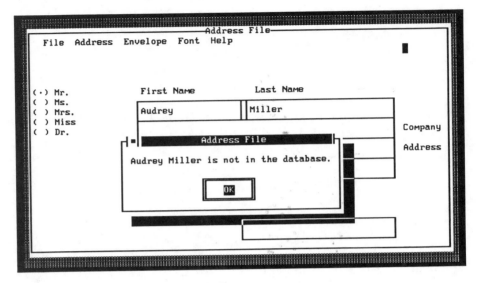

Figure 7-3 An unsuccessful record search

entry from the input form. The focus returns to the *First Name* text box, where you can begin a new entry.

Searching for and viewing an existing address is a two-step process. First you enter the full name—*First Name* and *Last Name*—of the person whose address you want to retrieve. Then you press the key that requests a record search: *Press F4 to retrieve an address.* In response, the program looks up the name in the index. The index in turn supplies the location of the address in the database. Given this location, the program reads the address and displays the complete record in the form. On the other hand, if the program cannot find the name entry in the index, a message box appears on the screen (Figure 7-3). When this happens, you should check the spelling of the name you have entered. If the spelling is correct, you can assume that there is not yet an address recorded for this person. (Alphabetic case is not significant in a record search. You can enter a name in any combination of uppercase or lowercase letters.)

Once you have retrieved an address record from the database, you can make revisions in the address and phone number and then save the revised address back to the database. Again, you simply press the F2 function key to save the address. In this case, the program recognizes that you are revising an existing record and asks you to confirm the *save* operation. Figure 7-4 shows the message box that appears on the screen. Click the **Yes** button to update the address record or click **No** to cancel the operation.

Before you print an envelope for a given address, you may want to create a record of your return address. To do so, you clear the input form (F3) and enter your name and address. Then you instruct the program to record

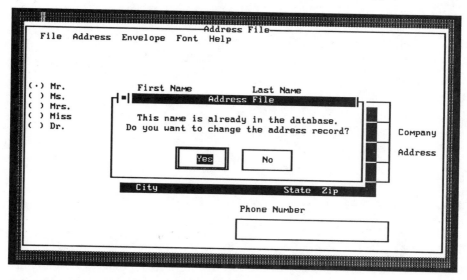

Figure 7-4 Updating an existing address record

the entry as the return address: *Press **Ctrl+R** to save the current address entry as the return address.* The program stores the return address in a separate file on disk. Once you have saved a return address, the program includes it on all envelopes that you print. You can view the recorded return address at any time: *Press **F8** to view the return address.* In response, the program displays a message box similar to the one in Figure 7-5. To change the return address, simply enter a new address in the input form and press Ctrl+R

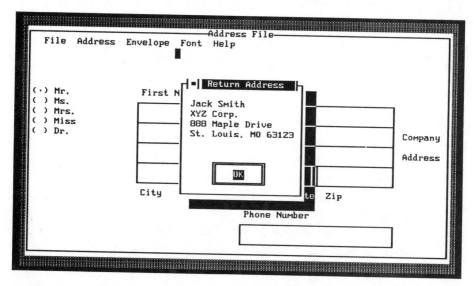

Figure 7-5 Viewing the return address

```
Jack Smith
XYZ Corp.
888 Maple Drive
St. Louis, MO 63123


                              Ms. Janet Doe
                              ABC Company
                              123 Main Street
                              Walnut Creek, CA 91234
```

Figure 7-6 *A printed envelope*

again. If you want to omit the return address from a printed envelope, save a blank address entry as the return address: Press F3 to clear the input form and then Ctrl+R to save the return address.

The *Address File* application offers three groups of options for printing envelopes: font, orientation, and envelope size. By default, the program is set up to do *landscape*-oriented printing in a fixed-space font, on a business-size envelope. (Under these default options, the program generates printer code commands that work on an HP LaserJet or compatible.) To print an envelope, you retrieve an existing address or enter a new address; then feed the envelope into the printer and instruct the program to begin printing: *Press **Ctrl+E** to print an envelope.* Figure 7-6 shows an example of the result.

The program's **Envelope** and **Font** menus provide other options for printing envelopes. In addition, the menu system supplies alternate ways of performing the program's other operations.

The Menu System

The **File** menu (Figure 7-7) and the **Address** menu (Figure 7-8) contain the commands for the program features you've seen up to now. The **File** menu has commands for saving an address to the database, clearing an address from the input form, and printing an envelope. The menu's final command is **Exit**, which terminates the program. *(Press **Ctrl+X** from the keyboard to end the program performance.)* The **Address** menu includes commands for retrieving an address from the database, for saving and viewing the return address, and for adding a new title to the list of option buttons at the left side of the form.

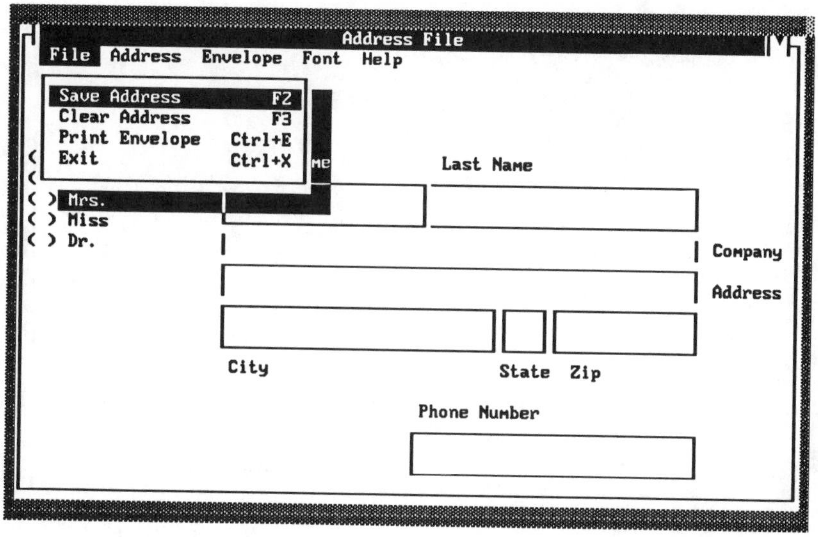

Figure 7-7 The **File** menu

The **Envelope** menu (Figure 7-9) offers three envelope-size settings, described as **Business, Home**, and **Personal**. There are also two orientation settings. For feeding envelopes sideways into a laser printer, use the default **Landscape Orientation** setting. For tractor-fed envelopes on other kinds of printers, use the **Portrait Orientation**. (The program's code—which you'll examine later in this chapter—illustrates two completely different

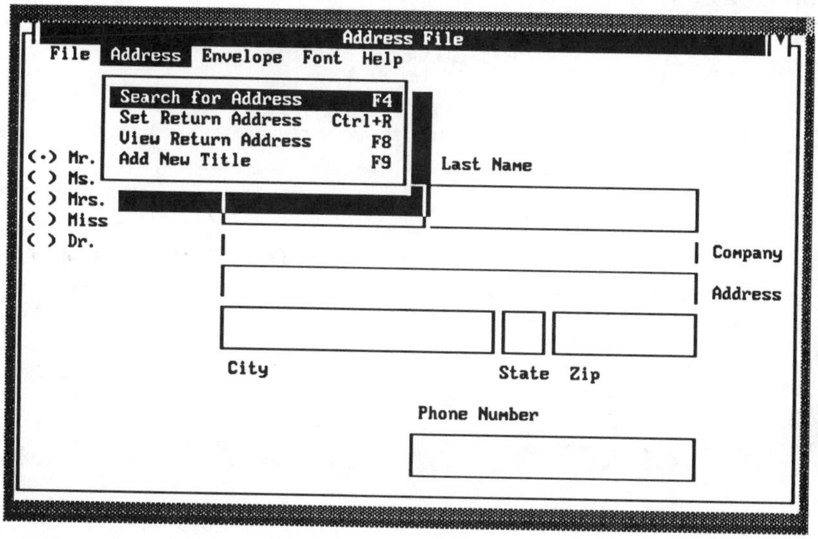

Figure 7-8 The **Address** menu

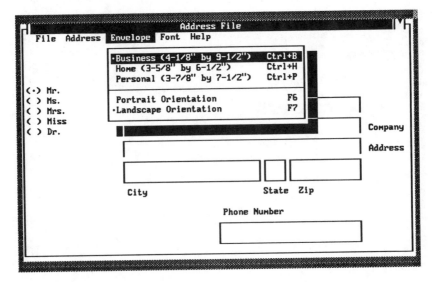

Figure 7-9 The **Envelope** menu

printing techniques corresponding to these two options. You may want to revise parts of the code to take advantage of the features of your own printer.) The **Font** menu contains two options (Figure 7-10)—**Fixed-Space Font** and **Proportional**. The second of these two options is dimmed if you choose the **Portrait Orientation** option in the **Envelope** menu.

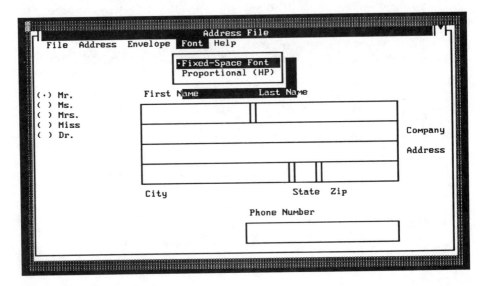

Figure 7-10 The **Font** menu

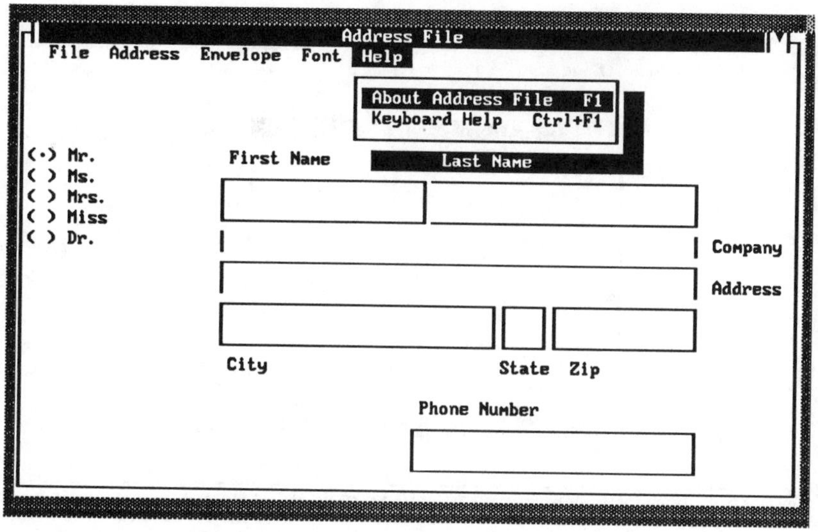

Figure 7-11 The **Help** menu

Finally, the **Help** menu (Figure 7-11) has two commands. The first, **About Address File**, gives a brief description of the program. The second, **Keyboard Help**, displays a message box (Figure 7-12) with a list of the special keys you use for the program's operations.

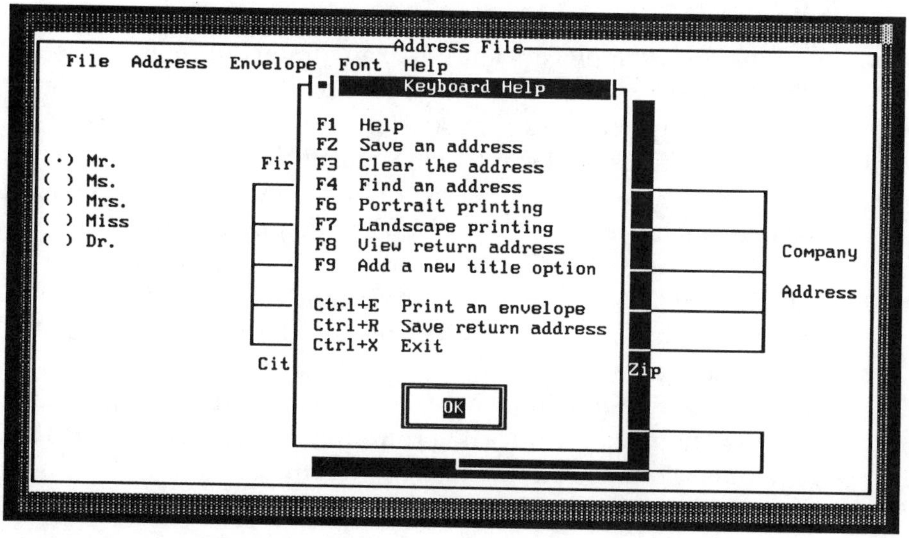

Figure 7-12 The **Keyboard Help** message box

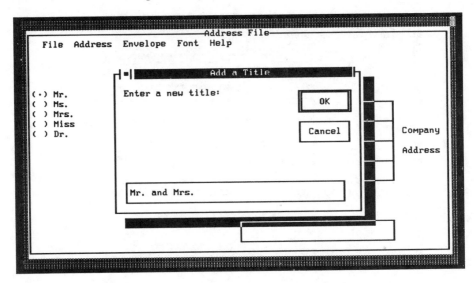

Figure 7-13 The Add a Title dialog box

Adding a Title

The program provides a special dialog box for adding a new title to the list of option buttons. *To add a new title, press the F9 function key.* The dialog box shown in Figure 7-13 appears on the screen. Enter a new title in the text box at the bottom of the dialog box and then click the **OK** button. In response, the program adds the new title to the bottom of the list of option buttons. For example, in Figure 7-14 an option button has been added for the title *Mr. and Mrs.* Once you add a new title, you can select it as the option for any new or existing address record.

The program allows you to add as many as ten new titles to the list. In addition, you can add the special option *(none)* to the list if your address database includes records for which you do not want to include a title. To add the *(none)* option, press F9 and enter any part of the label "(none)" into the text box—for example, enter **none**, or **no**, or simply **n**. When you later select this option for a given record, the program prints the record without a title.

The complete list of titles becomes a permanent part of your customized address database: The titles that you add to the list reappear in the *Address File* form each time you restart the program.

The Filing System for the Address Database

The *Address File* application creates and works with four files, all stored in the root directory of drive C. The main database, named ADDRESS.DAT,

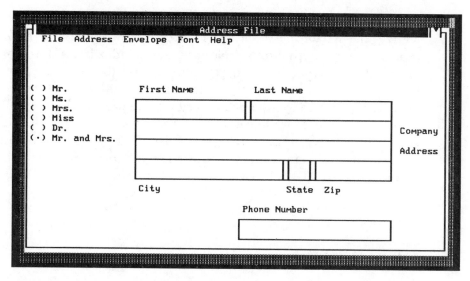

Figure 7-14 Adding a new title option

is opened as a *random-access* file. This means that the program can read any individual record directly from the file—or rewrite any record to the file—if the correct record number is available. For example, to read the tenth record in the file the program does *not* first have to read through the first nine records; rather, the program goes directly to the tenth record position and reads the address information.

The purpose of the index array is to supply the program with the record number for any address stored in the database. The index file, AD-DRESS.NDX, contains a list of the names from the database, along with the corresponding record numbers. Each time you store a new address record in the database, the program also appends another index line to the end of ADDRESS.NDX. Here is how the index might appear after you have stored a dozen addresses in your database file:

```
"MATSEN ELIZA",1
"HARRIS JOHN",2
"CLARK MARY",3
"WU NANCY",4
"ANDERSON SHEILA", 5
"DOE JANET",6
"BARTON RUDY",7
"JOHNSON DIANE",8
"SANDBERG TOM",9
"PETERSON SALLY",10
"VAN DYKE MARTHA",11
"SANCHEZ JACK", 12
```

Each line consists of a string and an integer. The string gives the last name and first name entries from a record in the database, and the integer represents the record number. Notice that the index is not stored on disk in alphabetical order. The program alphabetizes the index in memory at the beginning of a run and then realphabetizes the list each time a new name is added. Given this alphabetized list, the program uses an efficient search technique for finding a particular name whenever you press the F2 key. If the name is found in the index list, the program then reads the entire address directly from the specified record location in the database.

A file named ADDRESS.RTN stores your return address. Here is an example:

```
Mr. Jack Smith
XYZ Corp.
888 Maple Drive
St. Louis, MO 63123
```

This file contains three or four lines of text, depending on whether your return address includes a company name. The program rewrites the file whenever you record a new return address. When you print an envelope, the program reads the text of the return address directly from this file and prints it in the upper-left corner of the envelope.

Finally, the program creates a file named ADDRESS.TTL to save any new titles you add to the list of option buttons. This text file contains a line for each title you include in the list; for example:

```
Mr. and Mrs.
Madame
The Honorable
Professor
Dean
The Reverend
Rabbi
```

The program looks for this file each time you start the application. If the file exists, the program adds each title in the file to the list of option buttons in the **Title** array.

THE ELEMENTS OF THE ADDRESS FILE PROGRAM

The *Address File* project consists of a single form, stored on disk as IN-ADDR.FRM. The form contains a small variety of controls: eight text boxes, eight descriptive labels, and the array of option buttons.

The events in the program are primarily **Click** events for the menu commands. The program recognizes keyboard commands—such as F2, F4, or Ctrl+E—thanks to the shortcut keys defined for the menu system. Before examining the code, take a brief look at the application's controls and menu definition.

Controls, Properties, and Menus

The application's eight text boxes have predictable **CtlName** settings: **FirstName, LastName, Company, Address, City, State, Zip,** and **Phone.** Their **Text** settings all start out as empty strings. As you have seen, the group of option buttons located at the left of the text boxes is defined as a control array named **Title.** The five initial controls in the array have **Index** numbers from **0** to **4.**

The program's menu definition includes five menu lists. The **Envelope** menu illustrates the use of a *separator bar*—a line that separates two groups of commands in the menu. Turn back to Figure 7-9 to see what this line looks like in the menu display. It separates the three commands related to envelope size—**Business, Home,** and **Personal**—from the two printer orientation commands, **Portrait** and **Landscape.**

Figure 7-15 shows how the separator bar is created in the Menu Design Window. The **Caption** entry is blank, but the separator bar must have a distinct **CtlName** setting. You simply click the **Separator** option to define the entry as a separator bar.

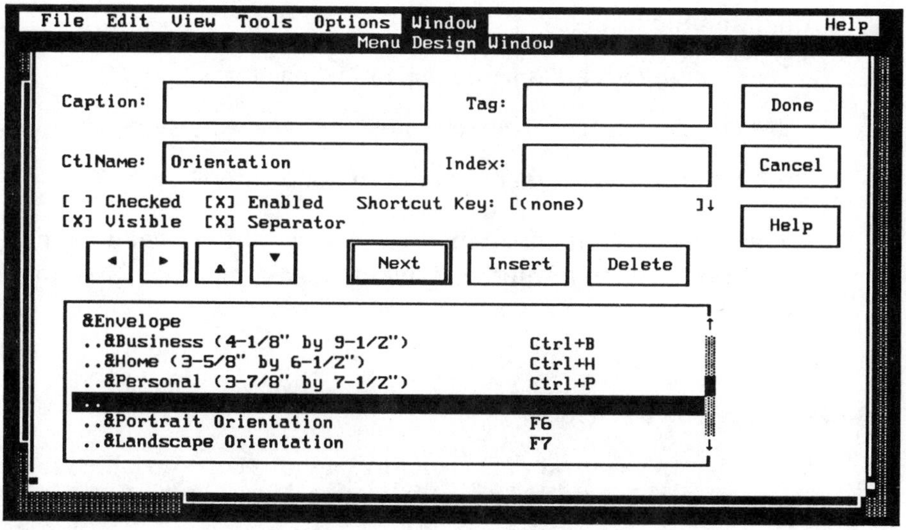

Figure 7-15 The separator bar for the **Envelope** menu

Events

Three categories of events occur in the *Address File* application:

- As usual, the **Form_Load** event is the first to take place. The program's **Form_Load** procedure performs a series of initializations and other startup tasks.

- A **GotFocus** event occurs each time the user selects one of the text boxes. As you have seen in other applications, each **GotFocus** procedure in the program arranges to highlight the contents of the text box that has received the focus.

- Finally, a **Click** event occurs whenever you select a command or an option from one of the program's menus. Keep in mind that the same **Click** event is triggered by any keyboard or mouse technique that you use to invoke a particular menu command. For example, any one of these operations results in a call to the event procedure named **PrintEnv_Click:** pressing the shortcut key Ctrl+E, typing the sequence of access keys Alt+F+P, or clicking the **Print Envelope** command with the mouse.

PROCEDURES AND METHODS

The complete code for the *Address File* application is shown in Listings 7-1 to 7-20. As you examine the code, you'll concentrate on three main programming topics:

1. Creating and managing dynamic data arrays

2. Using a control array to customize the application's options

3. Sending data and commands to the printer

The program contains about three dozen event procedures and general procedures. The following section guides you through a first brief look at the code.

An Overview of the Code

The program's central data structures are a record variable and an array of records. Accordingly, the program's form-level declarations (Listing 7-1) include two record types. The first, **AddrRecType**, outlines the structure of a database record:

```
TYPE AddrRecType
  TitleField AS INTEGER
  FirstField AS STRING * 20
  LastField AS STRING * 20
  CoField AS STRING * 50
  AddrField AS STRING * 50
  CityField AS STRING * 30
  StateField AS STRING * 2
  ZipField AS STRING * 10
  PhoneField AS STRING * 30
END TYPE
```

The second, **IndexType**, represents an element of the index array:

```
TYPE IndexType
  FullName AS STRING * 41
  RecNum AS INTEGER
END TYPE
```

Also in the form-level declaration section, two variables are created from these record types. The record variable named **AddrRec** is defined to store the current address record throughout the program performance:

```
DIM SHARED AddrRec AS AddrRecType
```

And the dynamic array of records named **AddrIndex** represents the database index:

```
DIM SHARED AddrIndex() AS IndexType
```

Notice that the length of the index array is not specified at this point.

The **Form_Load** procedure (Listing 7-2) opens the address database file and computes the number of records currently in the database. This number is stored in the global variable **AddrCount**. Assuming **AddrCount** is greater than zero, the program calls a general procedure named **ReadIndex** (Listing 7-3) to read the index file into memory.

Subsequent action depends on the user's activities and commands. For example, the user might begin by entering a new record in the input form and pressing F2 for a *save* operation. In response, the **SaveAddr_Click** procedure (Listing 7-4) saves the new record to the database file, first checking to make sure that the target name does not already exist in the database. After storing a new address record, the program also adds the current name to the index list. The **SortAddrIndex** procedure (Listing 7-6) realphabetizes the list.

When the user enters a name and presses F4 to retrieve the corresponding address record, the **SearchAddr_Click** procedure (Listing 7-5) reads the record from the database. This procedure in turn uses a function named **SearchIndex%** (Listing 7-6) to search efficiently through the index list for the target name.

Three procedures are in charge of saving and displaying the user's return address. The **SetRtnAddr_Click** procedure (Listing 7-8) writes the address to a text file on disk. The **ViewRtnAddr_Click** procedure (Listing 7-9) displays the address in a message box when the user presses F8. **ReadReturnAddr** (Listing 7-10) reads the address from disk and stores it in a special string array in memory, where it is available whenever the user wants to print an envelope.

A variety of simple **Click** procedures respond to the user's other menu choices. For example, **ClearAddr_Click** (Listing 7-12) blanks out all the text boxes in the input form when the user presses F3. **GeneralHelp_Click** and **KeyHelp_Click** (Listing 7-14) supply help messages if the user selects a command from the **Help** menu. The **Landscape_Click** and **Portrait_Click** procedures (Listing 7-15) make the appropriate changes in the menu system when the user selects one of the two orientation options from the **Envelope** menu. Likewise, **FixedFont_Click** and **PropFont_Click** (Listing 7-16) are in charge of adjusting the settings for fixed- or proportional-font printing.

The program's most detailed procedures are the ones that print envelopes. The **PrintEnv_Click** procedure (Listing 7-17) chooses between two different approaches for printing, depending on currently selected menu options. **PrintLandscapeEnv** (Listing 7-19) is the default printing procedure. It bypasses Visual Basic's **Printer** object, instead using the **PRINT#** statement to send text directly to the printer. This allows the program to send a greater variety of printer codes to a laser printer—including the code for landscape printing. In contrast, the **PrintPortraitEnv** procedure (Listing 7-20) takes the much simpler approach of printing data via the **Printer** object.

Finally, the three procedures that deal with additions to the **Title** array are shown in Listing 7-18. **AddTitle_Click** is called when the user presses F9 or chooses the **Add New Title** command from the **Address** menu. This procedure uses Visual Basic's **INPUTBOX$** function to display a dialog box on the screen, eliciting the text for the user's new title entry. When the entry is complete, the procedure calls the **LoadNewTitle** routine (also listed in Listing 7-18) to add the new option button to the *Address File* form and then opens ADDRESS.TTL to append the new entry to the file.

The program calls the **ReadTitleFile** procedure (Listing 7-18) at the beginning of each performance to read ADDRESS.TTL—if the file exists—and add the custom titles to the form.

Using a Dynamic Data Array

The **AddrIndex** array allows the program to locate address records or to determine whether a given name has been stored in the database. The **ReadIndex** procedure (Listing 7-3) is responsible for resizing this array whenever new records are added to the database. Two event procedures make calls to **ReadIndex**. First, the **Form_Load** procedure determines the initial size of the database; the number of records is stored in the global variable **AddrCount**. If **AddrCount** is greater than zero, the program calls **ReadIndex**:

```
IF AddrCount > 0 THEN ReadIndex
```

Each time the user adds a new record to the database, the **SaveAddr_Click** procedure increases the value of **AddrCount** by one:

```
AddrCount = AddrCount + 1
```

The **SaveAddr_Click** procedure then appends a new entry to the end of the index file and calls **ReadIndex** to rebuild the index array:

```
OPEN IndexFile FOR APPEND AS #1
  WRITE #1, BuildIndexName(), PutPos
CLOSE #1
ReadIndex
```

In short, the **AddrCount** variable always has a new value at the time **ReadIndex** is called. Accordingly, **ReadIndex** begins by defining a new size for the **AddrIndex** array:

```
REDIM AddrIndex(AddrCount) AS IndexType
```

The array now contains an element for each record in the database. To rebuild the index, the **ReadIndex** procedure reads the index file from disk and then makes a call to the **SortAddrIndex** procedure to alphabetize the new index:

```
OPEN IndexFile FOR INPUT AS #1
  FOR i% = 1 TO AddrCount
    INPUT #1, AddrIndex(i%).FullName, AddrIndex(i%).RecNum
  NEXT i%
CLOSE #1
SortAddrIndex
```

To summarize, here are the steps that the program uses to maintain the database index in the **AddrIndex** array:

1. Use a **DIM** statement to declare the dynamic array—without specifying a length—in the form-level declaration section.

2. After calculating the number of records in the database, define the initial length of the array in a **REDIM** statement. Read the index file into the array and alphabetize the list.

3. Perform the **REDIM** statement again each time the user adds a new address record. After redimensioning, reread the index file into the array and sort the array once again.

Using a Control Array to Customize the TITLE Options

As you've seen, the *Address File* application allows additions to the list of titles at the left side of the main dialog box. The three routines that manage this feature are all shown in Listing 7-18. When the user first presses F9 (or selects the **Add New Title** command), the **AddTitle_Click** procedure elicits the caption for a new option button and calls the **LoadNewTitle** procedure to add the new control to the form:

```
NewTitle$ = INPUTBOX$("Enter a new title:", "Add a Title")
  IF NewTitle$ <> "" THEN
    ' ...
    LoadNewTitle NewTitleIndex%, NewTitle$
```

The **LoadNewTitle** routine receives the index as **i%** and the title text as **TitleCaption$**. Accordingly, it uses the **LOAD** command to add a new element to the **Title** array and then sets the caption and other properties of the new option button:

```
SUB LoadNewTitle (i%, TitleCaption$)
  LOAD Title(i%)
  Title(i%).Visible = True
  Title(i%).Enabled = True
  Title(i%).Height = 1
  Title(i%).Width = 18
  Title(i%).Left = 0
  Title(i%).Top = 4 + i%
  Title(i%).Caption = TitleCaption$
```

Back in the **AddTitle_Click** procedure, the program increments the value of the **NewTitleIndex%** variable and stores the text of this new option button in the ADDRESS.TTL file:

```
NewTitleIndex% = NewTitleIndex + 1

OPEN TitleFile FOR APPEND AS #1
  PRINT #1, NewTitle$
CLOSE #1
```

These custom additions to the **Title** array are defined only during run time. (You can confirm that this is true by examining the *Address File* form again in the form development environment; you'll see that only the original five option buttons appear on the form.) But to maintain the integrity of the database, the application must redisplay these added titles whenever the user restarts the application. After all, the user can select any option button from the list as the title field for a given address record.

For this reason, the program makes a call to the **ReadTitleFile** procedure at the beginning of each program run. This routine checks to see if the ADDRESS.TTL file exists. If it finds the file, the routine reads each line of text and loads a new option button onto the *Address File* form for each custom title:

```
DO WHILE NOT EOF(1)
  LINE INPUT #1, NewTitle$
  LoadNewTitle NewTitleIndex%, NewTitle$
  NewTitleIndex% = NewTitleIndex% + 1
LOOP
```

Finally, the procedure checks to see if the **NewTitleIndex%** counter has gone past the maximum number allowed for the list of title options. If so, the program disables the **Add New Title** command in the **Address** menu:

```
IF NewTitleIndex% > MaxTitles THEN AddTitle.Enabled = False
```

This prevents any further additions to the **Title** array.

Printing Techniques

The **Printer** object is a versatile tool for sending information to the printer. Visual Basic defines three useful methods for this object to perform specific printing operations:

- The PRINT method sends lines of text to the printer.
- The NEWPAGE method feeds forward to the top of the next piece of paper.
- The ENDDOC method completes a printing operation and releases the entire job to the printer.

Despite the convenience of these tools, occasionally you may need a way to send printer-specific commands directly to the printer device, without passing through the **Printer** object. Your printer might have capabilities that are not supported by the **Printer** object. For example, Visual Basic does not supply a tool for switching between landscape and portrait orientation for a laser printer. You need a different technique for sending commands to the printer for these characteristics.

The solution to this problem lies with traditional I/O statements that Visual Basic inherits from previous versions of the language. Specifically, the following form of the **OPEN** command opens an output channel for sending text directly to the printer:

```
OPEN "Prn" FOR OUTPUT AS #1
```

Once this channel is open, you can use **PRINT #1** statements to send text output to the printer. The output can include lines of printable characters, along with control sequences and other special characters that your printer interprets as commands and option selections.

The *Address File* application illustrates both of these very different approaches to printing. The **PrintLandscapeEnv** procedure (Listing 7-19) uses **PRINT#** statements to send specific printing commands to a laser printer. In contrast, the **PrintPortraitEnv** procedure (Listing 7-20) takes advantage of the **Printer** object. Take a brief look at both of these procedures now.

Using the PRINT# Statement

The **PrintLandscapeEnv** procedure defines four string constants to represent specific command codes for the HP LaserJet printer:

```
CONST FixedCode = "(s0P"      ' Fixed-space font.
CONST PropCode = "(s1P"       ' Proportional font.
CONST LandCode = "&l1O"       ' Landscape printing.
CONST PortraitCode = "&l0O"   ' Portrait printing.
```

Given these codes, the routine begins its output to the printer with two command sequences:

```
PRINT #1, CHR$(27) + CurFont$
PRINT #1, CHR$(27) + LandCode
```

These commands represent a font setting and the landscape-orientation switch for the printer. Each begins with the escape character (**CHR$(27)**), which signals the beginning of a control command. The **CurFont$** string contains one of two settings—either **FixedCode** or **PropCode**, depending on the current setting in the **Font** menu.

After sending these two control commands, the **PrintLandscapeEnv** procedure writes the text for the return address and the destination address, again using the **PRINT#** statement. For example, here is the output for the return address:

```
FOR i% = 0 TO 3
  PRINT #1, Indent$; ReturnAddrLines(i%)
NEXT i%
```

A form-feed character completes the printing operation after text for the two addresses has been sent:

```
PRINT #1, CHR$(FormFeed)
```

(The procedure defines **FormFeed** as an integer constant with a value of 12. **CHR$(12)** is the form-feed character.)

Finally, when both addresses have been printed, the routine resets the printing modes and closes the output channel:

```
PRINT #1, CHR$(Esc) + PortraitCode
PRINT #1, CHR$(Esc) + FixedCode

CLOSE #1
```

This approach requires detailed understanding of your printer's command codes. Use the **OPEN** and **PRINT#** commands for printer output only when the **Printer** object does not meet your printing requirements.

Using the Printer Object

The **PrintPortraitEnv** procedure uses the **Printer.PRINT** method to send the two addresses to the printer. For example, here is the sequence for the return address:

```
FOR i% = 0 TO 3
  Printer.PRINT Indent$; ReturnAddressLines(i%)
NEXT i%
```

When both addresses have been printed, calls to the **NEWPAGE** and **ENDDOC** methods complete the output operation:

```
Printer.NEWPAGE
Printer.ENDDOC
```

ENDDOC sends a signal that the completed document can be released to the printer.

SUMMARY: DATA STRUCTURES AND CONTROL ARRAYS

Visual Basic's data arrays and control arrays give you flexible ways to manage data and controls in an application.

You can define data arrays as *static* or *dynamic* structures. The length of a static array remains fixed throughout program execution. In contrast, a program establishes the dimensions of a dynamic array at run time. Both kinds of arrays have important uses. In general, you should use static arrays whenever you can be certain of the amount of data that an application will generate; the *Sales Week* application contains examples. On the other hand, a dynamic array is the better choice when the dimensions of the data are not known until run time—or when the length of data can change one or more times during run time.

For example, the *Address File* application builds an index that increases in length each time the user adds a new record to the address database. Defining this index as a static array could cause two different problems:

- For a small address database, the array might actually be larger than necessary, and therefore waste memory space.

- As the address database grows over time, the array might at some point turn out to be too small, placing an upper limit on the number of records the program can handle.

The *Address File* program rereads the index list from disk after redimensioning the array.

Like data arrays, Visual Basic's control arrays have a built-in flexibility that proves very useful in applications that must respond dynamically to run-time events. You can use control arrays—along with the **LOAD** and **UNLOAD** statements—to add or remove controls during program execution.

Finally, this chapter's application example illustrates another Visual Basic data structure known as a *user-defined structure,* or simply a *record.* A record structure, representing multiple fields belonging to different data types, is an important structure in database management applications. You can learn more about records and databases by reviewing the *Real Estate* application. This program, originally introduced in Chapter 1, is described in much greater detail in Chapter 8.

Listing 7-1 Form-level declarations

```
' The Address Program (ADDRESS.MAK)

' INADDR.FRM
' Declarations.

DECLARE SUB ReadIndex ()
DECLARE SUB SortAddrIndex ()
DECLARE FUNCTION SearchIndex% ()
DECLARE FUNCTION BuildIndexName$ ()
DECLARE FUNCTION ReadReturnAddr () AS INTEGER
DECLARE SUB BusinessEnv_Click ()
DECLARE FUNCTION Trm$ (TextBox AS CONTROL)
DECLARE SUB Landscape_Click ()
DECLARE SUB PrintLandscapeEnv ()
DECLARE SUB PrintPortraitEnv ()
DECLARE SUB ReadTitleFile ()
DECLARE SUB LoadNewTitle (i%, TitleCaption$)
DECLARE SUB ClearAddr_Click ()
DECLARE SUB FixedFont_Click ()

' The address record type.

TYPE AddrRecType
  TitleField AS INTEGER
  FirstField AS STRING * 20
  LastField AS STRING * 20
  CoField AS STRING * 50
  AddrField AS STRING * 50
  CityField AS STRING * 30
  StateField AS STRING * 2
  ZipField AS STRING * 10
  PhoneField AS STRING * 30
END TYPE

' The index record type.

TYPE IndexType
  FullName AS STRING * 41
  RecNum AS INTEGER
END TYPE

' The names of the four files
```

(continued)

```
' this program creates and reads.

CONST AddrFile = "C:\ADDRESS.DAT"
CONST IndexFile = "C:\ADDRESS.NDX"
CONST ReturnAddr = "C:\ADDRESS.RTN"
CONST TitleFile = "C:\ADDRESS.TTL"

' The maximum number of titles in the
' list of option buttons.

CONST MaxTitles = 14

' Boolean values.

CONST False = 0
CONST True = NOT False

DIM SHARED AddrRec AS AddrRecType        ' An address record.
DIM SHARED AddrIndex() AS IndexType      ' The index array.
DIM SHARED AddrCount AS INTEGER          ' Current number of
records.

DIM SHARED TitleStr$                  ' "Mr. ", "Mrs. ", etc.
DIM SHARED NewTitleIndex%             ' Index for new title.
DIM SHARED ReturnAddrLines$(3)        ' Return address lines.
DIM SHARED NumPrintFonts AS INTEGER      ' Number of printer
fonts.

DIM SHARED CrLf$                        ' Carriage return, line feed.
```

Listing 7-2 The Form_Load procedure

```
SUB Form_Load ()

    ' Initialize variables and menu options and
    ' check the length of the address database.

    ' Carriage-return, line feed.
    CrLf$ = CHR$(13) + CHR$(10)
```

```
' Open the database file and find
' out how many records it contains.

OPEN AddrFile FOR RANDOM AS #1 LEN = LEN(AddrRec)
   AddrCount = LOF(1) / LEN(AddrRec)
CLOSE #1

' If the database is not empty, read the index.

IF AddrCount > 0 THEN ReadIndex

' Initialize the title list.

NewTitleIndex% = 5
ReadTitleFile
Title(0).Value = True

END SUB  ' Form_Load
```

Listing 7-3 The ReadIndex procedure

```
SUB ReadIndex ()

   ' Read the index file for the address database.

   ' First redimension the AddrIndex array for
   ' storing the index at its current length.

   REDIM AddrIndex(AddrCount) AS IndexType

   OPEN IndexFile FOR INPUT AS #1
      FOR i% = 1 TO AddrCount
         INPUT #1, AddrIndex(i%).FullName, AddrIndex(i%).RecNum
      NEXT i%
   CLOSE #1

   ' Arrange the index in alphabetical order.
   SortAddrIndex

END SUB  ' ReadIndex
```

Listing 7-4 The SaveAddr_Click procedure

```
SUB SaveAddr_Click ()

  ' Save the current address in the database.

  CONST Yes = 6, No = 7
  DIM LocPos AS INTEGER, PutPos AS INTEGER
  DIM DoSave AS INTEGER, NewRecord AS INTEGER

  ' Don't save a blank record.

  IF Trm$(FirstName) = "" OR Trm$(LastName) = "" THEN
     MSGBOX "Can't save a record without a name.", 48,
"Address File"
     EXIT SUB
  END IF

  ' Check index to see if this name already exists.

  LocPos = SearchIndex%()

  ' If so, give the user the options of writing over the
  ' existing record or abandoning the save operation.

  IF LocPos > 0 THEN
     Msg$ = "This name is already in the database." + CrLf$
     Msg$ = Msg$ + " Do you want to change the address
record? "

     IF MSGBOX(Msg$, 4, "Address File") = Yes THEN
       DoSave = True
       NewRecord = False
       PutPos = LocPos
     ELSE
       DoSave = False
     END IF

  ELSE  ' This is a new record.

     DoSave = True
```

```
   ' Increment the record count.

   AddrCount = AddrCount + 1
   PutPos = AddrCount
   NewRecord = True
 END IF


 ' Save the record.

 IF DoSave THEN
   AddrRec.TitleField = 0
   FOR i% = 0 TO NewTitleIndex% - 1
     IF Title(i%).Value THEN AddrRec.TitleField = i% + 1
   NEXT i%

   AddrRec.FirstField = FirstName.Text
   AddrRec.LastField = LastName.Text
   AddrRec.CoField = Company.Text
   AddrRec.AddrField = Address.Text
   AddrRec.CityField = City.Text
   AddrRec.StateField = State.Text
   AddrRec.ZipField = Zip.Text
   AddrRec.PhoneField = Phone.Text

   OPEN AddrFile FOR RANDOM AS #1 LEN = LEN(AddrRec)
     PUT #1, PutPos, AddrRec
   CLOSE #1

   ' If this is a new record, add a new entry to the index.

   IF DoSave AND NewRecord THEN
     OPEN IndexFile FOR APPEND AS #1
       WRITE #1, BuildIndexName(), PutPos
     CLOSE #1
     ReadIndex
   END IF

 END IF

END SUB  ' SaveAddr_Click
```

Listing 7-5 The SearchAddr_Click procedure

```
SUB SearchAddr_Click ()

  ' Search for the current address in the database.

  DIM TargetPos%

  ' Find the name in the index and read the record's
  ' position. (A return value of zero indicates that
  ' the record is not in the database.)

  TargetPos% = SearchIndex%()

  IF TargetPos% <> 0 THEN

    ' Read the record.

    OPEN AddrFile FOR RANDOM AS #1 LEN = LEN(AddrRec)
      GET #1, TargetPos%, AddrRec
    CLOSE #1

    ' Display the fields of the record in
    ' the appropriate text boxes.

    FirstName.Text = AddrRec.FirstField
    LastName.Text = AddrRec.LastField
    Company.Text = AddrRec.CoField
    Address.Text = AddrRec.AddrField
    City.Text = AddrRec.CityField
    State.Text = AddrRec.StateField
    Zip.Text = AddrRec.ZipField
    Phone.Text = AddrRec.PhoneField

    ' Display the title field as a selected option button.

    IF AddrRec.TitleField <> 0 AND AddrRec.TitleField <=
NewTitleIndex% THEN
        Title(AddrRec.TitleField - 1).Value = True
    END IF

  ' If the record does not exist, inform the user.

  ELSE
```

```
      Msg$ = FirstName.Text + " " + LastName.Text
      Msg$ = Msg$ + " is not in the database."
      MSGBOX Msg$, 48, "Address File"
   END IF

END SUB  ' SearchAddr_Click
```

Listing 7-6 The SortAddrIndex procedure and the SearchIndex% function

```
SUB SortAddrIndex ()

  ' Alphabetize the index.

  DIM TempAddrRec AS IndexType

  FOR i% = 1 TO AddrCount - 1
    FOR j% = i% + 1 TO AddrCount
      IF AddrIndex(i%).FullName > AddrIndex(j%).FullName THEN
        TempAddrRec = AddrIndex(i%)
        AddrIndex(i%) = AddrIndex(j%)
        AddrIndex(j%) = TempAddrRec
      END IF
    NEXT j%
  NEXT i%

END SUB  ' SortAddrIndex


FUNCTION SearchIndex% ()

  ' Search through the index for the name that
  ' the user has entered into the FirstName and
  ' LastName text boxes.

  DIM AddrFound%, StartPos%, EndPos%, CenterPos%, SearchName$

  AddrFound% = 0
  StartPos% = 1
  EndPos% = AddrCount
```

(continued)

```
' Build the target name in the format used in the index.

SearchName$ = BuildIndexName$()

' Perform a binary search.

DO WHILE ((AddrFound% = 0) AND (StartPos% <= EndPos%))
  CenterPos% = (StartPos% + EndPos%) \ 2

  SELECT CASE SearchName$
    CASE RTRIM$(AddrIndex(CenterPos%).FullName)
      AddrFound% = AddrIndex(CenterPos%).RecNum
    CASE IS > AddrIndex(CenterPos%).FullName
      StartPos% = CenterPos% + 1
    CASE ELSE
      EndPos% = CenterPos% - 1
  END SELECT
LOOP

' Return the record number if the name was found
' or a value of zero if the name was not found.

SearchIndex% = AddrFound%

END FUNCTION   ' SearchIndex%
```

Listing 7-7 The BuildIndexName$ and Trm$ functions

```
FUNCTION BuildIndexName$ ()

  ' Prepare the current name in the
  ' correct format for the index.

  DIM TempName$

  TempName$ = Trm$(LastName) + " " + Trm$(FirstName)
  BuildIndexName$ = UCASE$(TempName$)

END FUNCTION   ' BuildIndexName$
```

```
FUNCTION Trm$ (TextBox AS CONTROL)

  ' Trim spaces from the beginning
  ' and the end of a string.

  Trm$ = LTRIM$(RTRIM$(TextBox.Text))

END FUNCTION   ' Trm$
```

Listing 7-8 The SetRtnAddr_Click procedure

```
SUB SetRtnAddr_Click ()

  ' Save the current address as the return address.
  ' (Note: A blank address can be saved if the user does
  ' not want to print a return address on an envelope.)

  DIM Co$, Place$

  OPEN ReturnAddr FOR OUTPUT AS #1

    PRINT #1, TitleStr$;
    PRINT #1, Trm$(FirstName); " ";
    PRINT #1, Trm$(LastName)

    Co$ = Trm$(Company)
    IF Co$ <> "" THEN PRINT #1, Co$

    PRINT #1, Trm$(Address)
    Place$ = Trm$(City)
    IF Place$ <> "" THEN PRINT #1, Place$; ", ";
    PRINT #1, Trm$(State); " ";
    PRINT #1, Trm$(Zip)

  CLOSE #1

END SUB   ' SetRtnAddr_Click
```

Listing 7-9 The ViewRtnAddr_Click Procedure

```
SUB ViewRtnAddr_Click ()

  ' Display a message box with the return address.

  DIM temp$, maxLength%

  IF ReadReturnAddr() THEN

  ' Find the length of the longest line
  ' in the return address.

    maxLength% = 0
    FOR i% = 0 TO 3
      IF LEN(ReturnAddrLines$(i%)) > maxLength% THEN
        maxLength% = LEN(ReturnAddrLines$(i%))
      END IF
    NEXT i%

  ' Use LSET to left-justify the return address
  ' in the message box.

    Msg$ = ""
    FOR i% = 0 TO 3
      temp$ = SPACE$(maxLength%)
      LSET temp$ = ReturnAddrLines$(i%)
      Msg$ = Msg$ + temp$ + CrLf$
    NEXT i%
  ELSE
    Msg$ = "No return address found on disk."
  END IF

  MSGBOX Msg$, 64, "Return Address"

END SUB  ' ViewRtnAddr_Click
```

Listing 7-10 The ReadReturnAddr function

```
FUNCTION ReadReturnAddr () AS INTEGER

  ' Read the return address from its
  ' text file on disk.

  DIM OkReturn AS INTEGER, LineNum AS INTEGER

  ' First check to see if the file exists.

  OkReturn = True
  ON LOCAL ERROR GOTO NoReturnAddress
    OPEN ReturnAddr FOR INPUT AS #2
  ON ERROR GOTO 0

  IF OkReturn THEN

    ' Blank out any previous return address.

    FOR i% = 0 TO 3
      ReturnAddrLines$(i%) = ""
    NEXT i%

    LineNum = 0
    DO WHILE NOT EOF(2)
      LINE INPUT #2, ReturnAddrLines$(LineNum)
      LineNum = LineNum + 1
    LOOP
    CLOSE #2
  END IF

  ' Return a Boolean value indicating
  ' whether or not the file exists.

  ReadReturnAddr = OkReturn

  EXIT FUNCTION

' Error routine for missing file.

NoReturnAddress:
  OkReturn = False
RESUME NEXT

END FUNCTION   ' ReadReturnAddr
```

Listing 7-11 The GotFocus event procedures

```
SUB Address_GotFocus ()

  ' Highlight the contents of the text box.

  Address.SelStart = 0
  Address.SelLength = LEN(LTRIM$(RTRIM$(Address.Text)))

END SUB   ' Address_GotFocus


SUB City_GotFocus ()

  ' Highlight the contents of the text box.

  City.SelStart = 0
  City.SelLength = LEN(LTRIM$(RTRIM$(City.Text)))

END SUB   ' City_GotFocus


SUB Company_GotFocus ()

  ' Highlight the contents of the text box.

  Company.SelStart = 0
  Company.SelLength = LEN(LTRIM$(RTRIM$(Company.Text)))

END SUB   ' Company_GotFocus


SUB FirstName_GotFocus ()

  ' Highlight the contents of the text box.

  FirstName.SelStart = 0
  FirstName.SelLength = LEN(LTRIM$(RTRIM$(FirstName.Text)))

END SUB   ' FirstName_GotFocus
```

```
SUB LastName_GotFocus ()

  ' Highlight the contents of the text box.

  LastName.SelStart = 0
  LastName.SelLength = LEN(LTRIM$(RTRIM$(LastName.Text)))

END SUB  ' LastName_GotFocus


SUB Phone_GotFocus ()

  ' Highlight the contents of the text box.

  Phone.SelStart = 0
  Phone.SelLength = LEN(LTRIM$(RTRIM$(Phone.Text)))

END SUB  ' Phone_GotFocus


SUB State_GotFocus ()

  ' Highlight the contents of the text box.

  State.SelStart = 0
  State.SelLength = LEN(LTRIM$(RTRIM$(State.Text)))

END SUB  ' State_GotFocus


SUB Zip_GotFocus ()

  ' Highlight the contents of the text box.

  Zip.SelStart = 0
  Zip.SelLength = LEN(LTRIM$(RTRIM$(Zip.Text)))

END SUB  ' Zip_GotFocus
```

Listing 7-12 ClearAddr_Click and Quit_Click

```
SUB ClearAddr_Click ()

  ' Clear the current address.

  TitleStr$ = ""
  FirstName.Text = ""
  LastName.Text = ""
  Company.Text = ""
  Address.Text = ""
  City.Text = ""
  State.Text = ""
  Zip.Text = ""
  Phone.Text = ""

  ' Select the first option button and move the
  ' focus to the first text box.

  Title(0).Value = True
  FirstName.SETFOCUS

END SUB   ' ClearAddr.Click


SUB Quit_Click ()

  ' Terminate the program.

  END

END SUB   ' Quit_Click
```

Listing 7-13 Click event procedures for miscellaneous menu options

```
SUB BusinessEnv_Click ()

  ' Display a check next to the Business
  ' option in the Envelope menu.

  BusinessEnv.Checked = True
```

```
    HomeEnv.Checked = False
    PersonalEnv.Checked = False

END SUB  ' BusinessEnv_Click


SUB HomeEnv_Click ()

  ' Display a check next to the Home
  ' option in the Envelope menu.

  BusinessEnv.Checked = False
  HomeEnv.Checked = True
  PersonalEnv.Checked = False

END SUB  ' HomeEnv_Click


SUB PersonalEnv_Click ()

  ' Display a check next to the Personal
  ' option in the Envelope menu.

  BusinessEnv.Checked = False
  HomeEnv.Checked = False
  PersonalEnv.Checked = True

END SUB  ' PersonalEnv_Click
```

Listing 7-14 Click event procedures for Help menu options

```
SUB GeneralHelp_Click ()

    ' Display a message box describing the program.

    DIM Msg$

    Msg$ = "The Address File application manages an     " +
CrLf$
    Msg$ = Msg$ + "address database. You can press F2 to
" + CrLf$
```

(continued)

```
        Msg$ = Msg$ + "save an address, or F4 to find the " + CrLf$
        Msg$ = Msg$ + "address for a given name. The program also "
+ CrLf$
        Msg$ = Msg$ + "prints envelopes in a variety of sizes.      "

        MSGBOX Msg$, 64, "About Address File"

END SUB   ' GeneralHelp_Click




SUB KeyHelp_Click ()

   ' Display a list of special keys
   ' that the program uses.

   Msg$ = "F1   Help                          " + CrLf$
   Msg$ = Msg$ + "F2   Save an address          " + CrLf$
   Msg$ = Msg$ + "F3   Clear the address        " + CrLf$
   Msg$ = Msg$ + "F4   Find an address          " + CrLf$
   Msg$ = Msg$ + "F6   Portrait printing        " + CrLf$
   Msg$ = Msg$ + "F7   Landscape printing       " + CrLf$
   Msg$ = Msg$ + "F8   View return address      " + CrLf$
   Msg$ = Msg$ + "F9   Add a new title option " + CrLf$ + CrLf$

   Msg$ = Msg$ + "Ctrl+E  Print an envelope   " + CrLf$
   Msg$ = Msg$ + "Ctrl+R  Save return address" + CrLf$
   Msg$ = Msg$ + "Ctrl+X  Exit                "

   MSGBOX Msg$, 64, "Keyboard Help"

END SUB   ' KeyHelp_Click
```

Listing 7-15 The Landscape_Click and Portrait_Click procedures

```
SUB Landscape_Click ()

   ' Switch to the landscape printing mode.

   ' Make the switch only if the Landscape
   ' option is not currently checked.
```

```
   IF NOT Landscape.Checked THEN

     Landscape.Checked = True
     Portrait.Checked = False

     ' Enable the Home and Personal envelope options.

     HomeEnv.Enabled = True
     PersonalEnv.Enabled = True

     ' Enable the Proportional font option.

     PropFont.Enabled = True

   END IF

END SUB   ' Landscape_Click


SUB Portrait_Click ()

   ' Switch to the Portrait printing mode.

   ' Make the switch only if the Portrait
   ' option is not currently checked.

   IF NOT Portrait.Checked THEN

     Portrait.Checked = True
     Landscape.Checked = False

   ' Disable the Home and Personal envelope options.

     BusinessEnv_Click
     HomeEnv.Enabled = False
     PersonalEnv.Enabled = False

   ' Disable the Proportional font option.

     PropFont.Enabled = False
     FixedFont_Click

   END IF

END SUB   ' Portrait_Click
```

Listing 7-16 The FixedFont_Click and PropFont_Click procedures

```
SUB FixedFont_Click ()

  ' Change to the fixed-font option.

  PropFont.Checked = False
  FixedFont.Checked = True

END SUB   ' FixedFont_Click


SUB PropFont_Click ()

  ' Change to the proportional-font option.

  PropFont.Checked = True
  FixedFont.Checked = False

END SUB
```

Listing 7-17 The PrintEnv_Click procedure

```
SUB PrintEnv_Click ()

  ' Read the title selection.

  FOR i% = 0 TO NewTitleIndex% - 1
    IF Title(i%).Value THEN
      IF Title(i%).Caption <> "(none)" THEN
        TitleStr$ = Title(i%).Caption + " "
      ELSE
        TitleStr$ = ""
      END IF
    END IF
  NEXT

  ' Choose between two printing modes.

  IF Portrait.Checked THEN
```

```
      PrintPortraitEnv
   ELSE
      PrintLandscapeEnv
   END IF

END SUB   ' PrintEnv_Click
```

Listing 7-18 The AddTitle_Click, LoadNewTitle, and ReadTitleFile procedures

```
SUB AddTitle_Click ()

   ' Give the user the opportunity to add a new title
   ' to the list (Mr., Ms., Miss, etc.).

   NewTitle$ = INPUTBOX$("Enter a new title:", "Add a Title")

   IF RTRIM$(NewTitle$) <> "" THEN

      ' Test for an entry of "(none)"

      IF INSTR("(none)", NewTitle$) > 0 THEN NewTitle$ = "(none)"

      ' Load a new option button for the title.

      LoadNewTitle NewTitleIndex%, NewTitle$
      NewTitleIndex% = NewTitleIndex% + 1

      ' Save the title to ADDRESS.TTL

      OPEN TitleFile FOR APPEND AS #1
        PRINT #1, NewTitle$
      CLOSE #1

      ' Limit the number of new titles.

      IF NewTitleIndex% > MaxTitles THEN AddTitle.Enabled =
False
   END IF

END SUB   ' AddTitle_Click
```

(continued)

```
SUB LoadNewTitle (i%, TitleCaption$)

  ' Add a title to the list of option buttons.

    LOAD Title(i%)
    Title(i%).Visible = True
    Title(i%).Enabled = True
    Title(i%).Height = 1
    Title(i%).Width = 18
    Title(i%).Left = 0
    Title(i%).Top = 4 + i%
    Title(i%).Caption = TitleCaption$

END SUB   ' LoadNewTitle


SUB ReadTitleFile ()

  ' Read ADDRESS.TTL and add the titles
  ' to the list of option buttons.

  DIM TitleFileExists AS INTEGER

  ' First check to see if the file exists.

  TitleFileExists = True
  ON LOCAL ERROR GOTO NoTitleFile
    OPEN TitleFile FOR INPUT AS #1
  ON ERROR GOTO 0

  IF TitleFileExists THEN

    DO WHILE NOT EOF(1)
      LINE INPUT #1, NewTitle$
      LoadNewTitle NewTitleIndex%, NewTitle$
      NewTitleIndex% = NewTitleIndex% + 1
    LOOP
    CLOSE #1

    IF NewTitleIndex% > MaxTitles THEN AddTitle.Enabled =
False

  END IF
```

```
   EXIT SUB

' Error routine for missing file.

NoTitleFile:
  TitleFileExists = False
RESUME NEXT

END SUB   ' ReadTitleFile
```

Listing 7-19 The PrintLandscapeEnv procedure

```
SUB PrintLandscapeEnv ()

  ' Print the envelope in the landscape mode.
  ' (This routine uses HP LaserJet printer commands.)

  CONST FormFeed = 12   ' Chr$(12) is the form-feed character.
  CONST No = 7          ' The code for a "No" answer in a
message box.
  CONST Esc = 27        ' Escape code.

  ' HP printer commands:

  CONST FixedCode = "(s0P"      ' Fixed-space font.
  CONST PropCode = "(s1P"       ' Proportional font.
  CONST LandCode = "&l1O"       ' Landscape printing.
  CONST PortraitCode = "&l0O"   ' Portrait printing.

  DIM OkReturnAddr AS INTEGER, i%
  DIM Indent1$, Indent2$, CurFont$
  DIM FirstLine AS INTEGER, SkipLines AS INTEGER

  ' Read the setting for the envelope size and
  ' adjust the indent strings accordingly.

  IF BusinessEnv.Checked THEN
    Indent1$ = SPACE$(20)
  ELSEIF HomeEnv.Checked THEN
    Indent1$ = SPACE$(45)
```

(continued)

```
ELSE
  Indent1$ = SPACE$(35)
END IF

Indent2$ = SPACE$(70)

' Read the selection in the font menu and
' set the correct HP LaserJet code.

IF FixedFont.Checked THEN
  CurFont$ = FixedCode
ELSE
  ' Proportional font.
  CurFont$ = PropCode
  Indent1$ = Indent1$ + Indent1$
  Indent2$ = Indent2$ + Indent2$
END IF

FirstLine = 10
SkipLines = 6

' Set an error trap, in case the printer is
' not ready. Then attempt to print the envelope.

ON LOCAL ERROR GOTO NotReady
  OPEN "Prn" FOR OUTPUT AS #1

  ' Send the font code and the code
  ' for landscape printing.

  PRINT #1, CHR$(Esc) + CurFont$
  PRINT #1, CHR$(Esc) + LandCode

  FOR i% = 1 TO FirstLine
    PRINT #1,
  NEXT i%

  ' Print the return address if one exists.

  OkReturnAddr = ReadReturnAddr()
  FOR i% = 0 TO 3
    PRINT #1, Indent1$; ReturnAddrLines$(i%)
  NEXT i%
```

```
      FOR i% = 1 TO SkipLines
        PRINT #1,
      NEXT i%

      PRINT #1, Indent2$; TitleStr$;
      PRINT #1, Trm$(FirstName); " ";
      PRINT #1, Trm$(LastName)

      Co$ = Trm$(Company)
      IF Co$ <> "" THEN PRINT #1, Indent2$; Co$

      PRINT #1, Indent2$; Trm$(Address)

      PRINT #1, Indent2$; Trm$(City); ", ";
      PRINT #1, Trm$(State); " ";
      PRINT #1, Trm$(Zip)

      PRINT #1, CHR$(FormFeed)

      ' Restore portrait printing and fixed space.

      PRINT #1, CHR$(Esc) + PortraitCode
      PRINT #1, CHR$(Esc) + FixedCode

      CLOSE #1
    ON ERROR GOTO 0

    EXIT SUB

  ' Allow the user to abort the printing operation or try
  again.

  NotReady:
    Ans = MSGBOX("Printer not ready. Try again?", 4, "Printer
  Error")
    IF Ans = No THEN
      CLOSE #1
      EXIT SUB
    END IF

  RESUME

  END SUB   ' PrintLandscapeEnv
```

Listing 7-20 The PrintPortraitEnv procedure

```
SUB PrintPortraitEnv ()

  ' Print the envelope in the portrait mode.

  DIM OkReturnAddr AS INTEGER, i%

  Indent1$ = SPACE$(5)
  Indent2$ = SPACE$(50)

  ' Print the return address.

  OkReturnAddr = ReadReturnAddr()
  FOR i% = 0 TO 3
    Printer.PRINT Indent1$; ReturnAddrLines$(i%)
  NEXT i%

  FOR i% = 1 TO 6
    Printer.PRINT
  NEXT i%

  ' Print the destination address.

  Printer.PRINT Indent2$; TitleStr$;
  Printer.PRINT Trm$(FirstName); " ";
  Printer.PRINT Trm$(LastName)

  Co$ = Trm$(Company)
  IF Co$ <> "" THEN Printer.PRINT Indent2$; Co$

  Printer.PRINT Indent2$; Trm$(Address)

  Printer.PRINT Indent2$; Trm$(City); ", ";
  Printer.PRINT Trm$(State); " ";
  Printer.PRINT Trm$(Zip)

  Printer.NEWPAGE
  Printer.ENDDOC

END SUB  ' PrintPortraitEnv
```

8

Random-Access Files:
The Real Estate Application

INTRODUCTION

The random-access file structure is the key to creating efficient database management applications in Visual Basic. Thanks to a fixed-length record structure, a random-access file gives you direct access to individual data records in a database. Your programs can perform three essential input and output operations with such a file:

- Read a record directly from a target location in the database, without having to read any other records before or after.

- Write revised data over a target record position, without danger of destroying any other information in the database.

- Append a new record to the end of the database file.

The *Address File* application, presented in Chapter 7, is an example of a database application that creates and maintains a random-access file. Chapter 7 discusses the major data structures you are likely to use in this kind of application—a record variable, to represent individual records in the database (see **Review Box 7-1**), and an array, to store the index that the program builds for the database. The alphabetized index contains two items of information about each record in the database:

1. A unique key field for each record
2. Each record's numeric location in the database

With this index, the process of retrieving a target record is simple and direct: The program searches through the index for the key field and makes note of the record number that the index supplies. Given this record number, the program opens the database file and goes directly to the target record to perform an input or output operation.

Along with these two essential data structures, you use three major tools for working with a random-access file:

- An **OPEN** statement opens the file in the **RANDOM** mode and establishes the fixed record length.

- The **GET** statement reads a record from a target record position in the file.

- The **PUT** statement writes a record to the file—either appending a record to the end of the file, or overwriting an existing record.

Review Box 8-1 summarizes the use of these three Visual Basic statements.

In this chapter you'll return to another example of a database management program—the *Real Estate* application, first introduced in Chapter 1. The project is stored on the exercise disk under the name REALEST.MAK. Open the application now so that you can experiment with it and examine its code during the course of this chapter. You'll use this application to explore specific random-access file-handling techniques for a variety of tasks: reading records from the file, revising existing records, appending new records, and maintaining the database index.

THE REAL ESTATE APPLICATION

As you'll recall, the *Real Estate* program creates and maintains a residential real estate database. The program is useful when you are in the market for a new home. Each record in the database contains information about a particular home that is on the market. Figure 8-1 shows a sample record. The majority of the *Real Estate Database* form is taken up by the home description, where the fields include the address of the home, the asking price, the date you viewed the home, and additional details about the property for sale. There is also a **Comments** field in which you can record your own impressions and reactions to the home.

At the right side of the form is a simple calculator that you can use to anticipate the monthly payment on a mortgage for the home. Initially, the program copies the **Asking Price** field directly to the **Amount** text box in the payment calculator. But you can revise this amount if you expect to make an offer that is different from the asking price. You also can make

---

Review Box 8-1:

Random-Access Data Files

A random-access file is organized into individual units of data called *records*. Each record in a random-access file contains a structured group of data items known as *fields*. All the records in a given file have the same fixed length. Thanks to this characteristic, Visual Basic can provide direct access to any record in the file. A record is identified by its *record number*, an integer ranging from 1 up to the number of records currently stored in the file.

Visual Basic's *user-defined structure*, also known as a record structure, is the ideal data structure to use in the definition and creation of a random-access file. A **TYPE** statement defines a record structure, and a subsequent **DIM** statement creates a corresponding record variable. (See **Review Box 7-1** for details.) Along with a defined record structure, the major tools you are likely to use in a random-access file program are the **OPEN** and **CLOSE** statements, the **LOF** function, and the **GET** and **PUT** statements.

The following form of the **OPEN** statement opens a file in the random-access mode:

```
OPEN FileName FOR RANDOM AS #FileNum LEN =
LEN(RecordVariable)
```

In this syntax, *FileName* is the name of the file on disk, *FileNum* is an integer that identifies the open file in subsequent I/O statements, and *RecordVariable* is the name of a variable defined to represent records as they are read from the file or written to the file. This form of the **LEN** clause defines the file's fixed record length to be equal to the length of the record variable. Visual Basic's **LEN** function supplies the length, in bytes, of *RecordVariable*.

Once open, a random-access file is available for both reading and writing. At the outset a program typically needs to find out the number of records currently stored in the file. The following formula uses Visual Basic's **LOF** ("length of file") function to compute the record count:

```
RecordCount% = LOF(FileNum) / LEN(RecordVariable)
```

The **LOF** function takes an integer argument—the file number of the open file—and returns the length, in bytes, of the file. Dividing this value

---

Review Box 8-1: *(continued)*

by the length of the record structure gives the number of records in the file.

The **GET** statement reads a single record from a specified position in the open file:

```
GET #FileNum, RecordNumber, RecordVariable
```

The value of *RecordNumber* ranges from 1 up to the current *RecordCount*. As a result of this statement, the entire record stored at the *RecordNumber* position in the file is assigned to the fields of *RecordVariable*. You can use a **FOR** loop to read a random-access file sequentially:

```
FOR i% = 1 TO RecordCount
  GET #FileNum, i%, RecordVariable
  ' Process the record.
NEXT i%
```

The **PUT** statement writes a single record to a specified position in the open file:

```
PUT #FileNum, RecordNumber, RecordVariable
```

If *RecordNumber* is equal to *RecordCount* + 1, this **PUT** statement appends a new record to the end of the open file. On the other hand, if *RecordNumber* is in the range from 1 to *RecordCount*, **PUT** writes the current contents of *RecordVariable* over an existing record. In this case, the value of the record previously stored at *RecordNumber* is lost.

---

changes in the values of the down payment percentage (20% by default), the loan interest rate (10% by default), and the term of the loan (30 years by default). Each time you change the value in any of the four text boxes of the payment calculator, the program automatically recalculates the monthly mortgage payment amount shown at the lower-right corner of the form. (The values you enter into the mortgage calculator portion of the form are not included as fields in the real estate database.)

The *Real Estate* application performs the basic operations of a typical database management program. To create a new home record, you enter

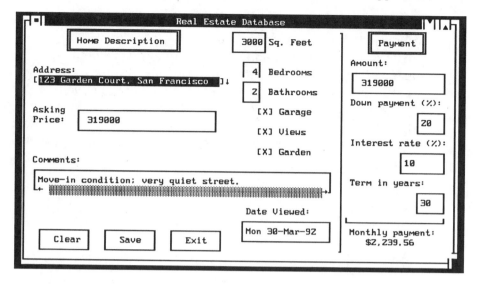

Figure 8-1 The *Real Estate* application

information about the home and click the **Save** button (or press Alt+S). You can easily retrieve an existing record by clicking the target address from the **Address** combo box list. When you do so, the program displays all the information about the home you have selected. You also can revise an existing record: Simply retrieve the record, make changes in any of the data fields other than the address, and click the **Save** button. The program saves your revisions as the new version of the record.

One of the important features of this application is its ability to check for appropriate input as you enter the fields of a home record into the main input form. Input validation applies to numeric fields and to the program's one date field, labeled **Date Viewed**. Take a moment to experiment with this feature now.

Entering the Fields of a Home Record

The main input form has four numeric fields—**Asking Price, Sq. Feet, Bedrooms,** and **Bathrooms**. When you enter a number into one of these text boxes and then move to another control on the form, the program checks your input. If you have entered a valid number, your input remains as it is. However, if you inadvertently enter a string that cannot be converted into a number, the program changes the entry to zero. Finally, if you enter a string of digits followed by a string of nonnumeric characters, the program drops the invalid characters from the entry. For example, an entry of **12345abc** becomes simply **12345**. You have seen this kind of numeric input validation before, in the *Sales Week* application.

The *Real Estate* application also checks dates. The default date entry in the **Date Viewed** field is always the current date. If you are entering a record into the database for a home you have looked at today, you don't have to change the date entry for the record. Otherwise, if you wish to enter a date other than today's date, the program is very flexible in the date input formats it recognizes. For example, any of the following input formats results in a date display of **Fri 3-Apr-92**, assuming the current year is 1992:

```
4/3/92
4/3
4-3
3 Apr
Apr 3, 92
```

Date formats that do not include a year—such as 4/3 and 4-3—are assumed to be in the current year. When you enter a date in any of these formats and then move to a new control on the input form, the *Real Estate* application automatically converts your entry into the program's standard date display format, represented generally as **ddd d-mmm-yy**.

On the other hand, if you enter a text value that the program cannot convert into a date, an error message appears on the screen, as shown in Figure 8-2. When you click OK to return to the input form, the program automatically resets the default date in the **Date Viewed** box. The program

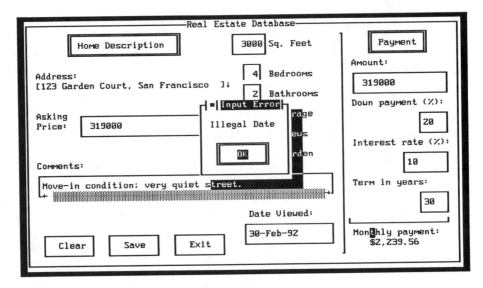

Figure 8-2 Error message for invalid date input

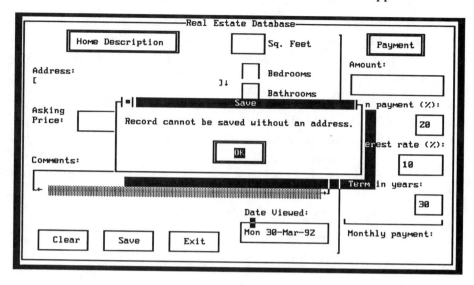

Figure 8-3 Error message for a missing address field

accomplishes its date validation and formatting with the help of built-in date functions that Visual Basic supplies. You'll examine these functions later when you turn to the program's code.

The program also produces an error message if you try to save a home record before entering an address field (Figure 8-3). Because the address is the key for retrieving a record, the program has to insist on a nonblank entry in the **Address** box before appending a new record to the database.

The Database File

The *Real Estate* application creates a single file on disk for the home database. The file's name is HOMES.DB, and it is stored in the root directory of drive C. Because HOMES.DB is structured as a random-access file, each home record takes up the same number of bytes. To maintain this fixed record length, Visual Basic stores each numeric field in a fixed-length binary format. For this reason, a random-access file is not like a text file; you cannot expect to load the file into a text editor and read the information contained in the file. Text fields in the database may be recognizable, but numeric fields will appear on the screen as unreadable sequences of characters. In short, a random-access file is designed to be read by a database program, not by a person.

Unlike the *Address File* application, this program does not maintain a separate disk file for storing the index to the database. Instead, the *Real Estate* application rebuilds the index from scratch at the beginning of each program run. This alternate program design is based on the assumption that the homes database will normally be relatively small—containing, say, dozens of records rather than many hundreds. Here are the initial steps that the program takes to build the index:

1. Open the database file and determine the number of records currently stored in the file.

2. Read through the entire database sequentially, from beginning to end, and build the index array with two items of information for each record: the address, which serves as the key field for retrieving records, and the numeric record number.

3. After reading these two data items from each record in the database, alphabetize the index array.

You'll see the code that performs these steps shortly.

THE ELEMENTS OF THE REAL ESTATE APPLICATION

The *Real Estate* project consists of a single input form, named REAL-EST.FRM on disk. The form contains the code both for maintaining the real estate database and for performing the mortgage payment calculations. The database operations are the main focus of your attention in this chapter.

Controls and Properties

The **RealEst** form contains a varied assortment of controls—text boxes, a combo box, check boxes, and command buttons, along with various labels that identify the controls. In order to follow the structure of the program's code, you'll need to be familiar with the **CtlName** settings of these controls:

- The text boxes in the home description area of the form represent the major features of a house, along with the date of your visit and your comments: **AskPrice**, **SqFeet**, **Bedrooms**, **Bathrooms**, **DateViewed**, and **Comments**.

- The combo box, with a **CtlName** of **Address**, represents the data field that is the key for retrieving records from the database.

- The three check boxes—each with a true or false setting that the user establishes at run time—complete the information about the home: **Garage**, **Views**, and **Garden**.

- The command buttons represent the program's database operations: **ClearButton**, **SaveButton**, and **ExitButton**.

- At the right side of the form the four text boxes have control names of **InPrice**, **InDown**, **InRate**, and **InTerm**. These are the four input values for a given mortgage calculation.

One of the text boxes has a special property setting you should notice. The **Comments** box has an attached horizontal scroll bar, giving the user an easy way to scroll through a comment that is too long to be displayed on the screen in its entirety. The **ScrollBars** property controls the presence of this feature. In the case of the **Comments** text box, the property's setting is **1-Horizontal**.

The **Address** combo box also has an important characteristic that makes the user-interface more convenient. Combo boxes have a property named **Sorted**, which determines whether or not the items in a drop-down list will appear in sorted order. The default setting for this property is **False**. The **Address** control's **Sorted** property has a nondefault setting of **True**. Under this setting, Visual Basic automatically alphabetizes the addresses in the drop-down list, even as the program adds new records to the database.

Events

The events recognized in the *Real Estate* application include:

- A **GotFocus** event for each of the text boxes. The corresponding event procedure arranges to highlight the entire current contents of the text box. This is an operation you have seen in other applications, including *Sales Week* and *Address File*.

- A **LostFocus** event for the text boxes that represent date and numeric fields. The **LostFocus** event procedures perform the application's input validations. In addition, the **LostFocus** procedures for the four text boxes of the mortgage payment calculator make calls to a procedure named **CalcPayment** whenever the user changes any of the four mortgage parameters.

- **Click** events for the command buttons.

- A **Click** event for the **Address** combo box. When the user selects an address from the drop-down list of addresses, the **Address_Click** event retrieves the corresponding home record and displays it in the input form.

Procedures and Methods

The event procedures and general procedures from the **RealEst** form appear in Listings 8-1 to 8-10. As you examine the **RealEst** procedures, you'll concentrate on the database operations they perform—saving, retrieving, and revising records. In addition, you'll learn how the program handles date input for the **Date Viewed** text box.

Opening the Database and Building the Index

The application's form-level declarations (Listing 8-1) include definitions for two record types: **HomeRecordType** and **IndexRecordType**. **HomeRecordType** identifies the ten fields of a record stored in the database itself. **IndexRecordType** defines the two fields of the index structure—the key address field (**AddressRef**) and the record number (**RecNo**):

```
TYPE IndexRecordType
   AddressRef AS String * 50
   RecNo AS Integer
END TYPE
```

The program creates a variable and an array belonging to these two record types. First, **HomeRecord** is the variable that will represent individual records read from or written to the database:

```
DIM SHARED HomeRecord AS HomeRecordType
```

The **AddressList** array serves as the index into the database:

```
DIM SHARED AddressList(MaxRecords) AS IndexRecordType
```

Unlike the *Address File* application, the *Real Estate* application uses a static array rather than a dynamic array to represent the index. The fixed length of the **AddressList** array is specified in the following constant definition:

```
CONST MaxRecords = 400
```

It is important to understand the significance of this definition. Because the index for the database has a fixed length, the program must place an upper limit on the number of records that can be entered into the database itself. In a practical sense this limitation is not likely to matter to users of the *Real Estate* application; there is, after all, an upper limit to the number of homes a house hunter will view before making a decision. However, if you find that you want to expand the home database beyond the length currently allowed by the program, you can make either of two revisions in the code:

- Increase the value of the **MaxRecords** constant.
- Restructure the database index, **AddressList**, as a dynamic array.

The second of these two revisions is a particularly interesting programming exercise, which you might want to try after you have finished studying the current version of the program.

The form-level declaration section also defines a string constant that represents the file name of the database:

```
CONST HomeDataBase = "C:\HOMES.DB"
```

The **Form_Load** procedure for the **RealEst** form (Listing 8-2) issues an **Open** statement to open this database as a random-access file:

```
OPEN HomeDataBase FOR RANDOM AS #1 LEN = LEN(HomeRecord)
```

Notice that this statement uses the length of the **HomeRecord** variable to define the record length inside the file. The program then divides the length of the file by the length of a single record to calculate the current number of records in the file.

```
RecCount = LOF(1) / LEN(HomeRecord)
```

The **RecCount** variable is declared at the form level, and is therefore available to all the procedures in the **RealEst** form.

After determining the size of the database, the **Form_Load** procedure reads sequentially through the entire file and builds the index. A **FOR** loop reads each record from the first to the last:

```
FOR i% = 1 TO RecCount
   GET #1, i%, HomeRecord
```

Immediately after reading a record, the program adds the record's address to the drop-down list attached to the **Address** combo box. The **AddItem** method accomplishes this task:

```
Address.ADDITEM HomeRecord.Address
```

Finally, the procedure assigns the address string to the **AddressRef** field of the current **AddressList** record and the record number to the **RecNo** field:

```
AddressList(i%).AddressRef = UCASE$(HomeRecord.Address)
AddressList(i%).RecNo = i%
```

The final step for building the index is to sort the list of addresses. A call to a general procedure named **SortAddressList** (Listing 8-4) does the job:

```
SortAddressList
```

This procedure uses a pair of nested **FOR** loops to compare each address in the index list with each address after it. Whenever two addresses are out of order, they are swapped. At the end of the looping, the addresses in the list are sorted in alphanumeric order. Now the index is ready to be used for retrieving records from the database.

The next events in the program depend upon the user's input activities and command choices.

Database Management Techniques

If the user enters the ten fields of a new home record and then clicks the **Save** button, the **SaveButton_Click** procedure (Listing 8-3) writes the record to the database. This procedure needs a way to distinguish between a new record that the user wants to append to the database and a revised record that the user wants to write over an existing record. To find out which of these is the situation for the current record, the program searches through the index for the current **Address** field. If the address already exists, the program assumes this is a revision; if not, this is a new record.

A call to the **SearchHomeRec%** function searches for the current address entry in the index:

```
CurRec% = SearchHomeRec%(HomeRecord.Address)
```

The **SearchHomeRec%** function (Listing 8-4) performs an efficient operation known as the *binary search*. This process continually divides the sorted address list into smaller and smaller pairs of sections, always focusing the search on the section in which the target address will ultimately be found if it exists. This approach minimizes the number of actual comparisons during the search. If the routine finds the address in the index list, **SearchHomeRec%** returns the corresponding record number—that is, the position of the record in the database. If the address is not found, **SearchHomeRec%** returns a value of zero. The **SaveButton_Click** procedure stores this return value in the **CurRec%** variable.

If **CurRec%** is zero, then the current text box entries represent a new home record. Accordingly, **SaveButton_Click** must perform several steps to add the record to the database:

1. Increase **RecCount** by 1:

```
RecCount = RecCount + 1
```

2. Copy the address and the record number to the index and then sort the index once again:

```
AddressList(RecCount).AddressRef = UCASE$(HomeRecord.Address)
AddressList(RecCount).RecNo = RecCount
SortAddressList
```

3. Copy all the fields of the new record to the **HomeRecord** variable. Some of these fields are copied by the appropriate **LostFocus** procedures as soon as the user completes a numeric data entry. For example, the **AskPrice_LostFocus** procedure copies the asking price into the **HomeRecord.AskPrice** field:

```
HomeRecord.AskPrice = VAL(AskPrice.Text)
```

Remaining fields are copied by the **SaveButton_Click** procedure:

```
HomeRecord.Comments = Comments.Text
HomeRecord.Garage = Garage.Value
HomeRecord.Views = Views.Value
HomeRecord.Garden = Garden.Value
```

4. Write the complete home record to the end of the database:

```
CurRec% = RecCount
'  ...
OPEN HomeDataBase FOR RANDOM AS #1 LEN = LEN(HomeRecord)
   PUT #1, CurRec%, HomeRecord
CLOSE #1
```

If the record already exists, **CurRec%** is the record's position in the database. In this case, the same **OPEN**, **PUT**, and **CLOSE** statements write the new version of the record to its correct place in the database.

SaveButton_Click anticipates one additional contingency. If the number of records in the database reaches the defined maximum—**MaxRecords**—the procedure cannot allow the user to save any new records:

```
ELSEIF CurRec% = 0 AND Reccount = MaxRecords THEN
```

The program displays an alert box on the screen and performs a premature exit from the **SaveButton_Click** procedure:

```
MSGBOX Msg$, 48, "Real Estate Database"
EXIT SUB
```

Figure 8-4 shows the message that appears on the desktop in this situation.

Of course, if you decide to revise the program—restructuring the database index as a dynamic array—you can eliminate this passage from

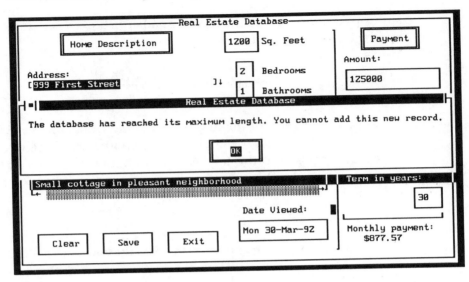

Figure 8-4 Error message displayed when database is "full"

the **SaveButton_Click** procedure. Here is an outline of the steps required for this revised version:

1. A **REDIM PRESERVE** statement increases the size of the **Address-List** array after each new record is added to the database.

2. The procedure next adds an index entry for the newly appended record.

3. Finally, a call to the **SortAddressList** procedure rearranges the index, using the address field as the key to the sort.

The action of selecting an address from the drop-down **Address** list triggers a call to the **Address_Click** event procedure (Listing 8-5). This procedure's job is to read the selected record from the database and then to display its fields in the **RealEst** form. The first step is to look up the record number from the index, a task performed by a call to the **SearchHomeRec%** function:

```
GetRec% = SearchHomeRec%((Address.Text))
```

This call illustrates an important detail regarding procedures and arguments. By default, an argument variable is passed to a procedure or a function *by reference* in Visual Basic. This means that the procedure receives the argument's *address* in memory and can potentially change the value of that variable. However, Visual Basic does not allow the value of a control property—for example, the **Text** property of a text box—to be sent by reference as an argument. Instead, a control property must be sent *by value*. This means that Visual Basic makes a copy of the argument and sends the copy to the procedure or function, thus protecting the original argument from changes.

There are two ways to send an argument by value in Visual Basic. One way is simply to enclose the argument in parentheses in the procedure call. This is the technique used in the call to the **SearchHomeRec%** function:

```
SearchHomeRec((Address.Text))
```

Notice the double parentheses. The outer parentheses are required in the syntax of any function call. The inner parentheses indicate that the argument **Address.Text** is to be sent by value.

The other technique is to use the keyword **BYVAL** in the argument list of the procedure or function itself. For example, here is how you could rewrite the first line of the **SearchHomeRec%** function:

```
Function SearchHomeRec% (BYVAL InAddress$)
```

Because this function makes no attempt to change the value of **InAddress$**, the **BYVAL** keyword is a reasonable alternative. But note that some procedures and functions are designed to use argument variables—specifically, arguments that are passed by reference—to send information back to the calling procedure. In these cases, you should use parentheses in the procedure call—rather than **BYVAL** in the procedure definition—if you want to protect a particular argument variable from changes.

After the call to the **SearchHomeRec%** function, the **Address_Click** procedure uses the record number—stored in the variable **GetRec%**—to read the selected record directly from its position in the database:

```
OPEN HomeDateBase FOR RANDOM AS #1 LEN = LEN(HomeRecord)
GET #1, GetRec%, HomeRecord
CLOSE #1
```

This **Get** statement reads the record stored at position **GetRec%** and stores the entire record in the fields of the **HomeRecord** variable. The procedure subsequently copies each field to its corresponding control in the **RealEst** form:

```
AskPrice.Text = LTRIM$(STR$(HomeRecord.AskPrice))
SqFeet.Text = LTRIM$(STR$(HomeRecord.SqFeet))
Bedrooms.Text = LTRIM$(STR$(HomeRecord.Bedrooms))
Bathrooms.Text = LTRIM$(STR$(HomeRecord.Bathrooms))
Garage.Value = HomeRecord.Garage
```

```
Garden.Value = HomeRecord.Garden
Views.Value = HomeRecord.Views
DateViewed.Text = FORMAT$(HomeRecord.DateViewed,
DateFormat)
Comments.Text = HomeRecord.Comments
```

The procedure uses the **STR$** function to convert numeric fields into string values. Only a string value can be assigned to the **Text** property of a text box.

Finally, note the use of Visual Basic's **FORMAT$** function to convert the **DateViewed** field into a displayable date format:

```
DateViewed.Text = FORMAT$(HomeRecord.DateViewed,
DateFormat)
```

HomeRecord.DateViewed is a serial date, stored in the database as a double-precision real value. As illustrated in the *Sales Week* application, the **FORMAT$** function supports a great variety of formats for converting serial dates into date display strings. In the *Real Estate* program, the following constant establishes the display format for any date that appears in the **Date Viewed** text box:

```
CONST DateFormat = "ddd d-mmm-yy"
```

In fact, the program takes care of converting any date entry into this standard date format.

Accepting Dates as Input from the Keyboard

The **DateViewed_LostFocus** procedure (Listing 8-7) validates any date that the user enters into the **Date Viewed** text box. If the entry is a valid date, the procedure copies the date to the **HomeRecord.DateViewed** field and then redisplays the value in the standard date format. If the entry is not valid, the procedure displays an error message (Figure 8-2) and instead stores today's date in the text box.

Visual Basic's **DATEVALUE** function accepts a date string as its argument and returns the equivalent serial date as its result. As you saw earlier in this chapter, **DATEVALUE** accepts date strings in a variety of recognizable formats. However, if the function receives a date string that cannot be converted into a date, Visual Basic generates a run-time error. For this reason, **DateViewed_LostFocus** requires an error trap to deal with the possibility of an invalid date entry:

```
ON LOCAL ERROR GOTO BadDate
```

Within the control of this error trap, the following statement attempts to convert value of **DateViewed.Text** to a serial date and to assign the value to the **HomeRecord.DateViewed** field:

```
HomeRecord.DateViewed = DATEVALUE(DateViewed.Text)
```

If an error occurs in this process—that is, if the user's date entry cannot be recognized—control jumps down to the error routine at **BadDate**:

```
BadDate:

  MSGBOX "Illegal Date", 48, "Input Error"
  DateError% = True


RESUME NEXT
```

This routine displays the error message and switches the **DateError%** flag to true. Back in the main part of the procedure, the following statement reinitializes the date if an error has taken place:

```
IF DateError% THEN InitDate
```

The **InitDate** procedure (Listing 8-7) simply assigns today's date to the **DateViewed** field:

```
HomeRecord.DateViewed = NOW
```

Then—whether the date is supplied by the user or reinitialized by the program—the following statement standardizes the display format:

```
DateViewed.Text = FORMAT$(HomeRecord.DateViewed,
DateFormat)
```

In short, the *Real Estate* application uses the following Visual Basic functions to handle date entries appropriately:

- The **DATEVALUE** function returns the serial date value from a date string.
- The **FORMAT$** function produces a formatted date string from a serial date.
- The **NOW** function supplies the serial date value for the current system date and time.

SUMMARY: DATABASE MANAGEMENT IN VISUAL BASIC

In any database programming environment, the first step in creating a successful database is to define an appropriate record structure. The user-defined record structure is the tool to use for this definition in Visual Basic. A **TYPE** statement outlines the fields of a record structure and a subsequent **DIM** statement creates a record variable.

References to this record variable appear in several different file statements. First, the statement that opens the database uses the variable to establish the fixed record length of a random-access file:

```
OPEN FileName FOR RANDOM AS #1 LEN = LEN(RecordVariable)
```

Once the file is open, the record variable also has a role in the calculation of the number of records currently in the database. The record count is equal to the length of the open file divided by the length of the record variable.

```
RecordCount = LOF(1) / LEN(RecordVariable)
```

Finally, the **GET** and **PUT** statements that perform input and output operations on the database use the record variable to represent individual record values. As a result of a **GET** statement, a record is read from the database and stored in the record variable:

```
GET #1, RecordNumber, RecordVariable
```

And a **PUT** statement writes a new record to the file:

```
PUT #1, RecordNumber, RecordVariable
```

In advance of the **PUT** statement, the program assigns a complete set of field values to the record variable.

A database management program typically builds an index structure to provide efficient access to records in the database. The index has at least two values for each record: a field value that serves as the key for a record search and the corresponding record number. The program keeps the index sorted by the key field. Given this sorted index, an algorithm known as the *binary search* performs an efficient search for a given record in the index. After a successful search, the index provides the numeric position in the database where the target record will be found.

Listing 8-1 RealEst form-level declarations

```
' The Real Estate Program (REALEST.MAK)

' REALEST.FRM
' Declarations

DECLARE SUB CalcPayment ()
DECLARE SUB ClearHomeRecord ()
DECLARE SUB InitDate ()
DECLARE SUB SortAddressList ()
DECLARE FUNCTION SearchHomeRec% (InAddress$)
DECLARE SUB HighlightEntry (InBox AS CONTROL)

' The record type definition for a home description:

TYPE HomeRecordType
  Address AS STRING * 50
  AskPrice AS LONG
  SqFeet AS INTEGER
  Bedrooms AS INTEGER
  Bathrooms AS INTEGER
  Garage AS INTEGER
  Views AS INTEGER
  Garden AS INTEGER
  DateViewed AS DOUBLE
  Comments AS STRING * 125
END TYPE

' The record type definition for the address index:

TYPE IndexRecordType
  AddressRef AS STRING * 50
  RecNo AS INTEGER
END TYPE

' Boolean constants.

CONST False = 0
CONST True = NOT False

' The program's standard date display format.

CONST DateFormat = "ddd d-mmm-yy"
```

(continued)

```
' The database file name.

CONST HomeDataBase = "C:\HOMES.DB"

' The maximum number of home records.

CONST MaxRecords = 400

' The HomeRecord and AddressList structures.

DIM SHARED HomeRecord AS HomeRecordType
DIM SHARED AddressList(MaxRecords) AS IndexRecordType
DIM SHARED RecCount AS INTEGER
```

Listing 8-2 The Form_Load Procedure

```
SUB Form_Load ()

   ' When the form is first loaded, initialize
   ' the date field and its display.

   InitDate

   ' Then open the home database file and read
   ' the records sequentially.

   OPEN HomeDataBase FOR RANDOM AS #1 LEN = LEN(HomeRecord)
   RecCount = LOF(1) / LEN(HomeRecord)

   ' Store the address field and the record number
   ' in the AddressList index.

   FOR i% = 1 TO RecCount
      GET #1, i%, HomeRecord
      Address.ADDITEM HomeRecord.Address
      AddressList(i%).AddressRef = UCASE$(HomeRecord.Address)
      AddressList(i%).RecNo = i%
   NEXT i%
   CLOSE #1

   ClearHomeRecord
```

```
' Alphabetize the index.

SortAddressList

END SUB   ' Form_Load
```

Listing 8-3 The SaveButton_Click procedure

```
SUB SaveButton_Click ()

  ' Save a new address in the database.

  DIM Msg$, CurRec%, HomeAddr$

  HomeAddr$ = LTRIM$(RTRIM$(Address.Text))
  IF HomeAddr$ = "" THEN

    ' Do not try to save without an address field.

    Msg$ = "Record cannot be saved without an address."
    MSGBOX Msg$, 48, "Save"
    Address.SETFOCUS

  ELSE

    HomeRecord.Address = HomeAddr$

    ' Find out if this record exists already.

    CurRec% = SearchHomeRec%(HomeRecord.Address)

    ' If not, create a new record.

    IF CurRec% = 0 AND RecCount < MaxRecords THEN

      ' First add the address to the index.

      RecCount = RecCount + 1
      AddressList(RecCount).AddressRef =
UCASE$(HomeRecord.Address)
      AddressList(RecCount).RecNo = RecCount
      SortAddressList
```

(continued)

```
    ' Add the address to the combo box list.

    Address.ADDITEM HomeRecord.Address
    CurRec% = RecCount

  ELSEIF CurRec% = 0 AND RecCount = MaxRecords THEN

    ' Display a message if the database is full,
    ' and go no further with the save operation.

    Msg$ = "The database has reached its maximum length. "
    Msg$ = Msg$ + "You cannot add this new record."
    MSGBOX Msg$, 48, "Real Estate Database"
    EXIT SUB

  END IF

  ' Read the fields that have not already been read.

  HomeRecord.Comments = Comments.Text
  HomeRecord.Garage = Garage.Value
  HomeRecord.Views = Views.Value
  HomeRecord.Garden = Garden.Value

  ' Write the record to the database. If this is a new
  ' record, CurRec% is the new length of the database.
  ' For revising a record, CurRec% is the numeric
  ' position of the existing record.

  OPEN HomeDataBase FOR RANDOM AS #1 LEN = LEN(HomeRecord)
    PUT #1, CurRec%, HomeRecord
  CLOSE #1
  END IF

END SUB   ' SaveButton_Click
```

Listing 8-4 The SortAddressList procedure and the SearchHomeRec function

```
SUB SortAddressList ()

  ' Alphabetize the database index.
```

```
    DIM TempAddressRec AS IndexRecordType

    FOR i% = 1 TO RecCount - 1
      FOR j% = i% + 1 TO RecCount
        IF AddressList(i%).AddressRef >
AddressList(j%).AddressRef THEN
          TempAddressRec = AddressList(i%)
          AddressList(i%) = AddressList(j%)
          AddressList(j%) = TempAddressRec
        END IF
      NEXT j%
    NEXT i%

END SUB   ' SortAddressList



FUNCTION SearchHomeRec% (InAddress$)

  ' Search for an address in the database index.

  AddrFound% = 0
  startPos% = 1
  endPos% = RecCount

  DO WHILE ((AddrFound% = 0) AND (startPos% <= endPos%))
    centerPos% = (startPos% + endPos%) \ 2
    SELECT CASE UCASE$(InAddress$)
      CASE AddressList(centerPos%).AddressRef
        AddrFound% = AddressList(centerPos%).RecNo
      CASE IS > AddressList(centerPos%).AddressRef
        startPos% = centerPos% + 1
      CASE ELSE
        endPos% = centerPos% - 1
    END SELECT
  LOOP

  ' Return the record number if the address was found;
  ' otherwise return a value of zero.

  SearchHomeRec% = AddrFound%

END FUNCTION   ' SearchHomeRec%
```

Listing 8-5 The Address_Click procedure

```
SUB Address_Click ()

  ' Retrieve an address record when the user selects
  ' an address from the Address combo box.

  GetRec% = SearchHomeRec%((Address.Text))
  IF GetRec% <> 0 THEN
    OPEN HomeDataBase FOR RANDOM AS #1 LEN = LEN(HomeRecord)
    GET #1, GetRec%, HomeRecord
    CLOSE #1

    ' Copy the fields of the address record to the
    ' appropriate controls on the input form.

    AskPrice.Text = LTRIM$(STR$(HomeRecord.AskPrice))
    SqFeet.Text = LTRIM$(STR$(HomeRecord.SqFeet))
    Bedrooms.Text = LTRIM$(STR$(HomeRecord.Bedrooms))
    Bathrooms.Text = LTRIM$(STR$(HomeRecord.Bathrooms))
    Garage.Value = HomeRecord.Garage
    Garden.Value = HomeRecord.Garden
    Views.Value = HomeRecord.Views
    DateViewed.Text = FORMAT$(HomeRecord.DateViewed,
DateFormat)
    Comments.Text = HomeRecord.Comments
  END IF

  ' Complete the Payment section of the form.

  InPrice.Text = AskPrice.Text
  CalcPayment

END SUB  ' Address_Click
```

Listing 8-6 The ClearButton_Click, ClearHomeRecord, and ExitButton_Click procedures

```
SUB ClearButton_Click ()

  ' Clear all the string and numeric text boxes,
  ' and reinitialize the date field.

  Address.Text = ""
```

```
      AskPrice.Text = ""
      Comments.Text = ""
      SqFeet.Text = ""
      Bedrooms.Text = ""
      Bathrooms.Text = ""
      InitDate
      Garage.Value = False
      Views.Value = False
      Garden.Value = False
      Address.SETFOCUS

      InPrice.Text = ""
      InDown.Text = "20"
      InRate.Text = "10"
      InTerm.Text = "30"
      MoPmt.Caption = ""

      ClearHomeRecord

  END SUB   ' ClearButton_Click


  SUB ClearHomeRecord ()

     ' Clear the fields of the HomeRecord variable.

     HomeRecord.Address = ""
     HomeRecord.AskPrice = 0
     HomeRecord.SqFeet = 0
     HomeRecord.Bedrooms = 0
     HomeRecord.Bathrooms = 0
     HomeRecord.Garage = False
     HomeRecord.Views = False
     HomeRecord.Garden = False
     HomeRecord.Comments = ""

  END SUB   ' ClearHomeRecord


  SUB ExitButton_Click ()

     ' Stop the program performance.

     END

  END SUB   ' ExitButton_Click
```

Listing 8-7 DateViewed_LostFocus and InitDate

```
SUB DateViewed_LostFocus ()

  ' Validate the user's date entry.

  DateError% = False
  ON LOCAL ERROR GOTO BadDate

    ' Attempt to convert the date input to a serial date.

    HomeRecord.DateViewed = DATEVALUE(DateViewed.Text)

    ' If an error occurs in the conversion attempt,
    ' reinitialize the date field to today's date.

    IF DateError% THEN InitDate
  ON ERROR GOTO 0

  ' Record the program's standard date format.

    DateViewed.Text = FORMAT$(HomeRecord.DateViewed,
DateFormat)

  EXIT SUB

BadDate:

  ' If the user has entered an invalid date, display an
  ' error message, and toggle the DateError flag to True.

  MSGBOX "Illegal Date", 48, "Input Error"
  DateError% = True

RESUME NEXT

END SUB   ' DateViewed_LostFocus


SUB InitDate ()

  ' Initialize the date field to today's date.

  HomeRecord.DateViewed = NOW
```

```
   ' Display this date in the program's standard date format.

   DateViewed.Text = FORMAT$(HomeRecord.DateViewed,
DateFormat)

END SUB   ' InitDate
```

Listing 8-8 The GotFocus event procedures

```
SUB AskPrice_GotFocus ()

   ' Highlight the contents of the text box.

   HighlightEntry AskPrice

END SUB


SUB Bathrooms_GotFocus ()

   ' Highlight the contents of the text box.

   HighlightEntry Bathrooms

END SUB   ' Bathrooms_GotFocus


SUB Bedrooms_GotFocus ()

   ' Highlight the contents of the text box.

   HighlightEntry Bedrooms

END SUB   ' Bedrooms_GotFocus

SUB Comments_GotFocus ()

   ' Highlight the contents of the text box.

   HighlightEntry Comments

END SUB   ' Comments_GotFocus
```

(continued)

```
SUB DateViewed_GotFocus ()

  ' Highlight the contents of the text box.

  HighlightEntry DateViewed

END SUB   ' DateViewed_GotFocus


SUB InDown_GotFocus ()

  ' Highlight contents of text box.

  HighlightEntry InDown

END SUB   ' InDown_GotFocus


SUB InPrice_GotFocus ()

  ' Highlight contents of text box.

  HighlightEntry InPrice

END SUB   ' InPrice_GotFocus


SUB InRate_GotFocus ()

  ' Highlight contents of text box.

  HighlightEntry InRate

END SUB


SUB InTerm_GotFocus ()

  ' Highlight contents of text box.

  HighlightEntry InTerm

END SUB
```

```
SUB SqFeet_GotFocus ()

  ' Highlight the contents of the text box.

  HighlightEntry SqFeet

END SUB   ' SqFeet_GotFocus


SUB HighlightEntry (InBox AS CONTROL)

  ' Highlight the contents of the text box
  ' that has just received the focus.

  InBox.SelStart = 0
  InBox.SelLength = LEN(LTRIM$(RTRIM$(InBox.Text)))

END SUB   ' HighlightEntry
```

Listing 8-9 The LostFocus event procedures

```
SUB AskPrice_LostFocus ()

  ' Validate the asking price entry when
  ' the user moves the focus to another control.

  HomeRecord.AskPrice = VAL(AskPrice.Text)
  AskPrice.Text = LTRIM$(STR$(HomeRecord.AskPrice))

  InPrice.Text = AskPrice.Text
  CalcPayment

END SUB   ' AskPrice_LostFocus


SUB Bathrooms_LostFocus ()

  ' Validate the entry for the number of bathrooms.

  HomeRecord.Bathrooms = VAL(Bathrooms.Text)
```

(continued)

```
    Bathrooms.Text = LTRIM$(STR$(HomeRecord.Bathrooms))

END SUB  ' Bathrooms_LostFocus


SUB Bedrooms_LostFocus ()

  ' Validate the entry for the number of bedrooms.

  HomeRecord.Bedrooms = VAL(Bedrooms.Text)
  Bedrooms.Text = LTRIM$(STR$(HomeRecord.Bedrooms))

END SUB  ' Bedrooms_LostFocus


SUB InDown_LostFocus ()

  ' Validate the Down payment entry and
  ' recalculate the payment.

  InDown.Text = LTRIM$(STR$(VAL(InDown.Text)))
  CalcPayment

END SUB  ' InDown_LostFocus


SUB InPrice_LostFocus ()

  ' Validate the Amount entry and recalculate the payment.

  InPrice.Text = LTRIM$(STR$(VAL(InPrice.Text)))
  CalcPayment

END SUB  ' InPrice_LostFocus


SUB InRate_LostFocus ()

  ' Validate the Rate entry and recalculate the payment.

  InRate.Text = LTRIM$(STR$(VAL(InRate.Text)))
  CalcPayment

END SUB  ' InRate_LostFocus
```

```
SUB InTerm_LostFocus ()

  ' Validate the Term entry and recalculate the payment.

  InTerm.Text = LTRIM$(STR$(VAL(InTerm.Text)))
  CalcPayment

END SUB   ' InTerm_LostFocus


SUB SqFeet_LostFocus ()

  ' Validate the entry for the square footage.

  HomeRecord.SqFeet = VAL(SqFeet.Text)
  SqFeet.Text = LTRIM$(STR$(HomeRecord.SqFeet))

END SUB   ' SqFeet_LostFocus
```

Listing 8-10 The CalcPayment procedure

```
SUB CalcPayment ()

  ' Calculate and display the monthly payment.

  d = VAL(InDown.Text) / 100
  p = VAL(InPrice.Text) * (1 - d)
  i = VAL(InRate.Text) / 1200
  t = VAL(InTerm.Text) * 12

  BadInput = (p = 0) OR (i = 0) OR (t = 0)

  IF BadInput THEN
    MoPmt.Caption = ""
  Else
    Pmt = (p * i) / (1 - (1 + i) ^ (-t))
    MoPmt.Caption = FORMAT$(Pmt, "$###,###.#0")
  END IF

END SUB   ' CalcPayment
```

9

Date and Time Values: The Work Day Application

INTRODUCTION

Chronological data—consisting of both date and time values—are important in a large variety of business applications. For example, a customer billing program might keep track of several dates for a given customer's account: a closing date, a billing date, a due date, and the actual payment date. The program may need to perform specific operations with these dates, such as finding the number of days between the due date and the payment date. Similarly, a time-sheet program calculates the amount of time that elapses between two time values—the time when an employee begins working on a particular job and the time when the work ends. These operations and others like them are sometimes called *date arithmetic* and *time arithmetic*.

To perform efficient arithmetic operations on chronological values, a program needs a system for translating dates and times into representative numeric values. For this purpose, dates are often represented as integers. In general, a given date-integer value is equal to the number of days elapsed since a fixed reference point in the past. Given two date integers, you can easily find the number of days between the two corresponding dates by subtracting one number from the other. A time value, on the other hand, can be conveniently represented as a fractional value, expressing the portion of a 24-hour day that has gone by at a given point in time. For example, 6:00 A.M. is represented by the decimal fraction .25—because one-fourth of a day is over at six in the morning.

Visual Basic uses a practical format known as the *serial number* to represent date and time values together. Specifically, a serial number is a double-precision floating-point value that Visual Basic interprets as a particular date and time. The integer portion of a serial number—that is, the sequence of digits located before the decimal point—represents a date. The fractional portion—located after the decimal point—represents the time of day.

The fixed reference date in the past that Visual Basic uses to calculate serial dates is December 30, 1899. This "starting date" has a serial value of zero. Subsequent dates—up to December 31, 2078—have positive serial values, and prior dates have negative values.

The exercise disk has a simple application named the *Date Converter* that you can use to explore Visual Basic's serial date system. The project is stored on disk as DATES.MAK. Load it now into the Visual Basic environment and press F5 to run it. The form that appears on the screen has five text boxes (Figure 9-1). In the two boxes at the left side of the form you can enter date strings in any recognizable format. (Enter a date and then press the Tab key to move the edit cursor to the next or previous text box.) In response, the program displays the corresponding serial date in the adjacent text box to the right. When you then enter a second date string, the program calculates the difference between the two dates in days and displays this value in the single text box at the right side of the form.

For example, in Figure 9-1 the dates 04-15-1992 and 12-31-1999 have been entered into the two text boxes. As you can see, the corresponding serial dates are **33709** and **36525**, respectively. In other words, the date April 14, 1992, is 33,709 days forward from December 30, 1899, the starting point of Visual Basic's serial date system. Likewise, December 31, 1999, is 36,525 days forward from the starting date.

The number of days between these two dates is equal to the difference between their serial date equivalents. In general, you compute the number of days between any two dates by first finding the equivalent serial dates, *SerialDate1* and *SerialDate2*, and then subtracting one serial date from the other:

```
DiffInDays = SerialDate2 - SerialDate1
```

Combined with a fractional value representing the time of day, a serial number is a complete date-and-time value. Consider the following example:

```
33709.75
```

You already know (from Figure 9-1) that 33709 represents the date 4-15-92. The decimal value .75 represents 6:00 P.M., the time when three-quarters

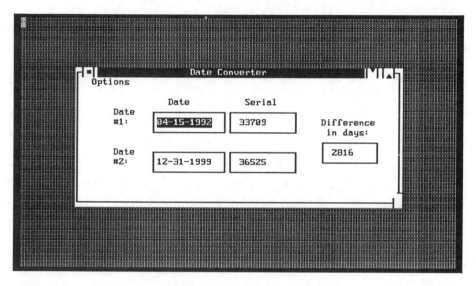

Figure 9-1 The *Date Converter* exercise

of the day is over. Consequently, Visual Basic interprets this serial number as April 15, 1992, at 6:00 P.M.

To use serial numbers effectively, you need convenient tools for converting string date formats—such as "April 15, 1992" or "4-15-92"—into serial dates and, conversely, for creating recognizable date strings from serial numbers. You also need tools for converting between time strings—such as "7:55 A.M." or "21:15:38"—and their equivalent serial time values. As you might expect, Visual Basic has a useful library of functions that relate to this subject. Here are four of the most important among them:

- The **DATEVALUE** function takes a date string as its argument and returns the equivalent serial date value.

- The **TIMEVALUE** function takes a time string as its argument and returns the equivalent serial time value.

- The **FORMAT$** function—useful for creating string displays in many different contexts—can produce date and time strings from serial numbers.

- The **NOW** function returns a serial number representing the current date and time.

You'll find illustrations of some of these tools in the code from the *Date Converter* exercise, shown in Listing 9-1. For example, here is how the program converts a date entry into a serial date value:

```
SerialDate = DATEVALUE(DateStr(Index).Text)
```

In the procedure named **CalcDiff**, you can see how the program calculates and displays the difference between two date entries:

```
Diff.Text = STR$(ABS(VAL(SerialNum(0).Text) - VAL(SerialNum(1).Text)))
```

The serial numbers are displayed in text boxes named **SerialNum**. The program uses the **VAL** function to convert each text value to a number and then subtracts one serial date from the other.

You'll see additional examples of these and other date and time operations in this chapter's major application, named *Work Day*. In addition, the *Work Day* application uses a Visual Basic control that you haven't seen yet in an application—the timer control. When activated, this control keeps track of a specific time interval and triggers an event at the end of the interval. In this chapter you'll learn the mechanical details of operating the timer and you'll see how it can prove useful in an application.

THE WORK DAY APPLICATION

Work Day is a time-sheet program, designed for tracking the amount of time spent working on particular jobs or projects during the course of a given business day. The application is suitable for a variety of businesspeople, including:

- Employees who are required to account in detail for time spent on the job.

- Managers who want to analyze the time requirements for a variety of tasks.

- Professionals who need to produce records of time billable to particular clients.

The *Work Day* project is stored on the the exercise disk under the name WORKDAY.MAK. When you load it into Visual Basic, you'll see that the project consists of three forms and a module (Figure 9-2). The main form is named **TimeSheet** (TMSHEET.FRM on disk), and the secondary forms are **TSPrint** (TSPRINT.FRM) and **TSOpen** (TSOPEN.FRM). The module is named TSPROCS.BAS.

Press the F5 function key to run the program, and the program's main form—titled *Daily Work Record*—appears on the screen. The form contains

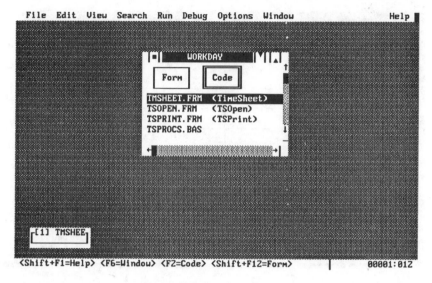

Figure 9-2   The WORKDAY.MAK project

a grid of text boxes organized for recording the details of a work day (Figure 9-3). The grid has five columns:

- The *Description* column is for the name or description of a given job, project, or client.

- The *Ref #* column is for a corresponding reference number.

- The *Start* and *Finish* columns are for recording the starting time and finishing time for work on a particular job.

- Finally, the *Time* column ultimately displays the total amount of time spent on a job. The *Work Day* program fills in this column after you supply values for *Start* and *Finish*.

Centered above the grid is the file name for the current time sheet. Although the program begins by displaying the time sheet for today's date, you can open and work with any time-sheet file stored on disk. Just beneath the time-sheet grid, the program displays today's date and the current time. This display is updated regularly from the system clock. Finally, there is a *subtotal* box at the lower-right corner of the form. The program uses this box to display the total hours of the jobs displayed on the current page of the time sheet. A time sheet for a given day consists of as many as ten pages, each containing up to eight lines of job descriptions. (You'll learn how to change the maximum number of pages per day when you examine the code for the *Work Day* application.)

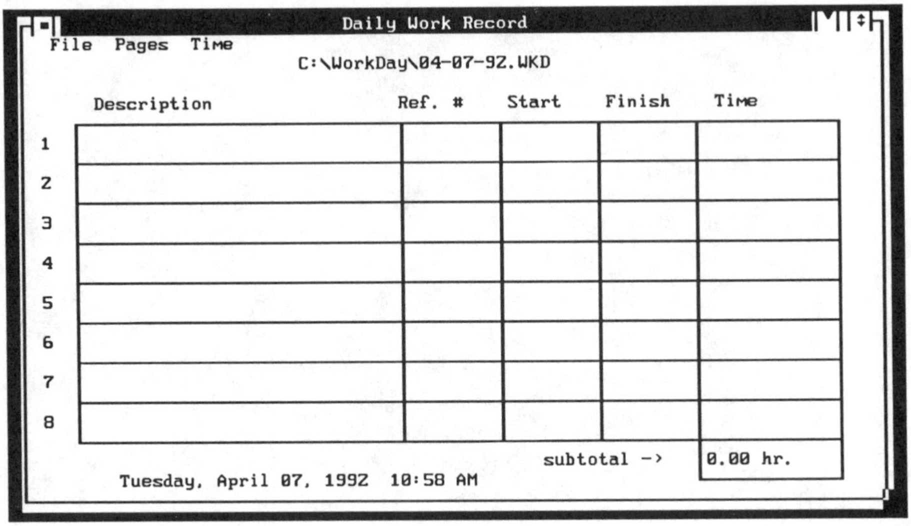

```
┌─■┐                    Daily Work Record                    ⌐M│‡┐
  File  Pages  Time
                     C:\WorkDay\04-07-92.WKD

         Description              Ref. #   Start   Finish    Time
   1
   2
   3
   4
   5
   6
   7
   8
                                          subtotal -> │0.00 hr. │
          Tuesday, April 07, 1992  10:58 AM
```

Figure 9-3 The *Daily Work Record* form

Figures 9-4 and 9-5 show an example of a two-page time sheet for a day's work. To scroll down to the next page of a time sheet, you can choose the **Next Page** command from the program's **Pages** menu, or you can simply press Ctrl-C from the keyboard. Conversely, to scroll up to the previous page, choose the **Previous Page** command or press Ctrl-R.

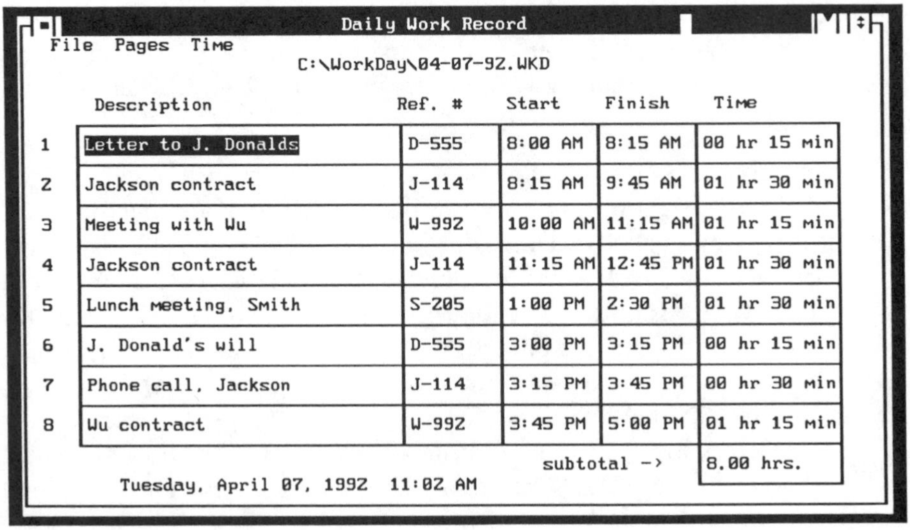

```
┌─■┐                    Daily Work Record               █    ⌐M│‡┐
  File  Pages  Time
                     C:\WorkDay\04-07-92.WKD

         Description              Ref. #   Start   Finish    Time
   1  Letter to J. Donalds       D-555   8:00 AM  8:15 AM  00 hr 15 min
   2  Jackson contract           J-114   8:15 AM  9:45 AM  01 hr 30 min
   3  Meeting with Wu            W-992  10:00 AM 11:15 AM  01 hr 15 min
   4  Jackson contract           J-114  11:15 AM 12:45 PM  01 hr 30 min
   5  Lunch meeting, Smith       S-205   1:00 PM  2:30 PM  01 hr 30 min
   6  J. Donald's will           D-555   3:00 PM  3:15 PM  00 hr 15 min
   7  Phone call, Jackson        J-114   3:15 PM  3:45 PM  00 hr 30 min
   8  Wu contract                W-992   3:45 PM  5:00 PM  01 hr 15 min
                                          subtotal -> │8.00 hrs.│
          Tuesday, April 07, 1992  11:02 AM
```

Figure 9-4 A page of time-sheet records

```
 ┌─■┐                      Daily Work Record                    ▐▐│ ╪┐
     File   Pages   Time
                        C:\WorkDay\04-07-92.WKD

         Description               Ref. #    Start    Finish    Time
    9  │Phone call, Donalds      │D-555   │5:00 PM │5:15 PM │00 hr 15 min│
   10  │Wu contract              │W-992   │5:15 PM │7:15 PM │02 hr 00 min│
   11  │                         │        │        │        │            │
   12  │                         │        │        │        │            │
   13  │                         │        │        │        │            │
   14  │                         │        │        │        │            │
   15  │                         │        │        │        │            │
   16  │                         │        │        │        │            │
                                               subtotal ->  │ 2.25 hrs. │
              Tuesday, April 07, 1992   11:04 AM
```

Figure 9-5 A second page of records

Notice the variety of formats in which the program displays time values. Times in the *Start* and *Finish* columns appear in AM/PM format—for example:

```
8:15 AM
```

In contrast, the elapsed time amounts in the *Time* column are expressed in hours and minutes, such as:

```
01 hr 30 min
```

Finally, the *subtotal* box shows the total working time for a given page, expressed as a decimal value:

```
2.25 hrs
```

You'll see how these displays are produced when you examine the program's code, later in this chapter.

The *Work Day* application has a number of features that make it particularly convenient for creating and using daily work records:

- The program allows you to enter times into the *Start* and *Finish* columns in two ways. If you type a time entry directly from the keyboard, the program checks your entry—making sure it represents a valid time value—and then converts it to a standard time display format. Alternatively, you can enter the *current* time into any *Start* or *Finish* box by selecting the box and pressing Ctrl-T from the keyboard.

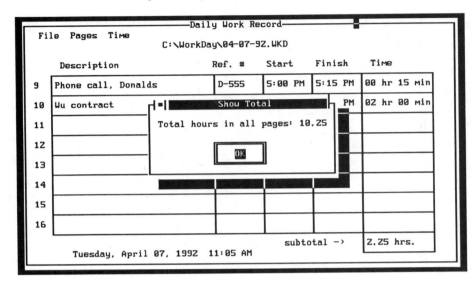

Figure 9-6 The total of both pages

- The times displayed in the *Time* column and *subtotal* column are updated automatically each time you complete a job line or change a *Start* or *Finish* time. Furthermore, you can view the total hours for all the pages in the current time sheet by choosing the **Show Total** command from the **Pages** menu or by pressing F6 from the keyboard. When you do so, the program displays a message box similar to the one shown in Figure 9-6. As you can see, the sample time sheet records a total of 10.25 hours.

- Options available in the program's **File** menu allow you to create new time sheets or open existing time-sheet files. Each day's time sheet is saved in its own file on disk.

- The program allows you to print a variety of reports from a time sheet. For a simple printout of the current time sheet, you can press Ctrl-P (or choose the **Print This Time Sheet** command from the **File** menu). In response, the program prints all the nonblank lines of the open time-sheet file, as shown in Figure 9-7. Alternatively, you can produce reports from any day's time-sheet file. These printed reports are sorted by reference numbers, and include subtotals and a total. The example shown in Figure 9-8 is created from the two-page time-sheet in Figures 9-4 and 9-5. You can send reports like this one directly to your printer, or you can save them to disk as text files for subsequent processing or editing.

```
Time Sheet File: C:\WorkDay\04-07-92.WKD

Letter to J. Donalds     D-555     08:00 AM   08:15 AM    00 hr 15 min
Jackson contract         J-114     08:15 AM   09:45 AM    01 hr 30 min
Meeting with Wu          W-992     10:00 AM   11:15 AM    01 hr 15 min
Jackson contract         J-114     11:15 AM   12:45 PM    01 hr 30 min
Lunch meeting, Smith     S-205     01:00 PM   02:30 PM    01 hr 30 min
J. Donalds' will         D-555     03:00 PM   03:15 PM    00 hr 15 min
Phone call, Jackson      J-114     03:15 PM   03:45 PM    00 hr 30 min
Wu contract              W-992     03:45 PM   05:00 PM    01 hr 15 min
Phone call, Donalds      D-555     05:00 PM   05:15 PM    00 hr 15 min
Wu contract              W-992     05:15 PM   07:15 PM    02 hr 00 min


                                   Total --> 10.25 hrs.
```

Figure 9-7 A printout from the current time sheet

```
                      Time Sheet for 04-07-92
                      =======================

Job Description          Ref.       Start      Finish     Total Time
---------------          ----       -----      ------     ----------

J. Donalds' will         D-555      03:00 PM   03:15 PM   00 hr 15 min
Letter to J. Donalds     D-555      08:00 AM   08:15 AM   00 hr 15 min
Phone call, Donalds      D-555      05:00 PM   05:15 PM   00 hr 15 min

                                    Total for D-555 -->  0.75 hrs

Jackson contract         J-114      08:15 AM   09:45 AM   01 hr 30 min
Jackson contract         J-114      11:15 AM   12:45 PM   01 hr 30 min
phone call, Jackson      J-114      03:15 PM   03:45 PM   00 hr 30 min

                                    Total for J-114 -->  3.50 hrs

Lunch meeting, Smith     S-205      01:00 PM   02:30 PM   01 hr 30 min

                                    Total for S-205 -->  1.50 hrs

Meeting with Wu          W-992      10:00 AM   11:15 AM   01 hr 15 min
Wu contract              W-992      03:45 PM   05:00 PM   01 hr 15 min
Wu contract              W-992      05:15 PM   07:15 PM   02 hr 00 min

                                    Total for W-992    -->  4.50 hrs

                                    *** Total Work Time --->  10.25 hrs
```

Figure 9-8 A sorted time-sheet report

- The program also can print summary reports for an entire week's work records. Weekly reports are sorted by reference numbers, and also include subtotals and a total.

You'll investigate these program features in the sections ahead.

Entering Data into the Work Record Form

In all but the last column of the time-sheet grid, you can enter and edit information in any way you wish. To select a text box, click it with the mouse or use the keyboard:

- Press the Tab key to move from one box to the next inside the first four columns.

- Press the up- or down-arrow key to move to the previous or next box in the current column.

To enter the current time into a box in the *Start* or *Finish* column, you select the box and press Ctrl-T. To see how this works, try the following exercise:

1. In the *Description* column of line 1, enter the following imaginary project name:

   ```
   Billing application
   ```

2. In the *Ref #* column, enter:

   ```
   B-112
   ```

3. Now select the *Start* box in line 1 and press Ctrl-T. The program enters the current time into the box (Figure 9-9).

These three steps simulate the actions you might take as you begin working on a particular project on the morning of a new work day. You enter your description of the project, and when you are ready to begin your work, select the *Start* box and press Ctrl-T. Then you go to work.

If you need to run other applications during your work, press Ctrl-X to close the *Work Day* application temporarily. When you later restart the application, the program automatically opens today's time sheet from its file on disk. Any entries you have already begun for today's work reappear on the screen.

When you finish your work on this first project—or when you need to move on to another job—you return to the *Work Day* application and select the *Finish* box in line 1. Then press Ctrl-T. The program enters the current

```
┌─■┐                    Daily Work Record                    │M│‡├
   File  Pages  Time
                    C:\WorkDay\04-08-92.WKD

        Description                Ref. #    Start    Finish    Time
   ┌───────────────────────────┬─────────┬────────┬────────┬─────────┐
 1 │ Billing application        │ B-112   │ 6:33 AM│        │         │
   ├───────────────────────────┼─────────┼────────┼────────┼─────────┤
 2 │                           │         │        │        │         │
   ├───────────────────────────┼─────────┼────────┼────────┼─────────┤
 3 │                           │         │        │        │         │
   ├───────────────────────────┼─────────┼────────┼────────┼─────────┤
 4 │                           │         │        │        │         │
   ├───────────────────────────┼─────────┼────────┼────────┼─────────┤
 5 │                           │         │        ■        │         │
   ├───────────────────────────┼─────────┼────────┼────────┼─────────┤
 6 │                           │         │        │        │         │
   ├───────────────────────────┼─────────┼────────┼────────┼─────────┤
 7 │                           │         │        │        │         │
   ├───────────────────────────┼─────────┼────────┼────────┼─────────┤
 8 │                           │         │        │        │         │
   └───────────────────────────┴─────────┴────────┴────────┴─────────┘
                                            subtotal ->  │ 0.00 hr. │
          Tuesday, April 07, 1992  11:10 AM
```

Figure 9-9 Entering a job description and a starting time

time into the box and instantly calculates the amount of time that has gone by since you began your work on the project. This elapsed time appears in the *Time* column. In addition, the program displays your current total work time in the *Total* box (Figure 9-10).

Sometimes you may prefer to enter time values manually into the time-sheet grid instead of using Ctrl-T. For example, you might forget to

```
┌─■┐                    Daily Work Record                    │M│‡├
   File  Pages  Time
                    C:\WorkDay\04-08-92.WKD

        Description                Ref. #    Start    Finish    Time
   ┌───────────────────────────┬─────────┬────────┬────────┬─────────────┐
 1 │ Billing application        │ B-112   │ 6:33 AM│ 8:45 AM│ 02 hr 12 min│
   ├───────────────────────────┼─────────┼────────┼────────┼─────────────┤
 2 │                           │         │        │        │             │
   ├───────────────────────────┼─────────┼────────┼────────┼─────────────┤
 3 │                           │         │        │        │             │
   ├───────────────────────────┼─────────┼────────┼────────┼─────────────┤
 4 │                           │         │        │        │             │
   ├───────────────────────────┼─────────┼────────┼────────┼─────────────┤
 5 │                           │         │        ■        │             │
   ├───────────────────────────┼─────────┼────────┼────────┼─────────────┤
 6 │                           │         │        │        │             │
   ├───────────────────────────┼─────────┼────────┼────────┼─────────────┤
 7 │                           │         │        │        │             │
   ├───────────────────────────┼─────────┼────────┼────────┼─────────────┤
 8 │                           │         │        │        │             │
   └───────────────────────────┴─────────┴────────┴────────┴─────────────┘
                                            subtotal ->  │ 2.20 hrs. │
          Tuesday, April 07, 1992  11:11 AM
```

Figure 9-10 Completing a job line

enter the finishing time for a particular job at the appropriate moment. When you finally get back to the *Work Day* application, several hours might have gone by since you actually completed the job. In this case, you can simply type the time directly into the appropriate *Finish* box. The program allows some flexibility in the format of time entries. For example, if you type "10 a" into a time text box, the program recognizes the entry and converts it to "10:00 AM." However, if you make an entry that cannot be recongized as a time value, the program erases your entry and leaves the text box blank.

The program fills in the *Time* column for a given line whenever you supply valid entries for both the *Start* and *Finish* columns. Significantly, if you enter a *Finish* value that is earlier in time than the *Start* value for a given job, the program assumes that your work went past midnight into the next day. For example, if you enter "10:00 PM" as the *Start* time and "1:30 AM" as the *Finish* time, the program calculates the elapsed time as 3 hours and 30 minutes.

Except for requiring valid time entries, the program leaves you free to fill in the time-sheet form in any way you want. You can make entries in any order, and you can even reserve blank lines for later entries.

The File Menu Options

The application's **File** menu contains commands that allow you to open a day's work record from disk, and to print reports from any day's work record. Here is the list of commands that appears in the menu:

```
Create a New Time Sheet          F2
Open Today's Time Sheet          F3
Open an Existing Time Sheet...   F4

Print This Time Sheet            Ctrl+P
Print a Time Sheet Report...     F5

Exit                             Ctrl+X
```

Notice that there is no **Save** command. This is because the program automatically takes care of creating files and saving your work at the appropriate moments. The program saves all files in a directory named WORKDAY, on drive C. (If this directory does not exist initially, the application creates it at the beginning of the first program run.) The file name for a particular day's time sheet consists of the day's date followed by an extension name of WKD (for "work day"). For example, here is the path and file name for April 16, 1992:

```
C:\WORKDAY\04-16-92.WKD
```

The **Create a New Time Sheet** command allows you to create a file for a time sheet that does not yet exist on disk. For example, you might want to use this command to record your work hours for a day in the past when you neglected to do your time sheet. When you select this command from the **File** menu—or press the F2 shortcut key—the dialog box shown in Figure 9-11 appears on the screen. In the text box at the bottom of the dialog box, you enter the date for which you want to create the new time-sheet file. (You can enter the date in any recognizable format, such as 04-15-92 or April 15, 1992.) Assuming the file for this date does not exist on disk, the program creates the file and displays a blank time-sheet grid on the screen, where you can begin recording your work hours for the day. Keep in mind that the currently open file name is displayed above the time-sheet grid, whereas today's date is displayed beneath the grid.

If you happen to enter a date in the *New Time Sheet* box for which a file exists, a message box appears on the screen with the following prompt:

```
This file already exists. Do you want to delete the
previous version?
```

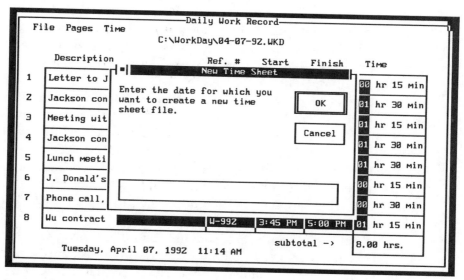

Figure 9-11 Creating a new time-sheet file

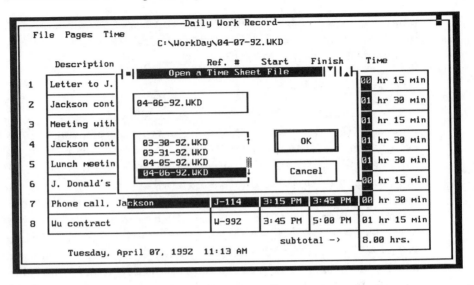

Figure 9-12 Opening an existing time-sheet file

The prompt is followed by two buttons labeled **Yes** and **No**. Click **Yes** to abandon the previous version of the time sheet and start with a blank grid. Click **No** to open the previous version and view its contents on the screen.

If you are working on a time sheet for a date other than today, you can quickly return to today's file by choosing the **Open Today's Time Sheet** command—or simply pressing F3. Alternatively, you can open any file by selecting the **Open an Existing Time Sheet** command. In response, the program displays the dialog box shown in Figure 9-12. To open a file, you select a name from the scrollable file list box and click **OK**. Before opening the newly selected file, the program saves any changes you may have made in the current open file.

The **File** menu offers two printing options. The first, **Print This Time Sheet**, sends the data to the printer from all the pages of the currently open time-sheet file. This option is useful if you simply want a quick printout of your current time sheet.

The second printing option, **Print a Time Sheet Report...**, gives you the opportunity to select a file from disk and create a printed report from data in the file. When you select this option, a new dialog box appears on the screen, as shown in Figure 9-13.

The **Print a Time Sheet** box contains a list of all the WKD files in the C:\WORKDAY directory. When you click a file in the list, the file name also appears on the text box above the file list. To print a report, you select a file and then click the **OK** button, or you can simply double-click a file name in the file list. In the resulting report, the job data is sorted by

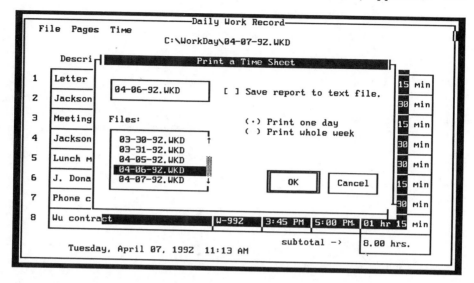

Figure 9-13 The **Print a Time Sheet** dialog box

reference numbers first and by descriptions within each reference number group. The report also shows a time subtotal for all the jobs of a given reference number. (Look back at Figure 9-8 to review the format of the printed report.)

The **Print a Time Sheet** dialog box contains two additional options:

- The **Save report to text file** option allows you to send the report to a text file on disk instead of printing it. To select this option, click the check box with the mouse or press Alt+S. An X appears inside the box. Use this option when you want to incorporate your report into a larger word-processed document or when you want to edit the report in some way before you print it. The application saves the report file in the WORKDAY directory, with a TXT extension.

- A pair of option buttons gives you a choice between printing a one-day report (**Print one day**) or a one-week summary report (**Print whole week**). By default, the application creates the output report from the single day's file that you select in the file list. However, if you select the **Print whole week** option, the program combines data from all the existing files of an entire week, Sunday through Saturday. To specify a week, you can select the file for any day that is in the week. The resulting report is in the same format as the one-day report (Figure 9-8), but contains data from as many as seven days. If you save this one-week summary report to disk instead of printing it, the application saves the file in the WORKDAY directory, with an extension of WK.

```
                    Time Sheet for 04-09-92
                    =======================

Job Description            Ref.        Start      Finish      Total Time
---------------            ----        -----      ------      ----------

Lunch with M. Smith        (no Ref #)  12:00 PM   01:30 PM    01 hr 30 min
Partners meeting           (no ref #)  09:30 AM   11:30 AM    02 hr 00 min

                            Total for (no ref #) -->  3.50 hrs

Carlson, cover letter      C-324                  04:00 PM
Carlson, new contract      C-324                  02:15 PM
Carlson, phone call        C-324       08:00 AM   08:30 AM    00 hr 30 min

                            Total for C-324          -->  0.50 hr

Wilson, meeting            W-882       04:00 PM   05:00 PM    01 hr 00 min
Wilson, review tax record  W-882       05:00 PM   06:30 PM    01 hr 30 min
Wilson, tax advice         W-882       08:30 AM   09:30 AM    01 hr 00 min

                            Total for W-882          -->  3.50 hrs

                            *** Total Work Time --->  7.50 hrs
```

Figure 9-14 A time-sheet report with missing data entries

The **Print whole week** option proves useful if you are keeping track of hours that are billable to a client. You can use the resulting report to produce detailed billing statements on a weekly basis.

The program can successfully generate time-sheet reports even from a file that has missing data values. For example, if you omit the reference number from one or more lines in a time-sheet file, the program creates a subgroup identified as *(no ref #)* and sorts the entries in this group by their job descriptions. Furthermore, if the starting or finishing time entry is missing from a given line in a time sheet, the program prints the line without including its time in the totals. You can see examples of both of these contingencies in the report shown in Figure 9-14.

THE ELEMENTS OF THE WORK DAY APPLICATION

Now that you've run the program, you can see the general purpose of each of the forms and modules contained in the *Work Day* project:

- The **TimeSheet** form displays the eight-line grid for entering a day's data. This form contains text boxes, labels, and a timer control. The code stored with this form responds to all the events that take place around the time-sheet grid itself and performs all menu commands except for the routines that print reports and control the Open dialog box. For input and output operations in the time-sheet files, this form defines a record-type definition named **WorkRecordType**. (The time sheets are saved as random-access files.) The same record-type definition is repeated in the **TSPrint** form and the TSPROCS.BAS module.

- The **TSPrint** form is the dialog box that appears when you select the **Print a Time Sheet Report...** command from the **File** menu. This form contains a text box, a check box, a pair of option buttons, two command buttons, and the *file list box* control from which you select a file to print. The code stored with this form is devoted to printing (or saving) data in the report formats.

- The **TSOpen** form appears when you select the **Open an Existing Time Sheet...** command, also from the **File** menu. This form has a framed label, two command buttons, and a file list box.

- Finally, the module TSPROCS.BAS contains two functions that are used in both the **TimeSheet** and **TSPrint** forms. A function named **BlankLine** checks to see if a particular time sheet line is blank; and a function named **DoLineTotal** calculates the difference between the *Start* and *Finish* times on a completed line. (Recall that the procedures and functions stored in a module are available to all forms in the application.)

The next sections of this chapter describe the program's organization and code, with a focus on the date and time operations the program performs.

Controls, Properties, and Menus

The data grid in the **TimeSheet** form consists of forty text boxes arranged in rows and columns and an additional text box for the total time. Here are the properties of these controls:

- Each column in the data grid is defined as a control array, with **Index** settings from **0** to **7**.

- The **CtlName** settings of the five control arrays are **Description, Ref, Start, Finish,** and **TotalTime**—similar to the label captions displayed at the top of the columns themselves.

- The eight text boxes in the **TotalTime** column have **Enabled** settings of **False**; this is because the program controls the contents of this particular column. The user never has access to these text boxes via the keyboard or the mouse.

- The text box at the lower-right corner of the form has a **CtlName** setting of **DayTotal** and an **Enabled** setting of **False**.

At the bottom of the **TimeSheet** form is an unframed label named **DayAndTime**, which displays the current date and time; and at the top of the form is a label named **TSFileName**, which displays the open file name.

As you can see in Figure 9-15, the timer control is represented by a box labeled Timer, at the upper-right corner of the form. This box disappears during run time. The *Work Day* application uses the timer control to update the date and time display every ten seconds. Visual Basic defines only a small number of properties—and a single event—for timer controls. Most important among the properties are **CtlName**, **Enabled**, and **Interval**. The timer in this application has a **CtlName** setting of **DayTimer**, and its **Enabled** setting is **True**.

The **Interval** property setting is an integer representing the number of milliseconds in the interval defined for the timer. In this application the **Interval** setting is **10000**, for ten seconds. The one event defined for this control is **Timer**. As long as the **Enabled** property remains **True**, the **Timer** event is called at the end of each time period defined by the **Interval** setting. Accordingly, the **DayTimer_Timer** event procedure is called every ten seconds in the *Work Day* application. This procedure's job is to update the

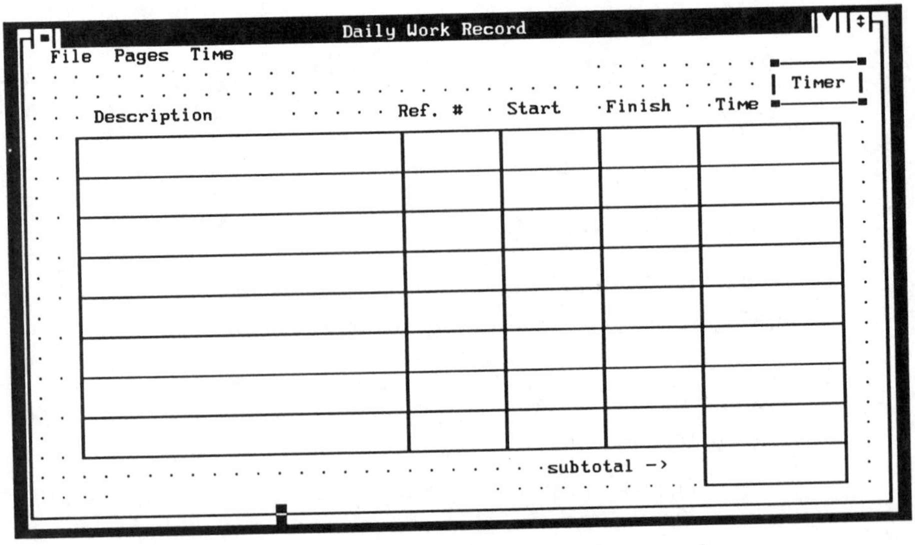

Figure 9-15 The timer control on the **TimeSheet** form

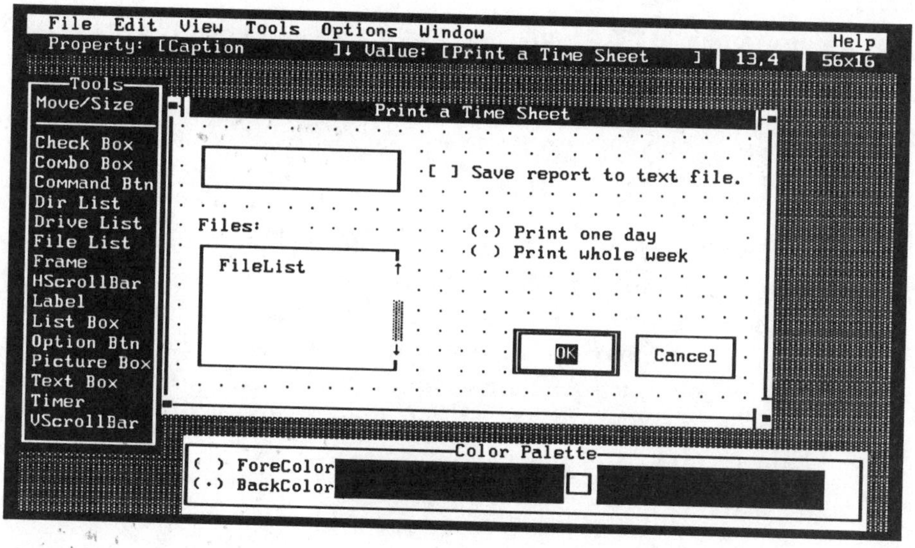

Figure 9-16 The controls on the **TSPrint** form

current date and time displayed as the **Caption** property of the **DayAnd-Time** label.

The **TSPrint** form (Figure 9-16) has a greater variety of controls than the **TimeSheet** form. The primary purpose of **TSPrint** is to prompt the user to select a file name for creating a report. In this context, the most important control in the form is the file list box, which displays the available file names.

Appropriately enough, the file list box has a **CtlName** setting of **FileList**. The program sets and reads other properties of this control at run time, starting in the **Form_Load** procedure of the **TSPrint** form (Listing 9-15). Three essential properties define the behavior and use of the file list box:

- The **Path** property specifies the path from which files will be accessed. (This property is available only at run time, not at design time.)

- The **Pattern** property gives the pattern of file names that will appear in the list.

- The **FileName** property (also available only at run time) provides the name of a file that the user has selected by clicking in the file list.

Here is how the program sets the **Path** and **Pattern** properties:

```
FileList.Path = PathName$
FileList.Pattern = "*." + ExtName$
```

PathName$** and **ExtName$ are string constants, defined in the form-level declarations for **TSPrint**:

```
Const PathName$ = "C:\WorkDay"
Const ExtName$ = "WKD"
```

As a result of these definitions, the **FileList** box displays the names of all WKD files in the C:\WORKDAY directory.

When the user clicks a file name, Visual Basic assigns the name of the file to the **FileName** property of the file list box. The *Work Day* program therefore gets the user's file selection from **FileList.FileName** and displays the file name in the text box located just above the file list box. The name of the text box is **DisplayFile**:

```
DisplayFile.Text = FileList.FileName
```

You'll learn more about the characteristics of file list boxes—and the companion controls known as *drive list boxes* and *directory list boxes*—in Chapter 10. The application presented there uses all three of these controls.

The remaining controls on the **TSPrint** form include:

- A check-box control named **SaveReport**. This control's initial **Value** setting is **0-Unchecked**. If the user checks this control, the program sends the report output to disk rather than to the printer.

- A pair of option buttons, organized as a control array. The buttons are named **WeekOrDay**, and they have **Index** settings of 0 and 1. The first of the two controls, **WeekOrDay(0)** has an initial **Value** setting of **True**, and the second is **False**. If the user accepts these default settings, the program creates a one-day report. Reversing the settings results in a one-week report.

- Two command buttons, named **OkButton** and **CancelButton**. The **CancelButton** control has a setting of **True** for a property named **Cancel**. When the **Cancel** setting is **True** for a given command button, the user can activate the button's **Click** event by pressing the Escape key on the keyboard.

The *Work Day* application's menu definitions (Figure 9-17) are simple and straightforward. The six commands in the **File** menu have **CtlNames** of **NewSheet**, **OpenToday**, **OpenPrevious**, **PrintRec**, **PrintPrevRec**, and **ExitCommand**. The **Pages** commands are named **NextPage**, **PreviousPage**, and **ShowTotal**; and the **Time** command is **CurTime**.

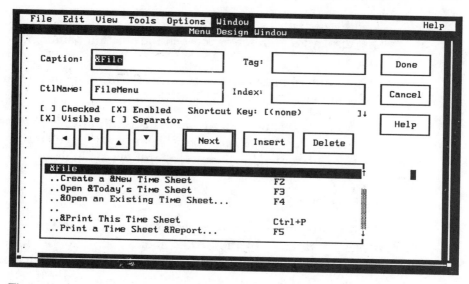

Figure 9-17 The menu design for the Work Day application

Events

Several types of events take place on the **TimeSheet** form:

- **GotFocus** and **KeyDown** events for each of the text boxes.
- **LostFocus** events for the **Start** and **Finish** text boxes.
- **Click** events for the menu commands.
- A **Timer** event for the **DayTimer** control.

The four **GotFocus** event procedures arrange to highlight the current contents of a newly selected text box so that the user can easily replace or revise an entry. The **KeyDown** event procedures (Listing 9-7) respond to the up- and down-arrow keys. If the user presses the up arrow or down arrow, these procedures move the focus to the text box just above or just below the current box.

The **Start_LostFocus** and **Finish_LostFocus** event procedures validate a new time entry when the user moves the focus away from a *Start* or *Finish* text box. In addition, these procedures update the hour values displayed in the *Time* column. Here is the sequence of steps performed by these two procedures:

1. Attempt to convert the user's entry to a serial time value.
2. If the conversion is successful, redisplay the time in a standard string format. (Otherwise, replace the entry with a blank string.)

3. If both time entries (*Start* and *Finish*) are available in the current line, display the difference between the two time values in the *Time* column.

4. Update the subtotal—that is, the number of hours on the current page of the time sheet.

The **Click** events for the menu commands result in calls to the event procedures that carry out the menu operations. Significantly, the **PrintPrevRec_Click** procedure consists of only two statements:

```
SavePage
TSPrint.SHOW 1
```

A call to the program's **SavePage** procedure writes the entries of the current page to disk. Then the **SHOW** method displays the previously hidden **TSPrint** form on the screen and temporarily transfers the program's focus to the controls contained in this secondary form.

The main events in the **TSPrint** form are:

- The initial **Form_Load** event, which establishes the path and the pattern characteristics of the file list box.

- The **Click** event for the **FileList** control, which copies the user's file selection—represented by **FileList.FileName**—to the **DisplayFile** text box.

- The **Click** event for the **OkButton**, which makes a call to the appropriate report-printing procedure.

Interestingly enough, the user can abbreviate this process by *double-clicking* a file name in the **FileList** box. The **FileList_DblClick** procedure simply makes a call to the **OkButton_Click** procedure to produce a report. But in Visual Basic's *event-ordering* protocol, a **DblClick** event always first triggers an automatic **Click** event. For this reason, the following three event procedures are called in response to a double-click:

```
FileList_Click
FileList_DblClick
OkButton_Click
```

The first of these procedures copies the selected file name to the **Display-File** text box, and the second and third procedures make the sequence of calls that results in the printing operation.

Finally, the **TSOpen** form recognizes **Click** events for its two command buttons and **Click** and **DblClick** events for its file list box. Once the user selects a file name from the *Open* dialog box, control of the program returns to the **TimeSheet** form, where the **OpenPrevious_Click** procedure arranges to open and display the selected time sheet file.

Procedures and Methods

The code for the *Work Day* application appears in Listings 9-2 to 9-24. More specifically, here is where you will find the code for each part of the program:

- The code from the **TimeSheet** form is in Listings 9-2 to 9-14.
- The code from the **TSPrint** form is in Listing 9-15 to 9-21.
- The code from the **TSOpen** form is in Listings 9-22 and 9-23.
- The two functions stored in the TSPROCS.BAS module appear in Listing 9-24.

Among the longest and most detailed routines in the program are the procedures that perform input and output operations. These include the **SavePage** procedure (Listing 9-11), responsible for saving the current time-sheet page to disk; the **OpenOnePage** procedure (Listing 9-10), which opens a time-sheet file and displays a page of records; the **PrintADay** and **PrintAWeek** procedures (Listings 9-17 and 9-18), which read data from disk in preparation for printing a report; and **PrintWorkRecordList** (Listing 9-19), which actually creates an output report, sending it either to the printer or to a text file on disk. The following discussion will give you a general sense of how these operations take place. Then you'll examine specific illustrations of date and time operations in the *Work Day* program.

Overview of File Procedures

The program defines a structured type named **WorkRecordType** as follows:

```
TYPE WorkRecordType
  DescriptField AS STRING * 25
  IDField AS STRING * 10
  StartField AS DOUBLE
  FinishedField AS DOUBLE
END TYPE
```

This record type—which appears in the form-level declarations of the **TimeSheet** and **TSPrint** forms and in the module-level section of the

TSPROCS.BAS file—contains four fields, representing a data entry from each of the four columns in the time sheet grid:

- **DescriptField** and **IDField** are string fields representing the description and reference number of a job.
- **StartField** and **FinishedField** are numeric fields representing the starting and finishing time for the job. The double-precision data type of these two fields accommodates Visual Basic's serial date and time format.

The **TimeSheet** form declares a single record variable belonging to this structured type:

```
DIM SHARED WorkRecord AS WorkRecordType
```

When the program saves a page of entries to a time-sheet file, this record variable is used in the process of opening the file and writing records to disk. Specifically, the **SavePage** procedure begins by copying the file name from the **Caption** property of the **TSFileName** label to the variable **CurFile$**:

```
CurFile$ = TSFileName.Caption
```

Then the procedure opens the file and initiates a **FOR** loop to write a page of records to the file:

```
OPEN CurFile$ FOR RANDOM AS #1 LEN = LEN(WorkRecord)
   FOR i% = FirstLine TO LastLine
      Ndx = (i% - 1) MOD 8
```

The four fields are initially read as strings, directly from the corresponding text boxes in the **TimeSheet** form:

```
WorkRecord.DescriptField = Description(Ndx).Text
WorkRecord.IDField = Ref(Ndx).Text

S$ = RTRIM$(Start(Ndx).Text)
F$ = RTRIM$(Finish(Ndx).Text)
```

Then the **StartField** and **FinishedField** entries have to be converted to numeric values. If a nonblank time entry exists, the program uses Visual Basic's **TIMEVALUE** function to convert it to a serial time; but if the entry is blank, the program stores a value of –1 (represented by the constant **NoTime**) as the time field:

```
IF LEN(S$) > 0 THEN
   WorkRecord.StartField = TIMEVALUE(S$)
```

```
ELSE
  WorkRecord.StartField = NoTime
END IF
```

Finally, when all four fields have been stored in the **WorkRecord** variable, a **PUT** statement writes the record to the file:

```
PUT #1, i%, WorkRecord
```

The **TSPrint** form declares two **WorkRecordType** structures—a dynamic array of records named **WorkRecordList** along with a single record variable named **WorkRecord**:

```
DIM SHARED WorkRecordList() AS WorkRecordType
DIM SHARED WorkRecord AS WorkRecordType
```

These structures are both used in the process of preparing data for output in reports. When the user requests a printed report, the **OKButton_Click** procedure (Listing 9-16) makes a call either to the **PrintADay** procedure or the **PrintAWeek** procedure, depending on which of the **WeekOrDay** option buttons has been selected:

```
IF WeekOrDay(0).Value THEN PrintADay ELSE PrintAWeek
```

The **PrintADay** procedure (Listing 9-17) opens a day's work file and calculates the number of records in the file, **RecCount**. Given this count, the procedure redimensions the **WorkRecordList** array accordingly and then reads the day's work data into the array:

```
REDIM WorkRecordList(RecCount) AS WorkRecordType

FOR i% = 1 TO RecCount
  GET #1, i%, WorkRecordList(i%)
```

If the **IDField** string is blank, the procedure replaces it with the string "(no ref #)":

```
IF RTRIM$(WorkRecordList(i%).IDField) = "" THEN
  WorkRecordList(i%).IDField = "(no ref #)"
```

Then a call to a procedure named **SortWorkRecordList** (Listing 9-21) sorts the array by the reference numbers—that is, the **IDField**—and a call to **PrintWorkRecordList** (Listing 9-19) prints the record or saves it as a text file on disk.

The **PrintAWeek** procedure (Listing 9-18) is slightly more complicated. It begins by determining the date of the first day of the week corresponding to the user's selected file. Then the procedure opens each of the week's seven files in turn and calculates **WeekRecCount**, the total number of records in all seven files. This value defines the dynamic size of the **WorkRecordList** array:

```
REDIM WorkRecordList(WeekRecCount)AS WorkRecordType
```

Next the procedure uses a pair of nested **For** loops to reopen each of the seven files in turn and read the records into the **WorkRecordList** array. Finally, a call to **SortWorkRecordList** sorts the array and a call to **PrintWorkRecordList** generates the one-week summary report.

The **PrintWorkRecordList** procedure (Listing 9-19) begins by reading the current **Value** setting of the check box control named **SaveReport**. A setting of **1** (which this program reads as *true*) means the user has requested text file output; a setting of **0** (which the program reads as *false*) means the user wants a printed report. Accordingly, the procedure assigns either a file name or the device name "Prn" to the string variable **Dest**:

```
IF SaveReport.Value THEN
   Dest = OutFile
ELSE
   Dest = "Prn"
END IF
```

(**OutFile**, the name used for a text file, is passed as an argument to the procedure.) Whichever destination has been selected, the following **Open** statement prepares for the output:

```
OPEN Dest FOR OUTPUT AS #1
```

Finally, a sequence of **Print #1** statements writes the report to the selected destination. As you can see, the use of the **Dest** variable in the **Open** statement simplifies the choice between printing or saving the report.

As the report is generated, the procedure tallies a running total of the hours recorded for a given reference number. Each time the reference number changes, a subtotal line is included in the report:

```
IF ThisRef <> NexRef THEN
   PRINT #1,
   PRINT #1, TAB(37); "Total for "; ThisRef; " -- > ";
   PRINT #1, FORMAT$(RefTot * 24, "##0.00"); " hr";
```

Date and Time Operations

The *Week Day* application often needs to convert time and date strings to serial numbers or serial numbers back to time and date strings. For example, time values are read from disk as double-precision numeric values but then are changed to a variety of display formats for the purpose of generating reports. When the program needs to perform an arithmetic operation on one or more chronological values, serial numbers are the most convenient way to store the data. However, a serial number would seem meaningless on a printed report and therefore needs to be converted to a readable string format.

For example, the first such conversion takes place in the routine that displays the date and time beneath the **TimeSheet** form. The **DayTimer_Timer** procedure (Listing 9-5) initially produces the display and then updates it every ten seconds:

```
DayAndTime.Caption = FORMAT$(NOW, "dddd, mmmm dd, yyyy
h:mm AM/PM")
```

In this statement, the **NOW** function supplies a complete serial number that represents the current date from the system calendar and time from the system clock. Given this argument, the **FORMAT$** function supplies a complete date-and-time display string, which the program assigns to the **Caption** property of the **DayAndTime** label. Notice the syntax of the **Format$** function for creating date-and-time displays:

```
FORMAT$(SerialNumber, "date-and-time format string")
```

You can use the **NOW** function in combination with the **INT** function to produce a serial date integer representing the current date. For example, consider this statement from the **OpenToday_Click** procedure (Listing 9-12):

```
Today = INT(NOW)
```

This statement assigns **Today** a serial number representing the current date, but with no record of the current time. The time portion is dropped from the number as a result of the **INT** function.

You also can use **Format$** to produce the date string or the time string alone from any serial number. In this case, the format string determines the content of the function's return value. For example, here is how the **Start_LostFocus** and **Finish_LostFocus** procedures display entries in the *Start* or *Finish* column of the time sheet grid:

```
Start(Index).Text = FORMAT$(S, "h:mm AM/PM")
Finish(Index).Text = FORMAT$(F, "h:mm AM/PM")
```

Another interesting example of the **Format$** function appears in the routine that builds the file names for saving time sheets to disk. The **FileName$** function (Listing 9-9) receives a serial date, **TargetDate**, as its argument and returns a string that includes the path name, file name, and extension name for saving the day's data to disk. In this case, the **Format$** function returns the date-string equivalent of its serial number argument:

```
TempName$ = PathName$ + "\"
TempName$ = TempName$ + FORMAT$(TargetDate, "mm-dd-yy")
FileName$ = TempName$ + "." + ExtName$
```

These lines produce a complete file name, such as:

```
C:\WORKDAY\04-17-92.WKD
```

The reverse operation—producing a serial number from a time string or a date string—is performed by Visual Basic's **TIMEVALUE** and **DATEVALUE** functions. Each of these functions takes one string argument—a time string or a date string—and returns the equivalent serial number:

```
SerialTime = TIMEVALUE(TimeString)
SerialDate = DATEVALUE(DateString)
```

Both functions are very flexible in the variety of string arguments that they will accept and recognize. For example, the **TIMEVALUE** function recognizes any of these time string formats:

```
6:35:15 PM
18:35:15
18:35
```

Likewise, **DATEVALUE** recognizes any of these date strings:

```
April 15, 1991
Apr 15, 91
15 April 91
4/15/91
4-15-91
```

As you might guess, **TIMEVALUE** gets more use than **DATEVALUE** in the *Work Day* application. For example, the **SavePage** procedure uses **TIMEVALUE** to store serial time values in the two time fields of the **WorkRecord** structure, **StartField** and **FinishedField**:

```
WorkRecord.StartField = TIMEVALUE(S$)
WorkRecord.FinishedField = TIMEVALUE(F$)
```

TIMEVALUE and **DATEVALUE** generate run-time errors if the functions receive unrecognizable time-string or date-string arguments. To avoid an interruption in your program's performance, you should write an error trap whenever there is a possibility that one of these functions will receive an invalid argument. For example, the **Start_LostFocus** and **Fin-**

ish_LostFocus event procedures read the user's entries into the **Start** and **Finish** text boxes. If the user enters a valid time string, the **TIMEVALUE** function successfully converts the entry. But if the user's input is not in a recognizable time string format, an error occurs when the program tries to convert the string to a serial time:

```
F = TIMEVALUE(Finish(Index).Text)
```

For this reason, the **LostFocus** routines include error traps to handle unpredictable problems in the user's input; for example:

```
OKTime = True
ON LOCAL ERROR GOTO BadFinishTime
  F = TIMEVALUE(Finish(Index).Text)
ON LOCAL ERROR GOTO 0
```

In this case, the error trap simply sets the variable named **OKTime** to false:

```
BadFinishTime:
  OKTime = False
RESUME NEXT
```

This causes the routine to reject the user's input and replace it with a blank string in the text box.

Once the user has successfully entered valid *Start* and *Finish* time strings for a given line in the time sheet grid, the *Work Day* application needs to compute the amount of time that has elapsed between the two time values and display the difference in hours and minutes. After using **TIMEVALUE** to convert each time string to a serial time, the program can simply subtract one time value from the other. This operation takes place in the function named **DoLineTotal**, stored in the TSPROCS.BAS module (Listing 9-24):

```
TempTotal = T2 - T1
```

The only complication is making the adjustment for a job entry that has gone past midnight. In this case, **T1**, the starting time, is greater than **T2**, the finishing time, and **TempTotal** is therefore a negative number. Adding 1 to this value gives the correct elapsed time:

```
IF T2 < T1 THEN TempTotal = TempTotal + 1
DoLineTotal = TempTotal
```

DoLineTotal therefore returns a double-precision number that represents the difference between two time values rather than an absolute time value. The program uses a string constant named **T$** to represent the format for converting these numbers to strings:

```
CONST T$ = "hh \hr mm \min"
```

For example, here is how the **Finish_LostFocus** procedure displays the total time for a job line:

```
LineTot = DoLineTotal(S, F)
TotalTime(Index).Text = FORMAT$(LineTot, T$)
```

As you have seen, this **Format$** function produces displays such as:

```
01 hr 30 min
```

The **UpdateDayTotal** procedure (Listing 9-13) tallies the total of all the times displayed on the current time sheet and displays the total in the **DayTotal** text box. In this case, the program displays the total time amount as a decimal value representing a number of hours; for example:

```
10.25 hrs
```

To produce this display, the program multiplies the total, **Tot**, by the number of hours in a day:

```
DispTot$ = FORMAT$(Tot * 24, "###0.00")
```

Finally, the *Work Day* application contains an interesting illustration of date arithmetic in the procedure that generates a one-week summary report, **PrintAWeek** (Listing 9-18). This procedure's first job is to determine the date of the first day of the week, given a date that the user has selected from the file list box. The user's selected date might be on any day of a given week, from Sunday to Saturday. **PrintAWeek** reads all the files for the corresponding week, beginning with the file for Sunday.

To find the date for the beginning of the week, **PrintAWeek** sends the user's selected date string to the **FirstDayOfWeek** function (Listing 9-20). This function begins by converting the date string to a serial date:

```
CurDate = DATEVALUE(DayInWeek)
```

Then the routine uses Visual Basic's **WEEKDAY** function in a formula that finds the date of the first day of the corresponding week:

```
FirstDayOfWeek = CurDate - (WEEKDAY(CurDate) - 1)
```

WEEKDAY returns an integer from 1 to 7, representing a day of the week from Sunday to Saturday. Subtracting 1 from the **WEEKDAY** value gives an integer in the range from 0 to 6. Reducing **CurDate** by this amount results in the serial date for Sunday.

The **PrintAWeek** procedure, in turn, assigns the serial date for Sunday to the variable **FirstDay** and then uses a **FOR** loop to go through an entire week of dates:

```
FOR i& = FirstDay TO FirstDay + 6
```

Notice that the counter variable for the loop is a long integer variable, **i&**, to accommodate the range of serial dates.

SUMMARY: DATE AND TIME VALUES

In other languages—including previous versions of Basic—programmers have to write their own procedures for performing such chronological operations as date and time arithmetic. But Visual Basic has built-in support for serial dates and serial time values, along with a library of functions for converting between strings and serial numbers. Functions such as **DATEVALUE**, **TIMEVALUE**—and the converse operations performed by **FORMAT$**—are simple to use but extremely valuable in any application where date and time values are significant.

Listing 9-1 Code from the Date Converter exercise

```
' The Date Converter Application
' DATES.MAK

' An experiment with date strings,
' serial numbers, and date arithmetic.

' DATES.FRM
' Declarations

DECLARE SUB CalcDiff ()

CONST False = 0
CONST True = NOT False
CONST DateFormat = "mm/dd/yyyy"


SUB CalcDiff ()

  ' Finds the difference in days between the two dates.

  IF DateStr(0).Text <> "" AND DateStr(1).Text <> "" THEN
    Diff.Text = STR$(ABS(VAL(SerialNum(0).Text) -
VAL(SerialNum(1).Text)))
```

(continued)

```
    END IF

  END SUB   ' CalcDiff



SUB ClearCommand_Click ()

  ' Clears all the text boxes.

  FOR i% = 0 TO 1
    DateStr(i%).Text = ""
    SerialNum(i%).Text = ""
  NEXT i%

  Diff.Text = ""

END SUB   ' ClearCommand_Click



SUB DateStr_GotFocus (Index AS INTEGER)

  ' Highlight the contents of the text box.

  DateStr(Index).SelStart = 0
  DateStr(Index).SelLength = LEN(DateStr(Index).Text)

END SUB   ' DateStr_GotFocus



SUB DateStr_LostFocus (Index AS INTEGER)

  ' Validates the user's date entry and displays
  ' the equivalent serial number in the adjacent text box.
  ' Also calls CalcDiff if both dates are available.

  DIM DateError%              ' Error flag for trap.
  DIM SerialDate AS LONG  ' Serial date value of entry.

  DateError% = False
  ON LOCAL ERROR GOTO BadDate
```

```
      SerialDate = DATEVALUE(DateStr(Index).Text)
    ON ERROR GOTO 0

    IF NOT DateError% THEN
      SerialNum(Index).Text = STR$(SerialDate)
      DateStr(Index).Text = FORMAT$(SerialDate, DateFormat)
      CalcDiff
    END IF

    EXIT SUB

  ' Error trap, activated if entry in DateStr box
  ' cannot be read as a date.

  BadDate:
    DateError% = True
    DateStr(Index).Text = ""
    SerialNum(Index).Text = ""
    Diff.Text = ""
  RESUME NEXT

  END SUB   ' DateStr().LostFocus



  SUB ExitCommand_Click ()

    END

  END SUB   ' ExitCommand_Click



  SUB TodayDate_Click (Index AS INTEGER)

    ' Enters today's date in the specified date box
    ' and the equivalent serial number in the adjacent box.

    DateStr(Index).Text = FORMAT$(INT(NOW), DateFormat)
    SerialNum(Index).Text = STR$(INT(NOW))
    CalcDiff

  END SUB   ' TodayDate_Click
```

Listing 9-2 Form-level declarations for TMSHEET.FRM

```
TMSHEET.FRM

' The Work Day Application (WORKDAY.MAK)

' TMSHEET.FRM
' Declarations.

DECLARE SUB DayTimer_Timer ()
DECLARE SUB UpdateDayTotal ()
DECLARE FUNCTION DoLineTotal (T1 AS DOUBLE, T2 AS DOUBLE) AS
DOUBLE
DECLARE SUB ClearLineTimes (WLineNum AS INTEGER)
DECLARE SUB SearchForPath ()
DECLARE FUNCTION FileName$ (TargetDate AS LONG)
DECLARE SUB OpenOnePage (FromLine%, ToLine%)
DECLARE SUB OpenToday_Click ()
DECLARE SUB ClearPage ()
DECLARE SUB SavePage ()
DECLARE FUNCTION CurTot () AS DOUBLE
DECLARE FUNCTION BlankLine (LineRec AS ANY) AS INTEGER

' Identify the other forms of the application.

'$FORM TSPrint
'$FORM TSOpen

' The record structure for one line on a time sheet.

TYPE WorkRecordType
  DescriptField AS STRING * 25
  IDField AS STRING * 10
  StartField AS DOUBLE
  FinishedField AS DOUBLE
END TYPE

' The path name for storing time sheet files.

CONST PathName$ = "C:\WorkDay"

' The extension name for time sheet files.

CONST ExtName$ = "WKD"
```

```
' Boolean values.

CONST False = 0
CONST True = NOT False

' Codes for the up- and down-arrow keys

CONST Up = &H26
CONST Down = &H28

' Constants for a blank time value and for
' formatting time strings.

CONST NoTime = -1#
CONST T$ = "hh \hr mm \min"

' The maximum number of lines in a time-sheet file.

CONST MaxLines = 80

DIM SHARED CurIndex AS INTEGER    ' The current line number
DIM SHARED Today AS LONG    ' Serial value for today's date.

DIM SHARED WorkRecord AS WorkRecordType   ' A file record.

' End of TMSHEET Declarations.
```

Listing 9-3 The Form_Load procedure for TMSHEET.FRM

```
SUB Form_Load ()

  ' Initialize the time sheet.

  DIM i%

  ' Make sure the directory exists for storing
  ' time sheet files. If not, create it.

  SearchForPath

  ' Display today's time sheet.
```

(continued)

```
    OpenToday_Click

    DayTimer_Timer
    CurIndex = 0
    CurTime.Enabled = False

END SUB  ' Form_Load (TimeSheet)
```

Listing 9-4 The ClearLineTimes and ClearPage Procedures

```
SUB ClearLineTimes (WLineNum AS INTEGER)

    ' Clear the time values from
    ' one line in the time sheet.

    Start(WLineNum).Text = ""
    Finish(WLineNum).Text = ""
    TotalTime(WLineNum).Text = ""

END SUB  ' ClearLineTimes


SUB ClearPage ()

  ' Clear all lines of the time sheet page.

  DIM i%

  FOR i% = 7 TO 0 STEP -1
    Ref(i%).Text = ""
    ClearLineTimes (i%)
    Description(i%).Text = ""
  NEXT i%

  DayTotal.Text = ""

  IF CurIndex <> 0 THEN
    CurIndex = 0
    Description(CurIndex).SETFOCUS
  END IF

END SUB   ' ClearPage
```

Listing 9-5 CurTime_Click, CurTot, and DayTimer_Timer

```
SUB CurTime_Click ()

  ' Enter the current time into a
  ' Start or Finished text box.

  SCREEN.ActiveControl(CurIndex).Text = FORMAT$(NOW,  "h:mm
AM/PM")

  ' Move the focus to trigger the LostFocus event.

  Ref(CurIndex).SETFOCUS

END SUB   ' CurTime_Click



FUNCTION CurTot () AS DOUBLE

  ' Find the total number of hours in all
  ' of the pages of the current time sheet.

  DIM S AS DOUBLE, F AS DOUBLE
  DIM TempTot AS DOUBLE

  ' First save the current page.

  SavePage
  TempTot = 0

  ' Open the current file and read each record.

  OPEN TSFileName.Caption FOR RANDOM AS #1 LEN =
LEN(WorkRecord)
  DO WHILE NOT EOF(1)
    GET #1, , WorkRecord
    S = WorkRecord.StartField
    F = WorkRecord.FinishedField

    ' Add to the total only if both time fields
    ' contain nonblank values.

    IF NOT (S < 0 OR F < 0) THEN TempTot = TempTot +
```

(continued)

```
DoLineTotal(S, F)
  LOOP
  CLOSE #1

  ' Multiply the time value by 24
  ' to compute the number of hours.

  CurTot = TempTot * 24

END FUNCTION   ' CurTot


SUB DayTimer_Timer ()

    ' Display the date and time on the
    ' TimeSheet form.

    DayAndTime.Caption = FORMAT$(NOW, "dddd, mmmm dd, yyyy
h:mm AM/PM")

END SUB   ' DayTimer_Timer
```

Listing 9-6 The GotFocus event procedures

```
SUB Description_GotFocus (Index AS INTEGER)

  ' Highlight the contents of a Description text box.

  Description(Index).SelStart = 0
  Description(Index).SelLength =
LEN(RTRIM$(Description(Index).Text))

  CurIndex = Index

END SUB   ' Description_GotFocus


SUB Finish_GotFocus (Index AS INTEGER)

  ' Highlight the contents of a Finish text box.
```

```
   IF RTRIM$(Finish(Index).Text) <> "" THEN
     Finish(Index).SelStart = 0
     Finish(Index).SelLength =
LEN(RTRIM$(Finish(Index).Text)) - 3
   END IF

   CurIndex = Index

   ' Enable the Current Time option in the Time menu.

   CurTime.Enabled = True

END SUB   ' Finish_GotFocus



SUB Ref_GotFocus (Index AS INTEGER)

   ' Highlight the contents of a Ref text box.

   Ref(Index).SelStart = 0
   Ref(Index).SelLength = LEN(RTRIM$(Ref(Index).Text))

   CurIndex = Index

END SUB   ' Ref_GotFocus



SUB Start_GotFocus (Index AS INTEGER)

   ' Highlight the contents of a Start text box.

   IF RTRIM$(Start(Index).Text) <> "" THEN
     Start(Index).SelStart = 0
     Start(Index).SelLength = LEN(RTRIM$(Start(Index).Text)) - 3
   END IF

   CurIndex = Index
   CurTime.Enabled = True

END SUB   ' Start_GotFocus
```

Listing 9-7 The KeyDown event procedures

```
SUB Description_KeyDown (Index AS INTEGER, KeyCode AS
INTEGER, Shift AS INTEGER)

  ' Respond to up- or down-arrow key.

  SELECT CASE KeyCode
  CASE Up
    IF CurIndex = 0 THEN
      Description(7).SETFOCUS
    ELSE
      Description(CurIndex - 1).SETFOCUS
    END IF
  CASE Down
    IF CurIndex = 7 THEN
      Description(0).SETFOCUS
    ELSE
      Description(CurIndex + 1).SETFOCUS
    END IF
  END SELECT

END SUB   ' Description_KeyDown


SUB Finish_KeyDown (Index AS INTEGER, KeyCode AS INTEGER,
Shift AS INTEGER)

  ' Respond to up- or down-arrow key.

  SELECT CASE KeyCode
  CASE Up
    IF CurIndex = 0 THEN
      Finish(7).SETFOCUS
    ELSE
      Finish(CurIndex - 1).SETFOCUS
    END IF
  CASE Down
    IF CurIndex = 7 THEN
      Finish(0).SETFOCUS
    ELSE
      Finish(CurIndex + 1).SETFOCUS
    END IF
  END SELECT

END SUB   ' Finish_KeyDown
```

```
SUB Ref_KeyDown (Index AS INTEGER, KeyCode AS INTEGER, Shift
AS INTEGER)

  ' Respond to up- or down-arrow key.

  SELECT CASE KeyCode
  CASE Up
    IF CurIndex = 0 THEN
      Ref(7).SETFOCUS
    ELSE
      Ref(CurIndex - 1).SETFOCUS
    END IF
  CASE Down
    IF CurIndex = 7 THEN
      Ref(0).SETFOCUS
    ELSE
      Ref(CurIndex + 1).SETFOCUS
    END IF
  END SELECT

END SUB   ' Ref_KeyDown



SUB Start_KeyDown (Index AS INTEGER, KeyCode AS INTEGER,
Shift AS INTEGER)

  ' Respond to up- or down-arrow key.

  SELECT CASE KeyCode
  CASE Up
    IF CurIndex = 0 THEN
      Start(7).SETFOCUS
    ELSE
      Start(CurIndex - 1).SETFOCUS
    END IF
  CASE Down
    IF CurIndex = 7 THEN
      Start(0).SETFOCUS
    ELSE
      Start(CurIndex + 1).SETFOCUS
    END IF
  END SELECT

END SUB   ' Start_KeyDown
```

Listing 9-8 The LostFocus procedures

```
SUB Finish_LostFocus (Index AS INTEGER)

  ' Validate a time entry.

  DIM OKTime AS INTEGER
  DIM S AS DOUBLE, F AS DOUBLE

  ' Attempt to convert the text value
  ' to a time value.

  OKTime = True
  ON LOCAL ERROR GOTO BadFinishTime
    F = TIMEVALUE(Finish(Index).Text)
  ON LOCAL ERROR GOTO 0

  IF OKTime THEN

    ' If the entry is valid, redisplay
    ' it in a standard time format.

    Finish(Index).Text = FORMAT$(F, "h:mm AM/PM")

    ' If the Start entry is also available,
    ' fill in the total hours value for this line.

    IF RTRIM$(Start(Index).Text) <> "" THEN
      S = TIMEVALUE(Start(Index).Text)
      LineTot = DoLineTotal(S, F)
      TotalTime(Index).Text = FORMAT$(LineTot, T$)
    END IF
  ELSE

    ' Otherwise, replace the current time and
    ' total with blank strings.

    Finish(Index).Text = ""
    TotalTime(Index).Text = ""
  END IF

  ' Recalculate the subtotal on the current page,
  ' and disable the Current Time option in the Time menu.

  UpdateDayTotal
```

```
   CurTime.Enabled = False

  EXIT SUB

BadFinishTime:
  OKTime = False
RESUME NEXT

END SUB   ' Finish_LostFocus


SUB Start_LostFocus (Index AS INTEGER)

  ' Validate a time entry.

  DIM OKTime AS INTEGER
  DIM S AS DOUBLE, F AS DOUBLE

  OKTime = True

  ' Attempt to convert the time entry to
  ' a numeric time value.

  ON LOCAL ERROR GOTO BadStartTime
    S = TIMEVALUE(Start(Index).Text)
  ON LOCAL ERROR GOTO 0

  ' If the entry is valid, redisplay it in
  ' a standard time format.

  IF OKTime THEN
    Start(Index).Text = FORMAT$(S, "h:mm AM/PM")
    IF RTRIM$(Finish(Index).Text) <> "" THEN
      F = TIMEVALUE(Finish(Index).Text)
      LineTot = DoLineTotal(S, F)
      TotalTime(Index).Text = FORMAT$(LineTot, T$)
    END IF

  ' Otherwise, replace the entry with a blank.

  ELSE
    Start(Index).Text = ""
    TotalTime(Index).Text = ""
  END IF
```

(continued)

```
    ' Update the total hours for the page.

    UpdateDayTotal

    CurTime.Enabled = False

    EXIT SUB

BadStartTime:
  OKTime = False
RESUME NEXT

END SUB   ' Start_LostFocus
```

Listing 9-9 The NewSheet_Click procedure and the FileName$ function

```
SUB NewSheet_Click ()

    ' Create a new time sheet file when the user
    ' chooses the New command from the File menu.

    ' Settings and return values for the
    ' INPUTBOX function.

    CONST YesNo = 4
    CONST Yes = 6
    CONST No = 7

    DIM NoAnswer AS INTEGER, OkDate AS INTEGER
    DIM NewDate AS LONG
    DIM NewFile$

    ' Input prompts.

    Prompt1$ = "Enter the date for which you want to"
    Prompt1$ = Prompt1$ + " create a new time sheet file."

    Prompt2$ = "This file already exists. Do you want to"
    Prompt2$ = Prompt2$ + " delete the previous version?"

    NoAnswer = False
```

```
' Display an input box and repeat the prompt until
' the user clicks Cancel or enters a valid date.

DO
  Answer$ = INPUTBOX$(Prompt1$, "New Time Sheet")
  IF Answer$ = "" THEN
    NoAnswer = True
  ELSE
    OkDate = True
    ON LOCAL ERROR GOTO BadDate
      NewDate = DATEVALUE(Answer$)
    ON LOCAL ERROR GOTO 0
  END IF
LOOP UNTIL OkDate OR NoAnswer

' If the user has entered a valid date,
' create the new time sheet file.

IF OkDate THEN
  NewFile$ = FileName$(NewDate)

  OPEN NewFile$ FOR RANDOM AS #1 LEN = LEN(WorkRecord)
    NumRecs% = LOF(1) / LEN(WorkRecord)
  CLOSE #1

  ' If this file already exists on disk, find out
  ' whether the user wants to replace it with a blank file.

  IF NumRecs% > 0 THEN
    ans% = MSGBOX(Prompt2$, YesNo, "New Time Sheet")
    IF ans% = Yes THEN KILL NewFile$
  END IF

  ' Save the current page of the previous file,
  ' display the new file name, and display its first page.

  SavePage
  TSFileName.Caption = NewFile$
  OpenOnePage 1, 8
END IF

EXIT SUB
```

(continued)

```
BadDate:
  OkDate = False
RESUME NEXT


END SUB   ' NewSheet_Click


FUNCTION FileName$ (TargetDate AS LONG)

    ' Create a file name from a serial date.
    ' Note: PathName$ and ExtName$ are global constants.

    DIM TempName$

    TempName$ = PathName$ + "\"
    TempName$ = TempName$ + FORMAT$(TargetDate, "mm-dd-yy")
    FileName$ = TempName$ + "." + ExtName$

END FUNCTION   ' FileName$
```

Listing 9-10 NextPage_Click, PreviousPage_Click, and OpenOnePage

```
SUB NextPage_Click ()

  ' Save the current page and then show
  ' the next page in the current time sheet file.

  SavePage
  FirstLine% = VAL(LineNum(0).Caption)

  ' Allow no more than MaxLines in the file.

  IF FirstLine% + 15 <= MaxLines THEN
    OpenOnePage FirstLine% + 8, FirstLine% + 15
  END IF

END SUB   ' NextPage_Click
```

```
SUB PreviousPage_Click ()

   ' Save the current page and then show
   ' the previous page in the current time sheet file.

   SavePage
   FirstLine% = VAL(LineNum(0).Caption)
   IF FirstLine% > 8 THEN OpenOnePage FirstLine% - 8,
FirstLine% - 1

END SUB   ' PreviousPage_Click


SUB OpenOnePage (FromLine%, ToLine%)

   ' Open a time sheet file and display a page of entries.

   DIM S AS DOUBLE, F AS DOUBLE

   CONST TimeFormat$ = "h:mm AM/PM"

   ClearPage

   ' Read the file name from the TSFileName label
   ' on the TimeSheet form. Then compute the number of
   ' records in the file.

   OPEN TSFileName.Caption FOR RANDOM AS #1 LEN =
LEN(WorkRecord)
   RecCount = LOF(1) / LEN(WorkRecord)

   ' Read and display a page of records.

   FOR i% = FromLine% TO ToLine%

      ' Calculate the index number for the text arrays
      ' and display the line number.

      LineNdx% = (i% - 1) MOD 8
      LineNum(LineNdx%).Caption = FORMAT$(i%, "## ")

      ' If this line contains a record, display it.
```

(continued)

```
    IF i% <= RecCount THEN
      GET #1, i%, WorkRecord
      Description(LineNdx%).Text = WorkRecord.DescriptField
      Ref(LineNdx%).Text = WorkRecord.IDField

      S = WorkRecord.StartField
      F = WorkRecord.FinishedField

      ' Display time entries or blanks.

      IF S >= 0 THEN
        Start(LineNdx%).Text = FORMAT$(S, TimeFormat$)
      ELSE
        Start(LineNdx%).Text = ""
      END IF

      IF F >= 0 THEN
        Finish(LineNdx%).Text = FORMAT$(F, TimeFormat$)
      ELSE
        Finish(LineNdx%).Text = ""
      END IF

      ' If both time entries are available,
      ' calculate the total for the line.

      IF NOT (S < 0 OR F < 0) THEN
        TotalTime(LineNdx%).Text = FORMAT$(DoLineTotal(S,
F), T$)
      END IF

    END IF
  NEXT i%

  CLOSE #1

  ' Display the subtotal for the page.

  UpdateDayTotal

END SUB   ' OpenOnePage
```

Listing 9-11 The SavePage procedure

```
SUB SavePage ()

  ' Save the displayed page of entries
  ' to the current time-sheet file.

  DIM CurFile$, S$, F$
  DIM FirstLine AS INTEGER, LastLine AS INTEGER
  DIM Ndx AS INTEGER

  ' Read the range of record numbers
  ' from the LineNum labels.

  FirstLine = VAL(LineNum(0).Caption)
  LastLine = VAL(LineNum(7).Caption)

  ' Read the file name from the TSFileName label.

  CurFile$ = TSFileName.Caption
  Description(0).SETFOCUS

  ' Open the random-access file
  ' and save each line as a record.

  OPEN CurFile$ FOR RANDOM AS #1 LEN = LEN(WorkRecord)
    FOR i% = FirstLine TO LastLine
      Ndx = (i% - 1) MOD 8
      WorkRecord.DescriptField = Description(Ndx).Text
      WorkRecord.IDField = Ref(Ndx).Text

      S$ = RTRIM$(Start(Ndx).Text)
      F$ = RTRIM$(Finish(Ndx).Text)

      ' Save each time entry as a double-precision
      ' numeric time value. For a blank time entry,
      ' save the value of the constant NoTime (-1).

      IF LEN(S$) > 0 THEN
        WorkRecord.StartField = TIMEVALUE(S$)
      ELSE
        WorkRecord.StartField = NoTime
      END IF
```

(continued)

```
      IF LEN(F$) > 0 THEN
         WorkRecord.FinishedField = TIMEVALUE(F$)
      ELSE
         WorkRecord.FinishedField = NoTime
      END IF

      PUT #1, i%, WorkRecord
   NEXT i%
 CLOSE #1

END SUB ' SavePage
```

Listing 9-12 Click event procedures for TMSHEET.FRM

```
SUB ExitCommand_Click ()

   ' Save the current page and
   ' end the program performance.

   SavePage
   END

END SUB   ' ExitCommand_Click


SUB OpenToday_Click ()

  ' Open the file for today's time sheet.

  IF LTRIM$(TSFileName.Caption) <> "" THEN SavePage
  Today = INT(NOW)

   ' Display the file name in the
   ' FSFileName label.

  TSFileName.Caption = FileName$(Today)

   ' Display the first page of the file.

  OpenOnePage 1, 8

 END SUB   ' OpenToday_Click
```

```
SUB PrintPrevRec_Click ()

    ' Prepare to print a time sheet or
    ' a week of time sheets from files
    ' stored on disk.

    ' First save the displayed page
    ' of the current file.

    SavePage

    ' Then show the TSPrint form to elicit
    ' the user's choice of a file name.

    TSPrint.SHOW 1

END SUB  ' PrintPrevRec_Click


SUB PrintRec_Click ()

    ' Print all the lines of the current time sheet.

    DIM S AS DOUBLE, F AS DOUBLE, Tot AS DOUBLE

    SavePage

    ' Set up an error trap to avoid a run-time
    ' error if the printer is not ready.

    ON LOCAL ERROR GOTO PrinterProblem

    ' Open the time sheet file as #2
    ' and the printer device as #3.

    OPEN TSFileName.Caption FOR RANDOM AS #2 LEN =
LEN(WorkRecord)
    OPEN "Prn" FOR OUTPUT AS #3
    NumRecs% = LOF(2) / LEN(WorkRecord)

    PRINT #3, "Time Sheet File: "; TSFileName.Caption
    PRINT #3,

    ' Print each line of the file.
```

(continued)

```
FOR i% = 1 TO NumRecs%
  GET #2, i%, WorkRecord

  ' Do not print blank lines. (The BlankLine
  ' function is in the TSProcs module.)

  IF NOT BlankLine(WorkRecord) THEN
    D$ = WorkRecord.DescriptField
    R$ = WorkRecord.IDField
    S = WorkRecord.StartField
    F = WorkRecord.FinishedField

    ' Print each field, or the appropriate
    ' number of spaces for a blank field.

    IF RTRIM$(D$) <> "" THEN
      PRINT #3, D$; "  ";
    ELSE
      PRINT #3, SPACE$(27);
    END IF

    IF RTRIM$(R$) <> "" THEN
      PRINT #3, R$; "   ";
    ELSE
      PRINT #3, SPACE$(12);
    END IF

    IF S < 0 THEN
      PRINT #3, SPACE$(11);
    ELSE
      PRINT #3, FORMAT$(S, "hh:mm AM/PM"); "    ";
    END IF

    IF F < 0 THEN
      PRINT #3, SPACE$(11);
    ELSE
      PRINT #3, FORMAT$(F, "hh:mm AM/PM"); "    ";
    END IF

    ' If both time entries are available,
    ' print the total number of hours for the line.

    IF NOT (S < 0 OR F < 0) THEN
      Tot = DoLineTotal(S, F)
      PRINT #3, FORMAT$(Tot, T$)
    ELSE
```

```
        PRINT #3,
      END IF
    END IF

  NEXT i%

  CLOSE #2

  ' Print the total hours for the file.

  PRINT #3,
  PRINT #3, SPACE$(46); "Total --> ";
  TempTot = CurTot
  PRINT #3, FORMAT$(TempTot, "###0.00"); " hrs."
  PRINT #3, CHR$(12) ' form-feed.
AbortPrint:
  CLOSE

EXIT SUB

PrinterProblem:
  MSGBOX "Check printer and try again.", 0, "Printer Problem"
RESUME AbortPrint

END SUB   ' PrintRec_Click
```

Listing 9-13 ShowTotal_Click and UpdateDayTotal

```
SUB ShowTotal_Click ()

  ' When the user chooses the Total command
  ' from the Pages menu, display a message box
  ' showing the total hours from in the current file.

  DIM TotStr$

  ' Prepare the message string. The CurTot function
  ' calculates the total hours for the file.

  TotStr$ = "Total hours in all pages: "
  TotStr$ = TotStr$ + FORMAT$(CurTot, "###0.00")
```

(continued)

```
    MSGBOX TotStr$, 0, "Show Total"

END SUB  ' ShowTotal_Click



SUB UpdateDayTotal ()

  ' Calculate the total hours for the
  ' current page of the time sheet file.

  DIM Tot AS DOUBLE, i%, DispTot$
  DIM S AS DOUBLE, F AS DOUBLE, T1$, T2$

  Tot = 0

  ' Step through each line of the time sheet.

  FOR i% = 0 TO 7

    T1$ = RTRIM$(Start(i%).Text)
    T2$ = RTRIM$(Finish(i%).Text)

    IF LEN(T1$) > 0 AND LEN(T2$) > 0 THEN
      S = TIMEVALUE(T1$)
      F = TIMEVALUE(T2$)
      Tot = Tot + DoLineTotal(S, F)
    END IF

  NEXT i%

  ' Display the Total value.

  DispTot$ = FORMAT$(Tot * 24, "###0.00")
  IF (Tot * 24) > 1 THEN
    DispTot$ = DispTot$ + " hrs."
  ELSE
    DispTot$ = DispTot$ + " hr."
  END IF

  DayTotal.Text = DispTot$

END SUB  ' UpdateDayTotal
```

Listing 9-14 The SearchForPath procedure

```
SUB SearchForPath ()

  ' Search for the directory in which work sheet files
  ' are to be stored. Create the directory (on drive C)
  ' if it does not exist yet.

  DIM CDir$

  ' Record the current directory.

  CDir$ = CURDIR$("C")

  ' Set up an error trap.

  ON LOCAL ERROR RESUME NEXT

  ' Attempt to change to the target directory.

  CHDIR PathName$

  ' If the directory doesn't exist, create it.

  MKDIR PathName$

  ' Restore the original directory.

  CHDIR CDir$

END SUB   ' SearchForPath
```

Listing 9-15 Form-level declarations and Form_Load procedure for TSPRINT.FRM

```
' TSPRINT.FRM
' Declarations

DECLARE SUB SavePage ()
DECLARE FUNCTION TimeStr$ (InTime AS DOUBLE)
DECLARE SUB OKButton_Click ()
```

(continued)

```
DECLARE SUB PrintADay ()
DECLARE SUB PrintAWeek ()
DECLARE SUB SortWorkRecordList (NumRecs AS INTEGER)
DECLARE SUB PrintWorkRecordList (Title AS STRING, NumRecs AS
INTEGER, OutFile AS STRING)
DECLARE FUNCTION FirstDayOfWeek! (DayInWeek AS STRING)
DECLARE FUNCTION DoLineTotal (T1 AS DOUBLE, T2 AS DOUBLE) AS
DOUBLE
DECLARE FUNCTION BlankLine (LineRec AS ANY) AS INTEGER


' The record structure for one line on a time sheet.

TYPE WorkRecordType
   DescriptField AS STRING * 25
   IDField AS STRING * 10
   StartField AS DOUBLE
   FinishedField AS DOUBLE
END TYPE

' Dynamic array of work records.

DIM SHARED WorkRecordList() AS WorkRecordType

' A single work record.

DIM SHARED WorkRecord AS WorkRecordType

' The path name for storing time sheet files.

CONST PathName$ = "C:\WorkDay"

' The extension name for time sheet files.

CONST ExtName$ = "WKD"

' Boolean constants.

CONST False = 0
CONST True = NOT False

' End of TSPRINT.FRM declarations.
```

```
SUB Form_Load ()

  ' Initialize the path and pattern
  ' of the file list box.

  FileList.Path = PathName$
  FileList.Pattern = "*." + ExtName$
  FileList.REFRESH

END SUB   ' Form_Load (TSPRINT.FRM)
```

Listing 9-16 Click procedures for TSPRINT.FRM

```
SUB CancelButton_Click ()

  ' Return to the time sheet without printing.

  UNLOAD TSPrint

END SUB   ' CancelButton_Click (TSPRINT.FRM)


SUB FileList_Click ()

  ' When the user clicks a file name in
  ' the file list, copy the file name to
  ' the DisplayFile text box.

  DisplayFile.Text = FileList.FileName

  ' Then enable the OK button.

  OKButton.Enabled = True

END SUB   ' FileList_Click (TSPRINT.FRM)


SUB FileList_DblClick ()

  ' If the user double-clicks a file name
```

(continued)

```
    ' in the file list, force a call to the
    ' OKButton_Click event procedure.

    OKButton_Click

END SUB   ' FileList_DblClick (TSPRINT.FRM)



SUB OKButton_Click ()

   ' When the user clicks the OKButton, call one
   ' of the two print procedures and then unload the
   ' TSPrint form.

   ' The choice between PrintADay and PrintAWeek
   ' depends on which of the two WeekOrDay option
   ' buttons is currently active.

   IF LTRIM$(DisplayFile.Text) <> "" THEN
      IF WeekOrDay(0).Value THEN PrintADay ELSE PrintAWeek
   END IF

   UNLOAD TSPrint

END SUB   ' OKButton_Click (TSPRINT.FRM)
```

Listing 9-17 The PrintADay procedure (TSPRINT.FRM)

```
   SUB PrintADay ()

      ' Print a single day of work records.

      DIM WorkFileName AS STRING, RecCount AS INTEGER
      DIM Heading AS STRING, DateStr AS STRING, OutFileName AS
   STRING

      ' Create the complete file name for the time sheet.

      WorkFileName = PathName$ + "\" + DisplayFile.Text

      ' Open the file and count its records.
```

```
OPEN WorkFileName FOR RANDOM AS #1 LEN = LEN(WorkRecord)
  RecCount = LOF(1) / LEN(WorkRecord)

  ' Redimension the array of records accordingly.

  REDIM WorkRecordList(RecCount) AS WorkRecordType

  ' Read the entire file into the array.

  FOR i% = 1 TO RecCount
    GET #1, i%, WorkRecordList(i%)

    ' If a reference entry is blank, store the
    ' string "(no ref #)" as the IDField value.

    IF RTRIM$(WorkRecordList(i%).IDField) = "" THEN
      WorkRecordList(i%).IDField = "(no ref #)"
    END IF
  NEXT i%
CLOSE #1

  ' Sort the array by the reference numbers (IDField)
  ' and descriptions (DescriptField).

SortWorkRecordList RecCount

  ' Print the one-day time sheet.

DateStr = LEFT$(DisplayFile.Text, 8)
Heading = "Time Sheet for " + DateStr
OutFileName = PathName$ + "\" + DateStr + ".TXT"
PrintWorkRecordList Heading, RecCount, OutFileName

END SUB   ' PrintADay (TSPRINT.FRM)
```

Listing 9-18 The PrintAWeek procedure (TSPRINT.FRM)

```
SUB PrintAWeek ()

  ' Print a week's summary of work records.

  DIM WorkFileName AS STRING, RecCount AS INTEGER
  DIM WeekRecCount AS INTEGER, Heading AS STRING
```

(continued)

```
DIM FirstDay AS LONG, FirstDayStr AS STRING, i&, j%
DIM FirstFileName AS STRING

' Find the serial number and the date string
' representing the first day of the target week.

FirstDay = FirstDayOfWeek(LEFT$(DisplayFile.Text, 8))
FirstDayStr = FORMAT$(FirstDay, "mm-dd-yy")

' Count the records in all the time sheet
' files for the week (Sunday through Saturday).

WeekRecCount = 0
FOR i& = FirstDay TO FirstDay + 6
   WorkFileName = PathName$ + "\" + FORMAT$(i&, "mm-dd-yy")
+ ExtName$
   OPEN WorkFileName FOR RANDOM AS #1 LEN = LEN(WorkRecord)
      WeekRecCount = WeekRecCount + LOF(1) / LEN(WorkRecord)
   CLOSE #1
NEXT i&

' Redimension the work record array accordingly.

REDIM WorkRecordList(WeekRecCount) AS WorkRecordType

' Read work records into the array, from as
' many as seven time sheet files.

ListNum = 1
FOR i& = FirstDay TO FirstDay + 6
   WorkFileName = PathName + "\" + FORMAT$(i&, "mm-dd-yy")
+ ExtName$
   OPEN WorkFileName FOR RANDOM AS #1 LEN = LEN(WorkRecord)
      RecCount = LOF(1) / LEN(WorkRecord)
      FOR j% = 1 TO RecCount
        GET #1, j%, WorkRecordList(ListNum)

        ' If a reference entry is blank, store the string
        ' "(no ref #)" as the IDField value.

        IF RTRIM$(WorkRecordList(ListNum).IDField) = "" THEN
           WorkRecordList(ListNum).IDField = "(no ref #)"
        END IF

        ListNum = ListNum + 1
      NEXT j%
```

```
      CLOSE #1
   NEXT i&

   ' Sort the array by the reference numbers (IDField)
   ' and the descriptions (DescriptField).

   SortWorkRecordList WeekRecCount

   ' Print the one-week time sheet summary.

   Heading = "Summary Time Sheet for the Week of " +
 FirstDayStr
   FirstFileName = PathName$ + "\" + FirstDayStr + ".WK"
   PrintWorkRecordList Heading, WeekRecCount, FirstFileName

 END SUB   ' PrintAWeek (TSPRINT.FRM)
```

Listing 9-19 The PrintWorkRecordList procedure (TSPRINT.FRM)

```
SUB PrintWorkRecordList (Title AS STRING, NumRecs AS
INTEGER, OutFile AS STRING)

   ' Print a daily or weekly report from a selected time
 sheet file.

   DIM T1 AS DOUBLE, T2 AS DOUBLE, RefTot AS DOUBLE
   DIM ThisRef AS STRING, NextRef AS STRING
   DIM TabForCenter AS INTEGER, Dest AS STRING
   DIM GrandTot AS DOUBLE

   ' Read the SaveReport value to determine
   ' whether the output should be printed or
   ' saved as a text file on disk.

   IF SaveReport.Value THEN
     Dest = OutFile
   ELSE
     Dest = "Prn"
   END IF

   ' In either event, set up an error trap and
```

(continued)

```
' use the Open statement to open the output file.

ON LOCAL ERROR GOTO DeviceNotReady
OPEN Dest FOR OUTPUT AS #1

' Print the title and the column headings.

TabForCenter = (75 - LEN(Title)) \ 2
PRINT #1, TAB(TabForCenter); Title
PRINT #1, TAB(TabForCenter); STRING$(LEN(Title), "=")
PRINT #1,
PRINT #1, "Job Description"; TAB(26); "  Ref.         ";
PRINT #1, "Start       Finish";
PRINT #1, "     Total Time"
PRINT #1, "---------------"; TAB(26); "  ----         ";
PRINT #1, "-----      ------";
PRINT #1, "     ----------"
PRINT #1,

RefTot = 0
GrandTot = 0

' Print the entire array of records.

FOR i% = 1 TO NumRecs

   ' Keep track of changes in the sorted
   ' column of reference numbers.

   IF NOT BlankLine(WorkRecordList(i%)) THEN
     ThisRef = WorkRecordList(i%).IDField
     IF i% <> NumRecs THEN
       NextRef = WorkRecordList(i% + 1).IDField
     ELSE
       NextRef = ""
     END IF

     ' Print a detail line.

     PRINT #1, WorkRecordList(i%).DescriptField; "   ";
     PRINT #1, ThisRef; "   ";
     T1 = WorkRecordList(i%).StartField
     T2 = WorkRecordList(i%).FinishedField
```

```
' If a time value is recorded as -1 (NoTime), the
' user has left this entry blank. Accordingly,
' print a space in the time column.

IF T1 >= 0 THEN
   PRINT #1, FORMAT$(T1, "hh:mm AM/PM"); "    ";
ELSE
   PRINT #1, SPACE$(11);
END IF

IF T2 >= 0 THEN
   PRINT #1, FORMAT$(T2, "hh:mm AM/PM"); "    ";
ELSE
   PRINT #1, SPACE$(11);
END IF

' Compute and print a total if
' both time values are available.

IF NOT (T1 < 0 OR T2 < 0) THEN
   PRINT #1, FORMAT$(DoLineTotal(T1, T2), "hh \hr mm
\min")

   ' Accumulate the total time for the
   ' current reference number.

   RefTot = RefTot + DoLineTotal(T1, T2)
ELSE
   PRINT #1,
END IF

' If the reference number changes, print
' a total line for the previous reference number.

IF ThisRef <> NextRef THEN
   PRINT #1,
   PRINT #1, TAB(37); "Total for "; ThisRef; " --> ";
   PRINT #1, FORMAT$(RefTot * 24, "##0.00"); " hr";
   IF RefTot * 24 > 1# THEN PRINT #1, "s" ELSE PRINT #1,
   PRINT #1,
   GrandTot = GrandTot + RefTot
   RefTot = 0
END IF
END IF
```

(continued)

```
    NEXT i%

    ' Print a total line for the entire report.

    PRINT #1,
    PRINT #1, TAB(37); "*** Total Work Time ---> ";
    PRINT #1, FORMAT$(GrandTot * 24, "##0.00"); " hr";
    IF GrandTot * 24 > 1# THEN PRINT #1, "s" ELSE PRINT #1,
    If Dest = "Prn" THEN PRINT #1, CHR$(12) ' form-feed.
AbortPrint:
    CLOSE #1

EXIT SUB

DeviceNotReady:
    MSGBOX "Check printer or disk and try again.", 0, "Device
Problem"
RESUME AbortPrint

END SUB   ' PrintWorkRecordList (TSPRINT.FRM)
```

Listing 9-20 The FirstDayOfWeek function

```
FUNCTION FirstDayOfWeek (DayInWeek AS STRING)

    ' Given a date string, find the serial date of
    ' the first day--Sunday--of the same week.

    DIM CurDate AS DOUBLE

    ' Find the serial date of the argument.

    CurDate = DATEVALUE(DayInWeek)

    ' Subtract enough days to reach Sunday.

    FirstDayOfWeek = CurDate - (WEEKDAY(CurDate) - 1)

END FUNCTION   ' FirstDayOfWeek (TSPRINT.FRM)
```

Listing 9-21 The SortWorkRecordList procedure

```
SUB SortWorkRecordList (NumRecs AS INTEGER)

  ' Sort the work record array, using the reference
  ' numbers (IDField) as the primary key, and the
  ' job description field as the secondary key.

  DIM i%, j%
  DIM TempWorkRec AS WorkRecordType

  FOR i% = 1 TO NumRecs - 1
    FOR j% = i% + 1 TO NumRecs

      ' Concatenate the primary and secondary key values.

      field1$ = WorkRecordList(i%).IDField +
WorkRecordList(i%).DescriptField
      field2$ = WorkRecordList(j%).IDField +
WorkRecordList(j%).DescriptField

      ' Compare the values, and swap the record positions if
necessary.

      IF field1$ > field2$ THEN
        TempWorkRec = WorkRecordList(i%)
        WorkRecordList(i%) = WorkRecordList(j%)
        WorkRecordList(j%) = TempWorkRec
      END IF

    NEXT j%
  NEXT i%

END SUB  ' SortWorkRecordList (TSPRINT.FRM)
```

Listing 9-22 Form-level declarations and Form_Load procedure for TSOPEN.FRM

```
' TSOPEN.FRM
' Declarations

' Identify the related form.

'$FORM TimeSheet
```

(continued)

```
DECLARE SUB OKButton_Click ()

' The path name for storing time sheet files.

CONST PathName$ = "C:\WorkDay"

' The extension name for time sheet files.

CONST ExtName$ = "WKD"

' Boolean constants.

CONST False = 0
CONST True = NOT False

' End of TSOPEN.FRM declarations.


SUB Form_Load ()

  ' Initialize the path and pattern
  ' of the file list box.

  TSFileList.Path = PathName$
  TSFileList.Pattern = "*." + ExtName$

  TSFileToOpen.Caption = ""
  OKButton.Enabled = False

  TSFileList.REFRESH

END SUB  ' Form_Load (TSOPEN.FRM)
```

Listing 9-23 Click event procedures for TSOPEN.FRM

```
SUB CancelButton_Click ()

  ' Return to the time sheet without opening a file.

  UNLOAD TSOpen

END SUB  ' CancelButton_Click (TSOPEN.FRM)
```

```
SUB OKButton_Click ()

  DIM TempName$

  ' Copy the selected file name to the TMSHEET form.

  TempName$ = PathName$ + "\" + TSOpen.TSFileToOpen.Caption
  TimeSheet.TSFileName.Caption = TempName$

  UNLOAD TSOpen

END SUB  ' OKButton_Click  (TSOPEN.FRM)



SUB TSFileList_Click ()

  ' When the user clicks a file name in the
  ' file list, copy the file name to the
  ' TSFileToOpen text box.

  TSFileToOpen.Caption = TSFileList.FileName

  ' Now enable the OK button.

  OKButton.Enabled = True

END SUB   ' TSFileList_Click (TSOPEN.FRM)



SUB TSFileList_DblClick ()

  ' If the user double-clicks a file name in
  ' the file list box, force a call to the
  ' OKButton_Click event procedure.

  OKButton_Click

END SUB  ' TSFileList_DblClick (TSOPEN.FRM)
```

Listing 9-24 TSPROCS.BAS Declarations and Functions

```
' The TSPROCS.BAS module.

' Declarations.

'$FORM TimeSheet
'$FORM TSPrint

DECLARE FUNCTION BlankLine (LineRec AS ANY) AS INTEGER
DECLARE FUNCTION DoLineTotal (T1 AS DOUBLE, T2 AS DOUBLE) AS
DOUBLE

' The record structure for one line on a time sheet.

TYPE WorkRecordType
  DescriptField AS STRING * 25
  IDField AS STRING * 10
  StartField AS DOUBLE
  FinishedField AS DOUBLE
END TYPE

' End of TSPROCS.BAS declarations.



FUNCTION BlankLine (LineRec AS WorkRecordType) AS INTEGER

  ' Check to see if the current
  ' time sheet line is blank.

  DIM D%, R%, S%, F%

  D% = (RTRIM$(LineRec.DescriptField) = "")
  R% = (RTRIM$(LineRec.IDField) = "") OR LineRec.IDField =
"(no ref #)"
  S% = (LineRec.StartField < 0)
  F% = (LineRec.FinishedField < 0)

  BlankLine = D% AND R% AND S% AND F%

END FUNCTION   ' BlankLine
```

```
FUNCTION DoLineTotal (T1 AS DOUBLE, T2 AS DOUBLE) AS DOUBLE

   ' Calculate the difference between two time
   ' values and return a serial time value.

   DIM TempTotal AS DOUBLE

   TempTotal = T2 - T1

   ' If the Finish value is earlier than the start,
   ' assume that the work continued past midnight.

   IF T2 < T1 THEN TempTotal = TempTotal + 1

   DoLineTotal = TempTotal

END FUNCTION   ' DoLineTotal
```

10

File-System Controls and Graphics: The Pie Chart Application

INTRODUCTION

An application that reads and writes disk files usually has an **Open** command that provides access to relevant data files stored on disk. In a typical **Open** dialog box, you can expect to accomplish three steps in the process of locating and opening a file:

1. Change the current disk drive if necessary—for example, to A, B, or C.

2. Find the directory where the file is stored.

3. Select the file itself and open it.

Each time you choose such an **Open** command, you can select the drive and directory for finding a particular file.

To match this capability in your own Visual Basic for DOS applications, you use three specially designed *file-system controls,* known as the *drive list box,* the *directory list box,* and the *file list box.* Examples of all three controls appear in Figure 10-1. Under the direction of a program's code, these three controls work together in a coordinated way to give the user access to any application-specific file on disk. The drive list box has a drop-down list displaying the drives on the current system. When the user clicks the name of a drive in this list, the directory list box in turn displays the hierarchy of directories available on the drive. Likewise, when the user selects and opens a directory, the file list box displays the names of files stored in the directory.

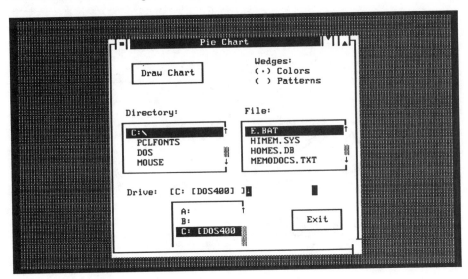

Figure 10-1 Examples of the three file-system controls

While the coordination between these three controls is not quite automatic in Visual Basic, nonetheless it requires very little programming on your part. To integrate the drive, directory, and file boxes, your program monitors the **Change** and **Click** events—and the resulting changes in property settings—that take place when the user makes selections in the boxes.

In particular, your program takes charge of exchanging specific items of information between the three controls:

- The drive list box has a **Drive** property that represents the name of the currently selected drive. When the user makes a new selection in the drive list box, the resulting **Change** event is an opportunity for your program to read the new **Drive** setting and pass it on to the directory list box.

- The directory list box has a property named **Path** that represents the current directory path. Your program assigns the **Drive** setting from the drive list box to the directory's **Path** property; this causes the directory box to display the directory hierarchy of the newly selected drive. When the user subsequently opens a directory, a **Change** procedure in your program can read the new setting of the directory control's **Path** property and pass the value to the file list box.

- The file list box has its own **Path** property. In this case the setting specifies the directory path from which the file list itself will be read.

Your program assigns the new **Path** setting from the directory list box to the **Path** property of the file list box; as a result, file names from the selected directory are displayed. The file list box also has a **Pattern** property to which your program can assign a specific wild-card string, thus restricting the displayed file list to a particular set of file names.

- Finally, when the user clicks a file name in the file list box, a **Click** event procedure in your program can read the new setting of the control's **FileName** property. This property supplies the name of the file that the user has selected.

Your code is *not* responsible for building the lists displayed in these three boxes. **ADDITEM**—the method used for building the list in a combo box—does not exist for the drive, directory, or file controls. Rather, these controls automatically read file-system information directly from the operating system. All your program has to do is orchestrate the changes in the three lists and read the user's file selections.

Clearly these three controls are among Visual Basic's most powerful tools. When you first add a set of them to a new form, their default **CtlName** values are **Drive1**, **Dir1**, and **File1**. In this chapter you'll learn to use the following properties and events:

- **Drive1.Drive**, the current drive name, and **Dir1.Path**, the current directory path.

- **File1.Path** and **File1.Pattern**, the properties that determine the contents of the file list.

- **File1.FileName**, the name of the currently selected file in the file list.

- **Drive1_Change**, **Dir1_Change**, **File1_Click**, and **File1_DblClick**, the event procedures that are called when the user makes new selections in the three file-system controls.

As an exercise with these controls, properties, and events, this chapter presents an application called *Pie Chart*. The application reads data files created by two other programs in this book—*Sales Week* (from Chapter 6) and *Work Day* (from Chapter 9)—and creates pie charts from the numeric information stored in the files.

Open the *Pie Chart* application now into the Visual Basic environment. The project is stored on the exercise disk as PIE.MAK and consists of a single form (Figure 10-2). Press F5 to run the program. You'll see that the three file-system controls from Figure 10-1 are part of this program's dialog box.

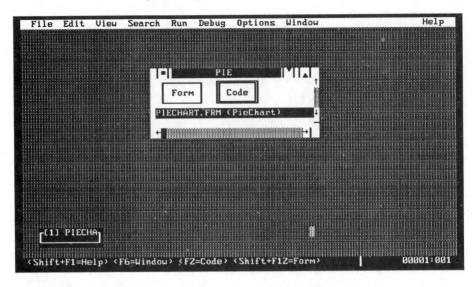

Figure 10-2 The PIE.MAK project

THE PIE CHART APPLICATION

A pie chart shows how individual numeric data items relate to the sum of all the items in a data set. Each number is represented by a wedge in a circular pie. The angle of a wedge—and therefore the size of the slice—is determined by the ratio of one numeric data item to the sum of all the data. In short, a pie chart gives you a useful picture of the parts that create a whole. The *Pie Chart* application draws pie charts for two familiar kinds of data files you have worked with in earlier chapters:

- The time-sheet files created by the *Work Day* program. You'll recall that these files have extension names of WKD. For a WKD file, the *Pie Chart* application draws a pie depicting the number of work hours recorded for a given day. Each wedge in the pie represents the number of hours recorded for one particular project, identified by the project's reference number.

- The weekly sales files created by the *Sales Week* program. These files have SLS extensions. For an SLS file, *Pie Chart* draws a pie depicting the total dollar sales for a given week. Each wedge in the pie thus represents one day's sales—from Sunday to Saturday.

The *Work Day* program creates random-access files, organized by individual job records. In contrast, the *Sales Week* program creates sequential-access text files consisting of a simple list of daily sales figures. The *Pie Chart* program therefore needs different procedures to read each kind of file. On the other hand, a single event procedure in the program draws the pie chart itself, regardless of the source of the data. For this reason you will find the application relatively easy to expand if you decide that you want to add other file types to the list of files that the program can recognize, read, and chart.

When you first run the application, the dialog box shown in Figure 10-1 appears on the screen. This form contains a variety of objects, including the trio of file-system controls. The application is very simple to use: To open a data file, you make appropriate changes in the current drive and directory if necessary, and then you select a WKD or SLS file name from the file list box. When you have made your selection, you click the **Draw Chart** button. (This button remains disabled until you select a file that the program can work with.) The application then switches your display screen to a graphics mode and draws a pie chart from the file you have selected. During a given run of the program you can examine charts for any number of different data files.

As a first exercise with the *Pie Chart* application, try the following sequence of steps:

1. Pull down the drive list, and note that the list contains the names of all the drives on your system. Drive C is currently selected. Assuming you have saved SLS and WKD files in directories on drive C, you do not need to change the drive.

2. In the directory list box, scroll down to the **WorkDay** directory, where the data files from the *Work Day* application are stored.

3. Double-click the directory name to open the directory. In response, the file list box displays a list of all the WKD files in the directory.

4. Click any one of the WKD files you have created with the *Work Day* program. When you do so, the **Draw Chart** button is enabled, and the name of your selected file appears just beneath the button in the dialog box (Figure 10-3).

5. Click the **Draw Chart** button. The application opens the selected file, reads and reorganizes its data, and draws the chart. If you are working with a color graphics monitor, you can view the chart in color. On a monochrome monitor, click the **Patterns** option at the top of the dialog box, and the wedges will be filled in with geometric patterns instead of colors. Figure 10-4 shows an example of the patterned pie chart.

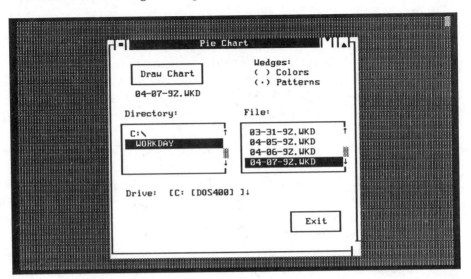

Figure 10-3 Selecting a WKD file name

At the right side of the chart, the program displays a *legend* for the pie chart. For a WKD file, the legend identifies the reference number corresponding to each wedge in the chart. The application allows a maximum of seven wedges for depicting the data in any given file. If a WKD file happens to have more than seven different reference numbers, the pie depicts the total hours for the seven most significant projects—that is, the

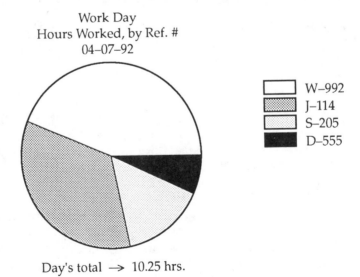

Figure 10-4 A pie chart created from a WKD file

```
                         Time Sheet for 04-07-92
                         =======================

Job Description                Ref.        Start       Finish      Total Time
---------------                ----        -----       ------      ----------

J. Donalds' will               D-555       03:00 PM    03:15 PM    00 hr 15 min
Letter to J. Donalds           D-555       08:00 AM    08:15 AM    00 hr 15 min
Phone call, Donalds            D-555       05:00 PM    05:15 PM    00 hr 15 min

                               Total for D-555        --> 0.75 hr

Jackson contract               J-114       08:15 AM    09:45 AM    01 hr 30 min
Jackson contract               J-114       11:15 AM    12:45 PM    01 hr 30 min
Phone call, Jackson            J-114       03:15 PM    03:45 PM    00 hr 30 min

                               Total for J-114        --> 3.50 hrs

Lunch meeting, Smith           S-205       01:00 PM    02:30 PM    01 hr 30 min

                               Total for S-205        --> 1.50 hrs

Meeting with Wu                W-992       10:00 AM    11:15 AM    01 hr 15 min
Wu contract                    W-992       03:45 PM    05:00 PM    01 hr 15 min
Wu contract                    W-992       05:15 PM    07:15 PM    02 hr 00 min

                               Total for W-992        --> 4.50 hrs

                               *** Total Work Time ---> 10.25 hrs
```

Figure 10-5 The time-sheet data from which the pie chart (Figure 10-4) was created

seven reference numbers with the greatest number of recorded work hours for the day.

Figure 10-5 shows a report produced by the *Work Day* application for the same day pictured in Figure 10-4. Examining the report, you can confirm that four projects with different reference numbers were recorded for the day. The total work time displayed on the bottom line of the report matches the total figure given at the bottom of the pie chart. Furthermore, you can see that each of the four subtotal amounts appears to be correctly represented by the size of the corresponding wedge.

Next try creating a pie chart for an SLS file from the *Sales Week* application:

1. If the previous chart is still displayed on the screen, press the space bar now to return to the Pie Chart form.

2.   In the directory list box, double-click the root directory, represented as **C:**. This action closes the **WorkDay** subdirectory and restores the full list of subdirectories on the C drive.

3.   Scroll down to the **SalesWk** directory, where the SLS files from the *Sales Week* application are stored. Double-click the directory name to open the directory. As a result, the file list box displays all the SLS files in the directory.

4.   Select a file name in the file list box. Double-click the file name. The *Pie Chart* application recognizes the double-click as a shortcut for two actions: selecting a file name and clicking the **Draw Chart** button. As a result of your double-click, the pie chart for the SLS file appears on the graphics screen, as shown in Figure 10-6.

This time the pie depicts an entire week's sales, and each wedge represents one day. The legend identifies the wedge pattern or wedge color for each day of the week, from Sunday to Saturday. The total sales amount for the week is displayed beneath the pie chart. Compare this chart with the bar graph created by the *Sales Week* application for the same week's sales (Figure 10-7). Clearly the two charts depict the same data set, but they focus on the data in different ways. While the bar graph shows the strength of each day's sales in relation to other days, the pie chart shows how each day relates to the whole week's sales.

If the *Pie Chart* program reads a *Sales Week* file containing fewer than seven sales figures—that is, if the sales amount is zero for one or more days in the week—the resulting pie chart includes only those days for which

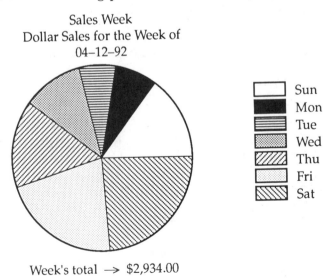

Sales Week
Dollar Sales for the Week of
04–12–92

□	Sun
■	Mon
☰	Tue
▦	Wed
▨	Thu
□	Fri
▧	Sat

Week's total → $2,934.00

Figure 10-6 A pie chart created from an SLS file

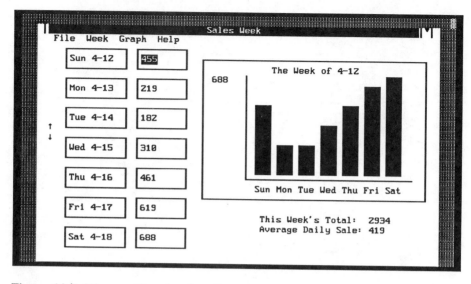

Figure 10-7 The weekly sales data from which the pie chart (Figure 10-6) was created

sales are recorded. For example, Figure 10-8 shows a pie chart for a week that has only three days of sales data. The corresponding *Sales Week* bar graph appears in Figure 10-9.

The *Pie Chart* program illustrates one way you can integrate the operations of different Visual Basic applications: By designing programs that recognize and read each other's data files, you can offer the user a variety of functions and operations to perform on shared data sets.

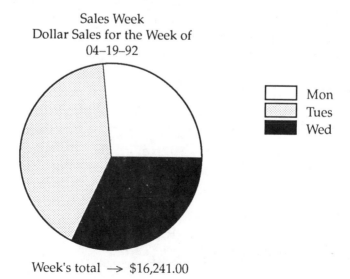

Figure 10-8 A pie chart representing three days of sales

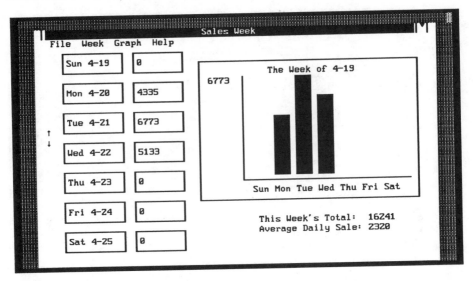

Figure 10-9 The bar graph representing three days of sales

THE ELEMENTS OF THE PIE CHART APPLICATION

As you examine the controls, properties, and code of the *Pie Chart* program, you'll focus on the three file-system controls included in the application. But *Pie Chart* also has some good examples of Visual Basic's extensive graphics tools. In particular, it demonstrates the use of the **CIRCLE** command for drawing the concentric wedges that make up a pie chart. The arithmetic algorithm for calculating the angles of wedges is also an interesting part of this program.

Controls and Properties

As you've seen, the application's single form, named **PieChart**, contains controls for selecting a file and for issuing the command to draw a chart. Most of the important properties for the file-system controls are set at run time rather than at design time. Describing the form's status at design time is therefore relatively simple. Here are the controls and their distinctive design-time properties:

- The three file-system controls have **CtlName** settings of **DirectoryList**, **FileList**, and **DriveList**. Each of these three controls is paired with a nearby label that identifies its purpose.

- A pair of option buttons is organized as a control array named **Wedges**. The index numbers of the two buttons are 0 and 1, and the captions are **Colors** and **Patterns**. These controls allow the user to choose between colored and patterned wedges.

- Two command buttons have the **CtlName** settings **DrawButton** and **ExitButton**. The user clicks the **DrawButton** control to request a pie chart for a selected file. Clicking the **ExitButton** control (or pressing the Esc key on the keyboard) terminates the program performance.

- Finally, a label named **FileDisplay** is located immediately beneath the **DrawButton** control. This label, which initially has a blank caption, is where the program displays a usable file name that the user has selected from the file list. Once a file name appears in this space, the user can either click the **Draw Chart** button or press the Enter key to open the file and view the pie chart.

Events

The program includes procedures for just a small number of events, most of them related to the file-system controls. As usual, a **Form_Load** event procedure performs initializations—in this case, defining the startup settings for the drive, directory, and file list boxes, and reading pattern strings for drawing the wedges of a pie chart. Subsequently, the program reacts to the following assortment of **Change**, **Click**, and **DblClick** events:

- **Change** events take place when the user makes new selections in the drive list box and the directory list box. The **DriveList_Change** and **DirectoryList_Change** procedures are therefore responsible for sending the user's drive and directory selections on to the file list box, so that the appropriate list of files will appear. Thanks to the sophistication of the three file-system controls, this task requires only a few lines of code.

- A **Click** event takes place when the user selects a file in the file list box. The **FileList_Click** procedure examines the selected file name and determines whether it is a file that the program can work with—that is, a WKD or SLS file. If so, the procedure copies the file name to the **FileDisplay** label and enables the **Draw Chart** button.

- A **DblClick** event occurs if the user double-clicks a file name in the file list box. In this case, the program automatically makes a call to **FileList_Click**. If the selected file is usable, the **FileList_DblClick** procedure then goes on to force a call to the **DrawButton_Click** event procedure.

- Other **Click** events take place when the user clicks either of the application's two command buttons, labeled **Draw Chart** and **Exit**. The **DrawButton_Click** procedure begins by making a call to one of two general procedures that are in charge of reading data files. Then the **Click** procedure actually draws the pie chart. The **ExitButton_Click** procedure terminates the program performance.

- Finally, the program recognizes a **Click** event when the user clicks either of the two option buttons, labeled **Colors** and **Labels**. The **Wedges_Click** procedure makes a call to **DrawButton_Click**, as long as the **DrawButton.Enabled** property setting is currently true. **DrawButton_Click**, in turn, reads the current settings of the option buttons to decide whether to fill the wedges with colors or with patterns.

Procedures and Methods

The code for the program appears in Listing 10-1 to 10-8. You'll concentrate first on the event procedures related to the three file-system controls (Listing 10-3). A large part of the listing is taken up by two general procedures—named **ReadSalesFile** and **ReadTimeFile**—that read the data files and organize the data into convenient formats. After a brief overview of these two procedures, you'll examine the **DrawButton_Click** procedure (Listing 10-4), which illustrates the **CIRCLE** command and other built-in Visual Basic graphics tools.

File, Directory, and Drive Procedures

Form_Load begins by calling a procedure named **Initialize** (Listing 10-2) to establish the default settings for the program's three file-system controls, **DriveList**, **DirectoryList**, and **FileList**. This is done simply by assigning string values to their **Drive**, **Path**, and **Pattern** properties. First the program selects drive C:

```
DriveList.Drive = "C:"
```

The initial directory list path is the root directory of drive C:

```
DirectoryList.Path = DriveList.Drive + "\"
```

Then the program explicitly assigns this path to the **Path** property of the file list box:

```
FileList.Path = DirectoryList.Path
```

As a result, the file list box initially displays file names from the root directory of drive C.

At the beginning, there is no reason to restrict the file list to any particular pattern of file names:

```
FileList.Pattern = "*.*"
```

However, until the user selects a file that the *Pie Chart* program can use, the **DrawButton** control is kept in a disabled state:

```
DrawButton.Enabled = False
```

By this simple mechanism, the program avoids trying to open and read any irrelevant files.

If the user makes a new selection in the drive list box, the program calls the **DriveList_Change** procedure (Listing 10-3). As a result of the **Change** event, Visual Basic automatically assigns the newly selected drive name to the control's **Drive** property. The **Change** procedure passes this change on to the directory list by simply assigning the new **Drive** setting to **Directory-List.Path**:

```
DirectoryList.Path = DriveList.Drive
```

Incidentally, this assignment results in an automatic **Change** event for the **DirectoryList** control. In other words, the **DirectoryList_Change** event procedure is called when the user makes a new selection either in the drive list box or the directory list box.

Notice that the **DriveList_Change** procedure uses an error trap to avoid an interruption in the program if the user selects a floppy drive that is open or contains no disk. In this case, the **DiskNotReady** routine simply calls **Initialize** to reestablish the default settings for the file-system controls.

The **Change** event for the directory list results in a new setting for the control's **Path** property. The first task of **DirectoryList_Change** is therefore to pass this new setting on to the file list box:

```
FileList.Path = DirectoryList.Path
```

As a result, the file list box displays the files in the newly selected drive or directory.

If the user opens one of this program's two target directories—**WorkDay** or **SalesWk**—the **DirectoryList_Change** procedure restricts the file list to names with the appropriate extensions. First the procedure assigns the new directory name to the string variable **DName$**. Then the **Pattern** property of the file list box is adjusted according to the value of this variable:

```
IF DName$ = "SALESWK" THEN
  FileList.Pattern = "*.SLS"
```

```
ELSEIF DName$ = "WORKDAY" THEN
   FileList.Pattern = "*.WKD"
ELSE
   FileList.Pattern = "*.*"
END IF
```

For the user's convenience, only SLS files appear in the file list when **SalesWk** is selected as the directory. Likewise, WKD files appear for the **WorkDay** directory. For any other directory, the program makes no special restriction on the **Pattern** property.

Finally, a **Click** event takes place when the user selects a file in the file list box. This event automatically changes the setting of the **FileName** property. In this case, the **FileList_Click** event examines the selected file name and determines whether the file is one that the *Pie Chart* program can use.

The first step in this task is to isolate the extension name of the current selection in the file list box:

```
Ext$ = UCASE$(RIGHT$(FileList.FileName, 3))
```

If the final three characters of this setting contain one of the two target extension names, this is a file the program can use:

```
IF Ext$ = "SLS" OR Ext$ = "WKD" THEN
```

The procedure copies the new **FileName** setting to the **Caption** property of the **FileDisplay** label and enables the **DrawButton** control:

```
FileDisplay.Caption = UCASE$(FileList.FileName)
DrawButton.Enabled = True
```

The user can now click the **Draw Chart** command button to instruct the program to draw a pie chart for the currently selected file.

However, if the current **FileName** selection does not contain one of the two target extension names, the program keeps the **FileDisplay** label blank and the **DrawButton** control disabled:

```
FileDisplay.Caption = ""
DrawButton.Enabled = False
```

The program also recognizes a **DblClick** event for the **FileList** control. When the user double-clicks a file name in the list, the **FileList_Click** procedure first examines the file name and determines whether it is usable. If the **FileList_DblClick** procedure subsequently finds a file name displayed in the **FileDisplay** label position, the routine makes a call to the **DrawButton_Click** procedure:

```
IF FileDisplay.Caption <> "" THEN DrawButton_Click
```

As you'll see shortly, the **DrawButton_Click** procedure calls one of two procedures to read a data file and then draws the pie chart.

Procedures that Read Data Files

Once the user selects a WKD or SLS file from the file list box, the program opens the file and reads the data. But then the data has to be reorganized for use in the pie chart. This task requires specific record-type data structures. Accordingly, the form-level declarations (Listing 10-1) include a record structure named **WedgeRecType**. It contains two fields—a single-precision numeric field named **Portion** and a string field named **LegendStr**:

```
TYPE WedgeRecType
  Portion AS SINGLE
  LegendStr AS STRING * 12
END TYPE
```

The program then defines an array of **WedgeRecType** records:

```
DIM SHARED WedgeRecs(6) AS WedgeRecType
```

This array is designed to store the information needed to draw a pie chart for either of the two file types. When the user selects a file and clicks the **Draw Chart** button, a call to either **ReadSalesFile** or **ReadTimeFile** fills the array with data.

Each record in the array describes one of the wedges in the chart:

- The **Portion** field is a decimal value representing the percentage of the pie to be taken up by a given wedge.

- The **LegendStr** field contains the legend caption for the wedge.

Two other form-level variables provide additional information about the chart:

```
DIM SHARED WedgeCount AS INTEGER
DIM SHARED Total AS DOUBLE
```

WedgeCount is the number of wedges, from 0 to 7. For a file created by the *Sales Week* application, **WedgeCount** is 7 if there are sales recorded for each day of the week or less than 7 if the sales figure is missing for one or more days. The **WedgeCount** for a *Work Day* file depends on the number of different reference numbers recorded in the file. The **Total** variable represents the sum of all the numeric data values that will be depicted in the pie chart—that is, the total dollar sales amount for an SLS file or the total work hours recorded in a WKD file.

The **ReadSalesFile** and **ReadTimeFile** procedures (Listings 10-6 and 10-7) read their respective data files and assign values to **WedgeCount**, **Total**, and the **WedgeRecs** array. These form-level variables therefore become the means of passing information about the data file to the **DrawButton_Click** procedure.

The **ReadSalesFile** has the relatively simple job of reading the seven daily sales amounts from an SLS file, calculating the total weekly sales, and assigning the **Portion** values to the **WedgeRecs** array. The variable **Count** keeps track of the number of nonzero daily sales amounts. The **Portion** for a given day is simply the ratio of the day's sales to the total sales for the week:

```
WedgeRecs(Count).Portion = SalesDay(i%) / WeekSales
```

The procedure also assigns day-of-the-week abbreviations to the **LegendStr** field of the **WedgeRecs** array.

The task of the **ReadTimeFile** procedure is somewhat more complex. The daily work records are stored in random-access files, and there is no fixed number of records in a file. The procedure opens a file, determines the number of records, and then reads all the records into a dynamic array named **WorkRecordList**. Then the procedure must accomplish a detailed sequence of steps:

1. Sort the **WorkRecordList** array by reference numbers and produce a count of the different reference numbers in the file. (These two tasks are performed by a call to the **SortWorkRecordList** function, shown in Listing 10-8.)

2. Copy the reference numbers and their subtotals into another dynamic array of records named **WorkTotals**.

3. Sort the **WorkTotals** array by the subtotal amounts. (This is done by a call to the **SortWorkTotals** procedure, also shown in Listing 10-8.) If there are more than seven reference numbers, select the top seven subtotals for the chart.

4. Calculate the **Portion** value for each subtotal. In this case, the **Portion** for a given reference number is the ratio of the subtotal to the total hours recorded for all the reference numbers.

5. Copy the reference numbers themselves to the **LegendStr** field of the **WedgeRecs** array.

When the **Portion** and **LegendStr** fields are available for each wedge, the program is ready to draw the pie chart.

Graphics Commands for Drawing a Pie Chart

In Visual Basic for DOS, you can switch into a graphics mode only when no forms are showing on the screen. Accordingly, the **DrawButton_Click** procedure (Listing 10-4) must begin by temporarily hiding the Pie Chart form:

```
PieChart.HIDE
```

Then the procedure switches to SCREEN mode 9 or 10, depending on the current setting of the **Wedges** options:

```
IF Wedges(0).Value THEN
   SCREEN 9
ELSE
   SCREEN 10
END IF
```

These two screen modes provide high-resolution graphics on EGA or VGA display systems.

To simplify the tasks of creating the pie chart and the legend in these screen modes, **DrawButton_Click** uses Visual Basic's **VIEW** and **WINDOW** commands to define custom coordinates within specific drawing areas. For example, before the program draws the pie chart, the following commands create a coordinate system that ranges from (-1, -1) to (1, 1) in the target drawing area:

```
VIEW (0, 0)-(500, 300)
WINDOW (-1, -1)-(1, 1)
```

Under the resulting coordinate system, the center point of this area is (0, 0) and the width and height of the area both have a scaled value of 2. These characteristics prove particularly convenient when the time comes to draw a wedge of the pie chart.

After selecting a graphics mode, the **DrawButton_Click** procedure displays titles at the top of the screen. The routine then calls either **ReadSalesFile** or **ReadTimeFile** to read a data file and assign values to the **Portion** and **LegendStr** fields of the **WedgeRecs** array.

Next a **For** loop draws the pie chart, wedge by wedge. The procedure uses three important numeric variables to keep track of the wedge angles:

- **W1** is the starting angle of a given wedge, relative to the full sweep of the circle.

- **W2** is the ending angle.

- **angle** is the actual angle measurement of the wedge—that is, the difference between **W1** and **W2**.

For the **CIRCLE** command, angles are measured in *radians* rather than degrees. The full sweep of 360 degrees is equal to a radian measurement of 2π. (The *Pie Chart* application includes a function named **Pi** that calculates and returns the value of π. You can examine this function in Listing 10-5.)

The first step in drawing a given wedge is to calculate the angle measurement that will determine the size of the wedge:

```
FOR i% = 0 To WedgeCount - 1
    angle = 2 * Pi() * WedgeRecs(i%).Portion
```

Multiplying the **Portion** field by the radian measurement of the full circle gives the angle measurement of the wedge. The next step is to calculate the starting angle, **W1**, and the ending angle, **W2**, of the wedge. The starting angle is equal to the ending angle of the previous wedge:

```
W1 = W2
```

And the ending angle is an offset of **angle** radians from the starting angle:

```
W2 = W1 + angle
```

The syntax of the **CIRCLE** command for drawing wedges is:

```
CIRCLE (x, y), Radius, Color, -StartAngle, -EndAngle
```

The coordinate address *(x, y)* is the center of the circle. To make the **Circle** method draw the radius sides of the wedge, you must express *StartAngle* and *EndAngle* as negative radian measurements. (This has no effect on the actual angle of the wedge.) Here, then, is how the **DrawButton_Click** procedure draws each wedge:

```
CIRCLE (0, 0), .5, QBColor(i% + 1), -W1, -W2
```

Thanks to the custom scaling done defined by the **VIEW** and **WINDOW** commands, the center of the drawing area has the coordinates (0, 0) and the shortest distance from the center to a side of the area is 1. This statement gives the circle a radius of .5, half the width of the area. The negative values of **W1** and **W2** are presented as the starting and ending angles.

Notice that the *Pie Chart* application uses Visual Basic's **QBCOLOR** function to specify colors for the pie chart and the legend. The **QBCOLOR** arguments and resulting color values appear in Table 10-1.

The **W1**, **W2**, and **angle** calculations are fine for all but the very first and the very last wedge of the pie. The **CIRCLE** command may behave unpredictably if the *StartAngle* or *EndAngle* value is equal to zero or 2π. Consequently the program instead uses a small nonzero number and a value

Table 10-1   QBCOLOR Arguments and Results

0	Black	8	Gray
1	Blue	9	Light Blue
2	Green	10	Light Green
3	Cyan	11	Light Cyan
4	Red	12	Light Red
5	Magenta	13	Light Magenta
6	Brown	14	Yellow
7	White	15	High-Intensity White

slightly decreased from 2π to represent these angles. For this purpose, the **DrawButton_Click** procedure defines a constant named **SmallDiff**:

```
CONST SmallDiff = .000001
```

Before calling the **CIRCLE** command for drawing the first and last wedges, the procedure makes a small change in the value of **W1** or **W2**:

```
SELECT CASE i%
  CASE 0
    W1 = W1 + SmallDiff
  CASE WedgeCount - 1
    W2 = W2 - SmallDiff
END SELECT
```

This small change results in properly drawn wedges for the pie.

Filling the Wedges with Color or Patterns

The **DrawButton_Click** procedure uses the **PAINT** command to fill the wedges and the legend boxes with colors or patterns. To decide between filling the wedges with color or patterns, the **DrawButton_Click** procedure reads the **Value** setting of **Wedges(0)**:

```
If Wedges(0).Value Then
```

If the value of this control element is true, the user has requested color wedges; if false, the user wants patterns.

For filling a shape with color, the **PAINT** command has the following general syntax:

```
PAINT (x, y), paintColor, borderColor
```

Given a point (*x, y*) inside the target shape, this command fills the area with *paintColor*. The shape itself must be fully enclosed by a border displayed in *borderColor*. The *Pie Chart* program uses the **SIN** and **COS** trigonometric functions to calculate a point (x, y) that is inside a given wedge of the pie chart:

```
a = W1 + angle / 2
y = .2 * SIN(a)
x = .2 * COS(a)
```

Given this interior point, the following **PAINT** statement fills the wedge with the same color as its border:

```
PAINT (x, y), QBCOLOR(i% + 1), QBCOLOR(i% + 1)
```

To fill a shape with a pattern, you express the pattern itself as a sequence of eight-bit characters, where each bit represents one on/off element of the pattern. Given such a pattern string, the general syntax for the **PAINT** command is:

```
PAINT (x, y), patternString, borderColor
```

Unfortunately, the task of developing a pattern string—and translating the binary digits into decimal values—can be long and tedious. To help you in this process, the program disk includes a tool called the *Patterns* application. (Listing 10-9 shows the code for the *Patterns* application.) When you load PATTERNS.MAK into Visual Basic and press F5 to run the program, you'll see a dialog box containing a grid of sixty-four small boxes. These boxes represent the on/off elements of a pattern. Initially they are all white, which signifies the *off* state. The program displays a numeric value at the right side of each row. This value is the decimal equivalent of the eight-digit binary number represented by the row of on/off boxes. At the beginning of the program, the value of each row is zero.

You can switch any box in the grid to its *on* state simply by clicking it with the mouse. When you do so, two things happen: First, the color of the box changes to black, signifying *on*; and second, the *Patterns* program recalculates the value of the binary pattern in the current row and displays the new value to the right of the row. To turn a box back to *off*, click the box again.

Figure 10-10 shows a sample bit pattern and the corresponding sequence of decimal numbers that represents this pattern. When you complete a pattern like this one, you can enter a short description of the pattern in the **Description** text box if you desire; then you can click the **File** menu command to save the description to disk. In response, the program ap-

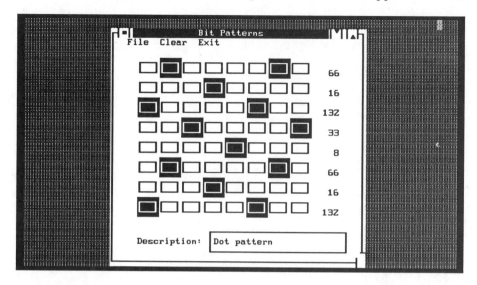

Figure 10-10 Using the *Patterns* application

pends the current description—in the form of a Visual Basic **DATA** line—
to a disk file named PATTERNS.TXT. For example, here is the line that
the program writes to the file for the pattern shown in Figure 10-10:

```
DATA 66, 16, 132, 33, 8, 66, 16, 132  : ' Dot pattern
```

To begin developing a new pattern, click the **Clear** menu command; the
program restores the original *off* status of the entire pattern grid. To end
the program performance, click the **Exit** menu command.

At the end of the form-level declarations in the *Pie Chart* program, you'll
find a group of **DATA** lines that represents the patterns in the wedges of a
pie chart:

```
DATA 0, 0, 0, 0, 0, 0, 0, 0              : ' All off
DATA  16,  16,  16,  16,  16,  16,  16,  16  : ' Vertical lines
DATA 0, 0, 0, 0, 0, 0, 255, 0           : ' Horizontal line
DATA 8,  8,  8,  8,  255,  8,  8,  8     : ' Crossing lines
DATA 8,  4,  2,  1,  128,  64,  32,  16  : ' Diagonals, down to right
DATA  16,  32,  64,  128,  1,  2,  4,  8  : ' Diagonals, down to left
DATA 255, 255, 255, 255, 255, 255, 255, 255  : ' All on
```

These lines were developed in the *Patterns* program and then copied from
PATTERNS.TXT to the program via the **Load Text...** command in Visual
Basic's **File** menu. The *Pie Chart* program uses a one-dimensional string
array named **Patterns$** to store these patterns. In the **ReadPatterns** proce-

dure (Listing 10-2) a pair of nested **FOR** loops reads the values, one byte at a time, into the **Patterns$** array:

```
FOR i% = 0 TO 6
  FOR j% = 1 TO 8
    READ bitLine%
    Patterns$(i%) = Patterns$(i%) + CHR$(bitLine%)
  NEXT j%
NEXT i%
```

Notice the use of the **CHR$** function to convert each decimal value into an ASCII character before it is concatenated to the end of the current **Pattern$** string.

SUMMARY: FILE-SYSTEM CONTROLS AND GRAPHICS COMMANDS

Visual Basic's three file-system controls are powerful tools to include in an application when you need to give the user access to files stored on disk. The drive and directory list boxes allow the user to select a new drive and directory during the process of searching for a file. The file list box then displays the files in the selected directory path.

Your program coordinates the activities of the three controls by reading and setting properties such as **Drive**, **Path**, **Pattern**, and **FileName**. However, your program is not responsible for building the lists displayed in the boxes. The controls read these lists directly from the operating system. In short, the file-system controls are easy to incorporate into a program and require little code. But they offer the user complete access to files wherever they are stored.

Along with some interesting examples of the file-system controls, the *Pie Chart* application also illustrates several of Visual Basic's built-in graphics commands. In particular, you have seen examples of the following:

- The **SCREEN** command, which switches your display hardware into a graphics mode.
- The **VIEW** and **WINDOW** commands, for establishing a custom coordinate system within a selected drawing area. (This is sometimes called a *viewport*.)
- The **CIRCLE** command, for drawing circles and wedges on a graphics screen.
- The **PAINT** command, for filling an enclosed shape with color or patterns.

Listing 10-1 Form-level declarations for the Pie Chart application

```
' The Pie Chart Program (PIE.MAK)
' Form-level declarations
' PIECHART.FRM

DECLARE SUB Initialize ()
DECLARE SUB ReadPatterns ()
DECLARE FUNCTION Pi () AS DOUBLE
DECLARE SUB DrawButton_Click ()
DECLARE SUB ReadSalesFile ()
DECLARE SUB ReadTimeFile ()
DECLARE SUB SortWorkTotals (NumRefs AS INTEGER)
DECLARE FUNCTION SortWorkRecordList (NumRecs AS INTEGER) AS
INTEGER

' Record type for wedge descriptions.

TYPE WedgeRecType
   Portion AS SINGLE    ' The decimal portion of a wedge.
   LegendStr AS STRING * 12  ' The caption of a legend entry.
END TYPE

' Record type for time-sheet files.

TYPE WorkRecordType
   DescriptField AS STRING * 25  ' Description of job.
   IDField AS STRING * 10   ' Reference number.
   StartField AS DOUBLE     ' Starting time.
   FinishedField AS DOUBLE    ' Ending time.
END TYPE

' Record type for time-sheet subtotals,
' organized by reference number.

TYPE WorkTotalType
   IDField AS STRING * 10   ' Reference number.
   TotalField AS DOUBLE   ' Total hours for this job.
END TYPE

' Boolean constants.

CONST False = 0
CONST True = NOT False
```

(continued)

```
' Day-of-the-week string.

CONST DayStr$ = "SunMonTueWedThuFriSat"

' Array of wedge-description records.

DIM SHARED WedgeRecs(6) AS WedgeRecType

' The number of wedges in the current chart
' and the total amount represented by the
' sum of the wedges.

DIM SHARED WedgeCount AS INTEGER
DIM SHARED Total AS DOUBLE

' Dynamic array of work records for
' reading a time-sheet file.

DIM SHARED WorkRecordList() AS WorkRecordType

' Dynamic array of subtotal records
' for a time-sheet file.

DIM SHARED WorkTotals() AS WorkTotalType

' Array of pattern strings.

DIM SHARED Patterns$(6)

' Data for patterns.

DATA 0, 0, 0, 0, 0, 0, 0, 0             : ' All off
DATA 16, 16, 16, 16, 16, 16, 16, 16    : ' Vertical lines
DATA 0, 0, 0, 0, 0, 0, 255, 0          : ' Horizontal line
DATA 8, 8, 8, 8, 255, 8, 8, 8          : ' Crossing lines
DATA 8, 4, 2, 1, 128, 64, 32, 16       : ' Diagonals, down to right
DATA 16, 32, 64, 128, 1, 2, 4, 8       : ' Diagonals, down to left
DATA 255, 255, 255, 255, 255, 255, 255, 255 : ' All on

' End of form-level declarations for Pie Chart.
```

Listing 10-2 Form_Load, Initialize, ReadPatterns, and ExitButton_Click

```
SUB Form_Load ()

  ' Initialize the drive, the path, and the pattern.

  Initialize

  ' Read the bit patterns for pie wedges.

  ReadPatterns

END SUB   ' Form_Load


SUB Initialize ()

  ' Initialize the file-system controls.

  DriveList.Drive = "C:"
  DirectoryList.Path = DriveList.Drive + "\"
  FileList.Path = DirectoryList.Path
  FileList.Pattern = "*.*"
  DrawButton.Enabled = False

END SUB   ' Initialize


SUB ReadPatterns ()

  ' Read the bit patterns and
  ' combine them into pattern strings.

  FOR i% = 0 TO 6
    FOR j% = 1 TO 8
      READ bitLine%
      Patterns$(i%) = Patterns$(i%) + CHR$(bitLine%)
    NEXT j%
  NEXT i%

END SUB   ' ReadPatterns
```

(continued)

```
SUB ExitButton_Click ()

  ' Terminate the program run.

  END

END SUB   ' ExitButton_Click
```

Listing 10-3 Event procedures for the file-system controls

```
SUB DirectoryList_Change ()

  ' Record the user's selections in the
  ' directory list box.

  DIM DName$   ' The current directory name.

  ' Copy the current path name to the Path
  ' property of the file list box.

  FileList.Path = DirectoryList.Path

  ' Blank out the FileDisplay control and
  ' disable the DrawButton command button.

  FileDisplay.Caption = ""
  DrawButton.Enabled = False

  ' If the current directory is SALESWK or
  ' WORKDAY, establish an appropriate file-name
  ' pattern for the file list box.

  DName$ = UCASE$(RIGHT$(DirectoryList.Path, 7))
  IF DName$ = "SALESWK" THEN
    FileList.Pattern = "*.SLS"
  ELSEIF DName$ = "WORKDAY" THEN
    FileList.Pattern = "*.WKD"
  ELSE
    FileList.Pattern = "*.*"
  END IF

END SUB   ' DirectoryList_Change
```

```
SUB DriveList_Change ()

  ' Record a change in the user's drive selection.

  ' Assign the new drive name to the Path property
  ' of the directory list box.

  ON LOCAL ERROR GOTO DiskNotReady
    DirectoryList.Path = DriveList.Drive
  ON LOCAL ERROR GOTO 0

  ' Blank out the FileDisplay control and
  ' disable the DrawButton command button.

  FileDisplay.Caption = ""
  DrawButton.Enabled = False

  EXIT SUB

DiskNotReady:

  ' If the selected disk is not ready,
  ' return to original file-system settings.

  Initialize

RESUME NEXT

END SUB   ' DriveList_Change



SUB FileList_Click ()

  ' Read the extension name of the user's selection
  ' from the file list box. If the extension is "SLS" or
  ' "WKD"--one of the two files that this application
  ' can work with--display the file name in the FileDisplay
  ' control and activate the DrawButton command button.

  Ext$ = UCASE$(RIGHT$(FileList.FileName, 3))
  IF Ext$ = "SLS" OR Ext$ = "WKD" THEN
    FileDisplay.Caption = UCASE$(FileList.FileName)
    DrawButton.Enabled = True
  ELSE
```

(continued)

```
        FileDisplay.Caption = ""
        DrawButton.Enabled = False
    END IF

END SUB   ' FileList_Click



SUB FileList_DblClick ()

  ' If a usable file has been selected from the
  ' file list box, accept a double-click as a command
  ' to create the pie chart.

  IF FileDisplay.Caption <> "" THEN DrawButton_Click

END SUB   ' FileList_DblClick
```

Listing 10-4 The DrawButton_Click event procedure

```
SUB DrawButton_Click ()

  ' Draw the pie chart, from information stored in the
  ' form-level WedgeRecs array and the form-level variables
  ' WedgeCount and Total.

  CONST SmallDiff = .000001  ' Small delta value for
                             ' first and last wedge angles.

  DIM W1, W2, angle  ' Wedge angle variables.
  DIM TtlStr$        ' The total line string.
  DIM ModeAvailable AS INTEGER  ' A flag for SCREEN mode
testing.

  ' Hide the PieChart form, and switch to one of two
  ' screen modes: SCREEN 9 for a color chart or
  ' SCREEN 10 for a black-and-white patterned chart.

  PieChart.HIDE

  ModeAvailable = True
  ON LOCAL ERROR GOTO NotAvailable
```

```
     IF Wedges(0).Value THEN
       SCREEN 9
     ELSE
       SCREEN 10
     END IF
  ON LOCAL ERROR GOTO 0

  IF ModeAvailable THEN
     OPEN "CON" FOR OUTPUT AS #2
     CLS

     ' Determine whether this is an SLS or WKD file
     ' and display the appropriate titles. Then
     ' call the procedure that opens and reads the file.

     IF RIGHT$(FileDisplay.Caption, 3) = "SLS" THEN
       PRINT #2, TAB(27); "Sales Week"
       PRINT #2, TAB(18); "Dollar Sales for the Week of"
       ReadSalesFile
     ELSEIF RIGHT$(FileDisplay.Caption, 3) = "WKD" THEN
       PRINT #2, TAB(28); "Work Day"
       PRINT #2, TAB(21); "Hours Worked, by Ref. #"
       ReadTimeFile
     END IF
     PRINT #2, TAB(28); LEFT$(FileDisplay.Caption, 8)

     W2 = 0
     FOR i% = 0 TO WedgeCount - 1

     ' Calculate the starting and ending
     ' angles for each wedge of the pie.

       angle = 2 * Pi() * WedgeRecs(i%).Portion
     W1 = W2
       W2 = W1 + angle

     ' Add or subtract the SmallDiff amount for
     ' the first and last wedges.

       SELECT CASE i%
         CASE 0
           W1 = W1 + SmallDiff
         CASE WedgeCount - 1
           W2 = W2 - SmallDiff
       END SELECT
```

(continued)

```
' Establish a convenient coordinate system
' for drawing the legend boxes.

  VIEW (500, 70)-(639, 165)
  WINDOW SCREEN (0, 0)-(9, 7)

' Display the legend.

  IF Wedges(0).Value THEN
     LINE (0, i%)-(1, i% + 1), QBCOLOR(i% + 1), BF
  ELSE
     LINE (0, i%)-(1, i% + 1), QBCOLOR(7), B
     PAINT (.5, i% + .5), Patterns$(i%), QBCOLOR(7)
  END IF

' Display the legend caption.

   LOCATE i% + 6, 68
   PRINT #2, WedgeRecs(i%).LegendStr

' Establish a convenient coordinate system
' for drawing a wedge.

  VIEW (0, 0)-(500, 300)
  WINDOW (-1, -1)-(1, 1)

' Draw and paint the wedge (or the entire circle if
' there is only one data value).

  IF WedgeCount > 1 THEN

   ' Calculate the location of a point
   ' inside the wedge (for the PAINT command).

     a = W1 + angle / 2
     y = .2 * SIN(a)
     x = .2 * COS(a)
  ELSE
     W1 = 0
     W2 = -2 * Pi
     x = 0
     y = 0
  END IF
```

```
         IF Wedges(0).Value THEN
            CIRCLE (0, 0), .5, QBCOLOR(i% + 1), -W1, -W2
            PAINT (x, y), QBCOLOR(i% + 1), QBCOLOR(i% + 1)
         ELSE
            CIRCLE (0, 0), .5, QBCOLOR(7), -W1, -W2
            PAINT (x, y), Patterns$(i%), QBCOLOR(7)
         END IF

      NEXT i%

      ' Display the total line at the bottom of the window.

      IF RIGHT$(FileDisplay.Caption, 3) = "SLS" THEN
         TtlStr$ = "Week's total -> " + FORMAT$(Total,
   "$##,###0.00")
      ELSEIF RIGHT$(FileDisplay.Caption, 3) = "WKD" THEN
         TtlStr$ = "Day's total -> " + FORMAT$(Total, "##0.00")
         IF Total > 1 THEN
            TtlStr$ = TtlStr$ + " hrs."
         ELSE
            TtlStr$ = TtlStr$ + " hr."
         END IF
      END IF

      LOCATE 20, 20
      PRINT #2, TtlStr$;

      ' Pause until user presses the space bar.

      DO WHILE INKEY$ <> " ": LOOP
      CLOSE
   END IF

   ' Switch back to text mode and show the PieChart form.

   SCREEN 0
   PieChart.SHOW
   EXIT SUB

NotAvailable:
  ModeAvailable = False
RESUME NEXT

END SUB   ' DrawButton_Click
```

Listing 10-5 The Pi function and the Wedges_Click event procedure

```
FUNCTION Pi () AS DOUBLE

  ' Return the value of Pi
  ' as a double-precision number.

  Pi = 4# * ATN(1)

END FUNCTION   ' Pi


SUB Wedges_Click (Index AS INTEGER)

  ' Redraw the pie chart when the user selects
  ' a new Wedge option button ("Colors" or "Patterns").

  IF DrawButton.Enabled THEN DrawButton_Click

END SUB   ' Wedges_Click
```

Listing 10-6 The ReadSalesFile procedure

```
SUB ReadSalesFile ()

  ' Read a weekly sales file and arrange the data
  ' in the following form-level variables:

  ' -- The WedgeRecs contains the sales portion represented
  '    by each wedge and the name of each legend entry.
  ' -- The WedgeCount variable gives the number of wedges
  '    (equal to the number of nonzero sales amounts).
  ' -- The Total variable gives the total weekly sales.

  ' The DrawButton_Click procedure creates the pie
  ' chart from the information stored in these variables.

  DIM SalesFile$    ' The name of the file.
  DIM SalesDay(6)   ' The daily sales data.
```

```
    DIM WeekSales        ' The week's total sales.
    DIM Count AS INTEGER   ' A temporary wedge count.

    ' Build the file name and open the file.
    ' (Weekly sales files, as created by the Sales Week
    ' application, are sequential-access files, with one
    ' numeric entry for each day of a given week.)

    SalesFile$ = DirectoryList.Path + "\"
    SalesFile$ = SalesFile$ + FileList.FileName
    OPEN SalesFile$ FOR INPUT AS #1

    ' Read the entire file.

    WeekSales = 0
    FOR i% = 0 TO 6
      INPUT #1, SalesDay(i%)
      WeekSales = WeekSales + SalesDay(i%)
    NEXT i%
    CLOSE #1

    ' Calculate the week's portion (WedgeRecs(i%).Portion)
    ' represented by each day of the week for which the sales
    ' figure is not zero.

    Count = -1
    FOR i% = 0 TO 6
      IF SalesDay(i%) <> 0 THEN
        Count = Count + 1
        WedgeRecs(Count).Portion = SalesDay(i%) / WeekSales
        WedgeRecs(Count).LegendStr = MID$(DayStr$, i% * 3 + 1,
3)
      END IF
    NEXT i%

    WedgeCount = Count + 1
    Total = WeekSales

END SUB  ' ReadSalesFile
```

Listing 10-7 The ReadTimeFile procedure

```
SUB ReadTimeFile ()

  ' Read a time-sheet file and arrange the data
  ' in the following form-level variables:

  ' -- The WedgeRecs contains the portion of the day
  '     represented by each wedge and the name of each
  '     legend entry.
  ' -- The WedgeCount variable gives the number of wedges:
  '     in this case, the number of different reference
  '     numbers in the time sheet. (The application includes
  '     a maximum of seven entries in the pie chart.)
  ' -- The Total variable gives the day's total hours worked.


  ' The DrawButton_Click procedure creates the pie
  ' chart from the information stored in these variables.

  ' A single work record variable.
  DIM WorkRecord AS WorkRecordType

  ' The file name and the number of records in the file.
  DIM WorkFileName AS STRING, RecCount AS INTEGER

  ' Reference number comparison variables.
  DIM ThisRef AS STRING, NextRef AS STRING

  ' Reference number counters.
  DIM RefIndex AS INTEGER, RefCount AS INTEGER, i%

  ' The subtotal for a given reference number.
  DIM RefTot AS DOUBLE

  ' Create the file name, open the file, and count its
  ' records.

  WorkFileName = DirectoryList.Path + "\" + FileList.FileName
  OPEN WorkFileName FOR RANDOM AS #1 LEN = LEN(WorkRecord)
  RecCount = LOF(1) / LEN(WorkRecord)

    ' Redimension the array of records accordingly and read
      the file.
```

```
REDIM WorkRecordList(RecCount) AS WorkRecordType
FOR i% = 1 TO RecCount
  GET #1, i%, WorkRecordList(i%)
  IF LTRIM$(WorkRecordList(i%).IDField) = "" THEN
    WorkRecordList(i%).IDField = "(no ref #)"
  END IF
NEXT i%
CLOSE #1

' Sort the array by the reference numbers (IDField)
' and count the reference numbers.

RefCount = SortWorkRecordList(RecCount)

' Redimension the array of totals accordingly.

REDIM WorkTotals(RefCount) AS WorkTotalType
RefTot = 0
RefIndex = 0

' Store the reference totals in the WorkTotals array.

FOR i% = 1 TO RecCount
  T1 = WorkRecordList(i%).StartField
  T2 = WorkRecordList(i%).FinishedField

  IF NOT (T1 < 0 OR T2 < 0) THEN
    RefTot = RefTot + (T2 - T1)
    IF T1 > T2 THEN RefTot = RefTot + 1
  END IF

' If the reference number changes, record
' the total for this reference number.

  ThisRef = WorkRecordList(i%).IDField
  IF i% <> RecCount THEN
    NextRef = WorkRecordList(i% + 1).IDField
  ELSE
    NextRef = ""
  END IF

  IF ThisRef <> NextRef THEN
    RefIndex = RefIndex + 1
    WorkTotals(RefIndex).IDField = ThisRef
```

(continued)

```
            WorkTotals(RefIndex).TotalField = RefTot
            RefTot = 0
      END IF
   NEXT i%


   ' Sort the WorkTotals array by the subtotal amounts.


   SortWorkTotals RefIndex

   ' If there are more than seven reference numbers,
   ' use the top seven--that is, the jobs with the
   ' greatest number of recorded work hours.

   IF RefIndex > 7 THEN RefIndex = 7

   ' Find the total hours as a serial time value.

   Total = 0
   FOR i% = 1 TO RefIndex
      Total = Total + WorkTotals(i%).TotalField
   NEXT i%

   ' Compute the wedge portions and record the legend captions.

   WedgeCount = RefIndex
   FOR i% = 0 TO RefIndex - 1
      IF WorkTotals(i% + 1).TotalField > 0 THEN
         WedgeRecs(i%).Portion = WorkTotals(i% + 1).TotalField
/ Total
         WedgeRecs(i%).LegendStr = WorkTotals(i% + 1).IDField
      ELSE

         ' Don't include a subtotal of zero.

         WedgeCount = WedgeCount - 1
      END IF
   NEXT i%

   ' Calculate the total time as a number of hours.

   Total = Total * 24

END SUB  ' ReadTimeFile
```

Listing 10-8 The SortWorkTotals procedure and the SortWorkRecordList function

```
SUB SortWorkTotals (NumRefs AS INTEGER)

  ' Sort the WorkTotals array by the subtotal amounts
  ' (TotalField). (Called from the ReadTimeFile procedure.)

  DIM TempTotRec AS WorkTotalType
  DIM i%, j%

  FOR i% = 1 TO NumRefs - 1
    FOR j% = i% + 1 TO NumRefs
      IF WorkTotals(i%).TotalField <
WorkTotals(j%).TotalField THEN
        TempTotRec = WorkTotals(i%)
        WorkTotals(i%) = WorkTotals(j%)
        WorkTotals(j%) = TempTotRec
      END IF
    NEXT j%
  NEXT i%

END SUB   ' SortWorkTotals


FUNCTION SortWorkRecordList (NumRecs AS INTEGER) AS INTEGER

  ' Sort the work record array by the reference numbers
  ' (IDField), and return a count of the different reference
  ' numbers in the file. (Called from the ReadTimeFile
  ' procedure.)

  DIM i%, j%, CountTemp AS INTEGER
  DIM TempWorkRec AS WorkRecordType

  FOR i% = 1 TO NumRecs - 1
    FOR j% = i% + 1 TO NumRecs
      IF WorkRecordList(i%).IDField >
WorkRecordList(j%).IDField THEN
        TempWorkRec = WorkRecordList(i%)
        WorkRecordList(i%) = WorkRecordList(j%)
        WorkRecordList(j%) = TempWorkRec
      END IF
    NEXT j%
  NEXT i%
```

(continued)

```
' Count the reference numbers.

CountTemp = 1
FOR i% = 1 TO NumRecs - 1
   IF WorkRecordList(i%).IDField <> WorkRecordList(i% +
1).IDField THEN
      CountTemp = CountTemp + 1
   END IF
NEXT i%

' Return the number of different reference numbers.

SortWorkRecordList = CountTemp

END FUNCTION   ' SortWorkRecordList
```

Listing 10-9 The code from the Patterns program

```
' The Patterns Program (PATTERNS.MAK)
' Declarations
' PATTERNS.FRM

DECLARE FUNCTION BDConvert% (inBin$)
DECLARE FUNCTION BinToDec% (inBin$)


FUNCTION BDConvert% (BinStr$)

' Convert a binary string to a decimal value.

  bitCount% = LEN(BinStr$)

  DecVal% = 0
  FOR i% = bitCount% TO 1 STEP -1
    digit% = VAL(MID$(BinStr$, i%, 1))
    DecVal% = DecVal% + digit% * 2 ^ (bitCount% - i%)
  NEXT i%

  BDConvert% = DecVal%

END FUNCTION   ' BDConvert%
```

```
SUB Bit_Click (Index AS INTEGER)

' Change the on-off status of a bit in the pattern.

  IF Bit(Index).Tag = "0" THEN
    Bit(Index).BackColor = 0
    Bit(Index).Tag = "1"
  ELSE
    Bit(Index).BackColor = 15
    Bit(Index).Tag = "0"
  END IF

' Form the new binary string resulting from this change.

  StartBit% = 8 * (Index \ 8)
  BitStr$ = ""
  FOR i% = StartBit% TO StartBit% + 7
    BitStr$ = BitStr$ + Bit(i%).Tag
  NEXT i%

' Convert the binary string to a decimal value
' and display it as the DecValue caption.

  DecValue(Index \ 8).Caption = STR$(BDConvert%(BitStr$))

END SUB  ' Bit_Click


SUB ClearCommand_Click ()

  ' Clear the current pattern to make way
  ' for a new pattern.

  FOR i% = 0 TO 63
    Bit(i%).BackColor = 15
    Bit(i%).Tag = "0"
  NEXT i%

  ' Clear the array of decimal values.

  FOR i% = 0 TO 7
    DecValue(i%).Caption = "0"
  NEXT i%

  ' Clear the description.
```

(continued)

```
   Description.Text = ""

END SUB  ' ClearCommand_Click


SUB ExitCommand_Click ()

  ' Terminate the Patterns program.

  END

END SUB  ' ExitCommand_Click


SUB FileCommand_Click ()

  ' Save the current pattern as a DATA line,
  ' appending the line to the end of PATTERNS.TXT.

  OPEN "PATTERNS.TXT" FOR APPEND AS #1
    PRINT #1, "DATA ";

    ' Save each of the eight bytes.

    FOR i% = 0 TO 7
      PRINT #1, DecValue(i%).Caption;
      IF i% < 7 THEN PRINT #1, ", ";
    NEXT i%

    ' Save the description as a comment.

    IF RTRIM$(Description.Text) <> "" THEN
      PRINT #1, "   :' "; Description.Text
    ELSE
      PRINT #1,
    END IF

  CLOSE #1

END SUB  ' FileCommand_Click
```

11

Multiline Text Boxes: The Memo Printer Application

INTRODUCTION

Visual Basic supports *multiline* text boxes, in which the user can enter, view, and edit multiple lines of text. Inside an appropriately designed text box, the user can perform several basic text-processing operations:

- Insert new lines of text, write over existing text, or delete text.
- Scroll vertically through the length of the text.
- Use standard keyboard operations to move the cursor to new locations inside the text—for example, Ctrl-Right Arrow or Ctrl-Left Arrow to move to the beginning of the next or previous word; Home or End to move to the beginning or end of the current line; and Ctrl-Home or Ctrl-End to move to the beginning or the end of the text box contents.
- Use the mouse or the keyboard to select and highlight any sequence of text. (On the keyboard, hold down the Shift key and press any combination of arrow keys to select a block of text.)
- Perform *copy* and *move* operations on a selection of text.
- Enter long lines of text in a text box that includes a horizontal scroll bar; or, alternatively, enter paragraphs of text with automatic *word wrap* in a text bar that does not have a horizontal scroll bar.

All these features are available automatically—without any extra programming on your part—once you design the text box itself appropriately. To create a multiline text box, you assign settings to several relevant properties in the Form Design environment. Most obviously, you should establish large enough **Height** and **Width** settings to give the user enough space for entering and editing multiple lines of text. In addition, the following properties have special settings for a text-processing application:

- The **Multiline** property setting is **True** for a multiple-line text box. (The default setting is **False**, for a single-line text box.)

- The **ScrollBars** property has four possible settings:

```
0 - None
1 - Horizontal
2 - Vertical
3 - Both
```

In a multiline text box, the **2 - Vertical** setting provides a vertical scroll bar, enabling the user to move easily up and down the text. Word wrap takes place in a multiline text box that *does not* include a horizontal scroll bar. The **1 - Horizontal** setting or the **3 - Both** setting allows the user to enter long lines of text without word wrap.

As always, the **Text** property represents the contents of a text box, whether the box is designed for single-line or multiple-line entries. For example, **MemoBox.Text** may refer to the entire text in a multiline text box. In your program code, you can add new lines to such a text box by concatenating a string to the end of the current **Text** value. In this context, you may also want to concatenate an end-of-line marker, represented by a combination of the carriage-return character (**CHR$(13)**) and the line-feed character (**CHR$(10)**); for example:

```
MemoBox.Text = MemoBox.Text + NewLine$ + CHR$(13) + CHR$(10)
```

The maximum length of the **Text** setting in any text box is 32 K bytes.

This chapter's sample project, called the *Memo Printer* application, illustrates techniques of multiple-line text processing. The application's main form includes a large text box in which you can write and edit an office memorandum directed to employees, colleagues, or co-workers. Listed above the memo box are the names of the people to whom you usually send memos. (You develop this list yourself when you first run the program, and then you revise the list whenever necessary.) To print copies of a particular memo, you simply click the names of the recipients—placing Xs in the corresponding check boxes—and then choose the program's print command. In effect, the *Memo Printer* carries out the equivalent of a print-merge operation, producing multiple personalized copies of a memo document.

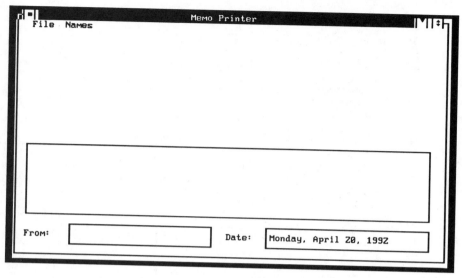

Figure 11-1 The startup form from the *Memo Printer* application

The *Memo Printer* project is stored on the exercise disk under the name MEMO.MAK. Open the project now and press the F5 key to run the program. The form shown in Figure 11-1 appears on the screen.

THE MEMO PRINTER APPLICATION

To set up the *Memo Printer* program for your own use, begin by creating a list of names—representing the people to whom you regularly send memos. You need to develop this list only once; the program saves your list on disk and automatically reads the list into the main dialog box when you next run the application. You can add new people to the list at any time—up to a maximum of thirty names. You can also delete names from the list.

For example, Figure 11-2 shows the *Memo Printer* form, complete with a list of imaginary names. Each name appears as the caption of a check box. You select the people who are to receive a copy of a given memo by clicking the corresponding check boxes.

As you can see in Figure 11-3, the application's **Names** menu gives you commands for building and using this list. To add a name to the list—or to begin building the list the first time you run the program—select the **Add a Name** command or press Ctrl+A. When you do so, the program displays a dialog box on the screen to elicit the first and last name of the person you want to include in the list (Figure 11-4). Each time you add a

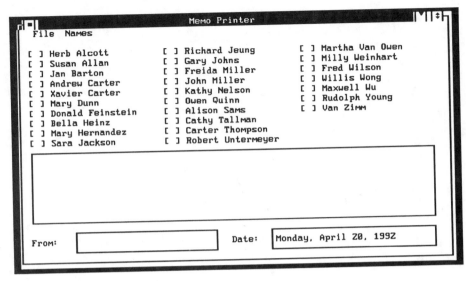

Figure 11-2 A list of names in the *Memo Printer* form

new name, the program alphabetizes the list and redisplays the names in the form. The list is saved on disk as MEMOLIST.TXT, in the root directory of the C drive.

The **Check All Names** and **Uncheck All Names** commands in the **Names** menu give you quick ways to select or deselect names for printing memos.

```
┌─┌─┐────────────────────Memo Printer───────────────────────┐M│↕┐
│ ┌─┐                                                        └─┘
│ │File  Names                                                    │
│    ┌────────────────────────────┐                              │
│ [ ] He│ Check All Names      F3 │ d Jeung       [ ] Martha Van Owen │
│ [ ] Su│ Uncheck All Names    F4 │ ohns          [ ] Milly Weinhart │
│ [ ] Ja│                         │ Miller        [ ] Jean Wexton    │
│ [ ] An│ Add a Name...    Ctrl+A │ iller         [ ] Fred Wilson    │
│ [ ] Xa│ Delete Unchecked Names...│ Nelson        [ ] Willis Wong   ■ │
│ [ ] Ma└─────────────────────────┘ uinn          [ ] Maxwell Wu     │
│ [ ] Donald Feinstein    [ ] Alison Sams          [ ] Rudolph Young │
│ [ ] Bella Heinz         [ ] Cathy Tallman        [ ] Van Zimm      │
│ [ ] Mary Hernandez      [ ] Carter Thompson                       │
│ [ ] Sara Jackson        [ ] Robert Untermeyer                     │
│    ┌──────────────────────────────────────────────────────────┐ │
│    │                                                          │ │
│    │                                                          │ │
│    │                                                          │ │
│    │                                                          │ │
│    └──────────────────────────────────────────────────────────┘ │
│    From: │ Jacqueline Sanders │      Date: │ Sunday, April 19, 1992 ││
└──────────────────────────────────────────────────────────────────┘
```

Figure 11-3 The **Names** menu

```
┌─────────────────────────Memo Printer─────────────────────────┐
│ File  Names                                                    │
│                                                                │
│  [ ] Herb Alcott        [ ] Richard Jeung      [ ] Martha Van Owen │
│  [ ] Susan Allan        [ ] Gary Johns         [ ] Milly Weinhart │
│  [ ] Jan Barton         [ ] Freida Miller      [ ] Fred Wilson │
│  [ ] Andrew Carter      [ ] John Miller        [ ] Willis Wong │
│  [ ] Xavier Carter      [ ] Kathy Nelson       [ ] Maxwell Wu │
│  [ ] Mary Dunn          [ ] Owen Quinn         [ ] Rudolph Young │
│  [ ] Donald Feinstein   [ ] Alison Sams        [ ] Van Zimm │
│  [ ] Bella Heinz        [ ] Cathy Tallman                      │
│  [ ] Mary Hernandez     [ ] Carter Thompson                   │
│  [ ] Sara Jackson       [ ] Robert Untermeyer                 │
│                                                                │
│        ┌──────────────────── Add a Name ────────────────────┐ │
│        │                                                     │ │
│        │   First Name:    ┌──────────────────────────────┐  │ │
│        │                  │ Jean                         │  │ │
│        │                  └──────────────────────────────┘  │ │
│        │   Last Name:     ┌──────────────────────────────┐  │ │
│        │                  │ Wexton                       │  │ │
│        │                  └──────────────────────────────┘  │ │
│        │                                                     │ │
│        │               ┌────────────┐   ┌────────────┐      │ │
│  From:           │       │    Add     │   │   Cancel   │      │ │
│         └────────│       └────────────┘   └────────────┘   0, 1992 │
│                  └─────────────────────────────────────────┘ │
└────────────────────────────────────────────────────────────────┘
```

Figure 11-4 Adding a name to the Memo Printer form

Press the F3 function key to check all the names if you want to print a copy
of a memo for each person on your list. Or press F4 to uncheck all the
names, and then click individual names with the mouse to select the people
who will receive your memo (Figure 11-5).

```
┌──────────────────────────Memo Printer──────────────────────────┐
│ File  Names                                                      │
│                                                                  │
│  [ ] Herb Alcott        [ ] Richard Jeung      [ ] Martha Van Owen │
│  [X] Susan Allan        [ ] Gary Johns         [ ] Milly Weinhart │
│  [X] Jan Barton         [X] Freida Miller      [ ] Jean Wexton  │
│  [ ] Andrew Carter      [ ] John Miller        [ ] Fred Wilson  │
│  [ ] Xavier Carter      [X] Kathy Nelson       [ ] Willis Wong  │
│  [X] Mary Dunn          [ ] Owen Quinn         [X] Maxwell Wu   │
│  [X] Donald Feinstein   [X] Alison Sams        [ ] Rudolph Young │
│  [ ] Bella Heinz        [X] Cathy Tallman      [X] Van Zimm     │
│  [ ] Mary Hernandez     [ ] Carter Thompson                     │
│  [ ] Sara Jackson       [X] Robert Untermeyer                   │
│                                                                  │
│  ┌────────────────────────────────────────────────────────────┐ │
│  │ Re: Staff meetings                                         │ │
│  │                                                            │ │
│  │ Please mark the following meetings on your calendar:       │ │
│  │                                                            │ │
│  │     Mon., 4/20, 10:30     Budget meeting                   │ │
│  │     Wed., 4/22,  9:00     Planning                         │ │
│  └────────────────────────────────────────────────────────────┘ │
│                                                                  │
│  From:  ┌────────────────────┐   Date:  ┌──────────────────────┐ │
│         │ Jacqueline Sanders │          │ Friday, April 17, 1992 │ │
│         └────────────────────┘          └──────────────────────┘ │
└──────────────────────────────────────────────────────────────────┘
```

Figure 11-5 Selecting names for the memo

The **Delete Unchecked Names** command deletes names from the list. To use this command, follow these steps:

1. Press F3 to check all the names in the list.

2. Use the mouse to uncheck the selected names that you want to delete from the list.

3. Pull down the **Names** menu and select **Delete Unchecked Names** command.

Before deleting any names, the program displays a dialog box asking you to confirm that you want to go ahead with the deletions (Figure 11-6).

Once you have developed a list of names, the next step in using the *Memo Printer* application is to type the memo itself into the memo box or to load a text file from disk as your memo document. The first three commands in the program's **File** menu (Figure 11-7) are designed to help you begin a memo. Choose the **Activate Memo Box** command (or simply press Ctrl+M at the keyboard) to move the focus to the memo text box. Or choose **Clear Current Memo** (or press Ctrl+C) to erase any text currently displayed in the memo box and to activate the box. Once the flashing cursor is displayed inside the box, you can begin composing your memo. As you can see back in Figure 11-5, the memo box shows only several lines of your document at a time, but you can use the scroll bar or the PgUp and PgDn keys to scroll up and down the document. Because the memo box has both vertical and horizontal scroll bars, word wrap does not take place for long lines of text. As you type your memo, press the Enter key to begin each new line.

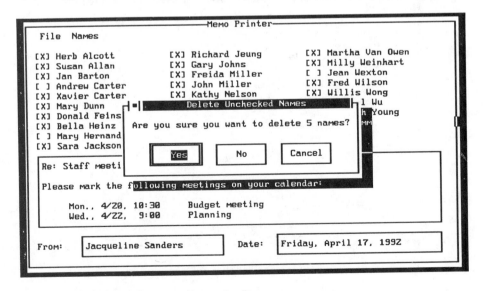

Figure 11-6 Deleting names from the list

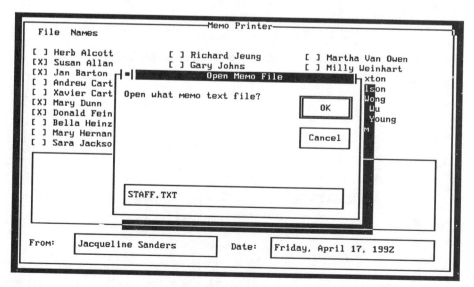

```
┌─■┐                         Memo Printer                                  ┌M┤─┐
│ File  Names                                                             │MI│‡│
│┌────────────────────────────────────┐                                  
││ Open Memo File...        Ctrl+O     │ Jeung     [ ] Martha Van Owen    
││ Activate Memo Box        Ctrl+M     │hns        [ ] Milly Weinhart     
││ Clear Current Memo       Ctrl+C     │Miller     [ ] Jean Wexton        
││                                     │ller       [ ] Fred Wilson        
││ Print or Save a Memo...  Ctrl+P     │elson      [ ] Willis Wong        ■
││                                     │inn        [ ] Maxwell Wu         
││ Exit                     Ctrl+X     │Sams       [ ] Rudolph Young      
│└────────────────────────────────────┘allman     [ ] Van Zimm           
│ [ ] Mary Hernandez       [ ] Carter Thompson                           
│ [ ] Sara Jackson         [ ] Robert Untermeyer                         
│                                                                         
│┌─────────────────────────────────────────────────────────────────────┐
││                                                                       │
││                                                                       │
││                                                                       │
│└─────────────────────────────────────────────────────────────────────┘
│ From:  ┌──────────────────────┐   Date:  ┌──────────────────────────┐ 
│        │ Jacqueline Sanders    │          │ Sunday, April 19, 1992    │ 
│        └──────────────────────┘          └──────────────────────────┘ 
└─────────────────────────────────────────────────────────────────────────┘
```

Figure 11-7 The **File** menu

If you have previously written a memo and saved it as a text file, you can load the memo directly into the memo box from disk. Choose the **Open Memo File** command from the **File** menu (or press Ctrl+O) and the input box shown in Figure 11-8 appears on the screen. Type the full name (and path if necessary) of the text file you want to read; the program opens your file and copies the text into the memo box. (If the program does not find the file name you enter, an error message appears on the screen.)

```
┌──────────────────────────Memo Printer──────────────────────────────┐
│  File  Names                                                        │
│  [ ] Herb Alcott      [ ] Richard Jeung    [ ] Martha Van Owen      │
│  [X] Susan Allan      [ ] Gary Johns       [ ] Milly Weinhart       │
│  [X] Jan Barton  ┌─■┐─────── Open Memo File ────────┐  xton          │
│  [ ] Andrew Cart │                                   │ lson          │
│  [ ] Xavier Cart │ Open what memo text file?         │ Wong          │
│  [X] Mary Dunn   │                        ┌────────┐ │ Wu            │
│  [X] Donald Fein │                        │   OK   │ │ Young         │
│  [ ] Bella Heinz │                        └────────┘ │ m             │
│  [ ] Mary Hernan │                        ┌────────┐ │               │
│  [ ] Sara Jackso │                        │ Cancel │ │               │
│                  │                        └────────┘ │               │
│                  │ ┌─────────────────────────────┐   │               │
│                  │ │ STAFF.TXT                    │   │               │
│                  │ └─────────────────────────────┘   │               │
│                  └───────────────────────────────────┘               │
│  From:  ┌──────────────────────┐   Date:  ┌────────────────────────┐ │
│         │ Jacqueline Sanders    │          │ Friday, April 17, 1992  │ │
│         └──────────────────────┘          └────────────────────────┘ │
└─────────────────────────────────────────────────────────────────────┘
```

Figure 11-8 Opening a memo text file

Before you begin printing copies of your memo, enter your own name in the **From** text box. (When you later choose the File Exit command, the program saves the current **From** name in a text file called MEMOFROM.TXT. In subsequent runs of the program, this name is read from disk into the **From** text box so that you don't have to retype your own name. However, you can *change* the name in this box at any time.) The **Date** text box displays the current date by default, but you can change this entry if you want to print some other date at the top of your memos.

The **Print or Save a Memo** command in the **File** menu displays yet another dialog box on the screen (Figure 11-9) to elicit your instructions for an upcoming output operation. Most commonly, you'll simply click OK or press Enter to accept the default options on the dialog box; when you do so, the program begins printing one copy of the memo for each person whose name you have checked in the list. As you can see in the example shown in Figure 11-10, each copy of the memo includes the date, a *To:* line that gives the name of the recipient, and a *From:* line that gives your name. These three items of information are copied from your selections and entries on the main *Memo Printer* form. The remaining text of the memo comes directly from the lines you have typed into the memo box.

But the **Print or Save a Memo** command offers you several other options. First, you can select the **Save as Text File** option if you want to store the memos in a text file instead of printing them. This gives you the opportunity to revise the memos in your word-processing program before you print them out. When you select this option, the program activates the **File Name** box. Enter a name for the file in which you want to save your memos and

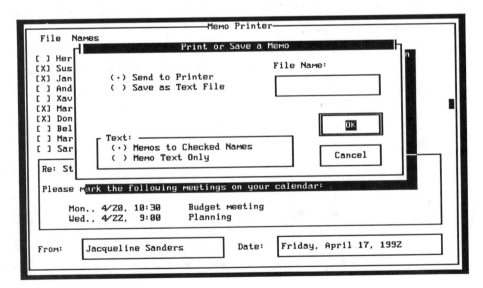

Figure 11-9 Printing the memos or saving them in a text file

```
*** Memo ***

Friday, April 17, 1992

To:    Susan Allan
From:  Jacqueline Sanders

Re: Staff meetings

Please mark the following meetings on your calendar:

     Mon., 4/20, 10:30    Budget meeting
     Wed., 4/22,  9:00    Planning
     Fri., 4/24,  3:00    Scheduling

It is very important that you attend these meetings.

                Thank you.

                J.S.
```

Figure 11-10 A sample of a printed memo

then click OK. If you enter an invalid file name—or, alternatively, if your printer is not ready when you select the **Send to Printer** option—the program displays the error message shown in Figure 11-11.

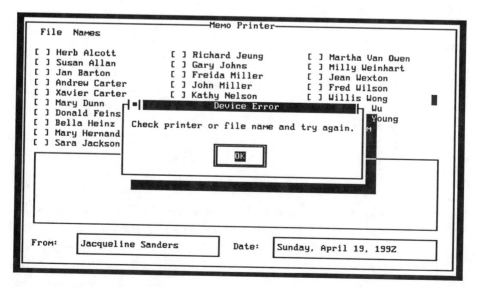

Figure 11-11 Error in printing or saving

Finally, the *Print or Save a Memo* dialog box allows you to specify what portion of the text will be sent to the printer or the text file. The default option, **Memos to Checked Names**, prints or saves a complete copy of the memo for each checked name in the list. The other available option, **Memo Text Only**, allows you to create a text file just for saving the current contents of the memo text box.

In summary, here are the steps for using the *Memo Printer* application:

1. When you run the application for the first time, use the **Add a Name** command in the **Names** menu to develop a list of people to whom you regularly send memos. You need do this only once, because the application saves the list to disk and rereads it each time you run the program.

2. Type the text of your memo, or choose the **Open Memo File** command from the **File** menu to read the memo from a text file stored on disk.

3. If necessary, enter or edit the items displayed in the **From** and **Date** text boxes.

4. When you are ready to print a memo, click the names of the people to whom you want to send the memo.

5. Select the **Print or Save a Memo** command from the **File** menu and click OK. The program prints one copy of the memo for each name that is checked in the names list. (Alternatively, use this same command to save the memos—or the memo text alone—to a text file on disk.)

THE ELEMENTS OF THE MEMO PRINTER APPLICATION

The *Memo Printer* project consists of three forms, as shown in Figure 11-12. The main form—which displays the list of names, the memo box, the **From** and **Date** boxes, and the program's menu bar—is named **MemoPrnt**. The two secondary forms, **MemoFile** and **MemoName**, are the dialog boxes for printing or saving a memo and for developing the name list.

The bulk of the application's code is devoted to three major tasks: managing the list of names that appears in the **MemoPrnt** form; performing input operations—most notably, reading memo files from disk; and performing output operations with the memos themselves—printing them or saving them to disk.

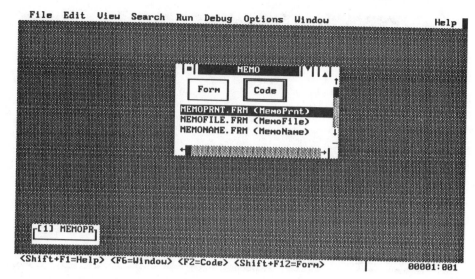

File   Edit   Uiew   Search   Run   Debug   Options   Window   Help

MEMO

Form   Code

MEMOPRNT.FRM (MemoPrnt)
MEMOFILE.FRM (MemoFile)
MEMONAME.FRM (MemoName)

[1] MEMOPR

<Shift+F1=Help> <F6=Window> <F2=Code> <Shift+F12=Form>   00001:001

Figure 11-12 The MEMO.MAK project

Controls, Menus, and Properties

The **MemoPrnt** form, shown in Figure 11-13, contains an array of check boxes along with three text boxes:

- The check box array has a **CtlName** setting of **SendTo**, with individual **Index** settings from **0** to **29**. Initially the **Caption** settings are blank. In addition, the program sets the **Visible** and **Enabled** settings to **False** for check boxes that are not in use—that is, when there are fewer than thirty names in the list. To fill in the captions, the program reads names from the MEMOLIST.TXT file on disk and changes **Visible** and **Enabled** to **True** for each check box that has a name caption.

- The memo box has a **CtlName** of **MemoText**, a **BackColor** setting of **15 - Bright White**, a **MultiLine** setting of **True**, and a **ScrollBars** setting of **3 - Both**.

- The remaining two text boxes have **CtlName** settings of **FromName** and **DateText**.

In addition to these controls, the **MemoPrnt** form has an important set of menus and menu commands. The Menu Design Window for the application appears in Figure 11-14. Because each of the menu commands

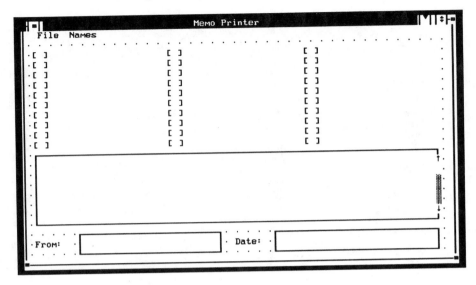

Figure 11-13 The **MemoPrnt** form

has a corresponding **Click** procedure in the program's code, you'll need to be familiar with the **CtlName** settings defined for the menu:

- The five commands in the **File** menu have **CtlName** settings of **OpenCommand** (for opening a memo file), **MemoCommand** (for activating the memo box), **ClearCommand** (for clearing the contents of the memo box), **PrintCommand** (for printing or saving a set of memos), and **ExitCommand** (for exiting from the program).

- The four commands in the **Names** menu have **CtlName** settings of **CheckCommand** and **UnCheckCommand** (for checking or unchecking all of the names in the list); and **AddCommand** and **DeleteCommand** (for adding or deleting names in the list).

The Data Files

The names of people who can receive copies of printed memos are stored on disk in a text file named MEMOLIST.TXT. Each line of this file contains a person's first name and last name; for example:

```
"Martha", "Van Owen"
"Jan", "Barton"
"Maxwell", "Wu"
"Milly", "Weinhart"
"John", "Miller"
```

The program appends lines of data to this file when the user adds a person to the name list. In contrast, when the user deletes a name, the program

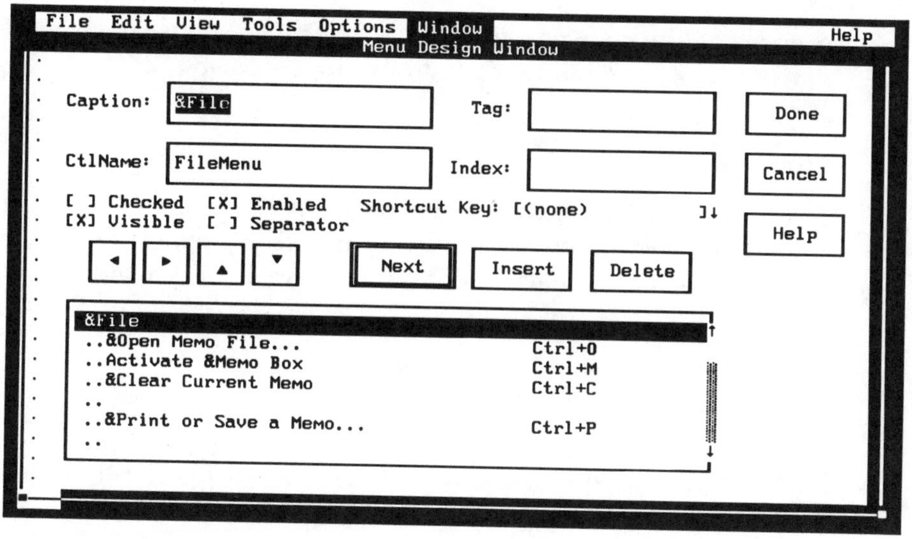

```
 File  Edit  View  Tools  Options  Window                            Help
                          Menu Design Window

   Caption: ▓File▓                      Tag: [            ]        [ Done ]

   CtlName: [FileMenu        ]         Index: [            ]        [ Cancel ]
   [ ] Checked  [X] Enabled    Shortcut Key: [(none)      ]↓
   [X] Visible  [ ] Separator                                     [ Help ]

   [ ◄ ] [ ► ] [ ▲ ] [ ▼ ]      [ Next ]  [ Insert ]  [ Delete ]

   ┌─────────────────────────────────────────────────────────┐
   │ &File                                                    │↑
   │ ..&Open Memo File...                        Ctrl+O       │
   │ ..Activate &Memo Box                        Ctrl+M       │
   │ ..&Clear Current Memo                        Ctrl+C      │▓
   │ ..                                                       │
   │ ..&Print or Save a Memo...                  Ctrl+P       │
   │ ..                                                       │↓
   └─────────────────────────────────────────────────────────┘
```

Figure 11-14 Menu design window for the MEMOPRINT form

completely rewrites the file. The names list contains a maximum of thirty first and last names.

The program creates an additional text file, MEMOFROM.TXT, to store the current name in the **From** text box.

Events

The program's **Form_Load** procedure initializes the names list by calling a routine that reads the MEMOLIST.TXT data file. Subsequently the program recognizes **Click** events for the menu commands and for the command buttons on the *Add a Name* and *Print or Save a Memo* dialog boxes.

When you run the program for the first time, you'll notice that certain menu commands are disabled—appearing in gray type in the menu lists—until you have created a names list and a document list. Specifically, the **Check All Names, UnCheck All Names**, and **Delete Unchecked Names** commands are dimmed until there are names in the list. Disabling these commands is a simple way to avoid inappropriate **Click** events during the program run.

Procedures and Methods

The form-level declarations for **MemoPrnt** appear in Listing 11-1, and the procedures from the **MemoPrnt** form are in Listings 11-2 through 11-9. Event procedures for the other two forms, **MemoFile** and **MemoName**, appear in Listings 11-10 and 11-11. The following sections give you a brief overview of the code and then a more detailed look at the routines that perform input and output operations with the **MemoText** box.

Overview

In the form-level declarations of **MemoPrnt,** the program defines a structured data type for storing the list of names in memory. The **NameRec** structure has string fields to represent a recipient's first and last names:

```
TYPE NameRec
   FirstName AS STRING * 20
   LastName AS STRING * 20
END TYPE
```

The program then creates an array of records for the list. A constant declaration establishes the maximum length of the list:

```
CONST MaxListLen = 30
```

Then the static array structure is declared:

```
DIM SHARED NameList(MaxListLen) AS NameRec
```

The **Form_Load** procedure (Listing 11-2) initializes this array by calling the procedure that reads the list of names from its file on disk:

```
ReadMemoOptions
```

The **ReadMemoNames** procedure (Listing 11-5) begins by setting the **Enabled** and **Visible** settings to **False** for the entire array of **SendTo** check boxes:

```
FOR i% = 1 TO MaxListLen
   SendTo(i%).Enabled = False
   SendTo(i%).Visible = False
NEXT i%
```

Then the procedure reads the MEMOLIST.TXT file if it exists. For each name in the list, the procedure displays and enables the corresponding check box and then copies the name to the **NameList** array:

```
SendTo(CurListLen).Enabled = True
SendTo(CurListLen).Visible = True
SendTo(CurListLen).Value = Unchecked
INPUT #1, NameList(CurListLen).FirstName
INPUT #1, NameList(CurListLen).LastName
```

After reading the entire list of names from the file, the procedure makes a call to **SortNameList** (Listing 11-6) to alphabetize the list by last and first names. Then each name appears on the form as the **Caption** property of one of the **SendTo** check boxes:

```
FOR i% = 1 TO CurListLen
  TempStr = RTRIM$(NameList(i%).FirstName) + " " +
RTRIM$(NameList(i%).LastName)
  SendTo(i%).Caption = TempStr
NEXT i%
```

If the list is at its maximum length, the program disables the **Add a Name** menu command:

```
IF CurListLen = MaxListLen THEN
  AddCommand.Enabled = False
ELSE
  AddCommand.Enabled = True
END IF
```

The **AddCommand_Click** procedure (Listing 11-4) reads a new name entry from the **MemoName** form and adds the entry to the name list. The first step in this process is to display the **MemoName** form on the screen as a dialog box for eliciting the new entry:

```
MemoName.SHOW 1
```

Notice that Visual Basic's **SHOW** method has an optional integer argument, representing an important *style* characteristic of the new form that appears on the screen:

```
FormName.SHOW style
```

Show accepts values of 0 or 1 for the *style* argument:

- With the default argument of 0, the newly displayed form is said to be *modeless*. As a result, the user can activate another form, even before completing the response to the newly loaded form.

- In contrast, an argument of 1 gives the newly displayed form a *modal* style. In effect, the new form takes control of the program. No events will be recognized on other forms until the user completes the input and/or closes the modal form.

When you design a form as a secondary dialog box, you will normally show the form in its modal style. This prevents the user from performing other actions until the new dialog box has received its required input response. The **MemoName** and **MemoFile** forms are both examples of modal-style dialog boxes.

When the user completes the input in the **MemoName** form, the **Add-Command_Click** procedure reads the input from the form and then appends the new name to the MEMOLIST.TXT file on disk:

```
OPEN NamesFile FOR APPEND AS #1
  WRITE #1, First, Last
CLOSE #1
```

Then the program calls a procedure named **UnloadAllNames** (Listing 11-4), which clears the current list of names from the **MemoPrnt** form. Finally, a call to **ReadMemoNames** alphabetizes and redisplays the list, including the new name that the user has just added.

The **DeleteCommand_Click** procedure (Listing 11-7) rewrites the MEMOLIST.TXT file, recording only those names that are currently checked in the names list on screen:

```
IF SendTo(i%).Value = Checked THEN
  First = RTRIM$(NameList(i%).FirstName)
  Last = RTRIM$(NameList(i%).LastName)
  WRITE #1, First, Last
END IF
```

Then, like **AddCommand_Click**, the delete procedure makes calls to **UnloadAllNames** and **ReadMemoNames** to display the new version of the names list on the **MemoPrnt** form.

Click procedures shown in Listing 11-2 are responsible for making selections in the list of names. For example, the **CheckCommand_Click** procedure puts an X in each **SendTo** check box:

```
FOR i% = 1 TO CurListLen
  SendTo(i%).Value = Checked
NEXT i%
```

Likewise, the **UnCheckCommand_Click** procedure loops through the entire list and removes all the Xs.

Text Processing

The **PrintCommand_Click** procedure (Listing 11-3) is called when the user selects the print command in the *Memo Printer* application's **File** menu. The procedure begins by establishing default settings on the **MemoFile** form and then shows the form as a *modal*-style dialog box:

```
MemoFile.SHOW 1
```

```
 File  Edit  View  Tools  Options  Window                    Help
 Property: [Caption        ]↓ Value: [Print or Save a Memo  ] | 9,2 | 61x14
┌─┐                           Print or Save a Memo                    ┌┐
│ ├Tools  . . . . . . . . . . . . . . . . . . . . . . . . . . . . . . ││
│ │Move/Siz . . . . . . . . . . . . . . . File Name: . . . . . . . . ││
│ │        . . . . . . . . . . . . . . . . . . . . . . . . . . . .   │
│ │Check Bo . . (·) Send to Printer   . . . . . ┌──────────────────┐ │
│ │Combo Bo . . ( ) Save as Text File . . . . . │                  │ │
│ │Command  . . ( ) None              . . . . . └──────────────────┘ │
│ │Dir List . . . . . . . . . . . . . . . . . . . . . . . . . . . . . │
│ │Drive Li . . . . . . . . . . . . . . . . . . . . . . . . . . . . . │
│ │File Lis ┌─ Text: ───────────────────────┐ . . ┌────────────────┐ │
│ │Frame    │ (·) Memos to Checked Names    │ . . │       OK       │ │
│ │HScrollB │ ( ) Memo Text Only            │ . . └────────────────┘ │
│ │Label    └───────────────────────────────┘ . . . . . . . . . . .  │
│ │List Box . . . . . . . . . . . . . . . . . . . ┌────────────────┐ │
│ │Option Btn                                     │     Cancel     │ │
│ │Picture Box                                    └────────────────┘ │
│ │Text Box                                                          │
│ │Timer                                                             │
│ │VScrollBar                                                        │
└─┘                                                                    
         ┌──────────────────────── Color Palette ──────────────────┐
         │ ( ) ForeColor                                           │
         │ (·) BackColor ██████████████████████ □ ░░░░░░░░░░░░░░░░  │
         └──────────────────────────────────────────────────────────┘
```

Figure 11-15 The MemoFile form

As you can see in Figure 11-15, the **MemoFile** form has the following controls:

- An array of option buttons named **Dest**, representing the possible output destinations.

- A second array of option buttons named **WhatText**, giving the user a choice between two output options.

- A text box named **OutFileName** for accepting a file name from the user.

- Two command buttons, **CancelButton** and **OKButton**.

The **Dest** array has three elements, although only the first two are visible to the user: **Dest(0)** represents the print option; **Dest(1)** is the save option; and **Dest(2)** is a hidden option that the program selects if the user clicks the Cancel button. Because **Dest(2)** is available exclusively for the program's internal use, the **Dest(2).Visible** and **Dest(2).Enabled** properties are both **False.** As you'll see shortly, **MemoFile** uses **Dest(2)** to instruct **MemoPrnt** to perform no output operation.

The user makes selections on the **MemoFile** dialog box and then clicks either OK or Cancel. Control of the program returns to the **PrintCommand_Click** procedure in **MemoPrnt.** On regaining control, the procedure first reads the setting that the user has selected for the output destination—that is, the choice between sending the memos to the printer or saving them in a text file on disk. Here is how **MemoPrnt** reads the selection in the **Dest** array:

```
IF MemoFile.Dest(0).Value THEN
  OutName$ = "Prn"
ELSE
  IF MemoFile.Dest(1).Value THEN
    OutName$ = MemoFile.OutFileName.Text
  ELSE
    EXIT SUB
  END IF
END IF
```

If the user has selected **Dest(0)**—that is, if the control's **Value** property is **True**—the procedure assigns the device name "Prn" to the string variable **OutName$**. For a selection of **Dest(1)**, this string variable receives the value that the user has entered into the file name text box, **MemoFile.Out-FileName.Text**.

But if the user has clicked the Cancel button—and **Dest(2).Value** is true—the current performance of **PrintCommand_Click** is terminated:

```
Else
  EXIT SUB
```

In Listing 11-10 you can see that the **CancelButton_Click** procedure in the **MemoFile** form takes care of setting the value of **Dest(2)** to **True** in response to a click of the Cancel button.

```
Dest(2).Value = True
```

Assuming the user has selected one of the two available output destinations, **PrintCommand_Click** opens the selected output device—the printer (Prn) or the named text file on disk:

```
OPEN OutName$ FOR OUTPUT AS #1
```

Then the procedure examines the selection in the **MemoFile.WhatText** array:

```
IF MemoFile.WhatText(0).Value THEN
```

If the user has chosen to print (or save) all the personalized memos, the procedure uses a **FOR** loop to produce a memo for each checked name in the **SendTo** array:

```
FOR i% = 1 TO CurListLen
  IF SendTo(i%).Value = Checked THEN
    PRINT #1, "*** Memo ***"
```

```
PRINT #1,
PRINT #1, DateText.Text
PRINT #1,
PRINT #1, "To:    "; SendTo(i%).Caption
PRINT #1, "From:  "; FromName.Text
PRINT #1,
PRINT #1, MemoText.Text
PRINT #1,
```

Alternatively, if the user has selected the **Memo Text Only** option, the contents of the **MemoText** box are sent alone as the output:

```
ELSE
   PRINT #1, MemoText.Text
END IF
```

In either event, you can see that the **MemoText.Text** property represents the user's entire multiline entry in the memo box.

Finally, another interesting text operation takes place in the **Open-Command_Click** procedure (Listing 11-8). This event procedure is called when the user chooses the **Open Memo File** command from the **File** menu. The procedure begins by using Visual Basic's INPUTBOX$ function to display a simple dialog box on the screen:

```
prompt$ = "Open what memo text file?"
title$ = "Open Memo File"
FileName$ = INPUTBOX$(prompt$, title$)
```

If the user's **FileName$** entry is valid, the procedure opens the file and reads its contents line by line:

```
OPEN FileName$ FOR INPUT AS #1
   DO WHILE NOT EOF(1)
      LINE INPUT #1, inLine$
```

Each line in turn is concatenated to the end of **MemoText.Text**:

```
   MemoText.Text = MemoText.Text + inLine$ + CrLf$
LOOP
```

The global string variable **CrLf$** represents the carriage-return and line-feed characters; its value is assigned in the **Form_Load** procedure:

```
CrLf$ = CHR$(13) + CHR$(10)
```

By inserting this combination of characters at the end of each concatenation, the program creates a multiline entry in the **MemoText** box.

SUMMARY: MULTILINE TEXT BOXES

By selecting appropriate settings for the **Height, Width, MultiLine,** and **ScrollBar** properties, you can design a text box that serves as a multiline editing environment in a Visual Basic application. The essential editing operations are built into the text box without the need for any detailed text-processing code. In addition, a program can access the entire contents of a multiline text box simply by referring to the control's **Text** property.

Listing 11-1 Form-level declarations for MEMOPRNT.FRM

```
' The Memo Printer Application (MEMO.MAK)
' MEMOPRNT.FRM
' Declarations

' $FORM MemoName
' $FORM MemoFile

DECLARE SUB ClearCommand_Click ()
DECLARE SUB SortNameList ()
DECLARE SUB UnLoadAllNames ()
DECLARE SUB ReadMemoNames ()


' Record type for name list.

TYPE NameRec
   FirstName AS STRING * 20 ' Person's first name.
   LastName AS STRING * 20 ' Person's last name.
END TYPE


' The file names for storing the two
' text files that the program creates
' and reads: NamesFile contains the list
' of people to whom memos can be sent, and
' FromFile contains the name of the person
' who is sending the memos.
```

```
CONST NamesFile = "C:\MemoList.TXT"
CONST FromFile = "C:\MemoFrom.TXT"

' The maximum number of "records" in
' the NamesFile list.

CONST MaxListLen = 30

' Boolean constants and
' Value-property constants for check boxes.

CONST False = 0
CONST True = NOT False

CONST Checked = 1
CONST Unchecked = 0

' Date format for the DateText box.

CONST DateFormat$ = "DDDD, MMMM DD, YYYY"

' Array for storing the list of people.

DIM SHARED NameList(MaxListLen) AS NameRec

' CurListLen is the number of people
' currently in the name list.

DIM SHARED CurListLen AS INTEGER

' Carriage-return/Line-feed codes.

DIM SHARED CrLf$

' End of form-level declarations
' for the MEMOPRNT form.
```

Listing 11-2 The Form_Load procedure and Click procedures

```
SUB Form_Load ()

  ' Initializations.

  ' Carriage-return/Line-feed.

  CrLf$ = CHR$(13) + CHR$(10)

  ' Display the current date.

  DateText.Text = FORMAT$(NOW, DateFormat$)

  ' Read and display the list of names

  ReadMemoNames

  ' Read the current FromFile if it exists.

  ON LOCAL ERROR GOTO NoFromName
      OPEN FromFile FOR INPUT AS #1
        INPUT #1, InName$
        FromName.Text = InName$
      CLOSE #1
  ON LOCAL ERROR GOTO 0

SkipFromName:
  EXIT SUB

NoFromName:
RESUME SkipFromName

END SUB  ' Form_Load


SUB CheckCommand_Click ()

    ' Place a check in all the check boxes
    ' in the list of names.

    DIM i%
```

```
  FOR i% = 1 TO CurListLen
    SendTo(i%).Value = Checked
  NEXT i%

END SUB   ' CheckCommand_Click



SUB ClearCommand_Click ()

  ' Clear the contents of the MemoText box.

  MemoText.Text = ""
  MemoText.SETFOCUS

END SUB   ' ClearCommand_Click



SUB ExitCommand_Click ()

  ' Terminate the program run.

  ' First save the current FromName entry.

  OPEN FromFile FOR OUTPUT AS #1
    WRITE #1, FromName.Text
  CLOSE #1

  END

END SUB   ' ExitCommand_Click



SUB MemoCommand_Click ()

  ' Move the focus to the MemoText box.

  MemoText.SETFOCUS

END SUB   ' MemoCommand_Click
```

(continued)

```
SUB UnCheckCommand_Click ()

  ' Uncheck the entire list of names.

  DIM i%
  FOR i% = 1 TO CurListLen
    SendTo(i%).Value = Unchecked
  NEXT i%

END SUB   ' UnCheckCommand_Click
```

Listing 11-3 The PrintCommand_Click procedure

```
SUB PrintCommand_Click ()

  ' Print memos to the checked names in the list
  ' or save the memos as a text file; alternatively,
  ' print or save the memo text alone.

  DIM i%, OutName$

  CONST NextPage = 12

  ' Establish the initial settings in the
  ' MemoFile form.

  IF CurListLen = 0 THEN
    MemoFile.WhatText(1).Value = True
    MemoFile.WhatText(0).Enabled = False
  ELSE
    MemoFile.WhatText(0).Enabled = True
    MemoFile.WhatText(0).Value = True
  END IF

  MemoFile.Dest(0).Value = True
  MemoFile.OutFileName.Text = ""

  ' Show the form and give it the focus
  ' until the user responds.
```

```
MemoFile.SHOW 1

' Read the option the user has selected
' for the destination of the text output.

IF MemoFile.Dest(0).Value THEN
  OutName$ = "Prn"
ELSE
  IF MemoFile.Dest(1).Value THEN
    OutName$ = MemoFile.OutFileName.Text
  ELSE

    ' If the user clicked Cancel, exit from
    ' this routine. (In this case, the hidden
    ' MemoFile.Dest(2) option button has a
    ' Value setting of true.)

    EXIT SUB
  END IF
END IF

ON LOCAL ERROR GOTO DeviceNotReady

' Open the file or the printer device for output.

OPEN OutName$ FOR OUTPUT AS #1

' If the user has selected the first WhatText
' option, print or save the memos to the
' checked names in the list.

IF MemoFile.WhatText(0).Value THEN
  FOR i% = 1 TO CurListLen
    IF SendTo(i%).Value = Checked THEN
      PRINT #1, "*** Memo ***"
      PRINT #1,
      PRINT #1, DateText.Text
      PRINT #1,
      PRINT #1, "To:    "; SendTo(i%).Caption
      PRINT #1, "From:  "; FromName.Text
      PRINT #1,
      PRINT #1, MemoText.Text
      PRINT #1,
```

(continued)

```
              ' Issue a form-feed at the end of
              ' each memo if the memos are being
              ' printed or a line of hyphens if
              ' the memos are being saved to disk.

              IF OutName$ = "Prn" THEN
                PRINT #1, CHR$(NextPage)
              ELSE
                PRINT #1, STRING$(65, "-")
              END IF

          END IF
        NEXT i%

     ' If the user has selected the second WhatText
     ' option, print or save only the text of the memo.

     ELSE
        PRINT #1, MemoText.Text
     END IF

  AbortPrint:
     CLOSE #1

  EXIT SUB

  DeviceNotReady:
     MSGBOX "Check printer or file name and try again.", 0,
  "Device Error"
  RESUME AbortPrint

  END SUB   ' PrintCommand_Click
```

Listing 11-4 AddCommand_Click and UnLoadAllNames

```
  SUB AddCommand_Click ()

     ' Add a person's name to the list of names.

     DIM First AS STRING
     DIM Last AS STRING
```

```
' Show the dialog box for eliciting a name.

MemoName.SHOW 1

' Read the name and then blank out the text
' boxes on the MemoName dialog box.

First = LTRIM$(RTRIM$(MemoName.NewFirstName.Text))
Last = LTRIM$(RTRIM$(MemoName.NewLastName.Text))
MemoName.NewFirstName.Text = ""
MemoName.NewLastName.Text = ""

' If the user entered a valid name, append
' it to the names file on disk.

IF First <> "" AND Last <> "" THEN
  OPEN NamesFile FOR APPEND AS #1
    WRITE #1, First, Last
  CLOSE #1

  ' Unload the current list and
  ' reread the entire list.

  UnLoadAllNames
  ReadMemoNames
END IF

END SUB   ' AddCommand_Click




SUB UnLoadAllNames ()

  ' Erase the check boxes in the
  ' SendTo control array.

  FOR i% = 1 TO CurListLen
    SendTo(i%).Enabled = False
    SendTo(i%).Visible = False
    SendTo(i%).Caption = ""
  NEXT i%

END SUB   ' UnloadAllNames
```

Listing 11-5 The ReadMemoNames procedure

```
SUB ReadMemoNames ()

  ' Read the file of names that will appear
  ' in this form's list.

  DIM TempStr AS STRING
  DIM i%, NoFile AS INTEGER

  CurListLen = 0
  NoFile = False

  FOR i% = 1 TO MaxListLen
    SendTo(i%).Enabled = False
    SendTo(i%).Visible = False
  NEXT i%

  ' Attempt to open the file, but go to the
  ' error-handling routine if the file does
  ' not exist. (NoFile then becomes True.)

  ON LOCAL ERROR GOTO NoNamesFile
    OPEN NamesFile FOR INPUT AS #1
  ON LOCAL ERROR GOTO 0

  ' If the file does not exist, there will
  ' be no names list in the form. Disable the
  ' menu commands that deal with the list and
  ' exit from this procedure.

  IF NoFile THEN
    DeleteCommand.Enabled = False
    CheckCommand.Enabled = False
    UnCheckCommand.Enabled = False
    EXIT SUB
  END IF

  ' If the file does exist, read it from beginning
  ' to end, or up to MaxListLen records.

  DO WHILE NOT EOF(1) AND CurListLen < MaxListLen
    CurListLen = CurListLen + 1
```

```
   SendTo(CurListLen).Enabled = True
   SendTo(CurListLen).Visible = True
   SendTo(CurListLen).Value = Unchecked

   ' Read the first name and the last name,
   ' and store them as a record in the
   ' NameList array.

   INPUT #1, NameList(CurListLen).FirstName
   INPUT #1, NameList(CurListLen).LastName

LOOP
CLOSE #1

' Alphabetize the list of names.

SortNameList

' Display the names as the caption properties
' of the check boxes.

FOR i% = 1 TO CurListLen
   TempStr = RTRIM$(NameList(i%).FirstName) + " " +
RTRIM$(NameList(i%).LastName)
   SendTo(i%).Caption = TempStr
NEXT i%

' If there are MaxListLen names in the list,
' disable the Add a Name menu command.

IF CurListLen = MaxListLen THEN
   AddCommand.Enabled = False
ELSE
   AddCommand.Enabled = True
END IF

' Now that there are names in the list,
' enable the appropriate menu commands.

DeleteCommand.Enabled = True
CheckCommand.Enabled = True
UnCheckCommand.Enabled = True

EXIT SUB
```

(continued)

```
' Error routine for a missing file.

NoNamesFile:
  NoFile = True
RESUME NEXT

END SUB   ' ReadMemoNames
```

Listing 11-6 The SortNameList procedure

```
SUB SortNameList ()

  ' Alphabetize the list of names.

  DIM i%, j%
  DIM FullName1 AS STRING
  DIM FullName2 AS STRING
  DIM TempNameRec AS NameRec

  FOR i% = 1 TO CurListLen - 1
    FOR j% = i% + 1 TO CurListLen

      ' Sort by last name and then first name,
      ' to allow for identical last names in the list.

      FullName1 = UCASE$(RTRIM$(NameList(i%).LastName) + " "
+ NameList(i%).FirstName)
      FullName2 = UCASE$(RTRIM$(NameList(j%).LastName) + " "
+ NameList(j%).FirstName)
      IF FullName1 > FullName2 THEN
        TempNameRec = NameList(i%)
        NameList(i%) = NameList(j%)
        NameList(j%) = TempNameRec
      END IF
    NEXT j%
  NEXT i%

END SUB   ' SortNameList
```

Listing 11-7 The DeleteCommand_Click procedure

```
SUB DeleteCommand_Click ()

  ' Delete all the names in the list that are
  ' not currently checked.

  CONST Yes = 6
  DIM i%, DelCount AS INTEGER
  DIM Ans AS INTEGER, Msg$
  DIM First AS STRING, Last AS STRING

  ' First count the unchecked names in the list.

  DelCount = 0
  FOR i% = 1 TO CurListLen
    IF SendTo(i%).Value = Unchecked THEN DelCount = DelCount
+ 1
  NEXT i%

  ' If the count is greater than zero, give the
  ' user a chance to back out of the delete operation.

  IF DelCount > 0 THEN
    Msg$ = "Are you sure you want to delete"
    Msg$ = Msg$ + STR$(DelCount)
    IF DelCount = 1 THEN
      Msg$ = Msg$ + " name?"
    ELSE
      Msg$ = Msg$ + " names?"
    END IF
    Ans = MSGBOX(Msg$, 3, "Delete Unchecked Names")

    ' If the user confirms, go ahead with the
    ' delete operation.

    IF Ans = Yes THEN

      ' If the entire list is unchecked,
      ' simply delete the names file.
```

(continued)

```
            IF DelCount = CurListLen THEN
              KILL NamesFile
            ELSE

              ' Otherwise, rewrite the checked names
              ' to a new version of the file.

              OPEN NamesFile FOR OUTPUT AS #1
                FOR i% = 1 TO CurListLen
                  IF SendTo(i%).Value = Checked THEN
                    First = RTRIM$(NameList(i%).FirstName)
                    Last = RTRIM$(NameList(i%).LastName)
                    WRITE #1, First, Last
                  END IF
                NEXT i%
              CLOSE #1
            END IF

            ' Unload the entire list of check boxes
            ' and then reread the name list.

            UnLoadAllNames
            ReadMemoNames
          END IF
        ELSE

          ' Display an error message if the user hasn't
          ' unchecked any names before selecting the Delete
          ' command.

          Msg$ = "To delete a name, first uncheck it in the " +
        CrLf$
          Msg$ = Msg$ + "list and then select the Delete " + CrLf$
          Msg$ = Msg$ + "Unchecked Names command again."
          MSGBOX Msg$, 64, "Delete Unchecked Names"
        END IF

      END SUB   ' DeleteCommand_Click
```

Listing 11-8 The OpenCommand_Click procedure

```
SUB OpenCommand_Click ()

  ' Open a text file and display the
  ' file's contents in the MemoText box.

  DIM prompt$, title$, FileName$

  ' Display an input box to elicit the file name.

  prompt$ = "Open what memo text file?"
  title$ = "Open Memo File"
  FileName$ = INPUTBOX$(prompt$, title$)

  ' If the user has entered a name,
  ' attempt to open the file.

  IF RTRIM$(FileName$) <> "" THEN
    ClearCommand_Click
    ON LOCAL ERROR GOTO NoMemoFile

    ' Read the file line by line and append
    ' each line to the end of the MemoText box.

    OPEN FileName$ FOR INPUT AS #1
      DO WHILE NOT EOF(1)
        LINE INPUT #1, inLine$
        MemoText.Text = MemoText.Text + inLine$ + CrLf$
      LOOP
    CLOSE #1
  END IF

AbortOpen:
  EXIT SUB

NoMemoFile:

  ' Display an error message if the file wasn't found.

  MSGBOX "Can't find " + UCASE$(FileName$) + ".", 0, "File
Name"

RESUME AbortOpen

END SUB  ' OpenCommand_Click
```

Listing 11-9 GotFocus and LostFocus procedures

```
SUB DateText_GotFocus ()

  ' Highlight the contents of the DateText box.

  DateText.SelStart = 0
  DateText.SelLength = LEN(DateText.Text)

END SUB   ' DateText_GotFocus


SUB DateText_LostFocus ()

  ' Validate a new date entry and redisplay
  ' the date in a standard date display format.

  DIM DateGood AS INTEGER
  DIM CurDate&

  ' Attempt to convert the date string to
  ' a serial date. If the attempt fails,
  ' go to error-handling routine at BadDate.

  DateGood = True
  ON LOCAL ERROR GOTO BadDate
    CurDate& = DATEVALUE(DateText.Text)
  ON LOCAL ERROR GOTO 0

  ' If new date is valid, display it;
  ' otherwise, display today's date.

  IF DateGood THEN
    DateText.Text = FORMAT$(CurDate&, DateFormat$)
  ELSE
    DateText.Text = FORMAT$(NOW, DateFormat$)
  END IF

  EXIT SUB

BadDate:
  DateGood = False
RESUME NEXT

END SUB   ' DateText_LostFocus
```

```
SUB FromName_GotFocus ()

  ' Highlight the current contents
  ' of the FromName box.

  FromName.SelStart = 0
  FromName.SelLength = LEN(FromName.Text)

END SUB   ' FromName_GotFocus
```

Listing 11-10 Event procedures for MEMOFILE.FRM

```
' MEMOFILE.FRM
' The dialog box for printing or saving memos.

' Form-level declarations

' $FORM MemoPrnt

CONST False = 0
CONST True = NOT False

' End of form-level declarations
' for MEMOFILE.FRM.

SUB CancelButton_Click ()

  ' If the user clicks Cancel, set the Value property
  ' of the hidden Dest(2) option button to True.
  ' (This is a signal to MEMOPRNT.FRM to
  ' perform no output operation.)

  Dest(2).Value = True

  ' Close the dialog box.

  HIDE

END SUB   ' CancelButton_Click
```

(continued)

```
SUB Dest_Click (Index AS INTEGER)

  ' Reset the OutFileName properties,
  ' depending on the Dest option that the
  ' user selects.

  IF Index = 0 THEN
    OutFileName.Enabled = False
    OutFileName.Text = ""
  ELSE
    OutFileName.Enabled = True
    OutFileName.SETFOCUS
  END IF

END SUB   ' Dest_Click

SUB OKButton_Click ()

  ' Close the dialog box. (The PrintCommand_Click
  ' procedure reads the user's selections from
  ' MEMOFILE.FRM and performs the requested output.)

  HIDE

END SUB   ' OKButton_Click
```

Listing 11-11 Event procedures for MEMONAME.FRM

```
' MEMONAME.FRM

' The dialog box for eliciting the first
' name and last name of a new person in the
' memo list.

' $FORM MemoPrnt

' End of form-level declarations
' for MEMONAME.FRM.
```

```
SUB AddButton_Click ()

  ' Validate and accept the user's entries.

  ' Display an error message if
  ' both name entries are not present.

  IF NewFirstName.Text = "" OR NewLastName.Text = "" THEN
    Msg$ = "Enter a first name and a last name."
    MSGBOX Msg$, 64, "Add a Name"
  ELSE
    NewFirstName.SETFOCUS

    ' Hide this form, returning control to
    ' the MEMOPRNT form.

    HIDE
  END IF

END SUB   ' AddButton_Click



SUB CancelButton_Click ()

  ' Respond to the user's cancel command.

  ' Blank out the two text boxes
  ' and reset the focus.

  NewFirstName.Text = ""
  NewLastName.Text = ""
  NewFirstName.SETFOCUS

  ' Hide this form, returning control
  ' to the MEMOPRNT form.

  HIDE

END SUB   ' CancelButton_Click
```

12

***

Drag-and-Drop Operations: The Program Summaries Application

INTRODUCTION

Visual Basic applications can include objects that you drag from one place to another on the desktop to achieve particular results. In an application that uses dragging as a meaningful operation, here is how you move an object from one place to another with the mouse:

1. Position the mouse pointer over the object on the screen.
2. Hold down the mouse button and move the mouse to a new position. The object on the screen moves along with the mouse pointer.
3. Release the mouse button at the screen position where you want to leave the object. This action is known as *dropping* the object.

The specific purpose of a *drag-and-drop* operation is defined by the application itself. A program might expect you to drag one object to a second object that represents a particular action or operation. In this context, the object you drag is known as the *source*, and the object where you drop the source is the *target*. For example, dragging an icon to a target object might represent an instruction to copy a document from one place to another or to merge one document with another.

Visual Basic defines tools for activating and recognizing drag-and-drop operations in an application. Except for timer controls and menu commands, all Visual Basic controls can become drag-and-drop objects.

The relevant property that you set either at design time or at run time is **DragMode**. The **DragMode** property has settings of **0-Manual** and **1-Auto-**

427

matic. In the manual mode, dragging is not generally available for the specified object. (However, your program can use a Visual Basic method named **Drag** to enable dragging in the manual mode.) In the automatic mode, dragging is always available for the specified object.

An event called **DragDrop** is another important feature in an application that uses dragging. This event occurs when the user drags a source object to a target object and then releases the mouse button. Because the target control is the object of this event, the corresponding event procedure has the following name:

```
TargetObject_DragDrop
```

One of the values that Visual Basic automatically passes to this procedure is a control-type argument identifying the source object. The code you write for the **DragDrop** event procedure therefore defines your program's specific reaction to the drag-and-drop operation.

This chapter's sample project, named the *Program Summaries* application, illustrates drag-and-drop operations. As its name suggests, this final program provides summaries of the major applications you have worked with in this book. It is also a convenient launch for running the programs. *Program Summaries* displays an icon for each of the book's nine major programs and offers you three options for any program you select. By dragging a program icon to a particular function box, you can:

- Request a description of the program.
- Request a list of the Visual Basic features illustrated in the program.
- Start a performance of the program.

With its nine program icons and three options, this application potentially performs twenty-seven different operations. This assortment could result in a confusing array of options if presented as command buttons or option buttons. But instead the program displays a row of drag-and-drop icons, along with three picture boxes that recognize the **DragDrop** event. As you'll see, this combination of controls results in a clear set of options that are easy to select.

THE PROGRAM SUMMARIES APPLICATION

The project is stored on the exercise disk under the name PRO-GRAMS.MAK. Load the project now and press F5 to begin a run. Figure

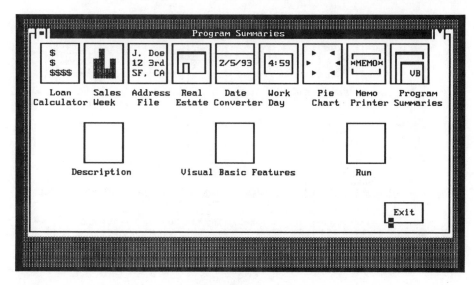

Figure 12-1 The *Program Summaries* Application

12-1 shows the form you see on the screen. The nine icons displayed in the upper half of the form represent the applications presented in Chapters 5 to 12. The three boxes in the lower half of the form—labeled **Description**, **Visual Basic Features**, and **Run**—represent the three functions of the *Program Summaries* application: describe a program, list the Visual Basic features of a program, or run a program. To select one of these functions for a given program, you drag the program icon and drop it into the box corresponding to the operation you want to perform.

For example, Figure 12-2 shows what happens when you drag the *Address File* icon down to the **Description** box. The image disappears from the row of program icons and appears inside the **Description** box . More important, the program displays a new form on the desktop that gives a brief description of the *Address File* application.

As long as this new **Description** form is on the screen, the controls on the main *Program Summaries* form are inactive. After you read the description, click the **OK** button on the second form. The description disappears and you can once again drag any of the nine icons to any of the three function boxes. Figures 12-3 to 12-11 show the **Description** forms and the **Visual Basic Features** forms that the program displays for the nine programs. These summaries serve as an informal reference to the work you've done with Visual Basic in this book.

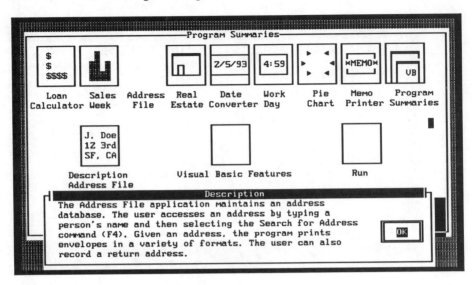

Figure 12-2 A **Description** form

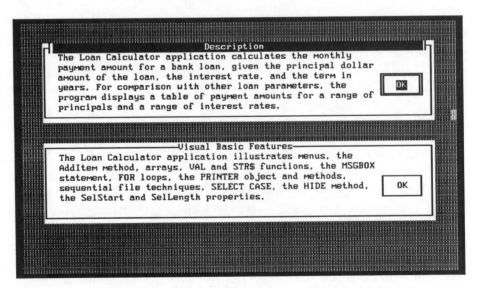

Figure 12-3 **Description** and **Features** of the *Loan Calculator* program

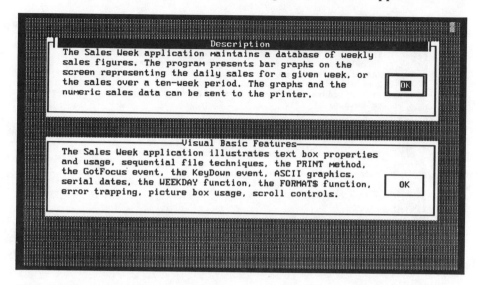

Figure 12-4 Description and **Features** of the *Sales Week* program

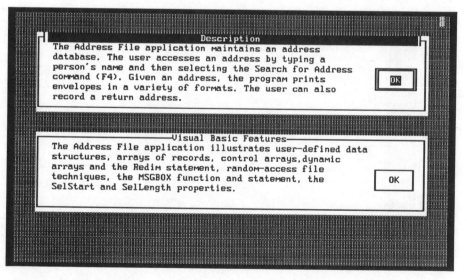

Figure 12-5 Description and **Features** of the *Address File* program

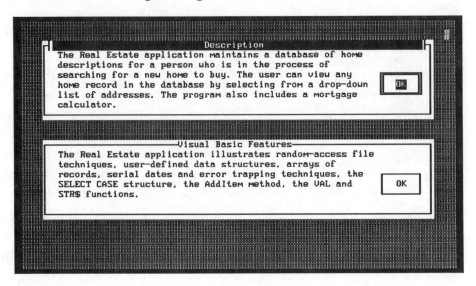

Figure 12-6 Description and **Features** of the *Real Estate* program

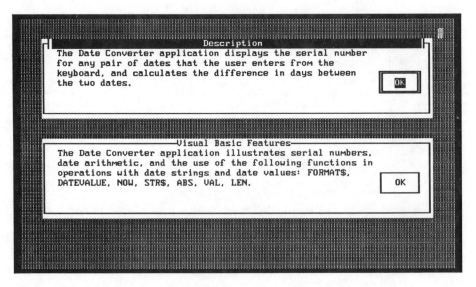

Figure 12-7 Description and **Features** of the *Date Converter* program

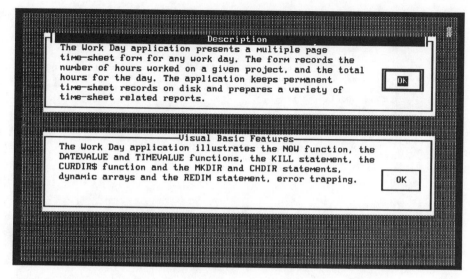

Figure 12-8   Description and **Features** of the *Work Day* program

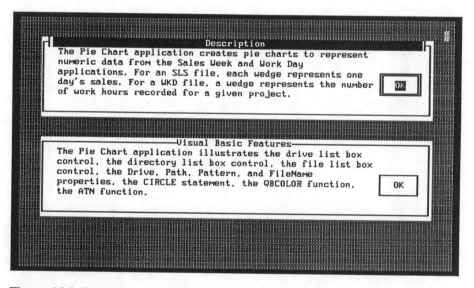

Figure 12-9   Description and **Features** of the *Pie Chart* program

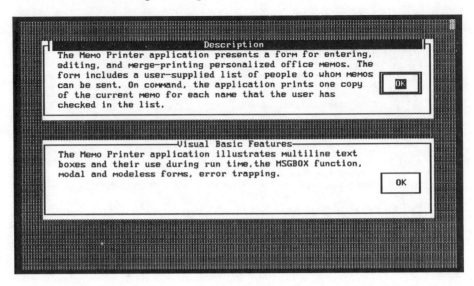

Figure 12-10 Description and **Features** of the *Memo Printer*

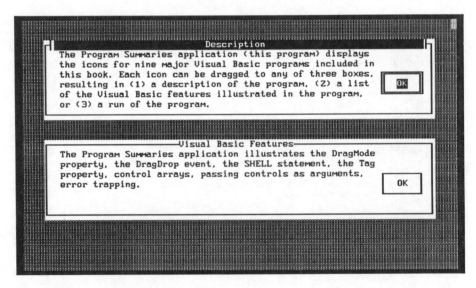

Figure 12-11 Description and **Features** of *Program Summaries*

To run a program, *Program Summaries* has to find the corresponding EXE file on disk in the root directory of the current disk. Here are the names of the EXE files you need to create in order to take advantage of this feature:

```
LOAN.EXE
SALESWK.EXE
ADDRESS.EXE
REALEST.EXE
DATES.EXE
WORKDAY.EXE
PIE.EXE
MEMO.EXE
```

If you haven't yet created the EXE file for a particular application, load the program into Visual Basic and select the **Make EXE File** from the **Run** menu.

THE ELEMENTS OF THE PROGRAM SUMMARIES APPLICATION

The *Program Summaries* application consists of two forms, named **Prog-Summ** and **ProgDesc** (Figure 12-12). The **ProgSumm** form contains two arrays of picture box controls and two arrays of labels. The **ProgDesc** form has one large label and a command button. Much of the program's code is devoted to preparing the messages that appear on the **ProgDesc** form. But the most important event procedure, named **DestFunction_DragDrop**, is the one that defines the program's response to a **DragDrop** event. This is the procedure that you'll be concentrating on in this chapter.

Controls and Properties

The *Program Summaries* application relies on interaction between different control arrays to simplify the operations performed in code. The **Prog-Summ** form contains four control arrays—two arrays of picture boxes and two arrays of labels. Here are descriptions of these four arrays:

- An array of picture boxes named **ProgIcon** displays the nine program icons. The **Index** settings of these controls range from **1** to **9**. To draw

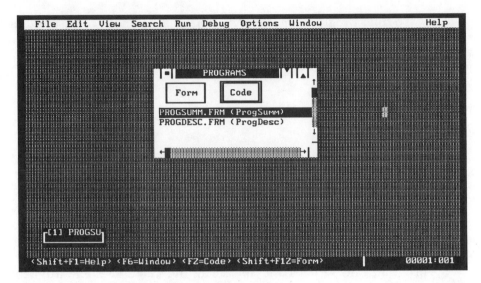

Figure 12-12 The PROGRAMS.MAK project

icons inside these picture boxes, the program displays ASCII characters in the three-row-by-six-column area inside the border of each box.
The sequences of ASCII codes are read from **DATA** lines in the
form-level declaration section and stored in a three-dimensional array
named **AsciiIcons**. A procedure named **DrawAnIcon** is called to place
each icon in its picture box.

- An array of labels named **ProgName** displays the names of the nine
  applications. Like the **ProgIcon** array, these controls have **Index**
  settings ranging from **1** to **9**. All nine labels have **Alignment** settings
  of **2-Center**.

- In the lower half of the **ProgSumm** form, the array of three bordered
  picture boxes is named **DestFunction**. These controls have **Index**
  settings ranging from **0** to **2**. When the user drags an icon to one of
  these boxes, the program calls the **DrawAnIcon** procedure to copy
  the relevant icon to the **DestFunction** box. (Immediately beneath
  each of these picture boxes is a label whose caption gives the program
  function represented by the box: **Description**, **Visual Basic Features**,
  and **Run**. These three labels are *not* part of a control array.)

- Finally, an array of three labels named **CopyName** is located at the
  bottom of the form. These labels have **Index** settings from **0** to **2**. They
  have no borders and blank **Caption** settings, and are therefore invisible at run time until the user performs a drag-and-drop operation.

When an icon is dropped into one of the **DestFunction** boxes, the application displays the corresponding program name as the **Caption** property of the **CopyName** label.

The **ProgSumm** form also has one command button named **ExitButton**.

The **ProgDesc** form has two controls. The large label named **DescriptLabel** is where the program displays program descriptions and Visual Basic feature lists. The user clicks the command button named **DoneButton** to return to the main dialog box.

Procedures and Methods

The program's code appears in Listings 12-1 to 12-8. As usual, a **Form_Load** event procedure performs several important initializations in this application. Subsequently the main action of the program is controlled by the **DragDrop** event procedure, along with **Click** procedures for the two command buttons.

Overview

The form-level declaration section for the **ProgSumm** form (Listing 12-1) includes **Dim** statements for three string arrays:

```
DIM SHARED Description(ProgCount) AS STRING
DIM SHARED Features(ProgCount) AS STRING
DIM SHARED ProgramNames(ProgCount) AS STRING
```

In the **Descriptions** and **Features** arrays, the program stores a description string and a list of features for each of the nine programs. The **ProgramNames** array stores the names of the EXE files in which the compiled programs are stored on disk. The **Form_Load** procedure (Listing 12-2) initializes these three arrays by making calls to the three procedures designed to prepare the string values:

```
WriteDescriptions
ListProgramNames
ListFeatures
```

The **Form_Load** procedure also reads ASCII characters into the **AsciiIcons** array. This array is defined globally as:

```
DIM SHARED AsciiIcons(ProgCount, IconRows, IconCols) AS
INTEGER
```

Because the array is three-dimensional, the program uses three nested **FOR** loops to read the ASCII codes for the program icons:

```
FOR i% = 1 TO ProgCount
  FOR j% = 0 TO IconRows
    FOR k% = 0 TO IconCols
      READ AsciiIcons(i%, j%, k%)
    NEXT k%
  NEXT j%
NEXT i%
```

Finally, **Form_Load** defines the characteristics of the **ProgIcon** control array. Within a **For** loop, the procedure assigns settings to properties and displays each icon. First, the **DragMode** property for each element of **ProgIcon** is given a setting of **1**, representing the automatic drag mode:

```
FOR i% = 1 TO ProgCount
  ProgIcon(i%).DragMode = 1
```

As a result, the user can perform drag-and-drop operations on all nine of the program icons. Then the procedure calls **DrawAnIcon** to display the correct sequence of ASCII characters inside the picture box:

```
DrawAnIcon ProgIcon(i%), i%
```

Notice that **DrawAnIcon** receives a control argument and an integer representing the icon that is to be drawn in the control. The procedure uses a pair of **FOR** loops and the **CHR$** function to display each character at its correct place within the box. Before printing a character, the procedure resets the **CurrentY** and **CurrentX** properties of the picture box:

```
FOR j% = 0 TO IconRows
  PicBox.CurrentY = j%
  FOR k% = 0 TO IconCols
    PicBox.CurrentX = k%
    PicBox.PRINT CHR$(AsciiIcons(n, j%, k%));
  NEXT k%
NEXT j%
```

Form_Load assigns settings to one additional property of each **ProgIcon** picture box—the **Tag** property. **Tag** is a string property that you can use in any way you wish to store text information about a control. Unlike other properties, **Tag** has no effect on the actual behavior or appearance of a control. In effect, **Tag** is simply a storage place for information that your program might need about a particular control.

The **Form_Load** procedure stores each program's application name—copied from the **Caption** property of the corresponding **ProgName** label—as the value of the **Tag** property:

```
ProgIcon(i%).Tag = ProgName(i%).Caption
```

Recording this value now as a property of each **ProgIcon** control is a convenience later in the program, as you'll see when you examine the **DragDrop** event procedure.

Responding to the DragDrop Event

The **DestFunction_DragDrop** procedure (Listing 12-3) is called when the user drags any one of the nine program icons to one of the three **DestFunction** picture boxes. This event procedure receives several important arguments:

```
SUB DestFunction_DragDrop (Index AS INTEGER,
                           Source AS CONTROL,
                           X AS SINGLE, Y AS SINGLE)
```

Because **DestFunction** is a control array, the procedure's first argument is **Index**, representing the number of the *target* object in the drag-and-drop operation. The second argument, **Source**, is a control argument representing the icon that the user has selected to drag. There is no argument that specifies the index number of the *source* icon, but the procedure can read this number from the **Source.Index** property. The third and fourth arguments are **X** and **Y**, representing the address of the drop operation. These final two arguments are not used in this application.

The procedure's first step is to produce the visual illusion that the selected icon has moved from its original position at the top of the form, down to the selected function box. To accomplish this, the program first copies the icon in the **Source** control to the selected **DestFunction** picture box:

```
DrawAnIcon DestFunction(Index), (Source.Index)
```

The next step is simply to set the **Visible** property of the **Source** control to **False**:

```
Source.Visible = False
```

Notice that the program does not *remove* the source icon, but simply makes it temporarily invisible. Later the icon will reappear in its original position.

In addition to displaying the selected icon inside the target picture box, the form displays the corresponding application name as a label beneath the picture box. To accomplish this, the program copies the value of **Source.Tag** to the **Caption** property of the **CopyName** label:

```
CopyName(Index).Caption = Source.Tag
```

This is the first of several uses of the **Source.Tag** setting that was assigned in the **Form_Load** procedure.

The next action depends on which of the three **DestFunction** picture boxes the user has selected. A **Select Case** decision structure uses the **Index** argument as the selector value:

```
SELECT CASE Index
```

If the user has requested a description or a list of Visual Basic features, the program moves its focus to the **ProgDesc** form. First the form's caption is changed to one of two titles:

```
ProgDesc.Caption = "Description"
```

or:

```
ProgDesc.Caption = "Visual Basic Features"
```

Then the program copies the appropriate text to the **Caption** property of the form's **DescriptLabel** control. This text comes either from the **Description** array:

```
ProgDesc.DescriptLabel.Caption = Description(Source.Index)
```

or from the **Features** array:

```
ProgDesc.DescriptLabel.Caption = Features(Source.Index)
```

Because these two assignments are made from within the **ProgSumm** form rather than the **ProgDesc** form, the procedure uses an extended reference notation. In general, one form refers to a control property on another form in the following way:

```
FormName.ControlName.PropertyName
```

Also notice the use of **Source.Index** to select the correct text from the **Description** or **Features** array.

Finally, once the **ProgDesc** form contains the information the user has requested, a call to the **SHOW** method displays the form on the desktop:

```
ProgDesc.SHOW 1
```

A **SHOW** argument of 1 displays **ProgDesc** as a *modal* form. While **ProgDesc** has the focus, the **ProgSumm** controls are temporarily frozen in place.

If the user drops a program icon into the **Run** box, the **DragDrop** event procedure makes an attempt to initiate a run of the selected program. The Visual Basic **SHELL** command runs a program. The syntax of the command is:

```
SHELL ProgramName
```

The argument gives the name of an executable program file, along with the directory location if necessary.

The **DestFunction_DragDrop** event procedure makes the following call to the **Shell** function:

```
SHELL Path + ProgramNames(Source.Index)
```

Path is a string constant defined in the form-level declaration section. The EXE program names are stored in the string array named **ProgramNames**. A reference to **Source.Index** selects the correct program name from the array.

If the user drags the *Program Summaries* application icon to the **Run** box, the program does not even attempt a call to the **SHELL** function. Instead a message appears on the desktop reminding the user that *Program Summaries* is already running.

When the action requested by the user's drag-and-drop operation has been completed, the program makes a call to a procedure named **RestoreIcons** (Listing 12-4) to restore the **ProgSumm** form back to its original appearance. This procedure begins by switching the **Visible** property back to **True** for the **ProgIcon** picture boxes—in effect, returning the source icon back to its place:

```
FOR i% = 1 To ProgCount
  ProgIcon(i%).Visible = True
NEXT i%
```

Because **RestoreIcons** does not know which icon was dragged, it switches **Visible** to **True** for all nine picture boxes.

Next the procedure uses the **CLS** method to remove the icon from the **DestFunction** picture box, and then blanks out the **Caption** property of the **CopyName** label:

```
DestFunction(i%).CLS
CopyName(i%).Caption = ""
```

These assignments restore the original appearance of the **ProgSumm** form. The program is now ready for the next drag-and-drop operation.

SUMMARY: DRAG-AND-DROP OPERATIONS

Drag-and-drop is a mouse action that you can employ as part of the user interface in a Visual Basic application you design. To plan for a drag-and-drop operation, you focus on the **DragMode** property and the **DragDrop** event procedure:

1. Activate the drag mode for an object by assigning a setting of 1 to the **DragMode** property. The object that the user drags is known as the *source* in the drag-and-drop operation.

2. Write a **DragDrop** procedure for the *target* object. This procedure defines your program's specific reaction to the user's drag-and-drop operation.

Drag-and-drop operations give the user a dramatically visual way of making selections and issuing instructions, simplifying the user interface for an application that contains a complex array of options.

Listing 12-1 The form-level declarations for ProgSumm

```
' The Program Summaries application (PROGRAMS.MAK)

' PROGSUMM.FRM
' Form-level Declarations

'$FORM ProgDesc

DECLARE SUB DrawAnIcon (PicBox AS CONTROL, n AS INTEGER)
DECLARE SUB RestoreIcons ()
DECLARE SUB WriteDescriptions ()
DECLARE SUB ListProgramNames ()
DECLARE SUB ListFeatures ()

' Boolean constants.

CONST False = 0
CONST True = NOT False
```

```
' The number of programs and the
' dimensions of each icon (starting from 0).

CONST ProgCount = 9
CONST IconRows = 2
CONST IconCols = 5

' The path for locating programs.

CONST Path = "\"

' The arrays of program descriptions.

DIM SHARED Description(ProgCount) AS STRING
DIM SHARED Features(ProgCount) AS STRING
DIM SHARED ProgramNames(ProgCount) AS STRING

' The three-dimensional array of ASCII icons.

DIM SHARED AsciiIcons(ProgCount, IconRows, IconCols) AS
INTEGER

' ASCII characters for creating icons.

DATA 0, 36, 0, 0, 0, 0, 0, 36, 0, 0, 0, 0, 0, 36, 36, 36, 36, 0
DATA 0, 0, 178, 0, 0, 0, 0, 178, 178, 0, 178, 0, 0, 178, 178, 178, 178, 0
DATA 74, 46, 0, 68, 111, 101, 49, 50, 0, 51, 114, 100, 83, 70, 44, 0, 67, 65
DATA 213, 205, 205, 205, 205, 184, 179, 218, 191, 0, 0, 179, 192, 193, 193,
196, 196, 217
DATA 196, 196, 196, 196, 196, 196, 50, 47, 53, 47, 57, 51, 196, 196, 196,
196, 196, 196
DATA 218, 196, 196, 196, 196, 191, 179, 52, 58, 53, 57, 179, 192, 196, 196,
196, 196, 217
DATA 0, 16, 0, 0, 17, 0, 16, 0, 0, 0, 0, 17, 0, 16, 0, 0, 17, 0
DATA 218, 196, 196, 196, 196, 191, 42, 77, 69, 77, 79, 42, 192, 196, 196,
196, 196, 217
DATA 213, 205, 205, 205, 205, 184, 179, 213, 205, 205, 205, 184, 179, 179, 0,
86, 66, 179

' End of form-level declarations
' for the PROGSUMM form.
```

Listing 12-2 The Form_Load procedure

```
SUB Form_Load ()

  ' Read the ASCII characters for the
  ' nine program icons.

  FOR i% = 1 TO ProgCount
    FOR j% = 0 TO IconRows
      FOR k% = 0 TO IconCols
        READ AsciiIcons(i%, j%, k%)
      NEXT k%
    NEXT j%
  NEXT i%

  ' Initialize the picture box properties and
  ' draw each ASCII icon in its respective box.

  FOR i% = 1 TO ProgCount

    ' The DragMode property determines the
    ' icon-dragging behavior.

    ProgIcon(i%).DragMode = 1
    DrawAnIcon ProgIcon(i%), i%
    ProgIcon(i%).Tag = ProgName(i%).Caption

  NEXT i%

  ' Call the three procedures that
  ' prepare program descriptions.

  WriteDescriptions
  ListProgramNames
  ListFeatures

END SUB  ' Form_Load
```

Listing 12-3 The DestFunction_DragDrop procedure

```
SUB DestFunction_DragDrop (Index AS INTEGER, Source AS
CONTROL, X AS SINGLE, Y AS SINGLE)

  ' Respond to the user's action of dragging and dropping
  ' an icon. First copy the icon to the destination picture
  ' box and temporarily set the Visible property of the
  ' source icon to false. Also, copy the program name to
  ' the label beneath the destination picture box.

  DrawAnIcon DestFunction(Index), (Source.Index)
  Source.Visible = False
  CopyName(Index).Caption = Source.Tag

  ' Select an action, depending on the destination box
  ' in which the user has dropped the icon.

  SELECT CASE Index
    CASE 0

      ' For the first destination box, display
      ' a description of the program.

      ProgDesc.Caption = "Description"
      ProgDesc.DescriptLabel.Caption =
Description(Source.Index)
      ProgDesc.SHOW 1

    CASE 1

      ' For the second destination box, display
      ' the list of Visual Basic features.

      ProgDesc.Caption = "Visual Basic Features"
      ProgDesc.DescriptLabel.Caption = Features(Source.Index)
      ProgDesc.SHOW 1

    CASE 2

      ' For the third destination box, attempt
      ' to run the program. If an error occurs,
      ' display an error message on the screen.
```

(continued)

```
        IF Source.Index <> ProgCount THEN
            ON LOCAL ERROR GOTO BadStart
                SHELL Path + ProgramNames(Source.Index)
            ON LOCAL ERROR GOTO 0
        ELSE

            ' The Program Summaries program is already running.

            MSGBOX "This program.", 64, Source.Tag
        END IF
    END SELECT

    ' Restore the original row of program icons.

    RestoreIcons
    EXIT SUB

' Display an error message if an error
' occurs during the attempt to run a program.

BadStart:
    MSGBOX "Can't start program.", 48, Source.Tag
RESUME NEXT

END SUB   ' DestFunction_DragDrop
```

Listing 12-4 The DrawAnIcon and RestoreIcons procedures

```
SUB DrawAnIcon (PicBox AS CONTROL, n AS INTEGER)

    ' Draw an ASCII icon in the picture box passed
    ' as the PicBox argument.

    ' First clear the current contents of the box.

    PicBox.CLS

    ' Then write individual characters from the
    ' AsciiIcons array to each (x, y) position of
    ' the box.
```

```
   FOR j% = 0 TO IconRows
     PicBox.CurrentY = j%
     FOR k% = 0 TO IconCols
       PicBox.CurrentX = k%
       PicBox.PRINT CHR$(AsciiIcons(n, j%, k%));
     NEXT k%
   NEXT j%

END SUB   ' DrawAnIcon



SUB RestoreIcons ()

  ' Move an icon from where it has been dropped,
  ' back to its place in the row of program icons.

  ' Restore the Visible property for all the icons.

  FOR i% = 1 TO ProgCount
    ProgIcon(i%).Visible = True
  NEXT i%

  ' Remove the icon from the function box.

  FOR i% = 0 TO 2
    DestFunction(i%).CLS
    CopyName(i%).Caption = ""
  NEXT i%

END SUB   ' RestoreIcons
```

Listing 12-5 The ListProgramNames and ExitButton_Click procedures

```
SUB ListProgramNames ()

  ' List the EXE program names for running
  ' each program from the Shell function.

  ProgramNames(1) = "Loan"
  ProgramNames(2) = "SalesWk"
```

(continued)

```
   ProgramNames(3)  =  "Address"
   ProgramNames(4)  =  "RealEst"
   ProgramNames(5)  =  "Dates"
   ProgramNames(6)  =  "WorkDay"
   ProgramNames(7)  =  "Pie"
   ProgramNames(8)  =  "Memo"
   ProgramNames(9)  =  "Programs"


END SUB   ' ListProgramNames




SUB ExitButton_Click ()

  ' Terminate the program performance.

  END

END SUB   ' ExitButton_Click
```

Listing 12-6 The WriteDescriptions procedure

```
SUB WriteDescriptions ()

  ' Prepare the program descriptions.

  DIM D AS STRING

  FOR i% = 1 TO ProgCount
    Description(i%) = "The " + ProgName(i%).Caption
    Description(i%) = Description(i%) + " application "
  NEXT i%


  D = "calculates the monthly payment "
  D = D + "amount for a bank loan, given the principal
dollar amount "
  D = D + "of the loan, the interest rate, and the term in
years. "
  D = D + "For comparison with other loan parameters, the
program "
```

```
   D = D + "displays a table of payment amounts for a range
of "
   D = D + "principals and a range of interest rates."
   Description(1) = Description(1) + D

   D = "maintains a database of weekly sales "
   D = D + "figures. The program presents bar graphs on the
screen "
   D = D + "representing the daily sales for a given week, or
the sales "
   D = D + "over a ten-week period. The numeric sales data
can be sent "
   D = D + "to the printer."
   Description(2) = Description(2) + D

   D = "maintains an address database. "
   D = D + "The user accesses an address by typing a person's
name "
   D = D + "and then selecting the Search for Address command
(F4). "
   D = D + "Given an address, the program prints envelopes in
a variety "
   D = D + "of formats. The user can also record a return
address."
   Description(3) = Description(3) + D

   D = "maintains a database of home "
   D = D + "descriptions for a person who is in the process
of "
   D = D + "searching for a new home to buy. The user can
view any "
   D = D + "home record in the database by selecting from a
drop-down "
   D = D + "list of addresses. The program also includes a
mortgage "
   D = D + "calculator."
   Description(4) = Description(4) + D

   D = "displays the serial number for "
   D = D + "any pair of dates that the user enters from the
keyboard, "
   D = D + "and calculates the difference in days between the
two dates."
   Description(5) = Description(5) + D
```

(continued)

```
   D = "presents a multiple page time-sheet form for "
   D = D + "any work day. The form records the number of
hours "
   D = D + "worked on a given project, and the total hours
for the day. "
   D = D + "The application keeps permanent time-sheet
records on disk "
   D = D + "and prepares a variety of time-sheet related
reports."
   Description(6) = Description(6) + D

   D = "creates pie charts to represent "
   D = D + "numeric data from the Sales Week and Work Day
applications. "
   D = D + "For an SLS file, each wedge represents one day's "
   D = D + "sales. For a WKD file, a wedge represents the
number of "
   D = D + "work hours recorded for a given project."
   Description(7) = Description(7) + D

   D = "presents a form for entering, editing, and
merge-printing "
   D = D + "personalized office memos. The form includes a
user-supplied "
   D = D + "list of people to whom memos can be sent. On
command, the "
   D = D + "application prints one copy of the current memo
for "
   D = D + "each name that the user has checked in the list. "
   Description(8) = Description(8) + D

   D = "(this program) displays the "
   D = D + "icons for nine major Visual Basic programs
included in "
   D = D + "this book. Each icon can be dragged to any of
three boxes, "
   D = D + "resulting in (1) a description of the program,
(2) a list "
   D = D + "of the Visual Basic features illustrated in the
program, "
   D = D + "or (3) a run of the program."
   Description(9) = Description(9) + D

END SUB   ' WriteDescriptions
```

Listing 12-7 The ListFeatures procedure

```
SUB ListFeatures ()

  ' List the Visual Basic features illustrated in
  ' each of the programs.

  DIM i%, F AS STRING

  FOR i% = 1 TO ProgCount
    Features(i%) = "The " + ProgName(i%).Caption
    Features(i%) = Features(i%) + " application illustrates "
  NEXT i%

  F = "menus, the AddItem method, arrays, VAL and STR$
functions, "
  F = F + "the MSGBOX statement, FOR loops, the PRINTER
object "
  F = F + "and methods, sequential file techniques, SELECT
CASE, "
  F = F + "the HIDE method, the SelStart and SelLength
properties."
  Features(1) = Features(1) + F


  F = "text box properties and usage, sequential file
techniques, "
  F = F + "the PRINT method, the GotFocus event, the KeyDown
event, "
  F = F + "ASCII graphics, serial dates, the WEEKDAY
function, "
  F = F + "the FORMAT$ function, error trapping, picture box
usage, "
  F = F + "scroll controls."
  Features(2) = Features(2) + F


  F = "user-defined data structures, arrays of records,
control arrays,"
  F = F + "dynamic arrays and the Redim statement, "
  F = F + "random-access file techniques, the MSGBOX
function and "
  F = F + "statement, the SelStart and SelLength properties."
  Features(3) = Features(3) + F
```

(continued)

```
   F = "random-access file techniques, user-defined data
structures, "
   F = F + "arrays of records, serial dates and error
trapping "
   F = F + "techniques, the SELECT CASE structure, "
   F = F + "the AddItem method, the VAL and STR$ functions."
   Features(4) = Features(4) + F

   F = "serial numbers, date arithmetic, and the use of the
following"
   F = F + " functions in operations with date strings and"
   F = F + " date values: FORMAT$, DATEVALUE, NOW, STR$, ABS,
VAL, LEN."
   Features(5) = Features(5) + F

   F = "the NOW function, the DATEVALUE and TIMEVALUE
functions, "
   F = F + "the KILL statement, the CURDIR$ function and the "
   F = F + "MKDIR and CHDIR statements, dynamic arrays and "
   F = F + "the REDIM statement, error trapping."
   Features(6) = Features(6) + F

   F = "the drive list box control, the directory list box
control, "
   F = F + "the file list box control, the Drive, Path,
Pattern, and "
   F = F + "FileName properties, the CIRCLE statement, the
QBCOLOR "
   F = F + "function, the ATN function."
   Features(7) = Features(7) + F

   F = "multiline text boxes and their use during run time,"
   F = F + "the MSGBOX function, modal and modeless forms, "
   F = F + "error trapping."
   Features(8) = Features(8) + F

   F = "the DragMode property, the DragDrop event, "
   F = F + "the SHELL statement, the Tag property, "
   F = F + "control arrays, passing controls as arguments, "
   F = F + "error trapping."
   Features(9) = Features(9) + F

END SUB  ' ListFeatures
```

Listing 12-8 The DoneButton_Click procedure

```
' PROGDESC.FRM
' Displays program descriptions
' and lists of Visual Basic features.

SUB DoneButton_Click ()

  ' Return control to the PROGDESC form.

  DescriptLabel.Caption = ""
  HIDE

END SUB   ' DoneButton_Click
```

Index

IBM Compatible 5.25", 1.2 MB Diskettes

This Bantam software product is also available in an IBM compatible 5.25", 1.2 MB disk format. If you'd like to exchange this software for the 5.25", 1.2 MB format, please:

- Package your original 3.5" diskette in a disk mailer.
- Include a check or money order for U.S. $7.95 ($9.95 Canadian) to cover media and postage and handling (California and Massachusetts residents, please add appropriate sales tax). Foreign orders: Please send international money orders; no foreign checks will be accepted.
- Include your completed warranty card.

Upon receipt, Bantam will immediately send your replacement disk via first-class mail.

Mail to: Bantam Electronic Publishing
666 Fifth Avenue
New York, NY 10103
Attn: VBDOS/5.25" Disk